Helicopt
Pilot

T0267353

ORAL
EXAM
GUIDE

RYAN DALE

THIRD EDITION

COMPREHENSIVE PREPARATION FOR THE
FAA PRIVATE HELICOPTER CHECKRIDE

AVIATION SUPPLIES & ACADEMICS, INC.
NEWCASTLE, WASHINGTON

Helicopter Pilot Oral Exam Guide
Third Edition
by Ryan Dale

Aviation Supplies & Academics, Inc.
7005 132nd Place SE
Newcastle, Washington 98059
asa@asa2fly.com | 425-235-1500 | asa2fly.com

See the Reader Resources at **asa2fly.com/oegh** for additional information and updates relating to this book.

ASA-OEG-H3
ISBN 978-1-64425-380-9

Additional formats available:
eBook EPUB ISBN 978-1-64425-381-6
eBook PDF   ISBN 978-1-64425-382-3

Printed in the United States of America
2028   2027   2026   2025   2024   9 8 7 6 5 4 3 2 1

Library of Congress Cataloging-in-Publication Data
Names: Dale, Ryan, author.
Title: Helicopter pilot oral exam guide : comprehensive preparation for the FAA private
    helicopter checkride / Ryan Dale.
Description: Third edition. | Newcastle, Washington : Aviation Supplies & Academics,
    Inc., 2024. | "ASA-OEG-H3"—Title page verso.
Identifiers: LCCN 2024014164 (print) | LCCN 2024014165 (ebook) | ISBN
    9781644253809 (trade paperback) | ISBN 9781644253816 (epub) | ISBN
    9781644253823 (pdf)
Subjects: LCSH: Helicopters—Piloting—Examinations—Study guides. | Helicopters—
    Piloting—Examinations, questions, etc. | LCGFT: Study guides.
Classification: LCC TL716.5 .D355 2024 (print) | LCC TL716.5 (ebook) | DDC
    629.132/5252076—dc23/eng/20240415
LC record available at https://lccn.loc.gov/2024014164
LC ebook record available at https://lccn.loc.gov/2024014165

Contents

About the Author

Ryan Dale is a helicopter and airplane certified flight instructor (CFI) who enjoys encouraging people as much as he enjoys flying. Ryan's aviation journey started in 2000, and he has personally trained hundreds of helicopter pilots and impacted thousands more through his written works.

At the start of his career, while Ryan was working toward his instructor certificate, he saw the need for more resources for aspiring helicopter pilots. He wrote the *Helicopter Oral Exam Guide* (2006) and *Helicopter Maneuvers Manual* (2011) to help other pilots pass exams and reach their goals in flying. Now, in view of the recent FAA update from Practical Test Standards (PTS) to Airman Certification Standards (ACS), Ryan felt the need to give the helicopter community an updated resource to integrate helicopter training and the new ACS.

In recent years, Ryan has extended his expertise beyond the flight deck to his online training platform *3G Heli Prep*, where he offers affordable, comprehensive helicopter pilot courses and personal tutoring. Ryan is dedicated to making the dream of flying accessible and affordable for everyone, from aspiring pilots taking their first discovery flight to seasoned pilots seeking advanced certifications.

Ryan currently resides in North Idaho with his wife, son, and daughter. When he's not in the air, writing, or developing coursework, you will find him sharing his journey on social media and encouraging others. For more information about Ryan and *3G Heli Prep* courses, visit 3GHeliPrep.com.

Introduction

This *Helicopter Pilot Oral Exam Guide* is designed for pilots who are involved with helicopter training. It provides information specific to helicopter operations, preparing you for the FAA practical exam (also called checkride), including the knowledge, risk management, and skills applicants will need to demonstrate. This guide will also prove beneficial to pilots who wish to refresh their knowledge or who are preparing for a flight review.

The *Private Pilot for Helicopter Airman Certification Standards* (FAA-S-ACS-15) specifies the areas in which knowledge and skills must be demonstrated by the applicant before issuance of a pilot certificate or rating. The *Helicopter Pilot Oral Exam Guide* is designed to evaluate a pilot's knowledge of those areas. You will find questions and appropriate responses for all Areas of Operations and Tasks required for the Private Pilot Certificate with a Helicopter Rating.

In this guide, questions and answers are organized into chapters that represent the areas of operations and tasks from the ACS, including knowledge, risk management and skills. At any time during the practical test, an examiner may ask questions pertaining to any of the subject areas within these divisions. This book provides you with the questions or topics commonly asked along with the information and/or appropriate reference necessary for a knowledgeable response.

Questions specific to aircraft operations refer to a Robinson R-22 helicopter. This guide does not take the place of the rotorcraft flight manual (RFM) for the helicopter in which your flight will take place.

You may supplement this guide with other comprehensive study materials as noted in brackets at the end of each answer; for example [PH.I.A.K1; 14 CFR 61.109]. The first of these items are ACS codes for the relevant Areas of Operation and Tasks from the *Private Pilot for Helicopter Airman Certification Standards* (FAA-S-ACS-15). Additional references pertaining to the questions can be found in the ACS listed under the Tasks corresponding to the provided ACS codes.

The next reference(s) in the brackets are other study materials for which abbreviations and corresponding titles are listed below.

Be sure that you use the latest revision of these references when reviewing for the test. Also, check the ASA website at asa2fly.com/oegh for the most recent updates to this book due to changes in FAA procedures and regulations as well as for Reader Resources containing additional relevant information and updates.

14 CFR Part 1	*Definitions and Abbreviations*
14 CFR Part 61	*Certification: Pilots, Flight Instructors, and Ground Instructors*
14 CFR Part 67	*Medical Standards and Certification*
14 CFR Part 68	*Requirements for Operating Certain Small Aircraft Without a Medical Certificate*
14 CFR Part 91	*General Operating and Flight Rules*
14 CFR Part 97	*Standard Instrument Approach Procedures*
14 CFR Part 133	*Rotorcraft External-Load Operations*
AC 68-1	*BasicMed*
AFM	*FAA-Approved Rotorcraft Flight Manual*
AIM	*Aeronautical Information Manual*
FAA-H-8083-1	*Aircraft Weight & Balance Handbook*
FAA-H-8083-2	*Risk Management Handbook*
FAA-H-8083-21	*Helicopter Flying Handbook*
FAA-H-8083-25	*Pilot's Handbook of Aeronautical Knowledge*
FAA-H-8083-28	*Aviation Weather Handbook*
FAA-S-ACS-15	*Private Pilot Helicopter Airman Certification Standards*
POH	*Pilot Operating Handbook* (be sure to reference the one specific to the helicopter you'll be flying for the checkride)
SFAR No. 73	*14 CFR Part 61, Special Federal Aviation Regulation No. 73—Robinson R–22/R–44 Special Training and Experience Requirements*

Most of these documents are available on the FAA website (faa.gov). Additionally, many of the publications are printed by ASA (asa2fly.com) and are available from aviation retailers worldwide.

A review of the information and references presented within this guide should provide the necessary preparation for the FAA Private Pilot Helicopter checkride.

Preflight
Preparation

1

A. Pilot Qualifications

1. What is the minimum age requirement to become a private helicopter pilot?

17 years old.

[PH.I.A.K1; 14 CFR 61.103]

2. What knowledge test must be passed for private helicopter pilot certification?

Private Pilot Helicopter (PRH) Airman Knowledge Test.

[PH.I.A.K1; 14 CFR 61.103]

3. What is the minimum flight experience required for a Private Pilot Helicopter Certificate?

40 total hours of flight time, including 20 hours of flight training with a flight instructor and 10 hours of solo flight time.

[PH.I.A.K1; 14 CFR 61.109]

4. What specific night flight experience is required for private pilot helicopter certification?

3 hours of night flight training, one cross-country flight over 50 nautical miles, 10 takeoffs, and 10 landings to a full stop.

[PH.I.A.K1; 14 CFR 61.109]

5. What are the cross-country flight training requirements for obtaining a Private Pilot Helicopter Certificate?

3 hours of cross-country flight training in a helicopter.

One solo cross-country flight that is at least 100 nautical miles total distance, with landings at a minimum of three points, and one leg of the flight consisting of a straight-line distance of more than 25 nautical miles between the takeoff and landing locations.

[PH.I.A.K1; 14 CFR 61.109]

6. What type of medical certificate is required to exercise the privileges of a Private Pilot Helicopter Certificate?

A Third Class Medical Certificate.

[PH.I.A.K1; 14 CFR 61.23]

7. What tests must a private pilot—helicopter applicant pass to obtain certification?

The knowledge test, oral exam, and practical test (commonly referred to as the checkride).

[PH.I.A.K1; 14 CFR 61.103]

8. What types of logs must helicopter pilots maintain according to FAA regulations?

Helicopter pilots must maintain logs recording detailed flight information including flight dates, aircraft types, total flight hours, pilot-in-command time, night flying hours, and instrument flying hours.

[PH.I.A.K1; 14 CFR 61.51]

9. How does recordkeeping relate to a pilot's currency under FAA regulations?

Recordkeeping is essential for establishing pilot currency as per FAA regulations. Pilots must log their flight activities to demonstrate compliance with currency requirements, including recent flight experience and periodic flight reviews.

[PH.I.A.K1; 14 CFR 61.51]

10. How long are pilots advised to keep their flight records, according to FAA guidelines?

The FAA suggests that pilots retain their flight records indefinitely for verification purposes. This recommendation aligns with the guidelines outlined in 14 CFR §61.51, ensuring that pilots can substantiate their experience and currency at any time.

[PH.I.A.K1; 14 CFR 61.51]

11. Are electronic logbooks recognized by the FAA for recordkeeping purposes?

The FAA recognizes electronic logbooks as valid for recordkeeping, provided they include all information required in traditional paper logs. This acceptance is in line with the FAA's modernization efforts and the increasing use of digital tools in aviation.

[PH.I.A.K1; 14 CFR 61.51]

12. What are the flying privileges of a private helicopter pilot according to FAA regulations?

A private helicopter pilot is authorized to act as pilot-in-command of a helicopter for any noncommercial purpose and can share operating expenses with passengers.

[PH.I.A.K2; 14 CFR 61.113]

13. Can a private helicopter pilot charge passengers for flights?

No, a private helicopter pilot cannot charge passengers for flights. They are only allowed to share operating expenses like fuel, oil, airport expenditures, or rental fees with passengers.

[PH.I.A.K2; 14 CFR 61.113]

14. Are private pilots allowed to fly in any airspace?

Private pilots are generally allowed to fly in most airspaces, provided they have the necessary endorsements and meet all airspace requirements, such as communication and equipment requirements for specific airspaces. Class A airspace requires pilots to have an instrument rating.

[PH.I.A.K2; 14 CFR 61.113]

15. Can a private pilot fly a helicopter under instrument flight rules (IFR)?

Yes, a private pilot can fly a helicopter under IFR, but only if they hold an instrument rating for helicopters.

[PH.I.A.K2; 14 CFR 61.113]

16. Can a private pilot act as a pilot-in-command of a helicopter for a business trip?

Yes, a private pilot can act as pilot-in-command of a helicopter for a business trip, as long as they do not receive compensation for the flight.

[PH.I.A.K2; 14 CFR 61.113]

17. Are there any restrictions on the type of helicopters a private pilot can fly?

Private pilots are restricted to flying helicopters for which they are rated. If they wish to fly a different type of helicopter, they must receive training and an endorsement for that specific helicopter type rating for helicopters above 12,500 lb.

[PH.I.A.K2; 14 CFR 61.113]

18. What are the currency requirements for private helicopter pilots to carry passengers?

Three takeoffs and landings within the preceding 90 days in a helicopter of the same category, class, and type (if required). Night passenger-carrying flights require these takeoffs and landings to be done at night.

[PH.I.A.K2; 14 CFR 61.57]

19. What are the different classes of medical certificates for private pilots?

Private pilots typically require a Third Class Medical Certificate. They may also obtain first or second class certificates, each with varying standards.

[PH.I.A.K3; 14 CFR 61.23]

20. How long does a Third Class Medical Certificate last for private pilots under 40? For those over 40?

For private pilots under 40, a Third Class Medical Certificate is valid for 60 calendar months from the month of issuance. For private pilots over 40, a Third Class Medical Certificate is valid for 24 calendar months from the month of issuance.

[PH.I.A.K3; 14 CFR 61.23]

21. Is it permissible to fly with an expired medical certificate?

No, a private pilot cannot legally fly with an expired medical certificate. Doing so may result in FAA enforcement action.

[PH.I.A.K3; 14 CFR 61.23]

22. What privileges does a First Class Medical Certificate grant to a pilot?

A First Class Medical Certificate allows a pilot to exercise the privileges of an Airline Transport Pilot (ATP) Certificate. ATPs typically operate in scheduled air carrier operations. This certificate is required for captains in airline operations and is valid for 12 months for ATP privileges if the pilot is under 40 years old, and for 6 months if over 40.

[PH.I.A.K3; 14 CFR 61.23]

23. Does a Second Class Medical Certificate allow a pilot to engage in commercial activities?

Yes, a Second Class Medical Certificate grants the privileges to exercise the duties of a commercial pilot, such as crop dusting, aerial photography, and charter operations. This certificate is valid for commercial pilot privileges for 12 months regardless of the pilot's age.

[PH.I.A.K3; 14 CFR 61.23]

24. Can a pilot with a Third Class Medical Certificate carry passengers?

Yes, a pilot with a Third Class Medical Certificate can carry passengers and act as pilot-in-command (PIC) for any private flying that does not require a higher-class medical certificate. This includes recreational and instructional flying.

[PH.I.A.K3; 14 CFR 61.23]

25. If a pilot's medical certificate expires, do they lose their pilot certificate?

No, the expiration of a medical certificate does not result in the loss of a pilot certificate. However, pilots cannot exercise the privileges of their pilot certificate without a valid medical certificate. They need to renew their medical certificate to regain those privileges.

[PH.I.A.K3; 14 CFR 61.23]

26. What conditions can temporarily disqualify someone from obtaining a medical certificate?

Temporary disqualifications include conditions like uncontrolled diabetes, certain psychiatric disorders, substance abuse, use of certain medications, or recent surgeries. The specific criteria depend on the certificate class and condition.

[PH.I.A.K3; 14 CFR 61.23]

27. Can a pilot with a medical condition obtain a medical certificate?

Yes, a pilot with a medical condition might obtain a medical certificate, possibly with limitations. The FAA may issue a special issuance certificate based on the condition and its management.

[PH.I.A.K3; 14 CFR Part 67]

28. What primary document must a private pilot possess to exercise flying privileges?

A current and valid pilot certificate issued by the FAA. This certificate serves as proof of the pilot's qualifications and privileges.

[PH.I.A.K4; 14 CFR 61.3]

29. What documentation is required to prove a private pilot's currency and competency?

A private pilot must maintain a logbook or other record showing recency of experience, including flight reviews, instrument proficiency checks (if applicable), and recent flight experience.

[PH.I.A.K4; 14 CFR 61.51]

30. Do private pilots need to carry photo identification when flying?

Yes, private pilots are required to carry a government-issued photo identification, such as a driver's license or passport, along with their pilot certificate and medical certificate when operating an aircraft.

[PH.I.A.K4; 14 CFR 61.3]

31. Are there specific documents a private pilot must have for cross-country flights?

For cross-country flights, a private pilot must have appropriate and current charts, the aircraft's registration, and airworthiness certificates. If the aircraft is not equipped with ADS-B Out, an operating transponder with an altitude reporting system is required in certain airspace.

[PH.I.A.K4; 14 CFR 91.103]

32. What documents are needed to show an aircraft's maintenance and airworthiness status?

The pilot must have access to the aircraft's maintenance logs to ensure compliance with all inspection and maintenance requirements. The logs should include records of the annual inspection, any applicable ADs, and the 100-hour inspection if the aircraft is used for hire.

[PH.I.A.K4; 14 CFR 61.45]

33. What is BasicMed, and who can use it?

BasicMed is an FAA alternative to traditional medical certification, allowing pilots to fly without a standard FAA medical certificate under certain conditions. Eligible pilots are those who have held a valid medical certificate within the past 10 years.

[PH.I.A.K5; AC 68-1]

34. Are there aircraft or operation limits under BasicMed?

BasicMed permits flying aircraft with a less than 6,000-pound maximum takeoff weight, carrying a maximum of five passengers, at altitudes below 18,000 feet MSL, and at speeds not exceeding 250 knots.

[PH.I.A.K5; AC 68-1]

35. To operate under BasicMed, how often is a pilot required to receive a comprehensive medical examination by a state-licensed physician?

Pilots must undergo a medical examination every 48 months.

[PH.I.A.K5; 14 CFR 61.113]

36. Is BasicMed valid for international flights?

BasicMed's acceptance varies by country. Pilots should verify with the aviation authorities of the destination country, as BasicMed is primarily for US domestic flights.

[PH.I.A.K5; AC 68-1]

37. How does one transition from a traditional medical certificate to BasicMed?

To switch to BasicMed, pilots must have had a valid FAA medical certificate after July 15, 2006, complete a medical examination as per BasicMed requirements, and finish an online medical course.

[PH.I.A.K5; AC 68-1]

38. What is the difference between *proficiency* and *currency* for a private pilot?

Currency refers to fulfilling the minimum legal requirements for flying, such as completing three takeoffs and landings within 90 days to carry passengers, as per 14 CFR §61.57. *Proficiency* involves a higher level of skill and understanding, ensuring safe and competent flight under various conditions. Proficiency goes beyond the basic legal requirements and focuses on a pilot's overall competence and comfort in various flying scenarios.

[PH.I.A.K5; FAA-H-8083-2]

39. How can a private pilot assess their proficiency versus just being current?

A private pilot can assess proficiency by self-evaluating their comfort and skill level in different flying situations, such as crosswind landings, instrument flying, or emergency procedures. This assessment involves honest reflection on one's abilities beyond the basic currency requirements. Regular training and flights with a certified flight instructor (CFI) can also provide valuable feedback on a pilot's proficiency.

[PH.I.A.K5; FAA-H-8083-2]

40. What risks are associated with confusing currency for proficiency?

Confusing currency for proficiency can lead to overestimating one's flying abilities, potentially leading to unsafe situations. A pilot might be legally current but may not have practiced certain skills or encountered specific scenarios recently, leading to inadequate preparation for unexpected conditions or emergencies.

[PH.I.A.K5; FAA-H-8083-2]

41. What role do flight reviews play in ensuring proficiency?

Flight reviews, required every 24 months as per 14 CFR §61.56, play a critical role in ensuring proficiency. They provide an opportunity for pilots to refresh their knowledge and skills under the guidance of a CFI. Flight reviews are tailored to address the specific needs and skill levels of pilots, helping to identify areas where they may need additional practice or training.

[PH.I.A.K5; FAA-H-8083-2]

42. How should a private pilot approach flying after a prolonged absence to ensure proficiency?

Pilots should take a cautious approach to regain proficiency. This might include reviewing pertinent aviation materials, taking additional training flights with an instructor, and gradually easing back into more challenging flying conditions. It's important to recognize that skills may degrade over time, and extra training may be necessary to regain proficiency levels previously attained.

[PH.I.A.K5; FAA-H-8083-2]

Skills to be demonstrated:

• Apply requirements to act as pilot-in-command (PIC) under visual flight rules (VFR) in a scenario given by the evaluator.

Example Scenario:

You're planning to fly a Robinson R22 helicopter for a proficiency flight from your local airfield to a nearby training area. The weather is favorable for VFR conditions: clear skies with good visibility and light winds. To act as pilot-in-command (PIC) under VFR in this scenario, you need to meet specific requirements, including those under Special Federal Aviation Regulation (SFAR) No. 73—Robinson R-22/R-44 Special Training and Experience Requirements:

1. *Pilot certification*—Confirm that you hold a valid Private Pilot Certificate with a rotorcraft category and helicopter class rating (FAA Requirement, 14 CFR Part 61).

2. *Medical certificate*—Ensure you have a valid medical certificate, at least a third-class, unless operating under BasicMed (FAA Requirement, 14 CFR §61.23).

3. *SFAR No. 73 ground training*—As you're flying a Robinson R22, complete SFAR No. 73 ground training for Robinson R22/R44 helicopters. This training covers unique characteristics and flight operations (SFAR No. 73 Requirement).

4. *Flight review compliance*—Verify completion of a flight review within the last 24 months, including 1 hour of ground instruction and 1 hour of flight instruction (FAA Requirement, 14 CFR §61.56).

5. *Recent flight experience*—If carrying passengers, ensure you've completed three takeoffs and landings in a helicopter within the last 90 days (FAA Requirement, 14 CFR §61.57).

6. *R22 specific experience*—Under SFAR No. 73, ensure you have logged the required flight experience in the R22, including instructional hours specific to this model if applicable.

7. *Preflight inspection*—Conduct a thorough inspection of the R22, checking all systems, fuel levels, and the helicopter's condition. Review weather, NOTAMs, and plan your route, considering any airspace restrictions.

(continued)

8. *Weather check*—Confirm that weather conditions meet VFR requirements, particularly staying clear of clouds for helicopter operations (14 CFR §91.155).

9. *Weight and balance*—Calculate the weight and balance for the R22 to ensure safe flight within operational limitations.

10. *Helicopter familiarity*—Be thoroughly familiar with the R22's operational procedures, emergency protocols, and flight characteristics, as outlined in the flight manual.

Incorporating SFAR No. 73 requirements is crucial when flying Robinson helicopters, ensuring compliance with specific safety guidelines and FAA regulations for PIC under VFR conditions.

B. Airworthiness Requirements

1. Where must the aircraft's airworthiness certificate be displayed?

In the aircraft's cabin or cockpit where it is clearly visible to all occupants. This requirement ensures that the certificate is easily accessible and can be inspected by passengers or aviation officials.

[PH.I.B.K1; 14 CFR 91.203]

2. What does a helicopter's airworthiness certificate include?

Aircraft's registration number, make, model, serial number, and airworthiness category.

[PH.I.B.K1; FAA-H-8083-25]

3. What is the expiration period for an aircraft's airworthiness certificate?

An aircraft's standard airworthiness certificate does not have a specified expiration date. It remains valid as long as the aircraft meets its approved type design, is in a condition for safe operation, and maintenance, preventive maintenance, and alterations are performed in accordance with applicable regulations.

[PH.I.B.K1; FAA-H-8083-25

4. Where is a helicopter's registration certificate located?

The registration certificate is carried onboard the helicopter, detailing the owner's information and aircraft specifics.

[PH.I.B.K1; 14 CFR 91.203]

5. When does an aircraft's registration certificate expire?

Seven years after the last day of the month in which it was issued. Upon expiration, the aircraft cannot be legally flown until the registration is renewed with the FAA.

[PH.I.B.K1; 14 CFR 47.31, 47.40]

6. Are airworthiness and registration certificates the same?

No, they are different. The airworthiness certificate confirms safety standards compliance, while the registration certificate shows ownership.

[PH.I.B.K1; FAA-H-8083-25]

7. How does a pilot verify the expiration of the aircraft's maintenance inspections?

The pilot must check the aircraft's maintenance records to verify the completion and expiration dates of required inspections, such as the annual and 100-hour inspections if applicable. The records should clearly indicate the dates these inspections were completed and when they are due again.

[PH.I.B.K1; 14 CFR 91.409]

8. What are the primary inspections required for an aircraft to be considered airworthy?

The primary inspections required include the annual inspection, which must be performed every 12 calendar months, and the 100-hour inspection for aircraft used for hire or flight instruction in the aircraft they provide. Additionally, transponder and static system inspections are required every 24 calendar months.

[PH.I.B.K1b; 14 CFR 91.409]

9. How are compliance with Airworthiness Directives (ADs) documented?

Compliance with Airworthiness Directives must be recorded in the aircraft's maintenance records. The record must include the AD number, the date of compliance, the method of compliance, and the signature of the person performing the work or the aircraft owner. This ensures that all mandatory modifications and repairs for safety are tracked.

[PH.I.B.K1b; 14 CFR 91.213]

10. What should be documented in the aircraft's engine logbook?

The aircraft's engine logbook should document all maintenance, preventive maintenance, and alterations performed on the engine. This includes dates, descriptions of the work performed, the name of the person performing the work, and the signature and certificate number of the person approving the aircraft for return to service.

[PH.I.B.K1b; 14 CFR 91.405]

11. Is documentation of fuel contamination checks required?

While regular fuel contamination checks are required for safe operation, the FAA does not mandate documentation of each fuel contamination check in the logbooks. However, it is recommended that fuel be checked prior to all flights and any maintenance or repairs related to fuel system issues should be recorded.

[PH.I.B.K1b; FAA-H-8083-25]

12. How often must emergency equipment be inspected, and is this documented?

The inspection frequency for emergency equipment like fire extinguishers and emergency locator transmitters varies based on the equipment's guidelines. Documentation of these inspections in the maintenance records is required to ensure readiness and compliance with safety regulations.

[PH.I.B.K1b; FAA-H-8083-25]

13. What is an Airworthiness Directive (AD), and why is it issued?

An Airworthiness Directive is a legally enforceable rule issued by the FAA to address a known safety issue in a particular model of aircraft, engine, avionics, or other systems. ADs are issued when an unsafe condition exists that could affect the safety of the aircraft and immediate action is required.

[PH.I.B.K1c; FAA-H-8083-25]

14. How are ADs categorized?

ADs are categorized as either emergency or non-emergency. Emergency ADs require immediate compliance before further flight, while non-emergency ADs have a specified compliance period. ADs can also be classified as one-time or recurring, indicating the frequency of required actions.

[PH.I.B.K1c; FAA-H-8083-25]

15. What is a Special Airworthiness Information Bulletin (SAIB), and how does it differ from an AD?

A Special Airworthiness Information Bulletin is an advisory issued by the FAA to inform aircraft operators of a noncritical airworthiness concern. Unlike ADs, SAIBs are not legally enforceable but provide important safety information and recommended actions. SAIBs address issues that don't warrant the issuance of an AD.

[PH.I.B.K1c; FAA-H-8083-25]

16. How can pilots and aircraft owners stay informed about ADs and SAIBs?

Subscribing to the FAA's email notification service, regularly checking the FAA's website, or consulting with maintenance professionals. Aircraft manufacturers and type clubs also disseminate this information to their members.

[PH.I.B.K1c; FAA-H-8083-25]

Example Scenario:

You are a private pilot preparing for a day VFR flight in a Robinson R44 helicopter from a small municipal airport in the Midwest to a nearby airfield for a leisure trip. The weather forecast is clear with light winds, ideal for VFR conditions. You last flew the helicopter two weeks ago, and it performed without any notable issues. Today, you arrive at the hangar and begin your preflight preparation.

Your task is to determine if the helicopter is airworthy for the planned flight. Consider the following points as you assess the helicopter's airworthiness:

1. *Aircraft documents*—Ensure the helicopter has its airworthiness certificate, registration, weight and balance information, and appropriate logbooks available and up to date.

2. *Maintenance records*—Review the helicopter's maintenance logbooks. Check for any overdue inspections, outstanding Airworthiness Directives (ADs), and the resolution of any previously noted discrepancies. Confirm the last date of the annual inspection and any applicable 100-hour inspections if the helicopter is used for instruction or hire.

3. *Physical inspection*—Conduct a thorough preflight inspection. Check for any visible damage or leaks, ensure all control surfaces are free and correct, and verify the integrity of the rotor system. Inspect the fuel level and quality, oil levels, and the condition of the landing gear.

4. *Instrument and equipment check*—Verify that all required instruments and equipment for day VFR flight are present and functioning correctly. This includes checking the functionality of the communication and navigation systems, engine gauges, and all cockpit controls.

5. *Pilot preparation*—Reflect on your own readiness. Ensure you have the necessary endorsements, meet recent flight experience requirements for carrying passengers if applicable, and are familiar with the helicopter's specific model and characteristics. In addition, pilots must meet the requirements set out by SFAR No. 73.

17. What is the purpose of a special flight permit?

A special flight permit, also known as a ferry permit, is issued
to allow an aircraft that may not currently meet airworthiness
requirements to be flown to a specific location for repairs,
alterations, maintenance, or storage. It's also used for delivering or
exporting an aircraft, or for evacuation from an area of impending
danger.

[PH.I.B.K1d; 14 CFR 21.197, 91.213]

18. Who is authorized to issue a special flight permit?

The FAA issues special flight permits. The request can be made
to the local Flight Standards District Office (FSDO) or through an
FAA-designated airworthiness representative who has the authority
to issue these permits.

[PH.I.B.K1d; 14 CFR 91.213]

19. What information is required when applying for a special flight permit?

Information such as the purpose of the flight, proposed itinerary,
a description of the aircraft's condition, and how the aircraft will
be made safe for the intended flight is required. This ensures that
the flight can be conducted safely under specific conditions and
limitations.

[PH.I.B.K1d; FAA-H-8083-25]

20. Are there any operational limitations imposed on flights under a special flight permit?

Yes, special flight permits may include operational limitations,
such as altitude restrictions, geographic limitations, crew
requirements, or specific equipment that must be operable. These
limitations are imposed to ensure the safety of the flight under the
aircraft's current condition.

[PH.I.B.K1d; FAA-H-8083-25]

21. Can a special flight permit be used for routine operations?

No, a special flight permit is not intended for routine operations. It is specifically for allowing a non-airworthy aircraft to be flown under controlled conditions to a location where it can be repaired, altered, or stored.

[PH.I.B.K1d; FAA-H-8083-25]

22. What are the primary responsibilities of an aircraft owner/operator?

The primary responsibilities of an aircraft owner/operator include ensuring the aircraft is maintained in an airworthy condition, complying with all airworthiness directives, maintaining the aircraft's registration, and keeping accurate maintenance records. The owner/operator must also make the aircraft available for required inspections.

[PH.I.B.K1e; FAA-H-8083-25]

23. What are the responsibilities of the pilot-in-command (PIC) before a flight?

Before a flight, the PIC is responsible for determining the aircraft's airworthiness, reviewing the maintenance and aircraft logs, checking the weather, preparing a flight plan, ensuring the aircraft is properly equipped for the intended flight, and conducting a preflight inspection. The PIC must also assess the weight and balance, fuel requirements, and passenger briefing.

[PH.I.B.K1e; 14 CFR 91.3]

24. How do PIC responsibilities differ from those of the owner/operator?

The owner/operator is responsible for the aircraft's overall maintenance and airworthiness, while the PIC is responsible for the safe operation of the aircraft during a specific flight. The PIC must verify the aircraft's condition for each flight and make operational decisions, whereas the owner/operator oversees long-term maintenance and compliance.

[PH.I.B.K1e; FAA-H-8083-25]

25. Who is responsible for ensuring the aircraft complies with noise regulations?

The owner/operator is responsible for ensuring the aircraft complies with applicable noise regulations. Compliance involves maintaining the aircraft's noise certification and operating it in accordance with established noise abatement procedures.

[PH.I.B.K1e; FAA-H-8083-25]

26. What is considered preventive maintenance that a pilot can perform?

Preventive maintenance includes simple or minor preservation operations and the replacement of small standard parts not involving complex assembly operations. This can include tasks like changing engine oil, replacing bulbs, batteries, tires, or packing wheel bearings. The FAA provides a specific list of such tasks.

[PH.I.B.K2; 14 CFR Part 43 Appendix A]

27. Who is authorized to perform preventive maintenance on an aircraft?

Certified pilots, excluding student pilots, sport pilots, and recreational pilots, are authorized to perform preventive maintenance on any aircraft owned or operated by them, provided the aircraft is not used under 14 CFR Part 121, 129, or 135 operations.

[PH.I.B.K2; 14 CFR 43.3, 43.17]

28. Are there specific recordkeeping requirements for pilot-performed preventive maintenance?

Yes, pilots performing preventive maintenance must make an entry in the maintenance records of the aircraft. The entry must include a description of the work, the date of completion, the pilot's name, and the pilot's certificate number and type.

[PH.I.B.K2; 14 CFR 43.12]

29. Can pilots perform preventive maintenance on any type of aircraft?

Pilots can perform preventive maintenance only on aircraft that are not used in air carrier service. This typically includes most general aviation aircraft used for private or business purposes.

[PH.I.B.K2; 14 CFR 43.1]

30. What training or qualifications are required for pilots to perform preventive maintenance?

The FAA does not require specific training or qualifications for pilots to perform preventive maintenance, but pilots must be competent to perform the tasks. Pilots are expected to follow manufacturer's guidelines and use proper tools and equipment.

[PH.I.B.K2; FAA-H-8083-25]

31. Is pilot-performed preventive maintenance allowed on aircraft under a continuous airworthiness maintenance program?

Pilot-performed preventive maintenance is generally not allowed on aircraft that are part of a continuous airworthiness maintenance program, such as those used in commercial operations under 14 CFR Part 121 or 135.

[PH.I.B.K2; FAA-H-8083-25]

32. What are the minimum equipment requirements for a private pilot to conduct day VFR flights?

For day VFR flights, private pilots must ensure their aircraft is equipped with certain items as specified in 14 CFR §91.205(b), including but not limited to: an airspeed indicator, altimeter, magnetic direction indicator, tachometer, oil pressure gauge, temperature gauge, fuel gauge, landing gear position indicator (if retractable gear), flotation gear (if over water), and seat belts.

[PH.I.B.K3; 14 CFR 91.205]

33. What additional equipment is required for night VFR flights?

In addition to the day VFR requirements, night VFR flights require the following additional equipment as per 14 CFR §91.205(c): approved position lights, anti-collision light system, a source of electrical energy adequate for all installed electrical and radio equipment, one spare set of fuses, or three spare fuses of each kind required, if fuses are used, landing light (if the aircraft is operated for hire), and an adequate source of electrical power for all installed electrical and radio equipment.

[PH.I.B.K3; 14 CFR 91.205]

34. Are there any specific instruments required for both day and night VFR flights?

Yes, certain instruments are required for both day and night VFR flights, such as an airspeed indicator, altimeter, and magnetic direction indicator. These instruments are essential for basic navigation and aircraft control.

[PH.I.B.K3; 14 CFR 91.205]

35. Is a transponder required for VFR flights?

A transponder with Mode C capability is required for VFR flights in certain controlled airspace, generally around busy airports and in Class B and C airspace, and above 10,000 feet MSL excluding the airspace at and below 2,500 feet AGL.

[PH.I.B.K3; 14 CFR 91.215]

36. What documents are required to be on board the aircraft for every flight?

The following documents (**A.R.R.O.W.P.D.C.**):

A – Airworthiness certificate

R – Registration certificate

R – Radio station license (if operating internationally)

O – Operating Limitations (usually found in POH/AFM)

W – Weight and balance sheet (specific for that aircraft, located in AFM)

P – Placards

D – Data plate

C – Compass deviation card

[PH.I.B.K3; 14 CFR 91.9, 91.203]

37. Can a private pilot operate an aircraft with inoperative equipment?

Yes, a private pilot can operate an aircraft with inoperative equipment, provided the equipment is not required by the type certificate, the Federal Aviation Regulations for the specific kind of flight operation, or the aircraft's equipment list or kinds of operations equipment list.

[PH.I.B.K3a; 14 CFR 91.213]

38. What steps must a pilot take if they discover inoperative equipment before a flight?

A pilot must first determine if the equipment is required for the flight. They can consult the aircraft's flight manual, the Federal Aviation Regulations or the minimum equipment list (MEL), if applicable. If the equipment is not required, it can either be repaired, removed, or deactivated and placarded as inoperative, in accordance with the procedures outlined in 14 CFR §91.213.

[PH.I.B.K3a; 14 CFR 91.213]

39. Is an aircraft considered airworthy if it has inoperative equipment?

An aircraft can be considered airworthy with inoperative equipment if the equipment is not required for safe flight, and the aircraft meets the conditions for operation with inoperative equipment under 14 CFR §91.213. The aircraft's maintenance records should reflect the deactivation and placarding of the inoperative equipment.

[PH.I.B.K3a; 14 CFR 91.213]

40. How should inoperative equipment be handled during preflight checks?

A pilot should identify any inoperative equipment and follow the procedures in 14 CFR §91.213. This includes determining whether the flight can proceed legally and safely, ensuring the equipment is appropriately placarded, and making an entry in the aircraft's maintenance records if necessary.

[PH.I.B.K3a; 14 CFR 91.213]

Example Scenario:

In the scenario where you are preparing for a day VFR flight in a Robinson R44 helicopter, you discover during your preflight checks that the VHF radio is not functioning. Here's how you should apply appropriate procedures for operating with this inoperative equipment:

1. *Regulations and documentation reference*—Check the Federal Aviation Regulations (FARs) and the helicopter's operating handbook to determine if a VHF radio is mandatory equipment for your planned day VFR flight. According to 14 CFR §91.205, a VHF radio is not explicitly required for VFR flight in uncontrolled airspace.

2. *Consult the minimum equipment list (MEL)*—If the R44 has an MEL, reference it to see if it allows flight without a functioning VHF radio and under what specific conditions. If no MEL exists, 14 CFR §91.213 provides guidance for operating without certain equipment.

3. *Risk assessment and flight plan adjustment*—Evaluate how the lack of a VHF radio affects your flight safety, especially communication with air traffic control, other aircraft, and for receiving updates on weather or airspace changes. Adjust your flight plan to avoid controlled airspace and areas where radio communication is typically required.

4. *Logbook entry and placarding*—Record the inoperative VHF radio in the maintenance logbook and place a placard in the cockpit indicating the radio is not to be used.

5. *Alternative communication methods*—Consider alternative means of communication if necessary, such as a portable handheld radio, as a backup.

6. *Final judgment on airworthiness*—Assess whether the helicopter is still airworthy for the intended flight considering the inoperative equipment and make a final decision. If unsure, consult with a certified aviation maintenance technician.

7. *Pilot-in-command decision*—As the pilot-in-command, your decision should prioritize safety and compliance with aviation regulations. Consider the importance of the flight versus the safety implications of flying without a VHF radio.

By carefully evaluating the implications of the inoperative VHF radio and taking the necessary steps as outlined, you ensure a responsible and compliant approach to managing inoperative equipment in aviation.

41. What is a minimum equipment list (MEL)?

An FAA-approved document specific to a particular aircraft make and model that lists equipment that can be inoperative while still maintaining the aircraft's airworthiness. It outlines the conditions and limitations under which a flight can be legally conducted even if certain equipment is not functional.

[PH.I.B.K3b; FAA-H-8083-25]

42. How is an MEL developed and approved?

An MEL is developed based on the master minimum equipment list (MMEL) for the aircraft type, which is provided by the FAA. Operators customize the MMEL to their specific aircraft and operational needs, and then submit it to the FAA for approval. The approved MEL becomes a binding document for that particular aircraft.

[PH.I.B.K3b; FAA-H-8083-25]

43. Is it mandatory for all aircraft to have an MEL?

No. However, for aircraft operated under certain regulations like 14 CFR Part 135, an MEL is typically required. For 14 CFR Part 91 operations, it's optional but beneficial as it provides clear guidance on managing inoperative equipment.

[PH.I.B.K3b; FAA-H-8083-25]

44. How does a pilot use an MEL during preflight planning?

During preflight planning, a pilot uses an MEL to determine if the aircraft is airworthy when certain equipment is inoperative. The pilot checks each inoperative item against the MEL to ensure compliance with the specified conditions and procedures, including any required placarding or maintenance actions.

[PH.I.B.K3b; FAA-H-8083-25]

45. What happens if an item not listed in the MEL is found inoperative?

If an inoperative item is not listed in the MEL, the aircraft may not be airworthy for flight. The pilot must consult the aircraft's equipment list, FARs, or other documentation to determine if the flight can proceed safely without that equipment.

[PH.I.B.K3b; FAA-H-8083-25]

46. What is the kinds of operation equipment list (KOEL)?

A specified inventory of equipment, instruments, and systems required for different types of operations (such as VFR, IFR, night, or high-altitude flight) for a particular aircraft, the KOEL ensures an aircraft is appropriately equipped for the intended operation.

[PH.I.B.K3c; FAA-H-8083-25]

47. How does the KOEL differ from the minimum equipment list (MEL)?

The KOEL specifies equipment necessary for various types of operations, whereas the MEL lists items that can be inoperative while still maintaining airworthiness. The KOEL focuses on operational requirements, while the MEL addresses equipment that, if inoperative, does not ground the aircraft.

[PH.I.B.K3c; FAA-H-8083-25]

48. Who is responsible for ensuring compliance with the KOEL?

The pilot-in-command (PIC).

[PH.I.B.K3c; FAA-H-8083-25]

49. Is the KOEL a mandatory document for all aircraft?

The KOEL itself is not a standalone mandatory document for all aircraft, but compliance with the equipment requirements for specific types of operations is mandatory. These requirements can be found in the aircraft's operating handbook, FARs, and other regulatory documents.

[PH.I.B.K3c; FAA-H-8083-25]

50. How is the KOEL used during preflight planning?

During preflight planning, the PIC uses the KOEL (or equivalent information) to verify that the aircraft is equipped for the specific type of flight planned, such as VFR or IFR. This includes checking for the presence and functionality of required navigation aids, communication equipment, lighting, and other systems as applicable.

[PH.I.B.K3c; FAA-H-8083-25]

51. What should a pilot do if the aircraft lacks equipment listed in the KOEL for a planned flight?

The pilot must either obtain the missing equipment before the flight, change the type of operation to one for which the aircraft is equipped, or postpone/cancel the flight. Flying without the required equipment for the intended operation is not permissible.

[PH.I.B.K3c; FAA-H-8083-25]

52. What are discrepancy records in aviation?

Logs or entries that detail any malfunctions, defects, or inoperative equipment found during aircraft inspections or operations. These records are essential for tracking maintenance needs and ensuring the continued airworthiness of the aircraft.

[PH.I.B.K3d; FAA-H-8083-25]

53. When must a placard be used in an aircraft?

A placard must be used to mark inoperative equipment or instruments in an aircraft when such items are not required for the safe operation of the flight and the flight operation is permitted under the aircraft's minimum equipment list (MEL) or as per 14 CFR §91.213 for aircraft without an MEL. The placard is used to inform the pilot and prevent the use of the inoperative item.

[PH.I.B.K3d; FAA-H-8083-25]

54. Who is responsible for ensuring that discrepancy records or placards are accurate and up to date?

The aircraft owner or operator is primarily responsible for ensuring that discrepancy records or placards are accurate, current, and reflect the true condition of the aircraft. It's also the responsibility of maintenance personnel to accurately log discrepancies and placard inoperative items.

[PH.I.B.K3d; FAA-H-8083-25]

55. What information must be included in a discrepancy record or placard?

A discrepancy record must include a description of the problem, the date it was observed, and any actions taken. A placard must clearly identify the inoperative equipment or instrument, be legible to the crew, and be placed in a position to prevent inadvertent operation of the inoperative item.

[PH.I.B.K3d; FAA-H-8083-25]

56. What is a special airworthiness certificate?

A special airworthiness certificate is an FAA-issued certificate that authorizes the operation of an aircraft that does not meet standard airworthiness requirements but is safe for specific operations. This certificate is commonly used for experimental, restricted, or light-sport aircraft.

[PH.I.B.K4; FAA-H-8083-25]

57. What are the pilot qualifications required to operate an aircraft with a special airworthiness certificate?

Pilot qualifications for operating an aircraft with a special airworthiness certificate include having the appropriate pilot certificate and ratings for the type of aircraft being flown. Additionally, pilots may need specific training or endorsements, especially for experimental or unusual aircraft.

[PH.I.B.K4; FAA-H-8083-25]

58. What should a pilot do upon discovering inoperative equipment before a flight?

Upon discovering inoperative equipment before a flight, a pilot should first consult the aircraft's minimum equipment list (MEL) or, if no MEL exists, follow the guidelines in 14 CFR §91.213 to determine if the flight can legally and safely proceed. The pilot must assess whether the inoperative equipment affects the aircraft's airworthiness or the safety of the flight.

[PH.I.B.R1; 14 CFR 91.213]

59. How does a pilot assess the risk associated with inoperative equipment?

A pilot assesses the risk associated with inoperative equipment by considering the equipment's function, the planned flight profile, and the prevailing conditions. Factors to consider include the necessity of the equipment for the specific type of operation (VFR or IFR), weather conditions, daylight versus night operations, and the availability of backups or alternatives.

[PH.I.B.R1; FAA-H-8083-25]

60. What are the mitigation strategies for flying with inoperative equipment?

Mitigation strategies include deferring the equipment under the MEL or 14 CFR §91.213 guidelines, using alternate or backup systems if available, adjusting the flight plan to avoid scenarios where the equipment would be critical, or deciding not to conduct the flight if safe operation is compromised.

[PH.I.B.R1; FAA-H-8083-25]

61. Is it mandatory to record inoperative equipment before a flight?

Yes, it is mandatory to record inoperative equipment in the aircraft's maintenance logbook, noting the nature of the defect, the date it was observed, and any action taken. The equipment should be placarded as inoperative to alert the crew.

[PH.I.B.R1; 14 CFR 91.213]

62. Can a pilot decide to fly without repairing inoperative equipment?

Only if the equipment is not required for the intended operation as per the MEL or 14 CFR §91.213, and if its absence does not compromise the safety of the flight. The pilot must still ensure that all regulatory and safety requirements are met.

[PH.I.B.R1; 14 CFR 91.213]

63. **What additional precautions should a pilot take when operating with inoperative equipment?**

Conducting a more thorough preflight check, briefing passengers about the inoperative equipment and any impact it may have, and being prepared with alternative procedures in case of unforeseen issues during the flight.

[PH.I.B.R1; FAA-H-8083-25]

Skills to be demonstrated:

• Locate and describe helicopter airworthiness and registration information.

• Determine the helicopter is airworthy in the scenario given by the evaluator.

• Apply appropriate procedures for operating with inoperative equipment in the scenario given by the evaluator.

C. Weather Information

1. **What are the primary sources of weather data for pilots during flight planning?**

National Weather Service (NWS), Flight Service Stations (FSS), Automated Flight Service Stations (AFSS), online aviation weather services, and 1800WXBRIEF. These sources provide forecasts, METARs, TAFs, significant weather charts, and personalized weather briefings essential for safe flight planning.

[PH.I.C.K1; FAA-H-8083-28]

2. **How does the National Weather Service contribute to aviation weather reporting?**

The National Weather Service provides extensive weather forecasting and reporting services crucial for aviation, offering products like METARs, TAFs, area forecasts, weather advisories, and radar imagery, which are vital for flight planning and decision-making.

[PH.I.C.K1; FAA-H-8083-28]

3. What role do Flight Service Stations (FSS) play in providing weather information?

Flight Service Stations offer personalized weather briefings to pilots, including en route weather information, destination forecasts, and weather-related advisories or warnings. Pilots can contact FSS for preflight briefings and updates during the flight.

[PH.I.C.K1; FAA-H-8083-28]

4. Can pilots use online weather services for flight planning?

Yes, pilots can utilize online weather services for flight planning. These services provide real-time weather data, forecasts, radar imagery, and other relevant tools for pilots to make informed decisions regarding their flights.

[PH.I.C.K1; FAA-H-8083-25]

5. What is the significance of 1800WXBRIEF for weather information?

1800WXBRIEF is a comprehensive source for pilots to access weather briefings and flight planning information. It offers services like flight plan filing, obtaining weather briefings, and accessing navigational aids, making it a vital tool for pilots in flight preparation.

[PH.I.C.K1; AIM 7-1-2]

6. Are there mobile applications available for aviation weather?

Yes, there are various mobile applications available that provide aviation weather information, featuring interactive weather maps, METARs, TAFs, NEXRAD radar imagery, and other important weather data. Pilots should choose apps from reliable sources to ensure accuracy and currency of the information.

[PH.I.C.K1; FAA-H-8083-28]

7. What is a METAR and what information does it provide?

A METAR is an aviation routine weather report that provides current weather conditions at an airport or airfield. It includes data on temperature, dew point, wind direction and speed, visibility, cloud cover, barometric pressure, and current weather phenomena. METARs are essential for understanding the latest weather conditions at specific locations.

[PH.I.C.K2a; FAA-H-8083-28]

8. How often are METARs issued, and where can pilots find them?

METARs are typically issued once an hour. However, in rapidly changing weather conditions, special weather reports (SPECI) can be issued in between regular METARs. Pilots can access METARs through Flight Service Stations, online aviation weather services, and various mobile applications including 1800wxbrief.com.

[PH.I.C.K2a; FAA-H-8083-28]

9. What is a PIREP, and why is it important for pilots?

A pilot report (PIREP) is a report submitted by pilots describing actual weather conditions encountered during their flight. PIREPs provide valuable information on weather phenomena like turbulence, icing, cloud heights, and visibility, which might not be fully captured by ground-based weather reporting systems. They are crucial for real-time weather assessment and for the safety of subsequent flights.

[PH.I.C.K2a; FAA-H-8083-28]

10. How can pilots submit a PIREP, and what information should it include?

Pilots can submit a PIREP during flight via radio communication with ATC or a Flight Service Station. A PIREP should include location, altitude, type of aircraft, and details about specific weather phenomena encountered, such as type and severity of turbulence, cloud cover, visibility, and any other significant weather observations.

[PH.I.C.K2a; FAA-H-8083-28]

11. Can PIREPs influence flight planning and decisions?

Yes, PIREPs can significantly influence flight planning and in-flight decisions. By providing real-time, firsthand accounts of weather conditions, PIREPs help pilots anticipate and prepare for similar conditions, adjust flight plans, and make informed decisions for safer flight operations.

[PH.I.C.K2a; FAA-H-8083-28]

12. What is a Terminal Area Forecast (TAF), and what information does it contain?

A Terminal Area Forecast (TAF) is a detailed weather forecast specifically for the area around an airport. It provides predicted weather conditions over a 24 or 30-hour period, including wind direction and speed, visibility, cloud cover, temperature, and the likelihood of significant weather phenomena like rain, snow, or thunderstorms.

[PH.I.C.K2b; FAA-H-8083-28]

13. How often are TAFs issued and for what duration do they provide forecasts?

TAFs are issued four times a day, every six hours, and typically provide weather forecasts for a 24- or 30-hour period. This regular issuance ensures that pilots have access to the most current and relevant forecast information for flight planning.

[PH.I.C.K2b; FAA-H-8083-28]

14. What are Graphical Forecasts for Aviation (GFAs), and how do they benefit pilots?

Graphical Forecasts for Aviation (GFAs) are a set of web-based displays that provide comprehensive weather information relevant to aviation. GFAs include data on cloud cover, flight category, precipitation, icing, turbulence, and winds aloft. They offer a visually intuitive way for pilots to assess weather conditions across large areas, aiding in flight planning and situational awareness.

[PH.I.C.K2b; FAA-H-8083-28]

15. How can pilots access TAFs and GFAs?

Pilots can access TAFs through Flight Service Stations, online aviation weather services, and various aviation weather apps. GFAs are available on the Aviation Weather Center's website and can be accessed through the internet, offering an interactive and user-friendly interface for weather analysis.

[PH.I.C.K2b; FAA-H-8083-28]

16. In what ways do TAFs and GFAs complement each other for flight planning?

TAFs provide detailed forecasts for specific airports, while GFAs offer a broader view of weather patterns over larger geographical areas. Together, they give pilots a comprehensive understanding of both local and regional weather conditions, which is critical for effective flight planning and decision-making.

[PH.I.C.K2b; FAA-H-8083-28]

17. Are there any limitations to using TAFs and GFAs for flight planning?

The limitations of TAFs include their focus on a specific airport area and the possibility of rapid weather changes not captured within the forecast period. GFAs, while providing a broad overview, may lack the localized detail of TAFs. Pilots should use these forecasts in conjunction with other weather reports and observations for a complete weather assessment.

[PH.I.C.K2b; FAA-H-8083-28]

18. What is an AIRMET, and what type of information does it provide?

An AIRMET (airman's meteorological information) is a weather advisory issued to alert pilots of weather conditions that may affect the safety of aircraft in flight. AIRMETs cover moderate icing, moderate turbulence, sustained winds of 30 knots or more at the surface, widespread areas of ceilings less than 1,000 feet and/or visibility less than 3 miles, and extensive mountain obscuration.

[PH.I.C.K2c; FAA-H-8083-28]

19. How frequently are AIRMETs issued, and for what duration?

AIRMETs are issued every six hours with intermediate updates, as necessary. Each AIRMET is valid for a six-hour period but may be updated more frequently if weather conditions change significantly.

[PH.I.C.K2c; FAA-H-8083-28]

20. What is a SIGMET, and what weather phenomena does it cover?

A SIGMET (Significant Meteorological Information) is a weather advisory that provides information on hazardous weather not covered by AIRMETs. SIGMETs are issued for severe icing, severe or extreme turbulence, dust storms, sandstorms, and volcanic ash that reduce visibility to less than 3 miles, and for thunderstorms that produce hail at the surface and/or wind gusts of 50 knots or more.

[PH.I.C.K2c; FAA-H-8083-28]

21. What is the difference between an AIRMET and a SIGMET?

The main difference between an AIRMET and a SIGMET is the severity of the weather conditions they report. AIRMETs inform pilots about moderate but potentially hazardous weather conditions, while SIGMETs are issued for severe weather phenomena that pose a significant risk to all aircraft.

[PH.I.C.K2c; FAA-H-8083-28]

22. How can pilots access AIRMETs and SIGMETs?

Pilots can access AIRMETs and SIGMETs through Flight Service Stations, online aviation weather services, aviation weather apps, and during preflight briefings from the weather briefer. These advisories are also available through in-flight communication with ATC.

[PH.I.C.K2c; FAA-H-8083-28]

23. Why are AIRMETs and SIGMETs crucial for in-flight decision-making?

AIRMETs and SIGMETs are crucial for in-flight decision-making because they provide timely and detailed information on potentially hazardous weather conditions. Pilots rely on these advisories to make informed decisions about route changes, altitude adjustments, or even delaying or diverting a flight for safety.

[PH.I.C.K2c; FAA-H-8083-28]

24. What is a winds and temperatures aloft forecast (FB), and what information does it provide?

A winds and temperatures aloft forecast (FB) is a weather product that provides predicted data for wind direction, wind speed, and temperature at various altitudes. These forecasts are essential for flight planning, as they help pilots anticipate wind conditions, calculate fuel requirements, and plan efficient flight paths.

[PH.I.C.K2d; FAA-H-8083-28]

25. How are the winds and temperatures in an FB forecast reported?

Winds are reported in knots, with direction given in degrees true. Temperatures are reported in degrees Celsius. For example, a forecast might read "27040 −02" indicating a wind from 270 degrees at 40 knots and a temperature of −2 degrees Celsius.

[PH.I.C.K2d; FAA-H-8083-28]

26. At what altitudes are wind and temperature forecasts provided in an FB?

Wind and temperature forecasts in an FB are typically provided for standard pressure altitudes starting from 3,000 feet above mean sea level (AMSL) and in 3,000 or 6,000-foot intervals up to 39,000 feet or higher.

[PH.I.C.K2d; FAA-H-8083-28]

27. How frequently are FBs issued, and for what duration do they forecast?

FBs are issued four times daily and provide forecasts that are valid for specific 12-hour periods. This regular issuance ensures that pilots have access to current and relevant wind and temperature data for their flight planning.

[PH.I.C.K2d; FAA-H-8083-28]

28. Why are FBs important for flight planning and enroute navigation?

FBs are important for flight planning and enroute navigation as they help pilots anticipate headwinds, tailwinds, and crosswinds, which can affect flight time and fuel consumption. Understanding temperature aloft is also crucial for performance planning and avoiding potential hazards like icing conditions.

[PH.I.C.K2d; FAA-H-8083-28]

29. Where can pilots access winds and temperatures aloft forecasts?

Pilots can access winds and temperatures aloft forecasts through Flight Service Stations, online at 1800WXBRIEF.com, and various aviation weather apps. These forecasts are also available during preflight briefings and can be a part of the weather package provided by flight planning tools.

[PH.I.C.K2d; FAA-H-8083-28]

30. What is a surface analysis chart, and what information does it provide?

A surface analysis chart is a graphical representation of current surface weather conditions over a large geographic area. It includes information on pressure systems, fronts, wind direction and speed, temperature, dew point, and significant weather phenomena like precipitation and thunderstorms. These charts are crucial for pilots to understand the broad weather patterns affecting their flight routes.

[PH.I.C.K2e; FAA-H-8083-28]

31. How often are surface analysis charts updated, and where can pilots access them?

Surface analysis charts are updated eight times daily, valid at 00, 03, 06, 09, 12, 15, 18, and 21 coordinated universal time (UTC). Pilots can access these charts through 1800WXBRIEF, and various aviation weather apps. They are also commonly available in preflight weather briefings provided by flight planning services.

[PH.I.C.K2e; FAA-H-8083-28]

32. What is a weather depiction chart, and how is it used in flight planning?

A weather depiction chart provides a visual summary of current weather conditions, including cloud cover, types of precipitation, visibility, and weather fronts across the United States. It's particularly useful for VFR pilots in determining areas of VFR and IFR conditions, helping them make informed decisions about flight routes and the need for alternate planning.

[PH.I.C.K2e; FAA-H-8083-28]

33. What are the primary features shown on a weather depiction chart?

Areas of VFR (visual flight rules), MVFR (marginal VFR), IFR (instrument flight rules), and LIFR (low IFR) conditions. It also shows weather fronts, high and low-pressure systems, and significant meteorological phenomena like thunderstorms and precipitation.

[PH.I.C.K2e; FAA-H-8083-28]

34. How do surface analysis and weather depiction charts complement each other in flight planning?

Surface analysis charts offer a broad view of the atmospheric pressure patterns and frontal systems, while weather depiction charts provide more specific information about cloud cover, visibility, and precipitation. Together, they give pilots a comprehensive understanding of current weather conditions, aiding in both VFR and IFR flight planning.

[PH.I.C.K2e; FAA-H-8083-28]

35. What is a significant weather prognostic chart?

Provides charts of surface pressure systems, fronts, and precipitation for a 2½-day period. The forecast area covers the CONUS, the coastal waters. The forecasted conditions are divided into five forecast periods: 12, 18, 24, 48, and 60 hours. Each chart depicts a snapshot of weather elements expected at the specified valid time.

[PH.I.C.K2f; FAA-H-8083-28]

36. What specific weather information is depicted on these charts?

Significant weather prognostic charts illustrate various weather phenomena including frontal systems, high and low-pressure areas, areas of expected thunderstorms or severe convection, regions of turbulence (light, moderate, severe), icing conditions, and areas with specific flight category conditions like IFR or MVFR.

[PH.I.C.K2f; FAA-H-8083-28]

37. What is a thunderstorm watch, and what does it signify for pilots?

A thunderstorm watch (often issued as a convective SIGMET in the United States) indicates that conditions are favorable for the development of thunderstorms over a large area. For pilots, it signifies a need for caution, as thunderstorms can produce severe turbulence, icing, hail, and strong winds, potentially impacting flight safety.

[PH.I.C.K2g; FAA-H-8083-28]

38. How do thunderstorm warnings differ from thunderstorm watches?

Thunderstorm warnings are issued when a thunderstorm is occurring or imminent in a specific area, indicating a more immediate and localized threat. Unlike a watch, which indicates potential development, a warning means that thunderstorm activity is already happening or expected shortly, requiring prompt action by pilots to avoid the affected area.

[PH.I.C.K2g; FAA-H-8083-28]

39. What information is provided on convective activity forecast charts?

Convective activity forecast charts provide information on areas where convective weather, such as thunderstorms or severe turbulence, is forecasted. These charts typically show areas of expected convective activity, including the severity and coverage, helping pilots to anticipate and plan for potential thunderstorm-related hazards during flight.

[PH.I.C.K2g; FAA-H-8083-28]

40. How frequently are convective activity forecast charts updated?

Convective activity forecast charts are updated regularly, typically every few hours, to reflect changing weather conditions and the latest forecasts. This frequent updating ensures that pilots have access to current information for flight planning and in-flight decision-making.

[PH.I.C.K2g; FAA-H-8083-28]

41. Where can pilots find information about thunderstorm watches, warnings, and convective forecasts?

Information about thunderstorm watches, warnings, and convective forecasts can be obtained from Flight Service Stations, online aviation weather services, aviation weather apps, and during preflight weather briefings. These sources provide up-to-date information essential for safe flight planning and operations.

[PH.I.C.K2g; FAA-H-8083-28]

42. How does atmospheric stability affect flying weather conditions?

Atmospheric stability influences weather; stable air suppresses cloud formation and leads to clear conditions, while unstable air promotes cloud development and weather disturbances like thunderstorms and turbulence.

[PH.I.C.K3a; FAA-H-8083-28]

43. What indicates a stable atmosphere in aviation?

Stratiform clouds, smooth air, poor visibility due to haze, and steady precipitation, suggesting limited vertical air movement and smoother flight conditions.

[PH.I.C.K3a; FAA-H-8083-28]

44. What characterizes an unstable atmosphere?

Cumuliform clouds, turbulence, good visibility except in precipitation, and showery precipitation, often leading to thunderstorms.

[PH.I.C.K3a; FAA-H-8083-28]

45. How does atmospheric stability relate to thunderstorm development?

In an unstable atmosphere, warm, moist air rises and cools, forming cumulus clouds that can develop into cumulonimbus clouds and thunderstorms, crucial for pilots to consider for safety.

[PH.I.C.K3a; FAA-H-8083-28]

46. Why is understanding atmospheric stability important for pilots?

Aids pilots in predicting weather changes, identifying turbulence, and making safe decisions about flight routes and altitudes.

[PH.I.C.K3a; FAA-H-8083-28]

47. What is wind shear, and why is it significant for aviation?

Wind shear is a sudden change in wind speed or direction over a short distance. It's significant in aviation due to its potential to cause rapid changes in aircraft performance, particularly during takeoff and landing phases.

[PH.I.C.K3b; FAA-H-8083-28]

48. What is a mountain wave, and how does it affect flying?

A mountain wave is a type of turbulence that occurs on the leeward side of mountains, caused by airflow disruption. It can lead to severe turbulence and altitude changes, challenging for pilots flying near mountainous terrain.

[PH.I.C.K3b; FAA-H-8083-28]

49. What factors affect wind patterns and behaviors in aviation?

Factors affecting wind include geographic features (like mountains and valleys), atmospheric pressure differences, temperature variations, and the Earth's rotation. These factors influence wind direction, speed, and patterns, impacting flight planning and operations.

[PH.I.C.K3b; FAA-H-8083-28]

50. How can pilots prepare for and manage wind-related flying challenges?

Pilots can prepare for wind challenges by studying weather forecasts, understanding local wind patterns, and receiving training on handling wind shear and turbulence. Good situational awareness and adherence to operational procedures are crucial for safely managing wind-related issues.

[PH.I.C.K3b; FAA-H-8083-28]

51. How does temperature affect aircraft performance?

Higher temperatures can reduce air density, leading to decreased engine efficiency, lift, and overall aircraft performance, especially during takeoff and climb.

[PH.I.C.K3c; FAA-H-8083-28]

52. What is heat exchange in the context of aviation, and why is it important?

Heat exchange in aviation refers to the transfer of heat between the aircraft and the surrounding environment. It's important for understanding engine cooling, cabin temperature control, and the effects of atmospheric conditions on aircraft systems.

[PH.I.C.K3c; FAA-H-8083-28]

53. How do temperature variations impact flight planning?

Temperature variations impact flight planning by affecting runway length requirements, climb performance, fuel efficiency, and altitude selection. Pilots must consider temperature in their calculations for safe and efficient flight operations.

[PH.I.C.K3c; FAA-H-8083-28]

54. What role does heat exchange play in aircraft engine operations?

Heat exchange is crucial in engine operations for maintaining optimal engine temperatures. Effective cooling systems are essential to prevent overheating, ensure efficient engine performance, and prolong engine life.

[PH.I.C.K3c; FAA-H-8083-28]

55. How does moisture in the atmosphere affect aviation?

Moisture in the atmosphere affects aviation by contributing to weather phenomena such as cloud formation, fog, precipitation, and icing conditions. These factors can impact visibility, aircraft performance, and flight safety.

[PH.I.C.K3d; FAA-H-8083-28]

56. Why is understanding precipitation important for flight planning and operations?

Understanding precipitation is important for flight planning and operations as it helps pilots anticipate weather-related challenges, choose suitable flight routes and altitudes, and make informed decisions about diversions or delays for safety.

[PH.I.C.K3d; FAA-H-8083-28]

57. How can pilots mitigate the risks associated with moisture and precipitation?

obtaining accurate weather briefings, using onboard weather radar (if available), applying anti-icing and deicing procedures, and practicing sound judgment in decision-making under adverse weather conditions.

[PH.I.C.K3d; FAA-H-8083-28]

58. What is an air mass, and how does it influence weather?

An air mass is a large body of air with relatively uniform temperature and humidity characteristics. It influences weather by determining the general temperature, humidity, and stability of the air over a region, affecting cloud formation, precipitation, and other weather phenomena.

[PH.I.C.K3e; FAA-H-8083-28]

59. How do fronts form, and what weather changes do they bring?

Fronts form at the boundary between two different air masses. A front brings significant weather changes as it passes, such as temperature shifts, wind changes, and precipitation. Types of fronts include cold fronts, warm fronts, stationary fronts, and occluded fronts, each associated with specific weather patterns.

[PH.I.C.K3e; FAA-H-8083-28]

60. What are the typical weather conditions associated with a cold front?

A cold front typically brings cooler air, clear skies after passage, and often leads to the development of cumulonimbus clouds, resulting in thunderstorms, heavy rain, or hail. Wind shifts and temperature drops are also common.

[PH.I.C.K3e; FAA-H-8083-28]

61. How do warm fronts affect aviation weather?

Warm fronts are associated with gradual temperature increases, widespread cloudiness, and prolonged precipitation. Stratus clouds and fog are common, leading to reduced visibility, which can impact flight operations, particularly during takeoff and landing.

[PH.I.C.K3e; FAA-H-8083-28]

62. What weather phenomena are associated with stationary and occluded fronts?

Stationary fronts can lead to prolonged periods of cloudiness and precipitation, similar to warm fronts. Occluded fronts, formed when a cold front overtakes a warm front, often bring complex weather patterns, combining characteristics of both cold and warm fronts, including varied precipitation types and temperature changes.

[PH.I.C.K3e; FAA-H-8083-28]

63. What are the different types of clouds, and how do they impact aviation?

Clouds are classified based on their appearance and altitude. Key types include:

- Cumulus (associated with fair weather or thunderstorms)
- Stratus (indicative of stable conditions, often bringing steady rain or drizzle)
- Cirrus (high-altitude, wispy clouds, usually signaling changes in weather)
- Cumulonimbus (thunderstorm clouds, associated with severe weather conditions)

Each type has different implications for aviation, affecting visibility, turbulence, and flight planning.

[PH.I.C.K3f; FAA-H-8083-28]

64. How do cloud formations influence a pilot's decision-making and flight strategy?

Pilots must navigate to avoid cumulonimbus clouds due to turbulence and icing risks, consider altitude adjustments for cloud layer avoidance, and prepare for instrument meteorological conditions when flying through extensive cloud cover. Understanding cloud types aids in anticipating weather changes and ensuring flight safety.

[PH.I.C.K3f; FAA-H-8083-28]

65. What is turbulence, and what causes it in aviation?

Turbulence is irregular atmospheric motion characterized by rapid changes in wind speed and direction. It's caused by various factors, including atmospheric pressure variations, jet streams, air around mountains, weather fronts, and thunderstorms.

[PH.I.C.K3g; FAA-H-8083-28]

66. How are different intensities of turbulence classified in aviation?

Turbulence is classified into four intensities:

- *Light turbulence* causes slight, erratic changes in altitude and/or attitude.
- *Moderate turbulence* causes changes that affect aircraft control but not violently.
- *Severe turbulence* causes large, abrupt changes in altitude and/ or attitude.
- *Extreme turbulence* involves the aircraft being violently tossed and practically impossible to control.

[PH.I.C.K3g; FAA-H-8083-28]

67. What operational considerations do pilots need to keep in mind when encountering turbulence?

Pilots should reduce airspeed to the turbulence penetration speed (or maneuvering speed V_A) recommended by the aircraft manufacturer, avoid thunderstorms and cumulonimbus clouds, maintain a level flight attitude, and inform passengers and crew. It's also crucial to report turbulence to air traffic control for the safety of other aircraft.

[PH.I.C.K3g; FAA-H-8083-28]

68. How can pilots anticipate and avoid areas of turbulence?

Studying weather forecasts, identifying areas prone to turbulence (like mountainous regions or near jet streams), and using onboard weather radar if available. Reviewing pilot reports (PIREPs) and ATC communications about reported turbulence can also provide crucial real-time information.

[PH.I.C.K3g; FAA-H-8083-28]

69. What are the primary hazards associated with thunderstorms for aviation?

The primary hazards of thunderstorms for aviation include severe turbulence, hail, lightning, heavy rain, strong winds, and reduced visibility. Thunderstorms can also produce dangerous wind shear and microbursts, posing significant risks to aircraft, especially during takeoff and landing.

[PH.I.C.K3h; FAA-H-8083-28]

70. How do microbursts form within thunderstorms, and why are they dangerous for aircraft?

Microbursts form within thunderstorms due to intense downdrafts. They are localized columns of sinking air that spread outwards upon reaching the ground, creating strong wind shear. Microbursts are dangerous for aircraft because they can cause rapid changes in wind speed and direction, leading to loss of control or altitude, particularly during the critical phases of takeoff and landing.

[PH.I.C.K3h; FAA-H-8083-28]

71. What are the signs of a developing thunderstorm a pilot should look for?

Large, towering cumulus clouds, darkening skies, increasing wind, and visible precipitation. Pilots may also notice lightning or hear distant thunder. These indicators suggest that a thunderstorm is forming, and caution should be exercised.

[PH.I.C.K3h; FAA-H-8083-28]

72. How can pilots avoid the risks associated with thunderstorms and microbursts?

Pilots should plan routes that circumvent thunderstorm activity, use onboard weather radar for real-time information, monitor weather reports and PIREPs, and adhere to ATC advisories. During flights, maintaining a safe distance from thunderstorms and being prepared for potential wind shear or turbulence is crucial.

[PH.I.C.K3h; FAA-H-8083-28]

73. What are the three stages of a thunderstorm's life cycle?

Cumulus stage, mature stage, and dissipating stage. The cumulus stage is characterized by updrafts and cloud formation. The mature stage involves both updrafts and downdrafts, producing the most severe weather phenomena like heavy rain, hail, and lightning. The dissipating stage is marked by weakening activity with predominant downdrafts.

[PH.I.C.K3h; FAA-H-8083-28]

74. During which stage of a thunderstorm is the risk of severe weather phenomena the highest?

The mature stage of a thunderstorm. This stage is when the storm is most intense, producing heavy precipitation, strong winds, lightning, hail, and possibly tornadoes. It's also when the danger of wind shear and microbursts is greatest.

[PH.I.C.K3h; FAA-H-8083-28]

75. How can pilots determine the freezing level and potential icing conditions for helicopter operations?

Pilots can determine the freezing level and potential icing conditions by reviewing weather forecasts, pilot reports (PIREPs), area forecasts (FA), and AIRMETs. Special attention should be paid to temperature and dew point spreads, and altitude-specific forecasts to assess the likelihood of icing conditions.

[PH.I.C.K3i; FAA-H-8083-28]

76. What are the indications of icing in helicopters, and what immediate actions should pilots take?

Indications of icing in helicopters include a decrease in rotor RPM, unusual vibrations, changes in control response, and an unexplained drop in altitude or airspeed. Upon detecting icing, pilots should immediately exit the icing conditions, preferably descending to a warmer altitude or moving to an area with higher temperatures.

[PH.I.C.K3i; FAA-H-8083-21]

77. What preventative measures can helicopter pilots take to avoid icing conditions?

To avoid icing conditions, helicopter pilots should conduct thorough preflight weather briefings, avoid flight in known icing conditions, especially in temperatures close to freezing with visible moisture present, and use deicing or anti-icing equipment if the helicopter is equipped. Staying informed about weather changes during flight and being prepared to alter the flight path as needed is also crucial.

[PH.I.C.K3i; FAA-H-8083-21]

78. What is fog, and how does it form in aviation contexts?

Fog is a cloud that forms at the Earth's surface, characterized by tiny water droplets suspended in the air, leading to reduced visibility. It forms when the air near the ground cools to the dew point or when moisture is added to the air near the ground, often occurring in calm or light wind conditions.

[PH.I.C.K3j; FAA-H-8083-28]

79. How does mist differ from fog, and what is its impact on aviation?

Mist is similar to fog but with greater visibility (between 1,000 and 5,000 meters). While mist does not reduce visibility as drastically as fog, it can still affect flight operations, particularly during takeoff and landing, by reducing the ability to see other aircraft, runway markings, and obstacles.

[PH.I.C.K3j; FAA-H-8083-28]

80. What are the common types of fog encountered in aviation, and how are they formed?

Radiation fog, which forms on clear nights with calm winds when the ground cools rapidly; advection fog, caused by moist air moving over cooler surfaces; and upslope fog, forming as moist air is forced up a slope and cools adiabatically. Each type affects visibility differently and requires specific considerations in flight planning.

[PH.I.C.K3j; FAA-H-8083-28]

81. How can pilots manage the risks associated with flying in fog and mist?

Pilots should obtain accurate weather briefings, use instrument approach procedures in low visibility, and be prepared for go-arounds if necessary. It's also important to be aware of the potential for rapid weather changes and have alternate plans in case of unexpected fog or mist.

[PH.I.C.K3j; FAA-H-8083-28]

82. What is frost, and how does it form on aircraft?

Frost is a crystalline ice deposit that forms when the temperature of the aircraft's surface drops below the dew point of the surrounding air and below freezing. It commonly forms on aircraft surfaces during clear, cold nights with calm winds.

[PH.I.C.K3k; FAA-H-8083-28]

83. How does frost affect an aircraft's performance and safety?

By disrupting the smooth flow of air over the wings and control surfaces, leading to reduced lift and increased drag. Even a thin layer of frost can significantly impair an aircraft's aerodynamic efficiency, increasing the risk of stalling and affecting takeoff performance.

[PH.I.C.K3k; FAA-H-8083-28]

84. What are the recommended procedures for dealing with frost on aircraft?

Thoroughly removing frost from the aircraft's wings, control surfaces, and other critical areas before flight. This can be done using deicing fluids, mechanical means, or by allowing the aircraft to warm up sufficiently to melt the frost naturally.

[PH.I.C.K3k; FAA-H-8083-25]

85. How does smoke from wildfires or industrial sources impact helicopter flight visibility?

Smoke can significantly reduce visibility for helicopter operations, particularly during low-altitude flights often associated with helicopter routes. The fine particles in smoke can obscure landmarks and terrain, complicating navigation and landing, especially in areas like wildfire zones where helicopters are frequently used for operations.

[PH.I.C.K3l; FAA-H-8083-28]

86. What specific risks does volcanic ash pose to helicopters, and why is avoidance crucial?

Volcanic ash poses risks to helicopters including engine damage from ash ingestion, abrasion of rotor blades, and damage to avionics and airframes. These risks are heightened in helicopters due to their reliance on rotor systems and often lower flying altitudes. Avoidance of volcanic ash clouds is crucial to prevent these potentially severe hazards.

[PH.I.C.K3I; FAA-H-8083-21]

87. What precautions should helicopter pilots take when flying in areas with reduced visibility due to smoke, haze, or volcanic ash?

Exercise caution when flying in areas with reduced visibility due to smoke, haze, or volcanic ash. This includes using instrument flight rules (IFR) techniques in low visibility, rerouting or altitude adjustments to avoid affected areas, and staying updated on weather forecasts and pilot reports. It's also important to regularly check and maintain helicopter engines and rotor systems for any signs of damage from these particulates.

[PH.I.C.K3I; FAA-H-8083-28]

88. How do digital weather displays on a helicopter's flight deck enhance situational awareness?

By providing real-time weather information such as storm tracking, wind speed, turbulence, and icing conditions. This information is crucial for helicopter pilots, who often operate at lower altitudes where weather changes can be more immediate and impactful.

[PH.I.C.K4; FAA-H-8083-21]

89. What types of aeronautical information can be accessed through digital displays in helicopters, and why is this important?

Digital displays in helicopters can provide aeronautical information including airport data, airspace boundaries, navigation aids, and flight plan routing.

[PH.I.C.K4; FAA-H-8083-21]

90. What are the limitations of digital weather and aeronautical information systems in helicopters, and how should pilots manage these?

Limitations of digital weather and aeronautical information systems in helicopters include potential delays in data updates, coverage gaps, and system malfunctions. Pilots should manage these limitations by cross-checking with other sources like ATC or pilot reports, understanding the data's timeliness, and not relying solely on digital information for critical decisions.

[PH.I.C.K4; FAA-H-8083-21]

91. What specific weather conditions should lead a helicopter pilot to consider diverting?

Reduced visibility due to fog, heavy precipitation, thunderstorms, and icing conditions. Helicopter pilots must also be wary of wind shear and turbulence, which can be more pronounced at lower flying altitudes.

[PH.I.C.R1a; FAA-H-8083-28]

92. In what circumstances would diverting be a prudent choice for helicopter pilots?

Deteriorating weather along the flight path, unexpected airspace closures, indications of mechanical problems, or when the intended landing zone becomes unsuitable due to factors like crowd gathering or surface changes. Timely decision-making is crucial in these situations to ensure safety.

[PH.I.C.R1a; FAA-H-8083-21]

93. What are personal weather minimums, and how should helicopter pilots establish them?

Personal weather minimums are self-imposed limits on weather conditions that a pilot sets for safe operation, above the regulatory minimums. Helicopter pilots should establish these based on their experience, proficiency, helicopter type, mission type, and comfort level with various weather scenarios.

[PH.I.C.R1b; FAA-H-8083-28]

94. How do personal weather minimums influence a helicopter pilot's go/no-go decision?

By providing a clear boundary of acceptable weather conditions for safe flight. If forecasted or actual weather conditions are worse than a pilot's personal minimums, it would warrant a no-go decision, especially in helicopters which often operate in more challenging environments.

[PH.I.C.R1b; FAA-H-8083-28]

95. When should a helicopter pilot consider diverting due to weather, in the context of personal weather minimums?

If in-flight weather conditions deteriorate below your personal weather minimums. This includes unexpected visibility reduction, cloud ceiling lowering, or encountering weather phenomena like thunderstorms or icing, which were not anticipated or are beyond the pilot's comfort level.

[PH.I.C.R1b; FAA-H-8083-28]

96. What factors should a helicopter pilot consider when setting personal weather minimums?

A helicopter pilot should consider factors such as their overall flying experience, specific experience in weather conditions, helicopter capabilities, terrain, type of operation (e.g., medical, search and rescue), and whether the flight will be under visual or instrument flight rules.

[PH.I.C.R1b; FAA-H-8083-28]

97. How should helicopter pilots assess go/no-go decisions in the presence of hazardous weather conditions like icing or turbulence?

By carefully evaluating weather forecasts for icing or turbulence. Factors like helicopter capability, route altitude, availability of alternate routes, and the pilot's experience with handling adverse weather conditions should be considered. If the risk of encountering hazardous weather is high and beyond the pilot's comfort level or helicopter's capability, a no-go decision is prudent.

[PH.I.C.R1c; FAA-H-8083-21]

98. What considerations are crucial for a helicopter pilot when deciding to continue a flight or divert due to turbulent conditions?

Helicopter pilots should consider the severity of the turbulence, helicopter performance characteristics, terrain, the potential for fatigue and disorientation, and available alternate routes or landing zones. If turbulence adversely affects aircraft control or passenger comfort, diversion or landing should be considered.

[PH.I.C.R1c; FAA-H-8083-21]

99. What are the common types of onboard weather equipment found in helicopters, and what information do they provide?

Weather radar systems, satellite weather systems, and lightning detection systems. Weather radar systems provide information on storm intensity and location, satellite weather systems offer a broader view of weather patterns, and lightning detectors help identify thunderstorm activity. This equipment aids in strategic planning and situational awareness during flight.

[PH.I.C.R2a; FAA-H-8083-21]

100. What limitations do onboard weather systems have, and how can pilots compensate for these?

Limitations include signal attenuation, radar shadows, and time delays in weather data updates. Pilots can compensate for these limitations by cross-checking with other sources like ATC, pilot reports, and ground-based weather updates. Understanding the capabilities and limitations of their specific equipment is also essential for accurate interpretation.

[PH.I.C.R2a; FAA-H-8083-28]

101. In what ways can onboard weather equipment impact decision-making during helicopter operations?

Providing timely and detailed weather information, allowing helicopter pilots to make informed decisions about route adjustments, altitude changes, or the need to divert. It enhances safety by enabling avoidance of hazardous weather conditions and helping to plan for contingencies.

[PH.I.C.R2a; FAA-H-8083-21]

102. What are the limitations of aviation weather reports and forecasts, and how can helicopter pilots mitigate these issues?

Potential delays in updates, and localized weather phenomena not captured in broader forecasts. Helicopter pilots can mitigate these issues by using real-time information sources like onboard weather systems, pilot reports, and ATC updates. Understanding the specific weather patterns of the operating area and maintaining flexibility in flight plans is also crucial.

[PH.I.C.R2b; FAA-H-8083-28]

103. How should helicopter pilots interpret discrepancies between weather forecasts and actual conditions encountered during flight?

With caution, pilots should be prepared to modify their flight plan based on real-time observations and reports. When actual conditions are worse than forecasted, pilots might need to consider alternate routes, delay, or even divert to ensure safety. Continuous monitoring and flexibility are key in responding to unexpected weather changes.

[PH.I.C.R2b; FAA-H-8083-28]

104. What in-flight weather resources are commonly used in helicopter operations, and how do they enhance safety?

Satellite weather services, onboard weather radar, automatic dependent surveillance-broadcast (ADS-B) weather, and pilot reports (PIREPs). These resources enhance safety by providing real-time weather updates, enabling pilots to avoid adverse weather conditions like storms, turbulence, and icing, and to make informed decisions about route adjustments or diversions.

[PH.I.C.R2c; FAA-H-8083-28]

105. How do helicopter pilots manage the limitations of in-flight weather resources?

Cross-referencing multiple sources to validate information, being aware of potential delays in data updates, and understanding the specific capabilities and limitations of their equipment. Pilots should also maintain communication with air traffic control (ATC) for additional weather information and updates.

[PH.I.C.R2c; FAA-H-8083-28]

Skills to be demonstrated:

• Use available aviation weather resources to obtain an adequate weather briefing.

• Analyze the implications of at least three of the conditions listed in PH.I.C.K3a through PH.I.C.K3l, using actual weather or weather conditions provided by the evaluator.

• Correlate weather information to make a go/no-go decision.

D. Cross-Country Flight Planning

1. How should you plan your route considering the different classes of airspace?

Consider the entry requirements for each airspace class:

• Class B, obtain ATC clearance before entry
• Class C, establish two-way radio communication with ATC
• Class D, establish two-way radio communication with ATC
• Class E, ensure you comply with VFR weather minimums.

Plan your altitude and headings to meet these requirements, and be prepared for potential reroutes by ATC, especially near Class B and C airspaces and their desired VFR checkpoints.

[PH.I.D.K1; FAA-H-8083-25]

2. What considerations should you make regarding the special use airspace along your route?

Check the status of the special use airspace before and during your flight. If it's active, plan a route that avoids it or seek clearance to transit, if applicable. Be aware of the type of SUA (e.g., restricted, prohibited, MOA) and the activities that might be conducted there. Ensure you have up-to-date information on the SUA's active times and altitudes.

[PH.I.D.K1; FAA-H-8083-25]

3. What are the primary functions of an EFB that a helicopter pilot can utilize during preflight planning and in-flight operations?

An EFB provides several key functions for helicopter pilots, including access to digital charts (sectional, terminal area, and helicopter route charts), real-time weather information, flight planning tools, weight and balance calculations, and electronic checklists. It can also store important documents like aircraft manuals and NOTAMs, enhancing preflight planning and in-flight decision-making efficiency.

[PH.I.D.K1a; FAA-H-8083-25]

4. How should a helicopter pilot ensure the reliability and compliance of their EFB for flight operations?

A helicopter pilot should ensure the EFB is updated with the latest software and chart versions, confirm that the device meets FAA regulations for electronic flight bags, and have backup power sources like extra batteries or charging options. Additionally, the pilot should be familiar with operating the EFB and have a contingency plan, such as paper charts, in case the EFB fails.

[PH.I.D.K1a; FAA-H-8083-21]

5. How should you determine the appropriate cruising altitudes considering the terrain and obstacles along the route?

When selecting cruising altitudes, consider the highest terrain and tallest obstacles along your route. Add a safety margin above these heights for clearance. In mountainous areas, this margin should be increased due to potential updrafts and downdrafts. Use topographical charts and helicopter performance charts to identify safe altitudes that provide ample clearance and allow for effective autorotation in case of an engine failure.

[PH.I.D.K2; FAA-H-8083-25]

6. What are the autorotation requirements for helicopters, and how do they influence altitude selection?

Autorotation requirements involve maintaining an altitude that allows for a safe autorotative descent and landing in case of engine failure. The altitude selected should provide enough height for the pilot to establish autorotation and navigate to a suitable landing area. This is especially critical in mountainous or densely populated areas where suitable landing spots may be limited.

[PH.I.D.K2; FAA-H-8083-21]

7. How should VFR cruising altitudes be selected for helicopter flights, and what regulations apply?

VFR cruising altitudes for helicopters should comply with FAA regulations, which state that when flying more than 3,000 feet above ground level (AGL), pilots should fly at odd thousand foot MSL altitudes plus 500 feet when on a magnetic course of 0–179 degrees, and even thousand foot MSL altitudes plus 500 feet when on a course of 180–359 degrees. However, helicopter pilots have more flexibility and may choose altitudes that are most suitable for the mission and safety, considering terrain and other factors.

[PH.I.D.K2; FAA-H-8083-21]

8. How does wind affect altitude selection in helicopter operations, and what should be considered?

Wind can significantly affect helicopter performance and flight path stability. When selecting altitude, consider the direction and speed of the wind. Higher altitudes might offer more favorable wind conditions and smoother flight but can also mean stronger winds. Headwinds may require higher power settings, while tailwinds can improve ground speed. Crosswinds might necessitate course adjustments. Always consider wind effects on endurance and fuel planning.

[PH.I.D.K2; FAA-H-8083-21]

9. How do you calculate the estimated time for a helicopter flight based on distance and cruising speed?

Calculate the estimated flight time by dividing the total distance by the helicopter's cruising speed. For instance, if flying 120 nautical miles at a cruising speed of 100 knots, the time would be $120/100$ = 1.2 hours or 72 minutes. This estimation should be adjusted for any expected delays due to climb, descent, or wind conditions.

[PH.I.D.K3a; FAA-H-8083-25]

10. What considerations are important for calculating climb and descent rates in helicopter operations?

When calculating climb and descent rates, consider the helicopter's performance data, which varies with weight, altitude, air temperature, and wind conditions. The climb rate should ensure safe obstacle clearance, and the descent rate should allow for a stable approach and landing. These rates are determined from the helicopter's performance charts.

[PH.I.D.K3a; FAA-H-8083-21]

11. How is the course and heading for a helicopter flight determined, especially with wind correction?

Determine the course by plotting the direct line between the departure and destination points on an aeronautical chart. The heading is the course adjusted for wind correction angle, which compensates for crosswind effects. This angle can be calculated using a flight computer or E6B calculator, factoring in wind direction, wind speed, and true airspeed.

[PH.I.D.K3a; FAA-H-8083-25]

12. How are true airspeed and groundspeed calculated for helicopter flights?

True airspeed is calculated by adjusting the indicated airspeed for altitude and temperature variations, often using performance charts or an E6B flight computer. Groundspeed is then determined by accounting for the wind's impact on true airspeed. Use a flight computer to calculate ground speed, considering whether you have a headwind (which decreases groundspeed) or tailwind (which increases it).

[PH.I.D.K3a; FAA-H-8083-25]

13. How do you calculate the estimated time of arrival (ETA) for a helicopter flight?

To calculate ETA, first determine the total flight time by dividing the distance by your groundspeed, adjusting for any wind effects. Then, add this flight time to your departure time. For example, if your departure time is 10:00 AM and the flight time is calculated as 1.5 hours, your ETA would be 11:30 AM local time.

[PH.I.D.K3b; FAA-H-8083-25]

14. What is the importance of converting ETA to Universal Coordinated Time (UTC) in aviation?

Converting ETA to UTC is important in aviation for standardized timekeeping, especially when flying across different time zones or when coordinating with international or military operations. UTC provides a common reference for pilots, air traffic control, and flight planning services, avoiding confusion and enhancing operational safety.

[PH.I.D.K3b; FAA-H-8083-25]

15. How can a helicopter pilot convert local time to UTC for ETA calculations?

To convert local time to UTC, a pilot must add or subtract the number of hours corresponding to their time zone difference from UTC. For example, if a pilot is in a time zone that is 4 hours behind UTC, they would add 4 hours to their local ETA. Daylight Saving Time should also be considered if applicable.

[PH.I.D.K3b; FAA-H-8083-25]

16. Are there any tools or resources helicopter pilots can use to assist with ETA and UTC conversions?

Helicopter pilots can use various tools for ETA and UTC conversions, including flight computers, E6B flight calculators, and mobile applications specifically designed for aviation time conversions. Additionally, online resources and world time zone maps can assist in accurately converting local time to UTC and vice versa.

[PH.I.D.K3b; FAA-H-8083-25]

17. How do helicopter pilots calculate the total fuel required for a flight?

To calculate total fuel requirements, pilots first determine the fuel consumption rate per hour based on the helicopter's performance data. Then, multiply this rate by the estimated flight time, including time for taxi, takeoff, climb, cruise, descent, and landing. For example, if a helicopter burns 20 gallons per hour and the estimated flight time is 1.5 hours, the total fuel required is 20 × 1.5 = 30 gallons.

[PH.I.D.K3c; FAA-H-8083-25]

18. What is the recommended fuel reserve for helicopter flights, and how is it calculated?

VFR flights are a minimum of 20 minutes of flight time at normal cruise speed. To calculate this, determine the fuel consumption rate and multiply it by the reserve time. For instance, if the helicopter consumes 20 gallons per hour, a 20-minute reserve would require 20/3 = 6.67 gallons.

[PH.I.D.K3c; FAA-H-8083-21]

19. How should helicopter pilots account for variables such as wind and flight conditions in fuel planning?

Pilots should consider variables like headwinds, which can increase flight time and fuel consumption, and tailwinds, which can decrease them. They should also factor in potential deviations for weather or air traffic, and any additional fuel required for holding, rerouting, or flying at less efficient altitudes. These considerations require adjusting the initial fuel calculation to ensure adequate fuel supply.

[PH.I.D.K3c; FAA-H-8083-25]

20. What are the regulatory requirements for fuel reserves in helicopter operations?

VFR daytime flights, the FAA requires enough fuel to fly to the first point of intended landing and, assuming normal cruising speed, to fly after that for at least 20 minutes. VFR night flights, the reserve requirement increases to 30 minutes. Pilots must always ensure they have enough fuel to complete the flight safely, considering all relevant factors.

[PH.I.D.K3c; 14 CFR 91.151]

21. What essential information must be included in a VFR flight plan for a helicopter?

The elements of a VFR (visual flight rules) flight plan, as detailed in the FAA Flight Plan Form 7233-1, include:

- *Type of flight plan*—Indicate whether the flight is VFR, IFR, or DVFR.
- *Aircraft identification*—Enter the complete aircraft identification, including the "N" prefix if applicable.
- *Aircraft type/special equipment*—Enter the aircraft's designator and any special equipment on board.
- *True airspeed*—Enter the aircraft's true airspeed in knots.
- *Departure point*—Enter the identifier code of the departure airport or, if unknown, the name of the airport.
- *Departure time*—Enter the proposed (Z) and, if applicable, actual (Z) departure times in Coordinated Universal Time (UTC).
- *Cruising altitude*—Enter the planned cruising altitude for the flight.
- *Route of flight*—Define the planned route of flight using navigational aid (NAVAID) identifier codes, airways, and waypoints.
- *Destination*—Enter the identifier code of the destination airport or, if unknown, the name of the airport and city.
- *Estimated time en route*—Enter the estimated time en route in hours and minutes.
- *Remarks*—Include any pertinent remarks that may aid in VFR search and rescue, such as planned stops en route or any clarifications regarding other flight plan information.
- *Fuel on board*—Specify the amount of fuel on board in hours and minutes.
- *Alternate airport(s)*—Specify an alternate airport(s) if desired.
- *Pilot's name, address & telephone number & aircraft home base*—Enter the pilot's complete information and aircraft home base.
- *Number aboard*—Enter the total number of persons on board, including crew.

(continued)

- *Color of aircraft*—Enter the predominant colors of the aircraft.
- *Destination contact/telephone (optional)*—Provide contact information at the destination if available.

[PH.I.D.K4; FAA-H-8083-25]

22. How does a helicopter pilot file a VFR flight plan?

A helicopter pilot can file a VFR flight plan via several methods: through a Flight Service Station (FSS) in person, by phone, or online through services like Leidos Flight Service. The flight plan should include the pilot's information, helicopter details, route, altitudes, estimated times, and emergency contact information. The plan must be filed at least 30 minutes before departure to ensure it is processed and available to ATC and search and rescue services.

[PH.I.D.K5; FAA-H-8083-25]

23. What is the process for activating a filed VFR flight plan for a helicopter flight?

On the ground the pilot can activate a flight plan online or by calling 1800WXBRIEF. In the air by contacting Flight Service over the radio.

[PH.I.D.K5; FAA-H-8083-25]

24. How should a helicopter pilot close their VFR flight plan upon completing the flight?

The pilot must close the VFR flight plan to prevent unnecessary search and rescue operations. This can be done by contacting the flight service by radio before landing if within radio range or by phone immediately after landing. Provide the helicopter's tail number and confirm that you have landed safely at your intended destination.

[PH.I.D.K5; FAA-H-8083-25]

25. What initial actions should a helicopter pilot take if intercepted in flight by a military or law enforcement aircraft?

If intercepted, the helicopter pilot should immediately try to establish radio communication with the intercepting aircraft or ATC on 121.5MHz. They should also follow standard visual signals used by the intercepting aircraft to understand their intentions. The pilot should maintain visual contact with the intercepting aircraft and prepare to follow their instructions, such as changing course or landing.

[PH.I.D.K6; AIM 5-6-4]

26. What are the standard visual signals a helicopter pilot should understand during an intercept?

A helicopter pilot should be familiar with standard visual signals, such as the intercepting aircraft rocking its wings or using flares, which signal the need to follow. If the intercepting aircraft circles around the helicopter, it generally indicates a request to follow. An intercepting aircraft lowering its landing gear or overflying an airfield can signal a directive to land. Knowing these signals is crucial for compliance and safety.

[PH.I.D.K6; AIM 5-6-4]

27. What types of risks should helicopter pilots identify and assess related to their personal proficiency and health?

Assess risks associated with personal proficiency, such as skill currency, familiarity with the helicopter type, and recent flight experience. Health risks include fatigue, illness, medication effects, alcohol consumption, and stress. Pilots should honestly evaluate their physical and mental state before each flight, considering factors like the IMSAFE checklist (Illness, Medication, Stress, Alcohol, Fatigue, and Emotion).

[PH.I.D.R1; FAA-H-8083-2]

28. **How can helicopter pilots mitigate risks associated with lack of recent flying experience?**

    To mitigate risks from lack of recent flying experience, pilots can undergo refresher training or flight reviews, practice maneuvers with a qualified instructor, and gradually reintroduce themselves to more complex flight scenarios. Pilots should start with familiar routes and conditions and avoid challenging operations until they regain proficiency.

    [PH.I.D.R1; FAA-H-8083-2]

29. **What strategies can pilots employ to manage risks associated with aeronautical decision making (ADM) under pressure?**

    Pilots can manage decision-making risks by using structured decision-making tools like the DECIDE model (Detect, Estimate, Choose, Identify, Do, Evaluate) and maintaining situational awareness. Regular training in emergency procedures and simulated pressure situations can enhance a pilot's ability to make sound decisions under stress. Building a habit of thorough preflight planning also helps in anticipating and managing potential in-flight challenges.

    [PH.I.D.R1; FAA-H-8083-2]

30. **How should helicopter pilots approach risk management related to external pressures, such as scheduling or passenger demands?**

    Prioritize safety over external pressures, such as tight schedules or passenger requests. Establishing personal minimums and adhering to them regardless of external factors is crucial. Pilots should communicate clearly with passengers or operators about safety concerns and the reasons for delays or changes in plans. Setting realistic expectations and being prepared to say no when safety is at stake are key risk management practices.

    [PH.I.D.R1; FAA-H-8083-2]

31. What are common risks associated with helicopter operations that pilots need to identify and assess?

Mechanical failures, weather-related hazards, operational risks like wire strikes or obstacles during low-level flight, and risks associated with specific missions such as emergency medical services or offshore operations. Pilots should also assess risks related to the helicopter's performance limitations, such as weight and balance issues, power available versus power required, and density altitude effects.

[PH.I.D.R2; FAA-H-8083-2]

32. How should helicopter pilots identify and assess weather-related risks before and during flights?

Helicopter pilots should assess weather-related risks by obtaining a comprehensive weather briefing before the flight, which includes information on visibility, wind, precipitation, cloud cover, and any significant weather phenomena like thunderstorms or icing conditions. During flight, pilots should continually monitor weather updates and changes, using onboard equipment if available, and remain vigilant for signs of deteriorating weather conditions.

[PH.I.D.R3; FAA-H-8083-2]

33. What considerations are important for mitigating risks related to airports and airspace in helicopter operations?

To mitigate risks related to airports and airspace, helicopter pilots need to be familiar with the types of airspace they will be operating in, including any restrictions or special requirements. They should also understand airport layouts, traffic patterns, and potential hazards such as bird activity. Effective communication with air traffic control and other aircraft is crucial, as is adherence to standard operating procedures and traffic regulations.

[PH.I.D.R3; FAA-H-8083-2]

34. How can pilots assess and mitigate risks associated with terrain and obstacles, including wire strike hazards?

Pilots can assess terrain and obstacle risks by thoroughly planning their flight path, considering terrain elevation, potential obstacles like towers, buildings, and wires, especially in low-level operations. To mitigate these risks, pilots should maintain a safe altitude, use obstacle databases or charts, and be trained in obstacle avoidance maneuvers. Awareness of wire strike hazards is particularly important, and pilots should be familiar with common locations for wires and appropriate avoidance techniques.

[PH.I.D.R3; FAA-H-8083-2]

35. What strategies can helicopter pilots employ to manage environmental risks in different types of operations?

Helicopter pilots can manage environmental risks by tailoring their strategies to the type of operation, such as EMS, offshore, or urban operations. This includes understanding the unique challenges of each environment, like confined area operations, over-water flights, or high-density altitudes. Continuous training, adherence to safety guidelines, and maintaining situational awareness are key to managing these environmental risks effectively.

[PH.I.D.R3; FAA-H-8083-21]

36. How does a pilot determine the cruising altitude or flight level to include in the VFR flight plan?

The cruising altitude in a VFR flight plan is determined based on the direction of flight, terrain, obstacles, weather, and helicopter performance. For eastbound flights (0–179 degrees), odd thousand-foot altitudes plus 500 feet are typical, and for westbound flights (180–359 degrees), even thousand-foot altitudes plus 500 feet are standard. However, helicopter pilots have more flexibility and may choose altitudes for optimal safety and efficiency.

[PH.I.D.R3; 14 CFR 91.159]

37. What are some common external pressures that helicopter pilots may face?

Tight schedules, demanding clients or passengers, pressure from employers or operators, and self-imposed pressures to complete missions, such as in medical evacuation or search and rescue operations. Other pressures may come from factors like fuel constraints, daylight limitations, or the desire to impress others.

[PH.I.D.R4; FAA-H-8083-2]

38. How can pilots identify and assess the impact of these external pressures on flight safety?

Pilots can identify and assess the impact of external pressures by being self-aware and acknowledging when they are being influenced by factors outside of safety considerations. Regular self-assessment, perhaps using tools like the PAVE checklist (Pilot, Aircraft, enVironment, External pressures), can help pilots recognize when external pressures are affecting their decision-making, potentially compromising safety.

[PH.I.D.R4; FAA-H-8083-2]

39. What strategies can helicopter pilots use to mitigate the risks associated with external pressures?

To mitigate these risks, helicopter pilots should set and adhere to personal minimums that account for their experience and skill level. They should be prepared to delay, divert, or cancel flights if conditions are unsafe. Effective communication with all stakeholders about safety concerns and the rationale for decisions is crucial. Pilots should also prioritize rest and stress management to maintain good judgment and decision-making abilities.

[PH.I.D.R4; FAA-H-8083-2]

40. What are some limitations of ATC services that helicopter pilots might encounter?

Coverage gaps in remote or low-altitude areas, communication difficulties, radar limitations, and delays in receiving clearances or responses due to high traffic volumes. ATC may also have limited ability to provide traffic advisories in uncontrolled airspace or during VFR flights where radar service isn't provided.

[PH.I.D.R5; AIM 4-3-17]

41. What strategies can helicopter pilots use to mitigate risks associated with ATC limitations?

maintain situational awareness, especially in areas with known ATC limitations. They should use available navigation aids and onboard equipment for traffic awareness and terrain avoidance. Pilots can plan routes that maximize ATC coverage and ensure they have alternative communication methods. Developing proficiency in non-radar navigation and self-separation techniques in VFR conditions is also crucial.

[PH.I.D.R5; AIM 4-3-17]

42. How should helicopter pilots handle situations where ATC services are unavailable or inadequate?

In situations where ATC services are unavailable or inadequate, helicopter pilots should rely on their training and skills in visual navigation, dead reckoning, and using onboard navigation systems. They should maintain a heightened level of vigilance for traffic and terrain, follow VFR flight rules, and make regular position reports on the appropriate frequency for traffic advisories, especially in uncontrolled airspace.

[PH.I.D.R5; FAA-H-8083-2]

43. What are common limitations in fuel planning that helicopter pilots might face?

Inaccuracies in fuel consumption estimates, unexpected changes in flight conditions like headwinds or rerouting, and limitations in fuel gauge accuracy. Other factors include failure to account for fuel needed for taxi, hover, and reserve requirements, as well as the inability to refuel at remote locations.

[PH.I.D.R6; FAA-H-8083-2]

44. How can pilots assess the impact of fuel planning limitations on their flight?

Considering various scenarios during preflight planning, such as changes in wind conditions, potential rerouting, and delays. They should also review historical fuel consumption data for their helicopter and consider the accuracy of fuel gauges. Assessing the availability of fuel at the destination and alternate airports is also crucial.

[PH.I.D.R6; FAA-H-8083-2]

45. What strategies can helicopter pilots use to mitigate risks associated with fuel planning limitations?

To mitigate risks, helicopter pilots should plan conservatively, factoring in additional fuel for unforeseen circumstances. They should calculate fuel requirements meticulously, including taxi, climb, cruise, descent, and reserve fuel. Pilots should also regularly monitor fuel levels during flight, adjust plans as needed, and always have an alternate plan that includes potential refueling stops.

[PH.I.D.R6; FAA-H-8083-2]

46. What are some limitations of using an electronic flight bag (EFB) that helicopter pilots should be aware of?

The potential for electronic failure or battery depletion, reliance on potentially outdated or incorrect information if not regularly updated, screen glare in bright light, and the possibility of becoming overly reliant on electronic data at the expense of basic pilotage and dead reckoning skills. Pilots must also be aware of the risk of distraction from flying the helicopter when interacting with the EFB.

[PH.I.D.R7; FAA-H-8083-25]

47. How can pilots assess the impact of EFB limitations on their helicopter operations?

A pilot should evaluate their dependence on the device for navigation, weather updates, and flight planning. They should consider backup options in case of EFB failure and be comfortable with traditional navigation methods. Regular checks for software and database updates are crucial to ensure the accuracy and reliability of the information provided by the EFB.

[PH.I.D.R7; FAA-H-8083-25]

48. What strategies can helicopter pilots use to mitigate risks associated with EFB limitations?

Helicopter pilots should ensure that their EFB is charged and in good working condition before each flight. They should have backup power sources and regularly update software and databases. Pilots should also maintain proficiency in traditional navigation and flight planning methods as backups. Importantly, pilots should manage cockpit workload to avoid becoming distracted by the EFB during critical phases of flight.

[PH.I.D.R7; FAA-H-8083-25]

49. How should helicopter pilots handle situations where the EFB becomes unavailable or unreliable during flight?

Pilots should rely on backup systems, such as paper charts, onboard navigation instruments, or a secondary electronic device. They should also be prepared to communicate with ATC for assistance with navigation or rerouting. Continuous training in manual navigation and flight planning ensures pilots are prepared to handle such scenarios effectively.

[PH.I.D.R7; FAA-H-8083-25]

Skills to be demonstrated:

- Prepare, present, and explain a cross-country flight plan assigned by the evaluator, including a risk analysis based on real-time weather, to the first fuel stop.

- Apply pertinent information from appropriate and current aeronautical charts, *Chart Supplement*; Notices to Air Missions (NOTAMs) relative to airport/heliport/helipad/landing area, runway, and taxiway closures; and other flight publications.

- Create a navigation plan and simulate filing a VFR flight plan.

- Recalculate fuel reserves based on a scenario provided by the evaluator.

- Use an electronic flight bag (EFB), if applicable.

E. National Airspace System

1. What are the VFR weather minimums in Class B airspace for helicopters?

3 statute miles visibility and must remain clear of clouds.

[PH.I.E.K1; 14 CFR 91.155]

2. What are the VFR weather minimums in Class C airspace for helicopters?

3 statute miles visibility, 500 feet below, 1,000 feet above, and 2,000 feet horizontal cloud clearance.

[PH.I.E.K1; 14 CFR 91.155]

3. What are the VFR weather minimums in Class D airspace for helicopters?

3 statute miles visibility, 500 feet below, 1,000 feet above, and 2,000 feet horizontal cloud clearance.

[PH.I.E.K1; 14 CFR 91.155]

4. What are the VFR weather minimums in Class E airspace below 10,000 feet MSL for helicopters?

3 statute miles visibility and cloud clearances of 500 feet below, 1,000 feet above, and 2,000 feet horizontally.

[PH.I.E.K1; 14 CFR 91.155]

5. What are the VFR weather minimums in Class E airspace above 10,000 feet MSL for helicopters?

5 statute mile visibility and cloud clearances of 1,000 feet below, 1,000 feet above, and 1 statute mile horizontally.

[PH.I.E.K1; 14 CFR 91.155]

6. What are the day VFR weather minimums in Class G airspace for helicopters?

½ statute mile, clear of clouds.

[PH.I.E.K1; 14 CFR 91.155]

7. What are the night VFR weather minimums in Class G airspace for helicopters?

1 statute mile, clear of clouds except provided that a helicopter may be operated clear of clouds in an airport traffic pattern within ½ mile of the runway or helipad of intended landing if the flight visibility is not less than ½ statute mile.

[PH.I.E.K1; 14 CFR 91.155]

8. What are the day VFR weather minimums in Class G airspace above 1,200 feet AGL, but less than 10,000 feet MSL for helicopters?

1 statute mile visibility and cloud clearances of 500 feet below, 1,000 feet above, and 2,000 feet horizontally.

[PH.I.E.K1; 14 CFR 91.155]

9. What are the night VFR weather minimums in Class G airspace above 1,200 feet AGL, but less than 10,000 feet MSL for helicopters?

3 statute mile visibility and cloud clearances of 500 feet below, 1,000 feet above, and 2,000 feet horizontally.

[PH.I.E.K1; 14 CFR 91.155]

10. What are the VFR weather minimums in Class G airspace more than 1,200 feet above the surface and at or above 10,000 feet MSL?

5 statute mile visibility and cloud clearances of 1,000 feet below, 1,000 feet above, and 1 statute mile horizontally.

[PH.I.E.K1; 14 CFR 91.155]

11. What equipment and communication requirements are necessary for helicopter operations in Class B airspace?

In Class B airspace, helicopters must be equipped with a Mode C transponder and an operable two-way radio. Pilots must obtain an ATC clearance before entering and maintain two-way radio communications with ATC throughout their time in the airspace.

[PH.I.E.K1; AIM 3-2-3]

12. What are the requirements and limitations for helicopter operations in Class B airspace?

Class B airspace surrounds the nation's busiest airports. Helicopter pilots flying in Class B airspace need to obtain an ATC clearance and maintain two-way radio communication. While a Mode C transponder is required, helicopters can sometimes operate under special VFR conditions, which can allow them to fly with lower weather minimums than fixed-wing aircraft.

[PH.I.E.K1; AIM 3-2-3]

13. What are the requirements for operating a helicopter in Class C airspace?

Class C airspace requires helicopters to have a Mode C transponder and a two-way radio. Pilots must establish two-way radio communication with ATC prior to entering and maintaining it while in the airspace. An ATC clearance is not required for entry, but communication with ATC is essential.

[PH.I.E.K1; AIM 3-2-4]

14. What should helicopter pilots understand about operating in Class C and Class D airspace?

In Class C airspace, helicopter pilots are required to establish two-way radio communication with ATC before entering and must operate with a Mode C transponder. Class D airspace, generally around smaller airports with operational control towers, also requires two-way radio communication prior to entry. Helicopter pilots should be aware of specific traffic patterns and altitude restrictions in these airspaces.

[PH.I.E.K1; FAA-H-8083-25]

15. What are the communication and equipment requirements for Class D airspace?

In Class D airspace, helicopters must have a two-way radio to establish and maintain communication with the control tower. While a mode C transponder is typically recommended, it is not always required unless the airspace is within the mode C veil of a Class B airport.

[PH.I.E.K1; AIM 3-2-5]

16. What should helicopter pilots be aware of when operating in Class E and G airspace regarding communication and equipment?

In Class E and G airspace, there are no specific equipment requirements for VFR flight. However, maintaining a two-way radio for communication, especially near airports, is advisable. In Class E airspace above 10,000 feet MSL, a mode C transponder is required.

[PH.I.E.K1; FAA-H-8083-25]

17. What are the operational considerations for helicopters in Class E and Class G airspace?

Class E airspace is controlled airspace not designated as Class A, B, C, or D, and generally does not require communication with ATC for VFR flights. Class G airspace is uncontrolled and also does not require ATC clearance or communication for VFR operations. However, helicopter pilots must be mindful of weather minimums and visibility requirements, which vary based on altitude and time of day. In both airspaces, pilots should exercise caution and maintain situational awareness due to the potential presence of other VFR traffic.

[PH.I.E.K1; FAA-H-8083-25]

18. In which types of airspace is ADS-B Out required for helicopter operations?

ADS-B out is required for helicopters operating in Class A, B, and C airspace, as well as in Class E airspace at and above 10,000 feet MSL, excluding airspace at and below 2,500 feet above the ground. It is also required within 30 nautical miles of most Class B primary airports, above the ceiling and within the lateral boundaries of Class B and Class C airspace up to 10,000 feet MSL, and in U.S. airspace over the Gulf of Mexico at and above 3,000 feet MSL.

[PH.I.E.K1; AIM 4-1-20]

19. What are the benefits of ADS-B for helicopter pilots?

ADS-B offers enhanced situational awareness, real-time precision, shared situational awareness with ATC and other aircraft equipped with ADS-B, and improved safety. It provides more accurate tracking of aircraft position and flight path, which is particularly beneficial in congested airspace, low-altitude operations, and areas with limited radar coverage. ADS-B can also facilitate more direct routes and efficient use of airspace.

[PH.I.E.K1; AIM 4-1-20]

20. What do blue and magenta colors represent on sectional aeronautical charts used by helicopter pilots?

blue symbols typically represent features and information related to controlled airspace, such as Class B, C, D, and E airspace boundaries and altitudes. Magenta is used for uncontrolled airspace, particularly Class E and G, and for depicting features like magenta circles around airports that indicate they are in uncontrolled airspace.

[PH.I.E.K2; Sectional Chart Legend]

21. How are different types of airports depicted on sectional charts?

Controlled airports with control towers are shown with blue symbols, while non-towered airports are shown in magenta. The layout of the runways is also depicted, and airports with hard-surface runways 1,500 feet or longer are shown with an outline of the runway layout. Smaller or private airports might be shown with simpler circle symbols.

[PH.I.E.K2; Sectional Chart Legend]

22. What do the various symbols for airspace boundaries and altitude limits mean on aeronautical charts?

Airspace boundaries are depicted with dashed, solid, or shaded lines in different colors, indicating the type of airspace (Class B, C, D, E, or restricted areas). Altitude limits for airspace are shown with numbers indicating the floor and ceiling of the airspace in hundreds of feet MSL. For example, a Class E airspace might be depicted with a floor of 700 feet AGL, shown as "70/SFC."

[PH.I.E.K2; Sectional Chart Legend]

23. How are obstacles, such as towers or tall structures, depicted on helicopter navigation charts?

Obstacles like towers, tall structures, or significant terrain features are marked with symbols such as dots or triangles, often accompanied by their height in feet above mean sea level (MSL) and/or above ground level (AGL). Obstacles of significant height may also have a flag symbol to indicate their presence. This information is crucial for helicopter pilots, especially those flying at low altitudes.

[PH.I.E.K2; Sectional Chart Legend]

24. What symbol indicates a VOR station on a sectional chart, and how can helicopter pilots identify it?

A VOR (VHF Omnidirectional Range) station is depicted on sectional charts as a hexagon with a solid blue color. Inside the hexagon, the VOR frequency and Morse code identifier are listed. Helicopter pilots use these symbols to identify VOR navigation aids for route planning and in-flight navigation.

[PH.I.E.K2; Sectional Chart Legend]

25. How are special use airspace areas like restricted areas or Military Operations Areas (MOAs) represented on aeronautical charts?

Special use airspace areas, such as restricted areas or MOAs, are depicted with hashed lines. Restricted areas are shown with blue hashed lines, and MOAs are depicted with magenta hashed lines. These symbols include the area name, operating hours, and altitudes, crucial for helicopter pilots to avoid unauthorized entry.

[PH.I.E.K2; Sectional Chart Legend]

26. What do the ticked lines around an airport symbol indicate on a sectional chart?

Class D airspace, which is controlled airspace extending upwards from the surface, usually up to 2,500 feet above the airport elevation. The ticks around the airport symbol help helicopter pilots recognize the boundaries and vertical limits of the Class D airspace for compliance with ATC communication requirements.

[PH.I.E.K2; Sectional Chart Legend]

27. How are heliports represented on aeronautical charts, and what information do they provide?

Heliports are represented on aeronautical charts with a circle and a letter *H* in the center. The symbol may include information about the heliport's name, location, and whether it is public or private. This information aids helicopter pilots in identifying suitable landing locations, particularly in urban or congested areas.

[PH.I.E.K2; Sectional Chart Legend]

28. What chart symbol is used to depict a non-towered airport with hard-surface runways, and what additional information does it provide?

A non-towered airport with hard-surface runways is depicted on sectional charts with a magenta open circle, and the runway layout is shown within the circle. Additional information, such as the airport's name, field elevation, runway lengths, and available services, may also be provided near the symbol. This information assists helicopter pilots in identifying suitable airports for landing, particularly in areas without air traffic control.

[PH.I.E.K2; Sectional Chart Legend]

29. What is special use airspace (SUA) and how is it categorized for helicopter pilots?

Special use airspace (SUA) is airspace where activities must be confined because of their nature, or where limitations are imposed on aircraft operations that are not a part of those activities. SUA includes prohibited areas, restricted areas, warning areas, military operation areas (MOAs), alert areas, and controlled firing areas. Each type has specific rules and requirements for entry and operation, which helicopter pilots must adhere to.

[PH.I.E.K3; AIM 3-4-1]

30. What are Special Flight Rules Areas (SFRA) and how do they impact helicopter flight operations?

Special Flight Rules Areas (SFRA) are designated regions of airspace with specific flight rules due to unique conditions or requirements, such as high traffic density or national security concerns. Pilots operating in an SFRA must follow the designated flight rules, which may include specific communication procedures, transponder settings, and flight paths. SFRAs are typically found around major metropolitan areas or sensitive locations.

[PH.I.E.K3; AIM 3-5-7]

31. How should helicopter pilots respond to temporary flight restrictions (TFR)?

Temporary flight restrictions (TFR) are imposed to restrict certain aircraft from operating within a defined area on a temporary basis. This is often for safety, security, or emergency reasons. Helicopter pilots must check for TFRs during preflight planning and avoid entering TFR areas unless they have the necessary authorization. Violating a TFR can lead to enforcement actions, including fines and suspension of pilot certificates.

[PH.I.E.K3; AIM 3-5-3]

32. What are other airspace areas that helicopter pilots need to be aware of?

Other airspace areas that helicopter pilots need to be aware of include National Security Areas (NSAs), where pilots are requested to voluntarily avoid flying due to national security concerns, and Parachute Jump Aircraft Areas, where increased vigilance is necessary due to parachute activities. Understanding these areas and their operational impact is crucial for safe helicopter flight operations.

[PH.I.E.K3; FAA-H-8083-25]

33. Can helicopter pilots request authorization to enter SUA or TFR areas, and if so, how?

Yes, helicopter pilots can request authorization to enter certain SUAs or TFRs by contacting the controlling agency or ATC responsible for the area. The request should be made well in advance and include the purpose of the flight, the desired time and duration, and the specific area of operation. However, authorization is not guaranteed and depends on the specific reason for the SUA or TFR and current conditions.

[PH.I.E.K3; FAA-H-8083-25]

34. What are the requirements for helicopter operations in special use airspace (SUA)?

Pilots must be aware of the types of SUA, such as restricted areas, MOAs, and prohibited areas, and understand the specific restrictions for each. Prior to flight, pilots should check NOTAMs for active times and areas. Some SUAs may require prior authorization from the controlling agency for entry, and all pilots must comply with any stated restrictions and procedures.

[PH.I.E.K3; AIM 3-4-1]

35. What are Special Air Traffic Rules (SATR), and how do they apply to helicopter pilots?

SATR are rules that apply to specific geographic areas and may include unique operating procedures, communication requirements, and flight rules. Helicopter pilots must be familiar with any SATR applicable to their flight route, such as specific altitude and airspeed restrictions or designated flight paths, to ensure safety and regulatory compliance.

[PH.I.E.K3; AIM 3-5-7]

36. How do helicopter pilots comply with operations in Special Flight Rules Areas (SFRA)?

In SFRAs, pilots must adhere to the specific flight rules designated for the area, which may include mandatory flight routes, communication procedures, and transponder settings. These areas often exist around major cities or sensitive locations for security or traffic management purposes. Pilots should thoroughly review the SFRA procedures during preflight planning and maintain strict adherence to the rules while operating within the SFRA.

[PH.I.E.K3; AIM 3-5-7]

37. What are the key considerations for helicopter pilots when operating in airspace with SATR or SFRA?

Pilots must be aware of the existence of SATR or SFRA along their flight route and understand the specific requirements of these areas, including communication protocols, flight paths, and transponder use. They should plan flights to accommodate these rules and be prepared for ATC instructions that may differ from standard VFR operations. Continuous situational awareness and adherence to the established procedures are critical for safe operations.

[PH.I.E.K3; AIM 3-5-7]

38. What conditions allow helicopters to operate under special VFR in controlled airspace?

Helicopters can operate under special VFR within controlled airspace extending to the surface for airports if they can maintain clear of clouds and with visibility of at least 1 mile during the day and 2 miles at night.

[PH.I.E.K4; AIM 4-4-6]

39. Are helicopters subject to the same VFR minimums as fixed-wing aircraft under special VFR conditions?

No, helicopters are allowed to operate under reduced visibility conditions compared to fixed-wing aircraft when flying under special VFR. They can operate with visibility of at least 1 mile during the day and 2 miles at night, which is less than the standard VFR minimums for fixed-wing operations.

[PH.I.E.K4; 14 CFR 91.157]

40. Is ATC clearance required for helicopters to operate under special VFR?

Yes, helicopters must obtain ATC clearance to operate under special VFR within controlled airspace extending to the surface for airports.

[PH.I.E.K4; 14 CFR 91.157]

41. What is the responsibility of the helicopter pilot when operating under special VFR?

The helicopter pilot is responsible for maintaining visual contact with the ground and navigating safely within the reduced visibility constraints allowed under special VFR conditions. It is subject to the pilot's discretion to ensure safe operation under the given conditions.

[PH.I.E.K4; 14 CFR 91.157]

42. What are the limitations and risks associated with flying under SVFR for helicopters?

While SVFR provides more flexibility for helicopter operations, it comes with increased risks such as reduced visibility, potential for disorientation, and increased workload due to the need for constant vigilance. Pilots must be mindful of obstacles like wires and towers, which are harder to see in reduced visibility. SVFR operations should only be conducted by experienced pilots familiar with the local area and weather conditions.

[PH.I.E.K4; FAA-H-8083-25]

43. What are the main risks associated with operating a helicopter in Class B airspace?

Class B airspace includes high air traffic density, strict adherence to ATC instructions, and potential for airspace incursions. Helicopter pilots must be vigilant in maintaining separation from other aircraft and have an understanding of the various VFR reporting points within that airspace.

[PH.I.E.R1; FAA-H-8083-25]

44. How can helicopter pilots mitigate risks in Class C and D airspace?

In Class C and D airspace, risks can be mitigated by maintaining continuous communication with ATC, following prescribed flight paths, and being aware of other traffic, especially during approach and departure phases.

[PH.I.E.R1; FAA-H-8083-25]

45. What challenges do helicopter pilots face in Class E and G airspace, and how are they addressed?

Challenges in Class E and G airspace include uncontrolled environments, varying weather conditions, and potential for traffic conflicts. Pilots should practice see-and-avoid techniques, adhere to VFR weather minimums, and maintain good situational awareness.

[PH.I.E.R1; FAA-H-8083-25]

46. How should helicopter pilots approach special use airspace (SUA) to minimize risks?

To minimize risks in SUA, pilots should be aware of the locations and active times of such airspaces, avoid unauthorized entry, and stay informed about any temporary changes or restrictions through preflight briefings and NOTAMs.

[PH.I.E.R1; FAA-H-8083-25]

47. What are the key risk mitigation strategies for helicopter operations in areas with temporary flight restrictions (TFR)?

Key strategies include checking for active TFRs during preflight planning, understanding the reasons behind the TFRs, maintaining up-to-date navigation charts, and having alternative routes in case of TFR activation during flight.

[PH.I.E.R1; FAA-H-8083-25]

Skills to be demonstrated:

- Identify and comply with the requirements for basic VFR weather minimums and flying in particular classes of airspace.

- Correctly identify airspace and operate in accordance with associated communication and equipment requirements.

- Identify the requirements for operating in SUA or within a TFR. Identify and comply with special air traffic rules (SATR) and SFRA operations, if applicable.

Limitations Review:

Pro Tip: Use the information from your helicopter to help you study by creating flashcards from the following questions/answers.

What is the normal takeoff speed? _____
What is the normal climb speed? _____
What is the normal cruise speed? _____
What is the best rate of climb speed? _____
What is the maximum range speed? _____
What is the autorotative descent speed? _____
What is the maximum glide speed (autorotations)? _____
What is the minimum rate of descent speed (autorotations)?_____
What is the V_{NE} speed? _____
What is the recommended hovering altitude? _____
What is the green arc for rotor RPM? _____ _____
What are the manifold pressure limits? _____
What are the cylinder head temperature limits? _____
What are the TOT limits? _____
What are the torque limits? _____
What is the make and model of the engine? _____
How much horsepower does the engine produce? _____
What is the minimum weight? _____
What is the maximum weight? _____
What is the maximum weight limit per seat? _____
How many usable gallons of fuel can you carry? _____
Where are the different tanks located and what are their capacities?
_____
Where are the fuel tanks vented? What kind of fuel can you use?
_____
How many and where are the fuel sump drains located?
_____
What are the minimum and maximum oil capacities? _____
What is the maximum oil temperature and pressure? _____
What kind of landing gear does the helicopter have? _____
What kind of rotor brake does your aircraft have?_____
What is the maximum useful load? _____
What is the OGE hover capability at max gross weight and +20°C?
_____
What is the IGE hover capability at max gross weight and +20°C?
_____

F. Performance and Limitations

1. How do helicopter pilots use performance charts to determine maximum takeoff weight?

Helicopter pilots refer to performance charts to determine the maximum takeoff weight by considering factors such as altitude, temperature, and wind conditions. These charts provide data on how these environmental conditions affect the helicopter's ability to generate lift and power, thereby influencing the maximum safe takeoff weight.

[PH.I.F.K1; FAA-H-8083-25]

2. How do pilots use data to calculate fuel consumption for a helicopter flight?

Pilots calculate fuel consumption by using performance data that includes fuel flow rates at various power settings and operational conditions. By estimating the duration of each phase of flight and the expected power setting, pilots can accurately calculate total fuel consumption for a flight.

[PH.I.F.K1; FAA-H-8083-25]

3. Why are weight and balance charts crucial for helicopter flight safety?

Weight and balance charts are crucial as they ensure the helicopter is loaded within its allowable weight and center of gravity limits. Improper weight and balance can affect the helicopter's stability and control, potentially leading to unsafe flight conditions. Pilots use these charts to plan loading and distribution of weight in the helicopter.

[PH.I.F.K1; FAA-H-8083-25]

4. How do helicopter performance charts assist in preflight planning?

Helicopter performance charts are crucial for determining factors like takeoff and landing distances, climb rates, and hover ceilings based on variables such as weight, altitude, and temperature. By consulting these charts, pilots can assess whether a helicopter can safely perform a flight under the given conditions, ensuring operational safety and regulatory compliance.

[PH.I.F.K1; FAA-H-8083-25]

5. **What information do density altitude charts provide to helicopter pilots?**

   Density altitude charts give pilots an understanding of the effective altitude at which the helicopter will be operating, considering temperature and atmospheric pressure. High density altitudes can significantly reduce aircraft performance by affecting lift, engine power, and rotor efficiency. Pilots use these charts to assess performance limitations and make informed decisions, especially when operating in hot and high conditions.

   [PH.I.F.K1; FAA-H-8083-25]

6. **Why is it important for helicopter pilots to understand performance limitations related to wind conditions?**

   Understanding performance limitations in various wind conditions is critical for helicopter safety. Tailwinds, crosswinds, and gusts can impact takeoff, landing, and hover performance. Pilots need to assess wind conditions and adjust their flight techniques accordingly to maintain control and avoid hazardous situations like loss of tail rotor effectiveness.

   [PH.I.F.K1; FAA-H-8083-25]

7. **How do temperature variations affect helicopter performance?**

   Increased temperatures can reduce air density, leading to decreased rotor efficiency, reduced lift, and diminished engine performance. This can affect a helicopter's ability to hover, especially at higher altitudes or when heavily loaded, and may require adjustments in power settings and operational planning.

   [PH.I.F.K2a; FAA-H-8083-25]

8. **What impact does altitude have on helicopter performance?**

   As altitude increases, air density decreases, which can lead to reduced rotor blade efficiency and lower engine power output. This affects the helicopter's hover ceiling, climb rate, and overall performance capabilities. Pilots must consider these altitude effects, particularly when operating in mountainous or high-altitude environments.

   [PH.I.F.K2a; FAA-H-8083-25]

9. **How does humidity influence helicopter flight characteristics?**

   High humidity reduces air density, which can decrease lift and engine power efficiency. While the effect of humidity is less pronounced than temperature or altitude, it still contributes to overall performance reduction, especially in combination with high temperatures and altitude.

   [PH.I.F.K2a; FAA-H-8083-25]

10. **In what ways do wind conditions affect helicopter operations?**

    Wind conditions, including wind speed and direction, significantly influence helicopter performance. Tailwinds can reduce performance during takeoff and climb, while headwinds can improve it. Crosswinds can challenge helicopter control during takeoff, landing, and hover. Understanding and adjusting for wind conditions are crucial for safe helicopter operations.

    [PH.I.F.K2a; FAA-H-8083-25]

11. **What role does atmospheric pressure play in helicopter performance?**

    Atmospheric pressure affects air density; lower pressure at higher altitudes leads to thinner air and reduced lift and engine power. Pilots need to be aware of the local barometric pressure, especially when operating from airports at higher elevations, to correctly calculate performance parameters like density altitude.

    [PH.I.F.K2a; FAA-H-8083-25]

12. **How does a pilot's control input technique affect helicopter performance?**

    A pilot's control input technique, including the manipulation of the cyclic pitch control, collective pitch control, and pedals, directly affects helicopter performance. Smooth and precise control inputs are essential for optimal performance, especially in hover and during transitions between flight regimes. Abrupt or excessive inputs can lead to inefficient operation and increased stress on the helicopter's systems.

    [PH.I.F.K2b; FAA-H-8083-21]

13. What impact does a pilot's decision-making have on fuel consumption and range?

A pilot's decision-making regarding route planning, altitude selection, and speed can significantly impact fuel consumption and range. Efficient route planning and optimal cruising speed selection help in conserving fuel, while poor decisions in these areas can lead to increased fuel usage and potentially critical situations, especially in remote operations.

[PH.I.F.K2b; FAA-H-8083-25]

14. How do external attachments or modifications impact helicopter performance?

External attachments or modifications, such as cargo hooks, skid extensions, or camera mounts, can alter the aerodynamics, increase drag, and affect weight distribution. Pilots must consider these changes in performance calculations and flight techniques, particularly regarding lift capacity and fuel consumption.

[PH.I.F.K2c; FAA-H-8083-21]

15. How do avionics and instrumentation setups affect a helicopter's operational performance?

Avionics and instrumentation setups, such as navigation systems, autopilot, and communication equipment, play a significant role in flight efficiency and safety. Advanced avionics can enhance situational awareness, reduce pilot workload, and improve navigational accuracy, thereby impacting overall operational performance.

[PH.I.F.K2c; FAA-H-8083-25]

16. How does operating at high-altitude airports affect helicopter performance?

Operating at high-altitude airports reduces air density, which can significantly impact engine power and rotor efficiency. This results in decreased lift and climb performance, requiring pilots to carefully calculate weight limits and takeoff or landing distances considering the higher density altitude.

[PH.I.F.K2d; FAA-H-8083-25]

17. What considerations must be made when operating helicopters from helipads?

When operating from helipads, especially those located on buildings or elevated structures, considerations include wind effects, such as turbulence and vortexes, and limited space for maneuvering. Pilots must be proficient in precision takeoff and landing techniques and aware of potential obstacles in the vicinity.

[PH.I.F.K2d; FAA-H-8083-25]

18. How does the environment of a heliport influence helicopter performance?

Heliport environments often involve confined areas surrounded by obstacles like trees, buildings, or power lines. These environments require knowledge of local wind patterns, careful power management and precise control to ensure safe takeoffs and landings. Pilots need to account for potential wind shear and turbulence when operating in such areas.

[PH.I.F.K2d; FAA-H-8083-25]

19. What performance factors are impacted when operating helicopters from unprepared surfaces?

Operating from unprepared surfaces, such as fields or uneven terrain, can present challenges like uneven lift distribution, foreign object damage, and brownout or whiteout conditions in dusty or snowy areas. Pilots must assess the suitability of the surface, considering weight-bearing capacity and obstacle clearance.

[PH.I.F.K2d; FAA-H-8083-25]

20. How does the surface condition of airports and heliports affect helicopter operations?

Surface conditions such as wet, icy, or uneven runways, taxiways and landing pads can affect helicopter ground handling. Pilots must be vigilant about potential sliding or skidding and adjust landing techniques accordingly, especially in adverse weather conditions.

[PH.I.F.K2d; FAA-H-8083-25]

21. Why is proper loading crucial for helicopter performance and safety?

To maintain the helicopter's center of gravity (CG) within allowable limits. Incorrect loading can lead to reduced control responsiveness, increased fuel consumption, and potential safety hazards, such as loss of control. Ensuring the load is within the helicopter's weight capacity and correctly distributed is vital for stable flight characteristics.

[PH.I.F.K3; FAA-H-8083-25]

22. How does weight distribution impact a helicopter's flight characteristics?

Weight distribution affects a helicopter's balance and CG position. An aft or forward CG can significantly alter handling characteristics, potentially leading to control difficulties. Correct weight distribution ensures optimal stability and control during various flight maneuvers, especially during takeoffs and landings.

[PH.I.F.K3; FAA-H-8083-25]

23. What is the significance of calculating the center of gravity (CG) for helicopters?

Calculating the CG is critical to determine the helicopter's balance point. A CG outside of the specified limits can result in inadequate control authority, increased stress on the airframe, and unsafe flight conditions. Pilots must calculate and verify CG before flight to ensure it falls within the permissible range for safe operations.

[PH.I.F.K3; FAA-H-8083-25]

24. How do changes in fuel load affect a helicopter's weight and balance?

Changes in fuel load alter the helicopter's weight and can shift the CG, especially in helicopters with large fuel capacities or multiple tanks. Pilots must account for fuel consumption during flight planning to ensure the CG remains within safe limits throughout the flight.

[PH.I.F.K3; FAA-H-8083-25]

25. What are the consequences of exceeding a helicopter's maximum gross weight?

Exceeding the maximum gross weight can lead to decreased performance, such as reduced climb rate, longer takeoff distances, and lower service ceiling. It also increases the risk of structural damage and can adversely affect flight safety. Pilots must adhere to weight limitations to ensure safe and efficient flight operations.

[PH.I.F.K3; FAA-H-8083-25]

26. How does rotor blade design influence helicopter lift and maneuverability?

Rotor blade design, including its airfoil shape, length, and pitch, directly impacts lift generation and maneuverability. Blades with optimized airfoil shapes and pitch control can enhance lift efficiency and responsiveness, enabling better control and handling during various flight maneuvers.

[PH.I.F.K4; FAA-H-8083-21]

27. What is the significance of dissymmetry of lift in helicopter flight?

Dissymmetry of lift occurs due to the differing airspeed of rotor blades in forward flight, with one side of the rotor disc advancing and the other retreating. This phenomenon can create an imbalance in lift across the rotor disc. Helicopters use blade pitch control mechanisms like cyclic feathering to compensate for this, ensuring balanced lift and stable flight.

[PH.I.F.K4; FAA-H-8083-21]

28. How does translational lift affect helicopter performance?

Translational lift is experienced as a helicopter moves through the air and begins to benefit from increased airflow and reduced rotor tip vortices. This results in improved rotor efficiency and lift, usually noticeable at speeds above 16–24 knots. It enhances climb performance and efficiency during the transition from hover to forward flight.

[PH.I.F.K4; FAA-H-8083-21]

29. What is the vortex ring state, and how does it affect helicopters?

Vortex ring state occurs when a helicopter descends into its own downwash, leading to a loss of rotor efficiency. It's characterized by increased vertical descent rates and reduced control effectiveness despite increased engine power. Avoiding steep descent rates and maintaining forward airspeed can prevent entering this hazardous flight condition.

[PH.I.F.K4; FAA-H-8083-21]

30. How do helicopters experience autorotation, and what is its significance?

Autorotation is a critical aerodynamic condition in helicopters, allowing controlled descent and landing in the event of engine failure. During autorotation, airflow from below turns the rotor blades, providing lift and control. Understanding and proficiency in autorotation are essential for helicopter pilots to safely handle engine-out scenarios.

[PH.I.F.K4; FAA-H-8083-21]

31. How does ground effect influence helicopter performance during takeoff and landing?

Ground effect occurs when a helicopter is hovering close to the ground, resulting in increased lift and decreased drag due to the interference of the ground with the rotor airflow. This effect enhances performance by reducing power requirements during takeoff and providing additional lift during landings, making hovering more efficient near the ground.

[PH.I.F.K4; FAA-H-8083-21]

32. What is the significance of retreating blade stall in helicopter flight?

Retreating blade stall occurs at high forward airspeeds when the retreating rotor blade experiences a higher angle of attack, leading to a stall on that side of the rotor disc. This can cause a roll to the retreating blade side and a loss of lift. Pilots must be aware of this limit and avoid excessive airspeeds to prevent retreating blade stall.

[PH.I.F.K4; FAA-H-8083-21]

33. How does torque effect impact helicopter control?

Torque effect is the helicopter's tendency to rotate in the opposite
direction of the main rotor due to Newton's third law of motion.
This is counteracted by the tail rotor or antitorque systems, which
provide directional control. Pilots must manage torque effects,
especially during power changes, to maintain heading and stability.

[PH.I.F.K4; FAA-H-8083-21]

34. What is the role of the tail rotor in helicopter aerodynamics?

The tail rotor provides counteractive thrust to offset the main
rotor's torque effect, enabling directional control and stability.
It allows the pilot to control the helicopter's yaw movement
and maintain heading. Efficient tail rotor function is crucial for
balanced flight, particularly during hovering and low-speed
maneuvers.

[PH.I.F.K4; FAA-H-8083-21]

35. How do helicopter pilots manage the effects of gyroscopic precession?

Gyroscopic precession is the phenomenon where a force applied to
a spinning object, like a rotor blade, is realized 90 degrees later in
the direction of rotation. Pilots must anticipate and manage these
effects, especially when making inputs to the cyclic pitch control
and the collective pitch control, ensuring timely and accurate
responses for maneuvering the helicopter.

[PH.I.F.K4; FAA-H-8083-21]

36. What is the purpose of the height/velocity (H/V) diagram in helicopter operations?

The H/V diagram, often referred to as the dead man's curve,
illustrates combinations of altitude and airspeed that should be
avoided during flight. It is designed to identify the safety envelope
for a helicopter, particularly highlighting the conditions where a
safe autorotation landing is less feasible in case of engine failure.

[PH.I.F.K5; FAA-H-8083-21]

37. How should pilots interpret the avoid areas depicted in the H/V diagram?

The avoid areas on the H/V diagram represent altitude and airspeed combinations where a successful autorotation landing following engine failure may be challenging or impossible. Pilots should minimize time spent in these zones, especially during low-altitude, low-speed flight, or high-altitude hover.

[PH.I.F.K5; FAA-H-8083-21]

38. Why is the H/V diagram particularly important for takeoff and landing?

During takeoff and landing phases, helicopters often pass through the critical regions depicted on the H/V diagram. Understanding the diagram helps pilots choose safer takeoff and landing profiles, avoiding conditions where engine failure would leave inadequate altitude or airspeed for autorotation.

[PH.I.F.K5; FAA-H-8083-21]

39. What precautions should pilots take when operating near the boundaries of the H/V diagram?

When operating near the boundaries of the H/V diagram, pilots should be particularly cautious and maintain awareness of their altitude and airspeed. They should plan maneuvers to quickly move out of hazardous zones and be prepared for immediate action in case of engine failure, prioritizing flight paths that remain within the safe envelope of the H/V diagram.

[PH.I.F.K5; FAA-H-8083-21]

40. What risks are associated with incorrect interpretation of helicopter performance charts?

Incorrect interpretation of performance charts can lead to errors in assessing the helicopter's capabilities, such as takeoff distance, weight capacity, or fuel consumption. This can result in unsafe flight conditions like overloading, insufficient fuel reserves, or inability to clear obstacles, posing significant risks to flight safety.

[PH.I.F.R1; FAA-H-8083-25]

41. What are the potential risks of not accounting for environmental factors in performance calculations?

Failing to account for environmental factors like temperature, altitude, and wind conditions can lead to inaccurate performance assessments. This oversight can result in reduced lift, inability to clear obstacles, or inadequate power, especially critical in high-density altitude or extreme weather conditions.

[PH.I.F.R1; FAA-H-8083-25]

42. What is the importance of contingency planning in relation to performance data?

Contingency planning is crucial when using performance data, as it prepares pilots for unexpected changes or inaccuracies in data. This includes planning for additional fuel reserves, alternative landing sites, and conservative weight limits to accommodate unforeseen conditions or performance discrepancies.

[PH.I.F.R1; FAA-H-8083-25]

43. What risks are associated with exceeding a helicopter's weight and balance limitations?

Exceeding weight and balance limitations can lead to reduced performance, such as impaired maneuverability, longer takeoff distances, and decreased climb rates. It also poses risks of structural overloading and loss of control. Pilots must adhere to specified limits to ensure safe handling and flight stability.

[PH.I.F.R2; FAA-H-8083-25]

44. How can pilots mitigate risks associated with helicopter engine limitations?

Pilots can mitigate risks by regularly monitoring engine parameters, such as temperature, pressure, and RPM, and adhering to operational limits specified in the rotorcraft flight manual (RFM). Regular maintenance and preflight inspections are also crucial to ensure engine reliability and performance within safe boundaries.

[PH.I.F.R2; FAA-H-8083-25]

45. What are the potential risks of operating in adverse weather beyond a helicopter's capability?

Operating in weather conditions beyond the helicopter's capability, such as high winds or icing conditions, can lead to decreased control, increased stress on the rotor system, and possible system failures. Pilots should assess weather forecasts and avoid flights in conditions that exceed the helicopter's certified limits.

[PH.I.F.R2; FAA-H-8083-25]

46. In what ways can effective preflight planning mitigate risks associated with helicopter operational limitations?

Effective preflight planning involves considering the helicopter's limitations in relation to the planned flight profile, including altitude, distance, and payload. By planning routes that accommodate limitations and having contingency plans for unexpected scenarios, pilots can significantly mitigate operational risks.

[PH.I.F.R2; FAA-H-8083-25]

47. What are the risks of discrepancies between calculated and actual helicopter performance?

Discrepancies between calculated and actual performance can lead to unexpected operational limitations, such as insufficient lift, longer than anticipated takeoff distances, or reduced climb rates. These differences pose risks of inadequate power for intended maneuvers, potential overloading, and safety hazards during critical phases like takeoff and landing.

[PH.I.F.R3; FAA-H-8083-25]

48. How can pilots assess the accuracy of performance calculations in helicopter operations?

Pilots can assess calculation accuracy by cross-referencing performance data with actual flight conditions and outcomes. Regularly comparing expected performance (like climb rate or fuel consumption) with in-flight results helps identify any deviations and adjust future calculations. Consistent monitoring of helicopter systems and environmental conditions also aids in accuracy assessment.

[PH.I.F.R3; FAA-H-8083-25]

49. What contingency plans should be in place for unexpected performance limitations?

Pilots should have contingency plans for scenarios like reduced lift in high-density altitude conditions or increased fuel consumption. These plans might include alternative landing sites, reduced payloads, additional fuel reserves, or modified flight paths to accommodate unforeseen performance limitations.

[PH.I.F.R3; FAA-H-8083-25]

50. What are the risks of exceeding a helicopter's maximum gross weight?

Exceeding the maximum gross weight can lead to compromised flight characteristics, including reduced lift, longer takeoff distances, diminished climb performance, and increased fuel consumption. It can also strain the helicopter's structure and systems, increasing the risk of mechanical failure and compromising overall flight safety.

[PH.I.F.R4; FAA-H-8083-25]

51. How can pilots assess the risk of weight-related performance issues?

Pilots can assess weight-related risks by meticulously calculating the total weight of the helicopter, including fuel, cargo, and passengers, before each flight. They should reference the rotorcraft flight manual (RFM) to ensure the weight does not exceed the helicopter's maximum gross weight and that the weight distribution maintains the center of gravity within specified limits.

[PH.I.F.R4; FAA-H-8083-25]

52. What are the consequences of consistently operating helicopters near or above maximum weight limits?

Consistently operating at or above maximum weight limits can lead to accelerated wear and tear on the helicopter, potentially reducing its operational lifespan and increasing maintenance requirements. It also habituates risky operational practices, which can compromise safety in varying flight conditions.

[PH.I.F.R4; FAA-H-8083-25]

53. What are the risks of operating a helicopter outside of its prescribed CG limits?

Operating outside of the CG limits can lead to poor handling characteristics, reduced controllability, and increased strain on the helicopter's structure. In extreme cases, it can result in a loss of control, particularly during critical phases of flight like takeoff and landing. It also affects the efficiency of rotor systems and can compromise the overall stability of the helicopter.

[PH.I.F.R5; FAA-H08083-25]

54. How can pilots accurately assess the helicopter's CG position before flight?

Pilots can assess the CG by calculating the weight distribution of the helicopter, including passengers, cargo, and fuel. This calculation involves using the weight and balance data provided in the rotorcraft flight manual (RFM) to ensure the CG is within the allowable range. Verifying the CG with each configuration change, such as fuel burn or passenger movement, is crucial for safe operations.

[PH.I.F.R5; FAA-H08083-25]

55. What are the long-term implications of frequently operating near the CG limits?

Regularly operating near the CG limits puts continuous stress on the helicopter's airframe and rotor system, potentially leading to increased maintenance needs and reduced aircraft longevity. It also cultivates a habit of operating in less stable conditions, which can compromise safety, especially in emergency situations or under adverse weather conditions.

[PH.I.F.R5; FAA-H08083-25]

56. What are the risks associated with shifting weight during helicopter flight?

Shifting weight during flight can alter the helicopter's center of gravity (CG), potentially moving it outside of the safe operational range. This can affect handling and stability, making the helicopter difficult to control, especially during maneuvers like hovering or sharp turns. It can also lead to unexpected pitch or roll movements.

[PH.I.F.R6; FAA-H-8083-25]

57. How can pilots assess the impact of adding weight to a helicopter?

Before adding weight, pilots should calculate the new total weight and ensure it remains within the helicopter's maximum allowable limit. They should also recompute the CG to confirm it stays within prescribed limits. Considering factors like fuel burn rate and duration of the flight is essential to maintain safe weight and balance throughout the journey.

[PH.I.F.R6; FAA-H-8083-25]

58. What strategies can mitigate risks when removing weight from a helicopter?

When removing weight, such as offloading cargo or passengers, pilots should reassess the helicopter's weight and balance. They may need to adjust the cargo or fuel distribution to maintain a proper CG. Continuous monitoring of the helicopter's performance after weight changes is crucial to detect and correct any balance issues promptly.

[PH.I.F.R6; FAA-H-8083-25]

59. What are the safety precautions to consider when shifting, adding, or removing weight?

Safety precautions include ensuring all cargo is properly secured to prevent in-flight shifting, adhering to weight limitations, and rechecking the CG after any significant weight change. Pilots should also be prepared to adjust flight controls and power settings to accommodate the new weight distribution and maintain optimal flight performance.

[PH.I.F.R6; FAA-H-8083-25]

60. What is retreating blade stall, and why is it a risk in helicopter flight?

Retreating blade stall occurs when the retreating side of the rotor disc, typically during high forward airspeeds, experiences a reduced airflow, leading to an increase in angle of attack and eventually a stall. This stall can cause a significant roll to the retreating blade side, loss of lift, and potential loss of control, especially at high airspeeds or in turbulent conditions.

[PH.I.F.R7; FAA-H-8083-21]

61. How can pilots identify the onset of a retreating blade stall?

Pilots can identify the onset of retreating blade stall by the presence of symptoms such as a distinct vibration, a nose-pitch-up attitude, and a rolling tendency toward the retreating blade side. The stall often begins at the blade tip and progresses inward as airspeed increases or altitude rises.

[PH.I.F.R7; FAA-H-8083-21]

62. What are effective strategies to mitigate the risk of retreating blade stall?

To mitigate the risk, pilots should avoid high-speed flight at high altitudes, especially in turbulent or high-density altitude conditions. Maintaining airspeeds below the maximum allowable, as specified in the rotorcraft flight manual, is crucial. Pilots should also be vigilant in monitoring airspeed and rotor RPM and be prepared to reduce airspeed if stall symptoms appear.

[PH.I.F.R7; FAA-H-8083-21]

63. What contingency plans should pilots have in place for retreating blade stall scenarios?

Pilots should have contingency plans that include immediate actions to reduce airspeed, descend to a lower altitude, and adjust the rotor RPM as necessary. Being prepared for a quick response in case of a stall, especially during flight in high-risk conditions, is a key part of safe helicopter operation.

[PH.I.F.R7; FAA-H-8083-21]

64. What is loss of tail rotor effectiveness (LTE) and its significance in helicopter flight?

LTE occurs when the tail rotor loses its ability to provide adequate yaw control, often due to specific aerodynamic conditions. It can result in an uncontrollable yaw or spin of the helicopter. Understanding and avoiding conditions that lead to LTE are crucial for safe helicopter operation.

[PH.I.F.R8; FAA-H-8083-21]

65. What are common situations that can lead to LTE?

Common situations leading to LTE include flying with a high tailwind, operating in areas of turbulent air, performing maneuvers that demand high tail rotor thrust, and vortex ring state conditions. Each of these scenarios can reduce the effectiveness of the tail rotor.

[PH.I.F.R8; FAA-H-8083-21]

66. How can pilots mitigate the risk of LTE during flight operations?

To mitigate the risk of LTE, pilots should avoid tailwind conditions during hover and low-speed maneuvers, be cautious in turbulent environments, and manage power settings carefully. Adequate preflight planning and situational awareness during operations in challenging conditions are also essential.

[PH.I.F.R8; FAA-H-8083-21]

67. What emergency procedures should a pilot follow if LTE occurs?

If LTE occurs, the pilot should immediately take corrective actions, such as reducing power to decrease the demand on the tail rotor, adjusting the collective to regain yaw control, and repositioning the helicopter to eliminate tailwind conditions. Quick and decisive actions are key to recovering from an LTE situation.

[PH.I.F.R8; FAA-H-8083-21]

Skills to be demonstrated:

• Compute the weight and balance, correct out-of-center of gravity loading errors and determine if the weight and balance remains within limits during all phases of flight.

• Use appropriate helicopter performance charts, tables, and data.

G. Operation of Systems

The following questions are specific to the R22 helicopter. Where possible the questions and their respective answers are kept as general as possible. When you're studying for your own checkride, be sure to substitute the information and limitations with the specific helicopter you'll be using for the checkride.

1. How do primary flight controls in a helicopter function and what are their roles?

Primary flight controls in a helicopter include the cyclic pitch control, the collective pitch control, the throttle control, and the antitorque pedals.

- The cyclic pitch control (also known as the cyclic stick or cyclic) modifies the helicopter's pitch and roll by changing the pitch angle of the rotor blades as they rotate.

- The collective pitch control adjusts the pitch angle of all rotor blades collectively to control vertical lift and descent.

- The throttle regulates engine RPM.

- The antitorque pedals control the yaw movement by adjusting the thrust of the tail rotor.

[PH.I.G.K1a; FAA-H-8083-21]

2. How does the cyclic pitch control affect a helicopter's movement?

The cyclic pitch control affects a helicopter's movement by tilting the rotor disc in the direction the pilot wishes to move. When the pilot moves the cyclic stick, it changes the pitch angle of the rotor blades cyclically as they revolve, resulting in a tilt of the rotor disc. This tilt causes the helicopter to move in the direction of the tilt, allowing for forward, backward, and sideways flight, as well as changes in pitch and roll attitudes.

[PH.I.G.K1a; FAA-H-8083-21]

3. **What is the purpose of collective pitch control in helicopter flight?**

   to control the helicopter's vertical lift and overall altitude. By pulling up on the collective lever, the pilot increases the pitch angle of all the rotor blades collectively, increasing lift and causing the helicopter to ascend. Pushing down on the collective decreases the pitch angle, reducing lift and causing the helicopter to descend. The collective pitch control allows the pilot to perform vertical takeoffs and landings, hover, and adjust altitude during flight.

   [PH.I.G.K1a; FAA-H-8083-21]

4. **Describe the function of the antitorque pedals in a helicopter.**

   The antitorque pedals in a helicopter control the pitch of the tail rotor blades, which counteracts the reactive torque produced by the main rotor and prevents the helicopter from spinning uncontrollably. By pressing the left or right pedal, the pilot can adjust the thrust produced by the tail rotor, controlling the helicopter's yaw (rotation around the vertical axis). This allows the pilot to steer the helicopter left or right, maintain directional control during takeoffs and landings, and perform precise maneuvers such as hovering in a fixed position.

   [PH.I.G.K1a; FAA-H-8083-21]

5. **How do the interactions between the cyclic, collective, and antitorque controls allow for helicopter maneuverability?**

   The interactions between the cyclic, collective, and antitorque controls allow for helicopter maneuverability by providing the pilot with the ability to control the helicopter's pitch, roll, yaw, and altitude simultaneously. The cyclic control tilts the rotor disc to achieve pitch and roll movements, the collective adjusts overall lift for altitude control, and the antitorque pedals manage yaw. This integrated control system enables the pilot to perform a wide range of maneuvers, from stable hovering to agile flight in any direction, making helicopters highly versatile aircraft.

   [PH.I.G.K1a; FAA-H-8083-21]

6. What is the purpose of trim systems in helicopters?

The trim system in helicopters is used to reduce pilot workload by maintaining a set attitude or flight condition without constant control inputs. It helps stabilize the helicopter in a desired position, allowing for smoother and more efficient flight, particularly during longer journeys or cruising phases.

[PH.I.G.K1a; FAA-H-8083-21]

7. How does a stability control system enhance helicopter flight operations?

A stability control system in a helicopter, if installed, enhances flight safety by providing additional control assistance or augmentation. It helps maintain a stable flight attitude and can aid in keeping the helicopter level, especially in turbulent conditions or during complex maneuvers. This system is particularly beneficial in reducing pilot workload and enhancing overall handling characteristics.

[PH.I.G.K1a; FAA-H-8083-21]

8. What are the common types of trim systems found in helicopters?

Common types of trim systems in helicopters include mechanical trim systems, which use springs or adjustable linkages, and electrical or hydraulic trim systems, which use servos to adjust control positions. Some advanced helicopters have an automatic trim system that adjusts to maintain the desired flight attitude without pilot input.

[PH.I.G.K1a; FAA-H-8083-21]

9. What are the two models of engines used in the R22 helicopter?

The R22 helicopter uses two models of Lycoming engines: the O-320 and the O-360.

[PH.I.G.K1b; FAA-H-8083-21]

10. Describe the type and key characteristics of the engine used in an R22 helicopter.

The engine in the R22 helicopter is a four-cylinder, horizontally opposed, direct drive, air-cooled, carbureted, and normally aspirated powerplant. The displacement for the O-320 model is 319.8 cubic inches, and for the O-360 model, it is 361.0 cubic inches.

[PH.I.G.K1b; FAA-H-8083-21]

11. What is the power rating for the R22 HP, Alpha, and Beta models?

The R22 HP, Alpha, and Beta models have a power rating of 160 BHP at 2700 RPM.

[PH.I.G.K1b; FAA-H-8083-21]

12. What is the derated power rating for the R22 Beta II model?

The R22 Beta II model has a derated power rating of 145 BHP at 2700 RPM.

[PH.I.G.K1b; FAA-H-8083-21]

13. What is the maximum continuous power rating in the R22 helicopter?

The maximum continuous power rating in the R22 helicopter is 124 BHP at 2652 RPM, which corresponds to 104% on the tachometer.

[PH.I.G.K1b; FAA-H-8083-21]

14. What is the 5-minute takeoff rating for the R22 Beta and Beta II models?

The 5-minute takeoff rating for the R22 Beta and Beta II models is 131 BHP at 2652 RPM.

[PH.I.G.K1b; FAA-H-8083-21]

15. What type of rotor system is used in the Robinson R22 helicopter?

The Robinson R22 helicopter utilizes two all-metal blades mounted to the hub by coning hinges. The hub is mounted to the shaft by a teeter hinge. The coning and teeter hinges use self-lubricated bearings.

[PH.I.G.K1c; FAA-H-8083-21]

16. What is the articulation type of the main rotor in the R22 helicopter?

The main rotor of the R22 helicopter is free to teeter and cone, and it is rigid in-plane.

[PH.I.G.K1c; FAA-H-8083-21]

17. How many blades does the main rotor of the R22 helicopter have?

The main rotor of the R22 helicopter has two blades.

[PH.I.G.K1c; FAA-H-8083-21]

18. What is the articulation type of the R22 helicopter's tail rotor?

The tail rotor of the R22 helicopter is free to teeter and is rigid in-plane.

[PH.I.G.K1c; FAA-H-8083-21]

19. How many blades does the R22 helicopter's tail rotor have?

The tail rotor of the R22 helicopter has two blades.

[PH.I.G.K1c; FAA-H-8083-21]

20. What type of clutch is used between the upper sheave and drive line in the R22 helicopter?

A sprag-type overrunning clutch is used between the upper sheave and drive line in the R22 helicopter.

[PH.I.G.K1d; FAA-H-8083-21]

21. What type of belts are used between the engine and upper sheave in the R22 helicopter's drive system?

Two double V-belts are used between the engine and upper sheave in the R22 helicopter's drive system.

[PH.I.G.K1d; FAA-H-8083-21]

22. How does the R22 helicopter transmit power from the drive line to the main rotor?

In the R22 helicopter, power is transmitted from the drive line to the main rotor using spiral-bevel gears.

[PH.I.G.K1d; FAA-H-8083-21]

23. What is the total fuel capacity of the R22 helicopter's main tank with bladders?

The total fuel capacity of the main tank with bladders in the R22 helicopter is 18.3 US gallons (69 liters).

[PH.I.G.K1e; FAA-H-8083-21]

24. What is the usable fuel capacity of the R22 helicopter's main tank with bladders?

The usable fuel capacity of the main tank with bladders in the R22 helicopter is 16.9 US gallons (64 liters).

[PH.I.G.K1e; FAA-H-8083-21]

25. What is the total fuel capacity of the R22 helicopter's auxiliary tank with bladders?

The total fuel capacity of the auxiliary tank with bladders in the R22 helicopter is 9.7 US gallons (37 liters).

[PH.I.G.K1e; FAA-H-8083-21]

26. What is the combined total fuel capacity of the R22 helicopter with tanks with bladders?

The combined total fuel capacity of the R22 helicopter with tanks with bladders is 20.8 US gallons (106 liters).

[PH.I.G.K1e; FAA-H-8083-21]

27. What is the combined usable fuel capacity of the R22 helicopter with tanks with bladders?

The combined usable fuel capacity of the R22 helicopter with tanks with bladders is 26.3 US gallons (100 liters).

[PH.I.G.K1e; FAA-H-8083-21]

28. What is the minimum oil pressure requirement during idle for the R22 helicopter?

The minimum oil pressure during idle for the R22 helicopter is 25 psi.

[PH.I.G.K1e; FAA-H-8083-21]

29. What is the required minimum oil pressure during flight in the R22 helicopter?

The required minimum oil pressure during flight in the R22 helicopter is 55 psi.

[PH.I.G.K1e; FAA-H-8083-21]

30. What is the maximum oil pressure allowed during flight in the R22 helicopter?

The maximum oil pressure allowed during flight in the R22 helicopter is 95 psi.

[PH.I.G.K1e; FAA-H-8083-21]

31. What is the maximum permissible oil pressure during start and warm-up in the R22 helicopter?

The maximum permissible oil pressure during start and warm-up in the R22 helicopter is 115 psi.

[PH.I.G.K1e; FAA-H-8083-21]

32. What is the oil quantity minimum for takeoff in the R22 helicopter?

The oil quantity minimum for takeoff in the R22 helicopter is 4 quarts (3.8 liters).

[PH.I.G.K1e; FAA-H-8083-21]

33. What is the normal operating range for the rotor tachometer in the R22 helicopter?

The normal operating range for the rotor tachometer in the R22 helicopter is 101% to 104% RPM.

[PH.I.G.K1f; RFM]

34. What is the caution range for the rotor tachometer in the R22 helicopter?

The caution range for the rotor tachometer in the R22 helicopter is 90% to 101% RPM and 104% to 110% RPM.

[PH.I.G.K1f; RFM]

35. What is the lower limit of the red arc for the rotor tachometer in the R22 helicopter?

The lower limit of the red arc for the rotor tachometer in the R22 helicopter is 90% RPM.

[PH.I.G.K1f; RFM]

36. What is the maximum allowable RPM for the rotor tachometer in the R22 helicopter?

The maximum allowable RPM for the rotor tachometer in the R22 helicopter is 110% RPM.

[PH.I.G.K1f; RFM]

37. What is the normal operating range for the engine tachometer in the R22 helicopter with the O-320 engine?

The normal operating range for the engine tachometer in R22 helicopters with the O-320 engine is 97% to 104% RPM.

[PH.I.G.K1f; RFM]

38. What is the minimum RPM indicated by the lower yellow arc on the R22 helicopter's rotor tachometer?

The lower yellow arc on the rotor tachometer indicates a minimum RPM of 90% for the R22 helicopter.

[PH.I.G.K1f; RFM]

39. What RPM range is indicated by the upper yellow arc on the R22 helicopter's rotor tachometer?

The upper yellow arc on the rotor tachometer indicates an RPM range of 104% to 110% for the R22 helicopter.

[PH.I.G.K1f; RFM]

40. What is the green arc range for the engine tachometer in the R22 helicopter?

The green arc range for the engine tachometer in the R22 helicopter is 101% to 104% RPM.

[PH.I.G.K1f; RFM]

41. What is the yellow arc range for the engine tachometer in the R22 helicopter?

The yellow arc range for the engine tachometer in the R22 helicopter is 90% to 101% RPM.

[PH.I.G.K1f; RFM]

42. What is the maximum limit indicated by the upper red arc on the engine tachometer in the R22 helicopter?

The upper red arc on the engine tachometer indicates a maximum limit of 110% RPM for the R22 helicopter.

[PH.I.G.K1f; RFM]

43. What is the normal operating range for oil temperature in the R22 helicopter?

The normal operating range for oil temperature in the R22 helicopter is 75°F to 245°F (24°C to 118°C).

[PH.I.G.K1f; RFM]

44. What is the maximum permissible oil temperature in the R22 helicopter?

The maximum permissible oil temperature in the R22 helicopter is 245°F (118°C).

[PH.I.G.K1f; RFM]

45. What is the normal operating range for cylinder head temperature in the R22 helicopter?

The normal operating range for cylinder head temperature in the R22 helicopter is 200°F to 500°F (93°C to 260°C).

[PH.I.G.K1f; RFM]

46. What is the normal operating range for carburetor air temperature in the R22 helicopter?

The normal operating range for carburetor air temperature in the R22 helicopter is −15°C to 5°C.

[PH.I.G.K1f; RFM]

47. What is the normal operating range (green arc) for the airspeed indicator in the R22 helicopter?

The normal operating range (green arc) for the airspeed indicator in the R22 helicopter is 50 to 102 KIAS.

[PH.I.G.K1f; RFM]

48. What is the never-exceed airspeed (red line) on the airspeed indicator for the R22 helicopter?

The never-exceed airspeed (red line) on the airspeed indicator for the R22 helicopter is 102 KIAS.

[PH.I.G.K1f; RFM]

49. What type of landing gear is used in the R22 helicopter?

The R22 helicopter uses a skid-type landing gear.

[PH.I.G.K1g; RFM]

50. How does the R22 helicopter's landing gear absorb the impact of hard landings?

In the R22 helicopter, most hard landings are absorbed elastically by the landing gear, and in extremely hard landings, the struts will hinge up and outward as the crosstube yields to absorb the impact.

[PH.I.G.K1g; RFM]

51. Is slight yielding of the crosstube acceptable in the R22 helicopter's landing gear?

Yes, slight crosstube yielding is acceptable in the R22 helicopter's landing gear.

[PH.I.G.K1g; RFM]

52. What happens to the R22 helicopter's landing gear in an extremely hard landing?

In an extremely hard landing, the struts of the R22 helicopter's landing gear hinge up and outward, and the crosstube becomes permanently bent to absorb the impact.

[PH.I.G.K1g; RFM]

53. What is the indication that the crosstube yielding in the R22 helicopter's landing gear is excessive?

Excessive yielding in the R22 helicopter's landing gear is indicated when the tail skid is within 34 inches of the ground.

[PH.I.G.K1g; RFM]

54. What type of electrical system is used in the R22 helicopter?

The R22 helicopter uses a 14-volt DC electrical system, which includes an alternator and a sealed lead-acid battery as standard components.

[PH.I.G.K1h; RFM]

55. Where is the battery located in the R22 helicopter?

In the R22 helicopter, the battery is located either in the engine compartment or beneath the instrument console.

[PH.I.G.K1h; RFM]

56. What is the purpose of the circuit breaker panel in the R22 helicopter?

The circuit breaker panel in the R22 helicopter, located just forward of the left seat, contains breakers marked to indicate function and amperage, and is used for protecting the electrical system.

[PH.I.G.K1h; RFM]

57. Is in-flight reset of circuit breakers recommended in the R22 helicopter?

In flight reset of circuit breakers is not recommended in the R22 helicopter.

[PH.I.G.K1h; RFM]

58. What components does the pitot-static system supply air pressure to in the R22 helicopter?

In the R22 helicopter, the pitot-static system supplies air pressure to operate the airspeed indicator, altimeter, and vertical speed indicator.

[PH.I.G.K1i; FAA-H-8083-25]

59. Where is the pitot tube located on the R22 helicopter?

The pitot tube is located on the front edge of the mast fairing in the R22 helicopter.

[PH.I.G.K1i; FAA-H-8083-25]

60. Where is the static source located in the R22 helicopter?

The static source in the R22 helicopter is located inside the aft cowling, inboard of the cowl door hinge.

[PH.I.G.K1i; FAA-H-8083-25]

61. What components are included in the R22 helicopter's environmental system?

The R22 helicopter's environmental system includes cabin heating and ventilation components.

[PH.I.G.K1j; RFM]

62. How is cabin temperature controlled in the R22 helicopter?

Cabin temperature in the R22 helicopter is controlled through the cabin heating and ventilation system.

[PH.I.G.K1j; RFM]

63. How is fresh air ventilation provided in the R22 helicopter?

Fresh air ventilation in the R22 helicopter is provided through adjustable vents that allow outside air to enter the cabin.

[PH.I.G.K1j; RFM]

64. How does the R22 helicopter's carburetor heat system prevent ice formation?

The carburetor heat system in the R22 helicopter prevents ice formation by heating the air entering the carburetor, which mitigates the cooling effect caused by pressure drops and fuel evaporation.

[PH.I.G.K1k; RFM]

65. What causes carburetor ice in the R22 helicopter?

In the R22 helicopter, carburetor ice is caused by pressure drops and fuel evaporation inside the carburetor, which leads to significant cooling. It can occur at outside air temperatures (OATs) as high as 30°C (86°F).

[PH.I.G.K1k; RFM]

66. What are common indications of a system failure in a helicopter?

Common indications of a helicopter system failure include unusual noises or vibrations, warning lights or alarms, abnormal gauge readings, changes in control responsiveness, or any unexpected changes in flight characteristics. Pilots should be familiar with their helicopter's normal operational sounds and behaviors to quickly recognize any abnormalities.

[PH.I.G.K2; RFM]

67. What are the key indicators a pilot should monitor to identify potential system malfunctions?

A pilot should regularly monitor engine performance indicators, such as temperature and pressure gauges, warning lights, abnormal sounds or vibrations, changes in control responsiveness, and unexpected alterations in flight characteristics. Recognizing deviations from normal readings or behaviors is crucial in early malfunction detection.

[PH.I.G.R1; FAA-H-8083-21]

68. How can a pilot assess the level of risk associated with a detected system malfunction?

To assess the risk level, the pilot should consider the nature and severity of the malfunction, its potential impact on flight safety, available redundancy in systems, and current flight conditions. Consulting the rotorcraft flight manual (RFM) for specific malfunction symptoms and recommended actions is critical in risk assessment.

[PH.I.G.R1; FAA-H-8083-21]

69. What are the immediate actions a pilot should take upon detecting a critical system failure?

Upon detecting a critical system failure, the pilot should follow the emergency procedures outlined in the RFM, which may include reducing power, adjusting the flight path, and preparing for an emergency landing. The priority is to maintain control of the helicopter, ensure the safety of onboard personnel, and navigate to the nearest suitable area for landing.

[PH.I.G.R1; FAA-H-8083-21]

70. How does effective preflight planning help in mitigating risks associated with system malfunctions?

Effective preflight planning, including thorough inspections and system checks, helps in identifying potential issues before takeoff. It also involves familiarizing oneself with the specific helicopter's systems, understanding emergency procedures, and having a clear plan for different malfunction scenarios.

[PH.I.G.R1; FAA-H-8083-21]

71. What role do training and proficiency play in managing risks associated with system malfunctions?

Regular training and maintaining proficiency are essential in managing risks associated with system malfunctions. This includes practicing emergency procedures, staying updated with the latest operational knowledge, and understanding the specific helicopter's systems. Simulated training scenarios can also prepare pilots for handling real-world malfunction situations effectively.

[PH.I.G.R1; FAA-H-8083-21]

72. What are the initial steps a pilot should take upon identifying a system failure in a helicopter?

Upon identifying a system failure, the pilot should first stabilize the helicopter and maintain control. They should then identify the failed system using cockpit indicators and warning systems. Once identified, the pilot should reference the rotorcraft flight manual (RFM) for the specific emergency or abnormal procedures for that system.

[PH.I.G.R2; FAA-H-8083-21]

73. How can a pilot assess the impact of a system failure on helicopter operations?

To assess the impact, the pilot should evaluate how the system failure affects the helicopter's ability to continue safe flight. This includes considering factors like flight conditions, remaining functional systems, the nature of the failure, and the helicopter's current location relative to a safe landing area.

[PH.I.G.R2; FAA-H-8083-21]

74. What risk mitigation strategies are effective during a system failure?

Effective risk mitigation strategies include following the RFM's emergency procedures, using redundant systems if available, reducing workload by simplifying operations, and if necessary, diverting to the nearest suitable landing area. Communication with air traffic control (ATC) for assistance and alerting emergency services if needed are also crucial steps.

[PH.I.G.R2; FAA-H-8083-21]

75. How does pilot proficiency in emergency procedures influence the management of system failures?

Pilot proficiency in emergency procedures greatly influences the effective management of system failures. Regular training and practice in handling various failure scenarios ensure that pilots can respond quickly and appropriately, reducing the risk of adverse outcomes. Proficiency provides the confidence and skill needed to manage emergencies effectively.

[PH.I.G.R2; FAA-H-8083-21]

76. What is the importance of monitoring automated systems in helicopters?

Monitoring automated systems in helicopters is crucial for ensuring they are functioning as intended and aiding in flight operations. Regular monitoring helps detect any anomalies or malfunctions early, allowing for timely intervention. It ensures that the automated systems complement the pilot's skills and enhance flight safety.

[PH.I.G.R3; FAA-H-8083-25]

77. How can a pilot effectively manage the risks associated with reliance on automated systems?

To manage risks associated with reliance on automated systems, a pilot should maintain proficiency in manual flight skills, understand the limitations and failure modes of the automated systems, and be prepared to take over control manually if needed. Regular training on automated system usage and emergency procedures is also important.

[PH.I.G.R3; FAA-H-8083-25]

78. What are common indicators of a malfunction in automated flight systems?

Common indicators of a malfunction in automated flight systems include unexpected changes in flight path, altitude, or speed, uncommanded control inputs, warning lights or messages, and discrepancies between the system's indications and expected performance. Pilots should be familiar with normal system operations to recognize these signs (Indicators of Malfunction, FAA Helicopter Flying Handbook).

[PH.I.G.R3; FAA-H-8083-25]

Skills to be demonstrated:

• Operate at least three of the helicopter's systems listed in PH.I.G.K1a through PH.I.G.K1k.

• Complete the appropriate checklist(s).

H. Human Factors

1. What are the symptoms of hypoxia in pilots?

Symptoms of hypoxia in pilots can include headache, dizziness, shortness of breath, fatigue, euphoria, impaired judgment, and a decrease in coordination and reaction time. As hypoxia progresses, it can lead to cyanosis (bluing of the skin, particularly fingertips and lips), unconsciousness, and in severe cases, death.

[PH.I.H.K1a; FAA-H-8083-25]

2. How can a pilot recognize the onset of hypoxia during flight?

Recognition of hypoxia during flight is based on being aware of its symptoms and understanding how they may manifest at altitude. Pilots should be vigilant for any signs of mental or physical impairment, especially during flights at higher altitudes or in unpressurized aircraft without supplemental oxygen.

[PH.I.H.K1a; FAA-H-8083-25]

3. What are the causes of hypoxia in aviation?

Hypoxia in aviation is primarily caused by a lack of oxygen at high altitudes. As altitude increases, the partial pressure of oxygen decreases, making it more difficult for the body to absorb sufficient oxygen. It can also be caused by factors such as carbon monoxide poisoning from engine exhaust, smoke, or inadequate pressurization in the aircraft cabin.

[PH.I.H.K1a; FAA-H-8083-25]

4. What are the symptoms of hyperventilation in pilots?

Symptoms of hyperventilation include rapid or deep breathing, dizziness, tingling in the extremities, lightheadedness, a feeling of suffocation, blurred vision, and disorientation. Pilots may also experience anxiety and a feeling of panic, which can exacerbate the condition.

[PH.I.H.K1b; FAA-H-8083-25]

5. How can a pilot recognize the onset of hyperventilation during flight?

A pilot can recognize hyperventilation by being aware of its symptoms, particularly during stressful situations or when experiencing anxiety. Recognizing an increased breathing rate or feeling the physical symptoms such as tingling or lightheadedness are key indicators. It is important to identify these symptoms early to prevent further complications.

[PH.I.H.K1b; FAA-H-8083-25]

6. What causes hyperventilation in aviation settings?

Hyperventilation in aviation settings is often caused by stress, anxiety, or fear. It can also be a reaction to perceived threats or emergency situations. Additionally, incorrect breathing techniques, especially during periods of high workload or concentration, can lead to hyperventilation.

[PH.I.H.K1b; FAA-H-8083-25]

7. What are common symptoms of middle ear and sinus problems in pilots?

Common symptoms include pain or discomfort in the ears or sinuses, hearing loss or muffled hearing, dizziness, and a feeling of fullness or pressure in the ears or face. These symptoms can be exacerbated during ascent and descent due to changes in atmospheric pressure.

[PH.I.H.K1c; FAA-H-8083-25]

8. What causes middle ear and sinus problems in an aviation environment?

These problems are often caused by changes in atmospheric pressure during ascent and descent, which can create a pressure differential between the air inside the middle ear or sinuses and the external environment. Congestion due to colds, allergies, or infections can exacerbate these issues, as it can block the Eustachian tubes or sinus openings.

[PH.I.H.K1c; FAA-H-8083-25]

9. **What are the effects of these problems on a pilot's ability to fly?**

   Middle ear and sinus problems can lead to discomfort, pain, and difficulty in focusing, which can distract a pilot and impair their ability to fly safely. Severe pain or dizziness can significantly degrade a pilot's situational awareness and decision-making capabilities.

   [PH.I.H.K1c; FAA-H-8083-25]

10. **What corrective actions should a pilot take if experiencing these issues during flight?**

    Corrective actions include trying to equalize ear pressure by swallowing, yawning, or performing the Valsalva maneuver (gently blowing with the nose pinched closed). If pain persists or if there are signs of infection, the pilot should consider descending to a lower altitude and seeking medical attention after landing. Pilots with known sinus or ear issues should avoid flying until these issues are resolved.

    [PH.I.H.K1c; FAA-H-8083-25]

11. **What are the symptoms of spatial disorientation in pilots?**

    Symptoms of spatial disorientation include a sense of confusion about the aircraft's attitude or motion, feelings of tilting or turning when the aircraft is flying straight, dizziness, and a mismatch between what the pilot feels and what the instruments show. In severe cases, it can lead to vertigo.

    [PH.I.H.K1d; FAA-H-8083-25]

12. **What causes spatial disorientation among pilots?**

    Spatial disorientation is often caused by flying in poor visibility conditions where visual cues are limited or absent, leading pilots to rely solely on vestibular and proprioceptive senses, which can be misleading. It can also occur due to sudden or unfamiliar movements, or when transitioning from visual to instrument flight.

    [PH.I.H.K1d; FAA-H-8083-25]

13. What corrective actions should a pilot take when experiencing spatial disorientation?

The primary corrective action is to trust the aircraft's instruments and disregard conflicting sensory perceptions. Pilots should maintain a straight-and-level flight attitude based on the instruments and avoid sudden or drastic maneuvers. If disorientation persists, it may be necessary to request assistance from air traffic control.

[PH.I.H.K1d; FAA-H-8083-25]

14. What are the symptoms of motion sickness in pilots?

Symptoms of motion sickness in pilots include nausea, dizziness, sweating, a general feeling of discomfort and unease, and in more severe cases, vomiting. Pilots may also experience headaches and a feeling of disorientation.

[PH.I.H.K1e; FAA-H-8083-25]

15. What causes motion sickness in aviation settings?

Motion sickness in aviation is often caused by a disconnect between the visual cues a pilot sees and the vestibular sensations in the inner ear, particularly during turbulent flights or when the visual horizon is obscured. Stress, anxiety, and certain medications can also increase susceptibility to motion sickness.

[PH.I.H.K1e; FAA-H-8083-25]

16. What corrective actions should a pilot take if they experience motion sickness during flight?

Corrective actions include opening air vents to increase ventilation, avoiding head movements that could worsen symptoms, focusing on a distant point or the horizon, and if possible, allowing another pilot to take control of the aircraft. Over-the-counter medications like antihistamines can be used as a preventative measure but should be tested before flight due to potential side effects.

[PH.I.H.K1e; FAA-H-8083-25]

17. What are the symptoms of carbon monoxide poisoning in pilots?

Symptoms of carbon monoxide poisoning in pilots can include headache, dizziness, weakness, nausea, confusion, blurred vision, shortness of breath, and loss of consciousness. Early symptoms are often nonspecific and can be mistaken for fatigue or mild illness.

[PH.I.H.K1f; FAA-H-8083-25]

18. What causes carbon monoxide poisoning in an aviation environment?

In aviation, carbon monoxide poisoning is typically caused by exhaust fumes entering the cabin or cockpit, often due to a faulty exhaust system or leaks. This is more common in piston-engine aircraft with cabin heating systems that use heat from the exhaust.

[PH.I.H.K1f; FAA-H-8083-25]

19. What corrective actions should a pilot take if carbon monoxide poisoning is suspected?

If carbon monoxide poisoning is suspected, the pilot should immediately shut off the cabin heater, open air vents to increase ventilation, and consider using supplemental oxygen if available. The pilot should land at the nearest suitable airport to seek medical attention and have the aircraft inspected for exhaust leaks.

[PH.I.H.K1f; FAA-H-8083-25]

20. What are common symptoms of stress in pilots?

Symptoms of stress in pilots can include increased heart rate, rapid breathing, muscle tension, sweating, fatigue, irritability, difficulty concentrating, and decision-making challenges. Chronic stress may lead to longer-term issues like anxiety, depression, and burnout.

[PH.I.H.K1g; FAA-H-8083-25]

21. How can a pilot recognize signs of stress during flight?

A pilot can recognize signs of stress by being aware of their own physical and emotional responses, such as feeling overwhelmed, anxious, or fatigued. Recognizing changes in behavior, such as becoming easily frustrated or making frequent errors, is also key.

[PH.I.H.K1g; FAA-H-8083-25]

22. What are the effects of stress on a pilot's ability to operate an aircraft?

Stress can significantly impair a pilot's ability to operate an aircraft safely. It can affect cognitive functions, impair judgment, decrease situational awareness, and increase the likelihood of errors. In extreme cases, it can lead to panic or an inability to make decisions.

[PH.I.H.K1g; FAA-H-8083-25]

23. What corrective actions should a pilot take to manage stress?

To manage stress, pilots should practice relaxation techniques, such as deep breathing or mindfulness, and ensure proper rest, nutrition, and hydration. Developing effective workload management strategies and seeking support from co-pilots or air traffic control when needed can also help. In the long term, addressing underlying causes and maintaining a healthy work-life balance are important.

[PH.I.H.K1g; FAA-H-8083-25]

24. What are common symptoms of fatigue in pilots?

Symptoms of fatigue in pilots include feelings of tiredness or exhaustion, lack of energy, difficulty focusing, slowed reaction times, memory lapses, impaired judgment, moodiness, and irritability. In advanced stages, fatigue can lead to microsleeps, brief periods of involuntary sleep.

[PH.I.H.K1h; FAA-H-8083-25]

25. What causes fatigue in aviation settings?

Fatigue in aviation can be caused by a variety of factors including long duty periods, insufficient rest or sleep, circadian rhythm disruptions due to night flying or time zone changes, monotonous or low-stimulus flight environments, and stress. Other contributors can include physical exertion and poor dietary habits.

[PH.I.H.K1h; FAA-H-8083-25]

26. What corrective actions should a pilot take if experiencing fatigue?

Corrective actions for fatigue include obtaining adequate rest before flying, managing workload to avoid excessive stress, taking breaks during long flights, staying hydrated, and consuming balanced meals. If fatigue is overwhelming, it's advisable to avoid flying until properly rested, or share or transfer piloting duties if flying with another qualified pilot.

[PH.I.H.K1h; FAA-H-8083-25]

27. What are common symptoms of dehydration in pilots?

Symptoms of dehydration in pilots can include thirst, dry mouth, fatigue, dizziness, decreased urine output, dark-colored urine, headache, and in severe cases, confusion and fainting. Chronic dehydration can lead to more serious health issues over time.

[PH.I.H.K1i; FAA-H-8083-25]

28. What causes dehydration and poor nutrition in aviation?

Dehydration in aviation can be caused by insufficient fluid intake, excessive sweating, and the dry air in aircraft cabins. Poor nutrition can result from irregular eating patterns, consuming low-quality meals, or skipping meals due to tight flight schedules or limited options.

[PH.I.H.K1i; FAA-H-8083-25]

29. What corrective actions should a pilot take to address dehydration and nutrition issues?

To address dehydration, pilots should ensure regular intake of fluids, particularly water, before and during flights. For nutrition, consuming balanced meals with adequate carbohydrates, proteins, and fats is important. Snacking on healthy options like fruits and nuts during flights can also help maintain energy levels.

[PH.I.H.K1i; FAA-H-8083-25]

30. What are common symptoms of hypothermia in pilots?

Symptoms of hypothermia in pilots can include shivering, numbness, pale and cold skin, fatigue, impaired judgment, drowsiness, slow or slurred speech, and in severe cases, loss of consciousness. Initial symptoms might be subtle, such as mild shivering or a feeling of cold.

[PH.I.H.K1j; FAA-H-8083-25]

31. What causes hypothermia in an aviation environment?

Hypothermia in aviation can be caused by prolonged exposure to cold temperatures, especially in unpressurized cabins at high altitudes. It can also occur due to inadequate insulation or heating in the aircraft, wet conditions, or insufficient personal protective gear against the cold.

[PH.I.H.K1j; FAA-H-8083-25]

32. What corrective actions should a pilot take if experiencing hypothermia?

If experiencing hypothermia, the pilot should increase the cabin temperature, if possible, and use additional layers of clothing or blankets to warm up. Consuming warm, sugary liquids (avoiding caffeine and alcohol) can help raise body temperature. In severe cases, land as soon as practical to seek medical treatment. Preventative measures include dressing appropriately for the cold and ensuring adequate heating in the aircraft.

[PH.I.H.K1j; FAA-H-8083-25]

33. What are common optical illusions experienced by pilots?

Common optical illusions experienced by pilots include runway width illusion, where a narrower-than-usual runway appears longer, and the runway slope illusion, where an upsloping runway appears longer than it is. Other illusions include false horizons, autokinesis (stationary lights appearing to move in dark conditions), and size-distance illusions affecting perception during landing.

[PH.I.H.K1k; FAA-H-8083-25]

34. What causes optical illusions in aviation?

Optical illusions in aviation are often caused by environmental factors like lighting conditions, atmospheric conditions (e.g., fog, haze), and the terrain or landscape over which the aircraft is flying. The design of the runway and airport environment can also contribute, as well as the pilot's angle of approach and altitude.

[PH.I.H.K1k; FAA-H-8083-25]

35. What corrective actions should a pilot take if experiencing optical illusions?

To counteract optical illusions, pilots should rely more on their flight instruments than on outside visual references, particularly in conditions where illusions are likely. Training and experience in different flying environments can help pilots anticipate and manage these illusions. In case of doubt, going around for a second approach is advisable.

[PH.I.H.K1k; FAA-H-8083-25]

36. What are common symptoms of excessive dissolved nitrogen in the bloodstream for pilots after scuba diving?

Symptoms can include joint pain, dizziness, extreme fatigue, numbness or tingling, shortness of breath, and in severe cases, paralysis or shock. These symptoms occur due to nitrogen bubbles forming in the bloodstream and tissues, a condition known as decompression sickness.

[PH.I.H.K1l; FAA-H-8083-25]

37. What causes excessive nitrogen buildup in a pilot's bloodstream after scuba diving?

Excessive nitrogen buildup occurs during scuba diving when a diver is exposed to high-pressure underwater environments, causing the body to absorb more nitrogen. Rapid ascent to high altitudes after diving can lead to decompression sickness as the reduced atmospheric pressure causes the excess nitrogen to form bubbles in the body.

[PH.I.H.K1l; FAA-H-8083-25]

38. What corrective actions should a pilot take to manage this risk?

Corrective actions include adhering to recommended waiting periods after scuba diving before flying. The FAA recommends a wait of at least 12 hours after a non-decompression dive and at least 24 hours after a decompression dive. If symptoms of decompression sickness occur, seek medical attention immediately and avoid flying until fully recovered.

[PH.I.H.K1l; FAA-H-8083-25]

39. What is the FAA regulation regarding the use of alcohol prior to flying?

FAA regulations state that no person may act as a crewmember of a civil aircraft within 8 hours after the consumption of alcohol (the 8-hour bottle to throttle rule). Additionally, a pilot cannot fly with a blood alcohol content of 0.04% or higher.

[PH.I.H.K2; 14 CFR 91.17]

40. Can pilots use prescription medications while flying?

Pilots can use certain prescription medications while flying, but it depends on the nature of the medication and its effects on the individual. The FAA requires that pilots not fly while using any medication that affects the body in any way contrary to safety. Pilots should consult an Aviation Medical Examiner (AME) to determine if a specific medication is safe to use while flying.

[PH.I.H.K2; FAA-H-8083-25]

41. What is the FAA's policy on marijuana use for pilots, given its legalization in some states?

Despite the legalization of marijuana in some states, the FAA prohibits its use for pilots. The FAA's policy is that marijuana remains a Schedule I controlled substance under federal law, and its use is disqualifying for medical certification. Pilots who test positive for marijuana are subject to FAA enforcement action.

[PH.I.H.K2; FAA-H-8083-25]

42. What are the primary effects of alcohol consumption on a pilot's abilities?

Alcohol can significantly impair a pilot's judgment, vision, coordination, and reaction times. It also affects the vestibular system, leading to disorientation and a decreased ability to process information, crucial for safe flight operations.

[PH.I.H.K3; FAA-H-8083-25]

43. How can prescription and over-the-counter medications affect a pilot's performance?

Prescription and over-the-counter medications can cause various side effects such as drowsiness, dizziness, vision impairment, and decreased cognitive functions, which can dangerously impair a pilot's ability to safely operate an aircraft. Some medications can also have delayed effects or interactions with other substances that can be hazardous while flying.

[PH.I.H.K3; FAA-H-8083-25]

44. What are the risks associated with using drugs, including cannabis, for pilots?

Drug use, including cannabis, can lead to impaired motor skills, altered perception of time and distance, impaired memory, decreased coordination, and impaired judgment. These effects can have a significant impact on a pilot's ability to operate an aircraft safely, regardless of the legality of the substance in certain areas.

[PH.I.H.K3; FAA-H-8083-25]

45. How do stimulants, such as caffeine or amphetamines, affect a pilot?

While stimulants like caffeine can temporarily increase alertness, excessive use can lead to restlessness, anxiety, and heart palpitations. Amphetamines and similar stimulants can cause overconfidence, risky decision-making, and after the effects wear off, result in severe fatigue and decreased mental clarity, impacting a pilot's abilities.

[PH.I.H.K3; FAA-H-8083-25]

46. What is aeronautical decision making (ADM) in the context of aviation?

Aeronautical decision making (ADM) is a systematic approach to the mental process used by pilots to consistently determine the best course of action in response to a given set of circumstances. It involves recognizing and managing risks effectively to make safe and sound decisions.

[PH.I.H.K4; FAA-H-8083-25]

47. How does single-pilot resource management (SRM) relate to ADM?

Single-pilot resource management (SRM) is an adaptation of crew resource management (CRM) principles for single-pilot operations. It involves the effective use of all available resources, including navigation tools, weather information, and the aircraft's systems and automation, to make informed decisions and manage flight safely.

[PH.I.H.K4; FAA-H-8083-25]

48. How can a pilot improve their ADM skills?

A pilot can improve ADM skills by practicing the use of decision-making models like the OODA loop (observe, orient, decide, and act) or the DECIDE model, engaging in regular training and simulations, learning from past experiences, and staying informed about new technologies and best practices in aviation safety.

[PH.I.H.K4; FAA-H-8083-25]

49. What role does risk management play in ADM and SRM?

Risk management is a critical element of both ADM and SRM. It involves identifying, assessing, and mitigating risks to reduce the likelihood of adverse events. Effective risk management allows a pilot to anticipate and address potential hazards proactively, ensuring a higher level of safety during flight.

[PH.I.H.K4; FAA-H-8083-25]

50. What are some common aeromedical factors that can affect a pilot's performance?

Common aeromedical factors include hypoxia, dehydration, fatigue, spatial disorientation, and the effects of medications or alcohol. These factors can impair cognitive functions, decision-making abilities, and motor skills, crucial for safe piloting.

[PH.I.H.R1; FAA-H-8083-25]

51. How does hypoxia impact a pilot in flight?

Hypoxia, a deficiency in oxygen, can lead to symptoms such as headache, dizziness, breathlessness, and impaired judgment. At higher altitudes, the risk of hypoxia increases, potentially leading to unconsciousness and loss of control of the aircraft.

[PH.I.H.R1; FAA-H-8083-25]

52. What is spatial disorientation and how does it affect pilots?

Spatial disorientation occurs when a pilot cannot correctly interpret aircraft attitude, altitude, or airspeed in relation to the Earth or other points of reference. It is especially prevalent in conditions of poor visibility or at night and can lead to loss of aircraft control.

[PH.I.H.R1; FAA-H-8083-25]

53. What role does fatigue play in pilot performance?

Fatigue can significantly impair a pilot's alertness, reaction time, coordination, and decision-making abilities. It can be caused by lack of sleep, long duty hours, or circadian rhythm disruptions. Fatigue management is crucial for maintaining safety in flight operations.

[PH.I.H.R1; FAA-H-8083-25]

54. How can a pilot manage the risks associated with physiological issues?

To manage these risks, pilots should ensure adequate rest, hydration, and nutrition; be aware of the symptoms of physiological issues; use supplemental oxygen as needed; and avoid flying under the influence of impairing substances or medications. Regular medical check-ups and staying informed about health-related aviation safety can also help.

[PH.I.H.R1; FAA-H-8083-25]

55. What is carbon monoxide poisoning and how can it affect pilots?

Carbon monoxide poisoning occurs when pilots are exposed to this odorless and colorless gas, often due to exhaust leaks or cabin heating systems. It can cause headache, dizziness, weakness, nausea, confusion, and even loss of consciousness, significantly impairing a pilot's ability to fly safely.

[PH.I.H.R1; FAA-H-8083-25]

56. How does motion sickness impact a pilot's ability to control the aircraft?

Motion sickness, caused by a mismatch between visual and vestibular inputs, can lead to symptoms like nausea, dizziness, and vomiting. It can distract pilots and impair their ability to focus on flying tasks, potentially leading to a loss of situational awareness and control of the aircraft.

[PH.I.H.R1; FAA-H-8083-25]

57. What are the effects of alcohol on a pilot's flying abilities?

Alcohol impairs a pilot's judgment, coordination, and reaction times. It can also lead to overconfidence and increased risk-taking. The FAA's 8-hour bottle to throttle rule is a minimum guideline, but the effects of alcohol can last much longer, depending on the amount consumed and individual tolerance.

[PH.I.H.R1; FAA-H-8083-25]

58. How can dehydration and nutrition affect a pilot's performance?

Dehydration can cause fatigue, decreased cognitive abilities, and dizziness. Poor nutrition can lead to low energy levels, decreased concentration, and slower reaction times. Pilots should ensure proper hydration and nutrition to maintain peak cognitive and physical performance while flying.

[PH.I.H.R1; FAA-H-8083-25]

59. What is the impact of stress on a pilot's performance?

Stress can negatively impact a pilot's decision-making ability, situational awareness, and reaction time. It can come from personal, environmental, or operational sources. Effective stress management, including recognizing stress symptoms and using coping strategies, is essential for safe flying.

[PH.I.H.R1; FAA-H-8083-25]

60. What are some common hazardous attitudes identified in pilots?

Common hazardous attitudes in pilots include invulnerability ("It won't happen to me"), macho ("I can handle it"), impulsivity ("Do it quickly"), resignation ("What's the use?"), and anti-authority ("Don't tell me"). These attitudes can compromise decision-making and increase the risk of accidents.

[PH.I.H.R2; FAA-H-8083-25]

61. How can the invulnerability attitude increase risk in flying?

The invulnerability attitude can lead pilots to underestimate risks and overestimate their ability to handle dangerous situations, potentially leading to poor decision-making and a disregard for safety protocols.

[PH.I.H.R2; FAA-H-8083-25]

62. What strategies can mitigate the risk associated with the macho attitude in pilots?

To mitigate the macho attitude, pilots should practice humility, recognize their limitations, and adhere to safety standards. Seeking feedback from instructors or peers and reflecting on past experiences can also help in overcoming this attitude.

[PH.I.H.R2; FAA-H-8083-25]

63. How does the anti-authority attitude impact a pilot's decision-making?

The anti-authority attitude can lead pilots to disregard rules, regulations, and advice from others, potentially resulting in non-compliance with safety procedures and increased risk of accidents or incidents.

[PH.I.H.R2; FAA-H-8083-25]

64. What are effective ways to address impulsivity in pilot decision-making?

Addressing impulsivity involves practicing patience, thorough planning, and considering the consequences of actions before making decisions. Pilots should develop a habit of analyzing situations carefully and consulting available resources before acting.

[PH.I.H.R2; FAA-H-8083-25]

65. How can the resignation attitude affect a pilot's performance and safety?

The resignation attitude can lead pilots to feel helpless and surrender control, believing that their actions do not have an impact on the outcomes. This attitude can result in a lack of proactive decision-making and reduced vigilance, increasing the risk of in-flight errors and accidents. Pilots should counter this by taking an active role in managing and controlling the flight, and by seeking opportunities for constructive participation in the flying process.

[PH.I.H.R2; FAA-H-8083-25]

66. What is the danger of a get-there-itis mindset in aviation, and how can it be mitigated?

Get-there-itis, or the desire to reach a destination at all costs, can lead to pushing the limits of safety, such as flying in poor weather conditions or when fatigued. This mindset can compromise a pilot's ability to make objective decisions. Mitigation includes setting personal minimums, having alternate plans, and being willing to delay, divert, or cancel a flight if conditions are not favorable.

[PH.I.H.R2; FAA-H-8083-25]

67. In what ways can a pilot effectively counter the impulsivity hazardous attitude?

To counter the impulsivity attitude, a pilot should focus on developing a disciplined approach to flying, such as following checklists and standard operating procedures, taking time to assess situations thoroughly, and not rushing into decisions. Seeking input from others and using a methodical decision-making process like the DECIDE model can also help in curbing impulsiveness.

[PH.I.H.R2; FAA-H-8083-25]

68. What are common distractions that can occur in the cockpit and how can they impact flight safety?

Common cockpit distractions include nonessential conversations, electronic devices, cockpit equipment issues, and external factors like weather or traffic. These distractions can lead to a loss of focus on primary flying tasks, potentially resulting in missed communications, navigational errors, or failure to monitor flight instruments.

[PH.I.H.R3; FAA-H-8083-25]

69. How can a pilot effectively prioritize tasks to avoid becoming overwhelmed?

Pilots can use the aviate, navigate, communicate hierarchy to prioritize tasks. This means first ensuring the aircraft is under control, then navigating along the planned route, and finally communicating with ATC or others, as necessary. Using checklists and dividing tasks into smaller, manageable steps can also help in effective task management.

[PH.I.H.R3; FAA-H-8083-25]

70. What strategies can help a pilot maintain situational awareness?

Strategies to maintain situational awareness include regularly scanning flight instruments and the external environment, staying updated on weather and traffic conditions, using navigational aids effectively, and anticipating future phases of flight. Continuous self-assessment and being aware of the current flight situation at all times are key.

[PH.I.H.R3; FAA-H-8083-25]

71. How can a pilot identify and recover from spatial disorientation?

Identifying spatial disorientation involves recognizing discrepancies between sensory perceptions and actual flight conditions, often indicated by conflicting information from flight instruments. Recovery includes trusting and relying on the aircraft's instruments, maintaining a stable attitude, and avoiding sudden or extreme maneuvers.

[PH.I.H.R3; FAA-H-8083-25]

72. What are the risks associated with task saturation, and how can they be mitigated?

Task saturation occurs when a pilot is overloaded with tasks, leading to errors, omissions, and poor decision-making. To mitigate this, pilots should delegate tasks when possible, use automation effectively, and not hesitate to ask ATC for assistance or relief, such as requesting delayed vectors or holding patterns to manage workload.

[PH.I.H.R3; FAA-H-8083-25]

73. What is confirmation bias and how does it affect pilot decision-making?

Confirmation bias is the tendency to search for, interpret, and recall information in a way that confirms one's preconceptions, leading to biased decision-making. In aviation, this bias can cause a pilot to disregard critical information or warning signs that contradict their initial beliefs or plans, potentially leading to unsafe situations.

[PH.I.H.R4; FAA-H-8083-2]

74. How can expectation bias impact a pilot's situational awareness?

Expectation bias occurs when a pilot's expectations about what should be happening influence their perception of what is actually happening. This can lead to misinterpreting information or missing important cues, such as misreading instruments or misunderstanding ATC instructions, due to expecting different information.

[PH.I.H.R4; FAA-H-8083-2]

75. What strategies can pilots use to mitigate the risk of confirmation bias?

To mitigate confirmation bias, pilots should actively seek out and consider information that challenges their assumptions, use checklists to ensure all procedures and checks are completed, and encourage open communication with co-pilots or ATC to gain different perspectives. Regular training on cognitive biases and their impact can also help.

[PH.I.H.R4; FAA-H-8083-2]

Skills to be demonstrated:

- Associate the symptoms and effects for at least three of the conditions listed in PH.I.H.K1a through PH.I.H.K1l with the cause(s) and corrective action(s).

- Perform self-assessment, including fitness for flight and personal minimums, for actual flight or a scenario given by the evaluator.

Preflight
Procedures

2

A. Preflight Assessment

1. Is there a self-assessment checklist to use that covers whether you're safe to fly?

There is, use the **I.M.S.A.F.E.** checklist:

I – Illness

M – Medication

S – Stress

A – Alcohol

F – Fatigue

E – Emotional health

[PH.II.A.K1; FAA-H-8083-25]

2. What is pilot self-assessment, and why is it important?

Pilot self-assessment is the process by which pilots evaluate their own fitness for flight, considering factors like health, skill level, knowledge, and emotional state. It's crucial because it allows pilots to identify potential issues that might affect their performance and make informed decisions about their ability to safely conduct a flight.

[PH.II.A.K1; FAA-H-8083-25]

3. What tools or methods can pilots use for effective self-assessment?

Pilots can use tools like the IMSAFE checklist (Illness, Medication, Stress, Alcohol, Fatigue, Eating/Emotion) to assess their readiness for flight. Additionally, regular proficiency checks, keeping a personal log of challenges faced during flights, and seeking feedback from instructors or peers are effective methods for ongoing self-assessment.

[PH.II.A.K1; FAA-H-8083-25]

4. How does a pilot's skill level and currency affect their self-assessment?

A pilot's skill level and currency, including recent flight experience and proficiency with specific aircraft types and operations, are critical components of self-assessment. Pilots need to honestly evaluate their skills and recency of experience to determine if they are competent to handle the planned flight, especially in challenging conditions or unfamiliar environments.

[PH.II.A.K1; FAA-H-8083-25]

5. What are the key elements a pilot should check to ensure a helicopter is airworthy?

To determine airworthiness, a pilot should check that the helicopter has a valid airworthiness certificate, registration, operating handbook, and weight and balance information. Additionally, the pilot should ensure that all required inspections (annual, 100-hour, etc.) are up to date and that there are no outstanding Airworthiness Directives (ADs) unaddressed.

[PH.II.A.K2; FAA-H-8083-21]

6. What is the role of preflight inspection in assessing helicopter airworthiness?

The preflight inspection is crucial in assessing a helicopter's airworthiness. It involves a thorough check of the helicopter's structure, control systems, fluid levels, powerplant, and avionics. Any anomalies or defects found during this inspection must be addressed before the flight.

[PH.II.A.K2; FAA-H-8083-21]

7. How do maintenance records influence the airworthiness of a helicopter?

Maintenance records provide a history of the helicopter's repairs, inspections, and compliance with Airworthiness Directives. These records must be reviewed to ensure that the helicopter has been maintained in accordance with regulatory requirements and manufacturer recommendations, which directly influence its airworthiness.

[PH.II.A.K2; FAA-H-8083-21]

8. What specific items should be inspected in a helicopter's powerplant during preflight?

In a helicopter's powerplant, the preflight inspection should include checking for leaks, ensuring proper oil and coolant levels, inspecting air filters and intakes, examining belts or transmissions for wear, and verifying the condition of exhaust systems and any visible engine components.

[PH.II.A.K3a; FAA-H-8083-21]

9. How is the helicopter's rotor system inspected during preflight?

The rotor system inspection includes examining rotor blades for damage or wear, checking blade bolts and grips for security, inspecting the rotor head for cracks or leaks, and ensuring that linkages and pitch-change mechanisms move freely and do not show signs of excessive wear or damage.

[PH.II.A.K3a; FAA-H-8083-21]

10. What should be checked in a helicopter's flight control system during preflight?

The flight control system inspection involves verifying the proper movement and security of cyclic, collective, and tail rotor pedals. It includes checking for full and free movement, ensuring that control linkages are secure and undamaged, and confirming that there are no obstructions or binding in the control paths.

[PH.II.A.K3a; FAA-H-8083-21]

11. What are some critical areas to inspect on the helicopter's exterior and interior?

On the exterior, critical areas include the fuselage for damage or cracks, landing gear or skids for integrity, antennas, lights, and external load attachments. Inside the helicopter, important checks include instrument functionality, proper seat adjustment and security, avionics settings, and ensuring emergency equipment is present and serviceable.

[PH.II.A.K3a; FAA-H-8083-21]

12. What should a pilot inspect in the helicopter's fuel system during preflight?

During preflight, a pilot should check the helicopter's fuel quantity indicators for accuracy, inspect for fuel leaks, verify the integrity of fuel lines, and ensure the fuel type and quality meet the requirements of the helicopter. The pilot should also check fuel filters and drains to ensure there are no contaminants in the fuel.

[PH.II.A.K3a; FAA-H-8083-21]

13. How important is it to inspect the helicopter's electrical system, and what should be included?

Inspecting the helicopter's electrical system is crucial for safe operation. This includes checking the battery condition and connections, ensuring proper operation of the alternator or generator, inspecting circuit breakers and wiring for signs of wear or damage, and verifying the functionality of the helicopter's lighting and avionics systems.

[PH.II.A.K3a; FAA-H-8083-21]

14. What checks should be performed on the helicopter's avionics and navigation equipment during preflight?

Preflight checks on avionics and navigation equipment include powering up the systems to verify their functionality, checking the settings and accuracy of navigation instruments, ensuring communication radios are operational, and verifying that GPS systems are updated and functioning correctly. It's also important to check that any emergency locator transmitter (ELT) is properly armed and in working condition.

[PH.II.A.K3a; FAA-H-8083-21]

15. What is the purpose of a preflight inspection for a helicopter?

The purpose of a helicopter preflight inspection is to ensure the aircraft is in a safe condition for flight.

[PH.II.A.K3b; FAA-H-8083-25]

16. How can a pilot detect defects in the helicopter's rotor system during preflight inspection?

During preflight, a pilot can detect rotor system defects by visually inspecting the rotor blades for any signs of damage like cracks, dents, or delamination. Checking for loose bolts or components and examining the rotor head and blade grips for leaks or unusual wear is also crucial. Listening for any unusual noises when moving the rotor blades can help identify internal issues.

[PH.II.A.K3c; FAA-H-8083-21]

17. What signs should a pilot look for to identify potential defects in the helicopter's engine and powerplant?

To identify defects in the engine and powerplant, a pilot should look for oil or fluid leaks, unusual stains, and cracks on the engine block or components. Checking for proper fluid levels, inspecting belts or hoses for wear and tension, and examining exhaust and intake areas for blockages or damage are also key indicators of potential issues.

[PH.II.A.K3c; FAA-H-8083-21]

18. How can defects in the helicopter's flight control system be detected during preflight?

Defects in the flight control system can be detected by ensuring all controls, including cyclic, collective, and pedals, move freely without binding or excessive play. Inspecting connecting rods, joints, and linkages for security and integrity, and checking for any abnormal looseness or stiffness in the control mechanisms can reveal potential problems.

[PH.II.A.K3c; FAA-H-8083-21]

19. What are common indicators of defects in a helicopter's fuel system during preflight checks?

Indicators of defects in the helicopter's fuel system include fuel leaks, dampness or staining around fuel lines and tanks, signs of fuel contamination in drains, and discrepancies in fuel gauge readings. Inspecting fuel caps for proper sealing and checking filters for blockages can also help identify issues.

[PH.II.A.K3c; FAA-H-8083-21]

20. **How does a pilot perform a preflight check for defects in the helicopter's electrical system?**

A preflight check for electrical system defects includes inspecting wiring for fraying or damage, ensuring all connections and terminals are secure, and checking battery condition and connections. Testing the operation of electrical components like lights, avionics, and instruments, and observing any abnormal readings or malfunctions can also reveal electrical issues.

[PH.II.A.K3c; FAA-H-8083-21]

21. **What regulation requires pilots to conduct a preflight inspection of a helicopter?**

While the Federal Aviation Regulations (FARs) do not explicitly state "preflight inspection" for helicopters, 14 CFR §91.103 requires the pilot-in-command to become familiar with all available information concerning the flight, which includes the condition of the aircraft. This regulation is commonly interpreted as mandating a thorough preflight inspection to ensure the aircraft is safe for operation.

[PH.II.A.K3d; FAA-H-8083-21]

22. **How does 14 CFR §91.7 relate to helicopter preflight inspections?**

14 CFR §91.7 addresses airworthiness, stating that no person may operate a civil aircraft unless it is in an airworthy condition. A preflight inspection is essential to determine the airworthiness of the helicopter, as it helps identify any conditions that would render the aircraft unairworthy.

[PH.II.A.K3d; FAA-H-8083-21]

23. What is the importance of a preflight inspection in relation to 14 CFR §91.13, which deals with careless or reckless operation?

Under 14 CFR §91.13, operating an aircraft in a careless or reckless manner is prohibited. Conducting a thorough preflight inspection helps ensure that the helicopter is operated safely and responsibly, thus adhering to this regulation by preventing potential accidents or incidents due to overlooked maintenance issues or aircraft defects.

[PH.II.A.K3d; FAA-H-8083-21]

24. Are there specific items listed in the regulations that must be inspected during a helicopter preflight?

The regulations do not specify exact items for preflight inspection. Instead, they emphasize the overall responsibility of the pilot to ensure the aircraft's airworthiness. Pilots should refer to their helicopter's specific rotorcraft flight manual (RFM) or pilot's operating handbook (POH) for detailed preflight inspection checklists and procedures.

[PH.II.A.K3d; FAA-H-8083-21]

25. How do weather conditions affect helicopter flight planning and operation?

Weather conditions significantly impact helicopter operations. Factors like visibility, wind speed and direction, precipitation, and cloud cover must be considered. Adverse weather, such as fog, thunderstorms, or high winds, can severely restrict visibility, alter flight performance, and increase the risk of encountering hazards like turbulence or icing. Proper weather assessment is crucial for safe route planning and decision-making.

[PH.II.A.K4; FAA-H-8083-25]

26. Why is terrain awareness crucial for helicopter pilots, and what should be considered during flight planning?

Terrain awareness is vital for avoiding obstacles and ensuring safe altitude clearance, particularly in low-altitude helicopter operations. Pilots must consider the elevation, contours, and type of terrain along their flight path. Mountainous or hilly areas, tall buildings, and other structures present potential hazards. Flight planning should include choosing routes that avoid difficult terrain and provide safe emergency landing options and adhere where possible to the VFR altitudes according to 14 CFR §91.159.

[PH.II.A.K4; FAA-H-8083-21]

27. How does route selection impact the safety and efficiency of a helicopter flight?

Route selection plays a critical role in safety and efficiency. Pilots should choose routes that minimize exposure to potential hazards, such as adverse weather, challenging terrain, and airspace restrictions. Considerations include ease of navigation, availability of emergency landing sites, and compliance with airspace regulations. Efficient routing also conserves fuel and reduces flight time.

[PH.II.A.K4; FAA-H-8083-21]

28. What types of obstructions pose risks to helicopter operations, and how can these risks be mitigated?

Obstructions like buildings, towers, power lines, and natural features such as trees pose risks to helicopters, especially during low-altitude flight. To mitigate these risks, pilots should conduct thorough preflight planning using updated charts, maintain vigilant lookout during flight, and adhere to recommended altitude and clearance guidelines.

[PH.II.A.K4; FAA-H-8083-21]

29. How should a pilot incorporate environmental factors into the decision-making process?

Incorporating environmental factors into decision-making involves assessing and mitigating risks associated with weather, terrain, route selection, and obstructions. Pilots should gather comprehensive information on these factors, consider their impact on the specific flight, and be prepared to alter plans as conditions change. Effective decision-making also involves recognizing personal limitations and opting for the safest course of action.

[PH.II.A.K4; FAA-H-8083-25]

30. What types of pilot-related risks should be identified during flight planning?

Pilot-related risks include factors like fatigue, stress, inexperience with the aircraft type or flight environment, and any potential health issues that could impair judgment or performance. It is crucial to assess personal physical and mental readiness, experience levels, and proficiency in the specific type of helicopter and flight conditions planned for the journey.

[PH.II.A.R1; FAA-H-8083-2]

31. How can a pilot assess their own fitness for flight?

A pilot can assess fitness for flight using the IMSAFE checklist: Illness, Medication, Stress, Alcohol, Fatigue, and Eating/Emotion. This tool helps evaluate whether any personal factors could impair the ability to safely operate the aircraft. If any element of the checklist raises concerns, the pilot should consider postponing the flight or seeking an alternative solution.

[PH.II.A.R1; FAA-H-8083-2]

32. In what ways can a pilot mitigate risks associated with personal limitations or lack of experience?

To mitigate risks associated with personal limitations or lack of experience, a pilot can seek additional training, use a more experienced co-pilot or flight instructor for support, and choose to fly in less demanding conditions. Limiting flights to familiar areas or under favorable weather conditions, and continuously striving to improve skills and knowledge are also effective strategies.

[PH.II.A.R1; FAA-H-8083-2]

33. How does a pilot's decision-making process affect flight safety, and what strategies can improve it?

A pilot's decision-making process is critical to flight safety, as it involves evaluating conditions, risks, and options to make informed choices. Strategies to improve decision-making include using structured frameworks like the DECIDE model, gaining experience, consulting with more experienced pilots, and staying updated with continuous education and training. Regularly practicing emergency procedures and scenarios also sharpens decision-making skills.

[PH.II.A.R1; FAA-H-8083-2]

34. What role does a pilot's situational awareness play in mitigating risks during flight?

Situational awareness is key to risk mitigation. It involves continuously monitoring the flight environment, weather, aircraft performance, and navigation. Maintaining situational awareness helps pilots anticipate and respond effectively to changing conditions or emergencies. Strategies to enhance situational awareness include thorough preflight planning, regular scanning of instruments and the environment, and avoiding distractions.

[PH.II.A.R1; FAA-H-8083-2]

35. How can a pilot manage the risk of becoming disoriented or losing situational awareness during flight?

A pilot can manage the risk of disorientation or loss of situational awareness by maintaining a systematic scan pattern, staying current with instrument proficiency, and using all available navigation aids. Regular training in different weather conditions and scenarios also helps. If disorientation occurs, relying on instruments and following standard procedures are key to regaining orientation.

[PH.II.A.R1; FAA-H-8083-2]

36. What steps can a pilot take to ensure proficiency in emergency procedures?

Ensuring proficiency in emergency procedures involves regular practice and training. Pilots should routinely review and train on emergency checklists and procedures for their specific helicopter. Participating in simulated emergency scenarios, either in actual flight or using flight simulators, and staying up to date with the latest best practices and manufacturer recommendations are also important.

[PH.II.A.R1; FAA-H-8083-2]

37. How can a pilot's overconfidence affect flight safety, and what are the ways to mitigate this risk?

Overconfidence can lead to underestimating risks and overestimating personal abilities, potentially resulting in poor decision-making. To mitigate this risk, pilots should adopt a culture of continuous learning and self-evaluation, seek feedback from instructors or peers, and avoid complacency by regularly reviewing procedures and staying informed about new developments in aviation.

[PH.II.A.R1; FAA-H-8083-2]

38. In what ways can peer pressure influence a pilot's decision-making, and how can this be managed?

Peer pressure can influence a pilot to make decisions that are not in line with safe flying practices, such as taking unnecessary risks to impress others or flying in adverse conditions to meet expectations. Managing this involves prioritizing safety over social factors, being assertive in decision-making, and being willing to decline suggestions that compromise safety. Building a network of supportive and safety-conscious peers also helps.

[PH.II.A.R1; FAA-H-8083-2]

39. What should a pilot do if their self-assessment reveals potential safety concerns?

If a pilot's self-assessment reveals any safety concerns, such as illness, high stress levels, or significant fatigue, the safest action is to postpone or cancel the flight. It is important for pilots to prioritize safety over the urgency of completing a flight. Consulting with medical professionals or seeking advice from other experienced pilots can also be helpful in such situations.

[PH.II.A.R1; FAA-H-8083-2]

40. Can self-assessment techniques differ depending on the type of flight or aircraft?

While the fundamental aspects of self-assessment, such as health and mental state, remain consistent, techniques may vary slightly based on the type of flight or aircraft. For example, pilots of complex aircraft or those undertaking longer, more demanding flights might place greater emphasis on fatigue and stress management. Similarly, different types of operations, like commercial or helicopter flights, may require specific considerations relevant to those operations.

[PH.II.A.R1; FAA-H-8083-2]

41. How can a pilot identify risks associated with a helicopter's mechanical condition before a flight?

Risks associated with a helicopter's mechanical condition can be identified through a thorough preflight inspection, reviewing maintenance logs, and checking for any outstanding airworthiness directives or service bulletins. Attention should be paid to the condition of critical systems like the engine, rotor system, and flight controls. Any signs of wear, damage, or irregularities should be investigated and resolved before the flight.

[PH.II.A.R2; FAA-H-8083-25]

42. What are the key factors a pilot should assess regarding aircraft performance capabilities and limitations?

Pilots should assess factors like the helicopter's weight and balance, power available versus power required, and performance charts for different environmental conditions. Understanding the limitations of the helicopter in various scenarios, such as high altitude or hot weather operations, is crucial. Knowledge of the helicopter's operational envelope helps in planning and executing the flight safely.

[PH.II.A.R2; FAA-H-8083-25]

43. How can a pilot mitigate risks associated with unfamiliar aircraft systems or avionics?

To mitigate risks associated with unfamiliar aircraft systems or avionics, a pilot should undergo thorough training and familiarization with the specific aircraft model. Reviewing the pilot's operating handbook (POH), practicing with flight simulators or training devices, and seeking instruction from qualified instructors or pilots experienced with the aircraft type are effective strategies. Familiarity with all systems and their backup procedures is key.

[PH.II.A.R2; FAA-H-8083-25]

44. What considerations should a pilot make regarding the fuel system to manage risk effectively?

Effective risk management regarding the fuel system includes ensuring proper fuel quantity and quality for the planned flight, understanding fuel consumption rates under different flight conditions, and being aware of the helicopter's fuel endurance. Regular checks for fuel contamination and understanding the fuel system's design and limitations are also important for preventing fuel-related issues.

[PH.II.A.R2; FAA-H-8083-25]

45. How does proper maintenance and compliance with airworthiness directives contribute to risk mitigation?

Proper maintenance and compliance with airworthiness directives are crucial in ensuring the helicopter's reliability and safety. Regular maintenance according to the manufacturer's schedule prevents mechanical failures, while adhering to airworthiness directives addresses safety issues identified by the manufacturer or aviation authorities. This proactive approach reduces the likelihood of in-flight emergencies related to aircraft malfunction.

[PH.II.A.R2; FAA-H-8083-25]

46. What role does understanding the weight and balance of a helicopter play in risk mitigation?

Understanding and correctly calculating the weight and balance of a helicopter is crucial for maintaining its stability and control. Overloading or improper distribution of weight can significantly affect performance, especially during takeoff, climbing, and maneuvering. Pilots should always ensure the helicopter's weight is within the permissible limits and the center of gravity is correctly positioned according to the aircraft's specifications.

[PH.II.A.R2; FAA-H-8083-25]

47. How can pilots mitigate risks associated with environmental effects on aircraft performance?

Pilots can mitigate risks due to environmental effects by understanding how factors like temperature, altitude, and humidity impact helicopter performance. These conditions can affect lift, engine power, and rotor efficiency. Pilots should use performance charts to determine the helicopter's capabilities under expected environmental conditions and plan flights accordingly, including selecting appropriate takeoff and landing sites and flight routes.

[PH.II.A.R2; FAA-H-8083-25]

48. In what ways can a pilot ensure the helicopter's avionics and navigation systems are functioning properly to reduce risk?

To ensure avionics and navigation systems are functioning properly, pilots should perform thorough preflight checks, including testing communication and navigation equipment. Regular maintenance and updates of these systems are also vital. Pilots should be familiar with the operation of all avionics equipment and, if possible, have a backup plan in case of system failure, such as using traditional navigation methods or portable navigation devices.

[PH.II.A.R2; FAA-H-8083-25]

49. How does staying informed about airworthiness directives (ADs) and service bulletins contribute to aircraft safety?

Staying informed about airworthiness directives and service bulletins is essential for maintaining aircraft safety. ADs are legally enforceable regulations issued by the FAA to correct unsafe conditions in an aircraft. Service bulletins, while not mandatory unless referenced in an AD, provide important safety recommendations from the manufacturer. Compliance with these directives and considering service bulletin recommendations ensure that known safety issues are addressed promptly, thus reducing the risk of in-flight incidents.

[PH.II.A.R2; FAA-H-8083-25]

50. How can a pilot assess and mitigate risks associated with weather conditions for a helicopter flight?

Pilots can assess weather risks by obtaining thorough weather briefings from reliable sources, such as the FAA or National Weather Service, and reviewing forecasts, METARs, and TAFs. Mitigation involves planning flights to avoid adverse weather conditions like thunderstorms, high winds, or low visibility, and having alternate plans in case weather changes en route. Understanding the helicopter's limitations in various weather conditions is crucial for safe decision-making.

[PH.II.A.R3; FAA-H-8083-28]

51. What considerations should be made when operating helicopters in areas prone to icing conditions?

In areas prone to icing conditions, pilots should assess the likelihood of encountering icing based on temperature, humidity, and cloud types. Avoiding flight in conditions conducive to icing, especially if the helicopter is not equipped or certified for icing conditions, is key. Pilots should be familiar with deicing/anti-icing systems if available and have a plan for exiting icing conditions promptly if encountered.

[PH.II.A.R3; FAA-H-8083-28]

52. What factors should be considered when choosing airports, heliports, helipads, or landing areas for helicopter operations?

When choosing landing areas, factors to consider include the size and condition of the landing area, presence of obstructions, wind direction and speed, terrain, and proximity to populated areas. Airports and heliports should be selected based on facilities and services available, such as fuel and maintenance. Compliance with noise abatement procedures and local regulations is also important.

[PH.II.A.R3; FAA-H-8083-28]

53. How does a pilot mitigate risks associated with airspace constraints during helicopter flight planning?

To mitigate risks associated with airspace constraints, pilots should thoroughly understand airspace classifications and requirements. This includes identifying restricted areas, controlled airspace, and special use airspace on the route. Compliance with airspace rules, obtaining necessary clearances, and maintaining communication with air traffic control help in managing airspace-related risks effectively.

[PH.II.A.R3; FAA-H-8083-25]

54. How should a pilot assess and address the risks associated with flying in mountainous terrain?

When flying in mountainous terrain, pilots should assess risks such as rapidly changing weather, high altitude, updrafts, downdrafts, and terrain-induced turbulence. Mitigation strategies include thorough preflight weather checks, choosing routes that offer safe altitudes and escape options, understanding the helicopter's performance limitations at higher altitudes, and being prepared for wind variations and potential loss of lift.

[PH.II.A.R3; FAA-H-8083-25]

55. What considerations should be made for helicopter operations over water, especially in areas without suitable emergency landing spots?

For overwater operations, especially where emergency landing spots are scarce, pilots should carry approved flotation gear readily available to each occupant and at least one pyrotechnic signaling device. Flight planning should include evaluating the distance from shore, available altitude for safe autorotation, and weather conditions over the water.

[PH.II.A.R3; FAA-H-8083-25]

56. What are external pressures in the context of helicopter flight, and how can they impact pilot decision-making?

External pressures refer to factors outside the immediate flight operation that influence a pilot's decisions, such as time constraints, expectations from passengers or employers, or the desire to complete a mission. These pressures can lead to rushed decisions, skipping critical procedures, or flying in unsafe conditions. Recognizing and managing these pressures is vital for maintaining safety.

[PH.II.A.R4; FAA-H-8083-2]

57. How can a pilot effectively manage the risks associated with get-there-itis or destination pressure?

To manage get-there-itis, pilots should prioritize safety over the urge to reach a destination by a certain time. This involves setting personal minimums, being willing to delay, divert, or cancel a flight if conditions are not favorable, and not allowing external factors, like the need to be at a destination for an event, to override safety concerns. Developing a flexible plan that accounts for potential delays can help mitigate this risk.

[PH.II.A.R4; FAA-H-8083-2]

58. What steps can a pilot take to resist pressure from passengers or employers to undertake a risky flight?

Pilots can resist pressure from passengers or employers by firmly communicating the safety risks involved and the importance of adhering to regulations and safety standards. Educating passengers or employers about the potential consequences of risky flights and the pilot's responsibility for safety can also be effective. In professional settings, having a clear company policy that supports pilot discretion in decision-making helps.

[PH.II.A.R4; FAA-H-8083-2]

59. How can helicopter pilots avoid the risks associated with scud running or flying too low to avoid bad weather?

To avoid the risks of scud running, pilots should have alternate plans ready in case of unexpected weather changes, including potential landing areas or alternate routes. Regular weather checks, both preflight and in-flight, help in avoiding situations where flying low to evade bad weather becomes a consideration. Training in instrument flight rules (IFR) can also prepare pilots for unexpected deteriorations in weather.

[PH.II.A.R4; FAA-H-8083-2]

60. What strategies can a pilot employ to manage the risks associated with financial or business pressures in aviation?

Pilots facing financial or business pressures should separate these concerns from operational decisions. Establishing clear operational guidelines that prioritize safety, regardless of financial implications, is crucial. Seeking support from peers or mentors in the aviation community can provide perspective and help manage these pressures. In commercial operations, fostering a safety-first culture within the organization helps alleviate business-related pressures on pilots.

[PH.II.A.R4; FAA-H-8083-2]

61. How can a pilot handle the pressure of flying to maintain currency or proficiency, especially when weather or other factors are marginal?

To handle the pressure of flying for currency or proficiency, pilots should have strict personal minimums that go beyond legal requirements, especially for weather conditions. If the weather or other factors are marginal, it is safer to postpone the flight rather than risk flying in unsafe conditions. Utilizing flight simulators or training devices can be an alternative way to maintain proficiency without actual flight risks.

[PH.II.A.R4; FAA-H-8083-2]

62. What approach should a pilot take to mitigate the risk of succumbing to peer pressure in aviation?

Pilots can mitigate the risk of succumbing to peer pressure by maintaining a strong commitment to safety standards and personal minimums. Building confidence in decision-making skills helps pilots stand firm on safety decisions, even when facing contrary opinions from peers. Seeking advice from experienced pilots and mentors and participating in regular safety meetings or seminars can reinforce a safety-oriented mindset.

[PH.II.A.R4; FAA-H-8083-2]

63. How can scheduling pressures influence a pilot's decision-making, and what strategies can be used to mitigate this risk?

Scheduling pressures can lead to rushed preflight procedures, skipping essential checks, or deciding to fly in suboptimal conditions. To mitigate these risks, pilots should plan flights with ample buffer time for unexpected delays and be prepared to adjust schedules if necessary. Communicating the importance of safety and the potential impact of rushed decisions on passengers or clients helps manage their expectations and reduces pressure.

[PH.II.A.R4; FAA-H-8083-2]

64. What are common aviation security concerns that pilots should be aware of?

Common aviation security concerns include unauthorized access to aircraft, tampering or sabotage, potential threats from unruly or suspicious passengers. Pilots should also be aware of the risks associated with flying into or near sensitive areas or during heightened security alerts.

[PH.II.A.R5; FAA-H-8083-25]

65. How can pilots ensure the security of their aircraft when unattended?

To ensure the security of an aircraft when unattended, pilots should use locks on cockpit doors, control locks, and propeller or throttle locks. Parking in well-lit, secure areas, and at airports with security personnel or surveillance systems can also deter unauthorized access. Regular inspection of the aircraft for signs of tampering before each flight is crucial.

[PH.II.A.R5; FAA-H-8083-25]

66. What steps should a pilot take if they encounter a suspicious person or activity at an airport?

If a pilot encounters a suspicious person or activity at an airport, they should immediately report it to airport authorities or law enforcement. Providing detailed descriptions and avoiding confrontation are important. Pilots should also inform other pilots and airport personnel to raise awareness and prevent potential security breaches.

[PH.II.A.R5; FAA-H-8083-25]

67. How can pilots contribute to overall aviation security while operating at airports?

Pilots can contribute to aviation security by being vigilant and reporting any unusual activities or security breaches. Participating in airport watch programs, staying informed about current security procedures, and adhering to identification and access control measures at airports are also key contributions. Collaboration with airport management and security personnel enhances the security environment.

[PH.II.A.R5; FAA-H-8083-25]

68. What precautions should pilots take when flying in areas with increased security measures or temporary flight restrictions (TFRs)?

When flying in areas with increased security measures or TFRs, pilots should thoroughly check NOTAMs and flight advisories before flight. Compliance with all TFR requirements and understanding the reasons for restrictions, such as VIP movement or security events, are essential. Maintaining clear communication with air traffic control and following their instructions helps avoid inadvertent violations.

[PH.II.A.R5; FAA-H-8083-25]

69. What role does pilot identification play in aviation security, and how can pilots comply with identification requirements?

Pilot identification plays a crucial role in aviation security by ensuring that only authorized individuals have access to aircraft and airport facilities. Pilots must carry government-issued photo identification along with their pilot certificate while operating an aircraft. Compliance with identification checks and displaying proper credentials at security checkpoints and restricted areas are essential for maintaining secure operations.

[PH.II.A.R5; FAA-H-8083-25]

70. How should pilots handle in-flight security issues, such as threats from passengers or hijack attempts?

In the event of in-flight security issues, such as threats from passengers or hijack attempts, pilots should remain calm, assess the situation, and attempt to de-escalate if possible. Utilizing crew resource management (CRM) techniques, following established protocols for handling in-flight disturbances, and communicating with air traffic control for assistance are critical. A pilot notifies ATC of a hijacking situation by squawking code 7500.

[PH.II.A.R5; FAA-H-8083-25]

Skills to be demonstrated:

- Inspect the helicopter with reference to an appropriate checklist.

- Verify the helicopter is in condition for safe flight and conforms to its type design.

- Perform self-assessment.

- Continue to assess the environment for safe flight.

B. Flight Deck Management

1. What are the key elements that should be included in a passenger briefing before a helicopter flight?

A comprehensive passenger briefing should include information on the use and operation of safety restraints, location and operation of emergency exits, emergency procedures and equipment, communication with the pilot during flight, and any specific safety concerns related to the flight. The briefing should be clear and understandable, ensuring that passengers know how to act in both normal and emergency situations.

[PH.II.B.K1; FAA-H-8083-25]

2. Why is it important for passengers to understand the operation of safety restraint systems?

Understanding the operation of safety restraint systems is crucial for passenger safety. Proper use of these systems ensures that passengers are securely fastened during takeoff, flight, and landing, reducing the risk of injury in the event of turbulence, sudden movements, or an emergency. Passengers need to know how to fasten and release the restraints quickly and correctly.

[PH.II.B.K1; FAA-H-8083-25]

3. How should a pilot address the use of emergency equipment in the passenger briefing?

In the passenger briefing, the pilot should explain the location, operation, and purpose of all emergency equipment onboard, such as life vests, fire extinguishers, first aid kits, and emergency locator transmitters. The briefing should include instructions on when and how to use these items. Pilots should also ensure that passengers understand their roles during an emergency evacuation.

[PH.II.B.K1; FAA-H-8083-25]

4. Why is the use of checklists considered essential in helicopter operations?

The use of checklists is essential in helicopter operations because they ensure that all necessary procedures are completed accurately and consistently. Checklists serve as a reminder for critical steps in preflight, startup, in-flight, emergency, and shutdown procedures, helping to prevent oversight and errors that could compromise safety. They provide a systematic approach to verifying that the helicopter is ready for operation.

[PH.II.B.K2; FAA-H-8083-25]

5. How should a pilot determine which checklists are appropriate for a specific helicopter?

A pilot should determine the appropriate checklists by referring to the manufacturer's rotorcraft flight manual (RFM) or pilot's operating handbook (POH) for the specific helicopter model. These documents provide standardized checklists that are tailored to the helicopter's systems and operational requirements. Pilots must ensure they are using the most current version of these checklists.

[PH.II.B.K2; FAA-H-8083-25]

6. In what situations would a pilot use an emergency checklist, and how do they differ from normal operation checklists?

A pilot would use an emergency checklist in situations such as engine failure, system malfunctions, fire, or other urgent scenarios that require immediate and specific actions. Emergency checklists are designed to guide pilots through the necessary steps to manage and resolve the situation safely. They differ from normal operation checklists in their focus on rapid response and critical procedures to mitigate emergencies.

[PH.II.B.K2; FAA-H-8083-25]

7. What is the recommended way for a pilot to use a checklist during different phases of flight?

The recommended way for a pilot to use a checklist is to follow the challenge-response method, where each item on the checklist is read (challenge) and the action is performed and verified (response). This should be done methodically and without rushing, especially during critical phases such as preflight, startup, and before takeoff. During flight, checklists should be used as needed, such as when transitioning between different flight operations or in response to changes in flight conditions.

[PH.II.B.K2; FAA-H-8083-25]

8. Why is it important for pilots to have current and appropriate navigation data for their flights?

Having current and appropriate navigation data is crucial for pilots to ensure safe and efficient navigation. Up-to-date data provide accurate information on airspace structures, navigational aids, airport facilities, and potential hazards, which is essential for flight planning, situational awareness, and compliance with air traffic control instructions. Outdated data can lead to navigation errors, airspace violations, or safety risks.

[PH.II.B.K3; FAA-H-8083-25]

9. What types of navigation data should a pilot ensure are current before a flight?

A pilot should ensure that they have the most current versions of sectional charts, terminal area charts, enroute charts, approach plates, airport facility directories, and NOTAMs. If using an electronic flight bag (EFB) or GPS, the pilot must also ensure that the software and navigational databases are updated to the latest available version.

[PH.II.B.K3; FAA-H-8083-25]

10. How can a pilot verify the currency of their navigation data?

A pilot can verify the currency of navigation data by checking the publication dates and effective periods on physical charts and approach plates. For electronic data, pilots can check the update status on their GPS or EFB systems, which typically display the last update date and the next scheduled update. Pilots should also regularly check NOTAMs and 1800WXBRIEF.com website for the latest information and updates.

[PH.II.B.K3; FAA-H-8083-25]

11. What are the potential consequences of using outdated navigation data during a flight?

Using outdated navigation data can lead to several consequences, including navigational errors, inadvertent airspace violations, missed communication frequencies, incorrect approach procedures, and unawareness of recent changes such as temporary flight restrictions or altered runway configurations. These issues can compromise flight safety and lead to legal ramifications for failing to comply with aviation regulations.

[PH.II.B.K3; FAA-H-8083-25]

12. How does the requirement for current navigation data differ for VFR and IFR flights?

For VFR flights, current navigation data requirements focus on up-to-date sectional charts, terminal area charts, and NOTAMs to navigate safely and avoid restricted areas. For IFR flights, the requirements are more stringent, including current enroute charts, instrument approach procedures, and any relevant navigation database updates in addition to VFR requirements. IFR flights rely more heavily on precise navigation data for approaches, departures, and enroute navigation under instrument meteorological conditions.

[PH.II.B.K3; FAA-H-8083-25]

13. Why is securing items and cargo crucial in helicopter operations?

Securing items and cargo in helicopters is crucial to prevent shifts during flight that could affect the aircraft's center of gravity and stability. Unsecured items pose a safety risk as they can move around, potentially causing distractions, obstructing controls or emergency exits, and in extreme cases, leading to loss of control of the aircraft.

[PH.II.B.K4; FAA-H-8083-25]

14. What are the best practices for securing cargo inside a helicopter?

Best practices for securing cargo inside a helicopter include using appropriate restraints like nets, straps, or tie-downs to ensure cargo is firmly anchored.

[PH.II.B.K4; FAA-H-8083-25]

15. How does improperly secured cargo affect helicopter flight characteristics?

Improperly secured cargo can shift during flight, altering the helicopter's center of gravity. This can affect the helicopter's handling characteristics, making it difficult to control. A shift in cargo can also lead to uneven weight distribution, potentially causing hazardous flight conditions such as an unanticipated roll, pitch, or yaw.

[PH.II.B.K4; FAA-H-8083-25]

16. How can a pilot identify risks associated with using onboard systems and equipment, including automation, in helicopters?

A pilot can identify risks by thoroughly understanding the capabilities and limitations of the helicopter's systems and automation features. This involves staying updated with the aircraft's operating manual and training materials. Risks can also be identified by regularly testing systems and monitoring for any signs of malfunction or abnormal behavior during use.

[PH.II.B.R1; FAA-H-8083-25]

17. What are common risks associated with the use of portable electronic devices (PEDs) in helicopter operations?

Common risks associated with PEDs include potential interference with aircraft navigation and communication systems, distractions during critical phases of flight, and the possibility of PEDs becoming unsecured projectiles in the event of turbulence. Additionally, reliance on PEDs for navigation or flight-related calculations without cross-checking against aircraft systems can lead to errors.

[PH.II.B.R1; FAA-H-8083-25]

18. How can pilots assess the risk level when using automation in helicopters?

Pilots can assess risk levels by considering factors such as their proficiency with the automation system, the complexity of the flight environment, and the reliability and condition of the automation equipment. They should evaluate whether the use of automation enhances safety and workload management or introduces potential for complacency and loss of situational awareness.

[PH.II.B.R1; FAA-H-8083-25]

19. What strategies can be employed to mitigate risks when using helicopter automation?

Pilots should also ensure that automation is used to enhance, not replace, their airmanship skills.

[PH.II.B.R1; FAA-H-8083-25]

20. What precautions should be taken to mitigate risks when using PEDs during flight?

Pilots should ensure that these devices do not interfere with aircraft operations or distract from flight responsibilities. PEDs should be secured to prevent movement during turbulence. Use of PEDs should be limited to necessary flight-related activities, and pilots should avoid becoming overly reliant on them for navigation or decision-making, cross-checking with onboard systems.

[PH.II.B.R1; FAA-H-8083-25]

21. How should a pilot identify risks associated with inoperative equipment in a helicopter?

A pilot identifies risks by conducting a thorough preflight inspection, noting any equipment that is not functioning as intended. They should refer to the helicopter's minimum equipment list (MEL) or equivalent documentation to understand the impact of inoperative equipment on flight safety.

[PH.II.B.R2; FAA-H-8083-2]

22. What is the first step in assessing the risk posed by inoperative equipment?

The first step in assessing risk is determining whether the flight can be conducted safely and legally without the inoperative equipment. This involves checking the MEL or kinds of operation equipment list (KOEL) for the specific helicopter model to ascertain if the equipment is required for the intended flight.

[PH.II.B.R2; FAA-H-8083-2]

23. What should a pilot do if they discover inoperative equipment during flight?

If a pilot discovers inoperative equipment during flight, they should assess the impact on the flight's safety and continue only if it is safe to do so. The pilot should inform air traffic control if necessary, adjust the flight plan accordingly, and follow any relevant emergency or abnormal procedures outlined in the aircraft's operating manual.

[PH.II.B.R2; FAA-H-8083-2]

24. How important is it for a pilot to report inoperative equipment postflight?

Reporting inoperative equipment postflight is crucial. It ensures that maintenance personnel are aware of and can address the issue before the aircraft's next flight. This reporting is not only essential for the safety of future flights but is also a regulatory requirement under FAA regulations.

[PH.II.B.R2; FAA-H-8083-2]

25. What are common passenger distractions a pilot may encounter during helicopter flights?

Common passenger distractions include excessive talking, movement within the cabin, use of electronic devices, and questions or actions that divert the pilot's attention from flying.

[PH.II.B.R3; FAA-H-8083-25]

26. How can a pilot assess the risk of passenger distractions before and during a flight?

A pilot assesses this risk by considering the number of passengers, their familiarity with flight procedures, and their behavior during preflight. During flight, the pilot should be aware of passenger activities and any signs of anxiety or discomfort that could lead to distractions.

[PH.II.B.R3; FAA-H-8083-25]

27. What strategies can pilots use to mitigate passenger distractions?

To mitigate passenger distractions, pilots should provide a thorough preflight briefing, setting clear expectations about behavior and communication during the flight. Establishing a sterile cockpit rule during critical phases of flight, where only essential communication is allowed, is also effective.

[PH.II.B.R3; FAA-H-8083-25]

28. How should a pilot handle an unexpected distraction from passengers while in flight?

If faced with an unexpected distraction, the pilot should first ensure the helicopter is in a stable flight condition. Then, address the distraction by calmly but firmly reminding passengers of the importance of minimizing nonessential interactions, especially during critical phases of flight.

[PH.II.B.R3; FAA-H-8083-25]

29. What role do preflight briefings play in managing passenger distractions?

Preflight briefings play a crucial role in managing passenger distractions. During these briefings, pilots can educate passengers about the importance of minimizing distractions, discuss when it is safe to talk or move around, and explain how to communicate with the pilot if necessary. This sets clear expectations and promotes a safer flight environment.

[PH.II.B.R3; FAA-H-8083-25]

Skills to be demonstrated:

- Secure all items in the aircraft.

- Conduct an appropriate passenger briefing, including identifying the pilot-in-command (PIC), use of safety belts, shoulder harnesses, doors, passenger conduct, rotor blade avoidance, and emergency procedures.

- Properly program and manage helicopter automation, as applicable.

- Appropriately manages risks by utilizing ADM, including SRM/CRM.

C. Powerplant Starting and Rotor Engagement

1. What are the key considerations for starting a helicopter's powerplant in cold weather?

In cold weather, it is important to allow for adequate warm-up time for the engine oil to reach the proper temperature. Pilots should follow the manufacturer's guidelines for cold starts, which may include using preheating equipment, and be attentive to any abnormal sounds or indications that could signal difficulty with the start.

[PH.II.C.K1; FAA-H-8083-21]

2. How does a pilot ensure safe rotor engagement during a powerplant start?

Safe rotor engagement involves gradually increasing engine power while monitoring rotor RPM and ensuring that the rotor system engages smoothly without excessive vibration or noise.

[PH.II.C.K1; FAA-H-8083-21]

3. **How does a pilot manage rotor engagement in high-wind conditions?**

In high-wind conditions, rotor engagement must be done with caution to avoid excessive blade flapping or loss of control. Pilots of fully articulated rotor systems should exercise extreme caution for ground resonance when engaging the rotor system in high-wind conditions.

[PH.II.C.K1; FAA-H-8083-21]

4. **What are key considerations for a pilot when positioning a helicopter near structures?**

Key considerations include accounting for rotor downwash effects, maintaining a safe distance to prevent rotor strike or vortex ring state, and being aware of wind interactions with structures. Pilots must understand the environmental impact on helicopter stability in these situations.

[PH.II.C.K1; FAA-H-8083-21]

5. **How do surface conditions affect helicopter positioning during takeoff and landing?**

Surface conditions such as uneven terrain, loose gravel, snow, or water can impact helicopter stability. Pilots should choose appropriate surfaces and be cautious of debris caused by rotor wash. The FAA advises assessing and adapting to these conditions for safe operation.

[PH.II.C.K1; FAA-H-8083-21]

6. **What factors should be considered when positioning a helicopter in proximity to other aircraft?**

Proximity to other aircraft requires careful consideration of rotor wash interference and maintaining safe spacing. Coordination with air traffic control and other pilots is crucial for managing safe distances.

[PH.II.C.K1; FAA-H-8083-21]

7. **What are the standard procedures for starting a helicopter's powerplant?**

Standard procedures include conducting a pre-start check, ensuring the area is clear, setting the throttle to the appropriate position, and engaging the starter. The pilot should monitor engine gauges for proper indications and be prepared for immediate shutdown if abnormalities are detected.

[PH.II.C.K2; FAA-H-8083-21]

8. **How does the use of external power sources impact the starting procedure of a helicopter?**

When using external power, the procedure includes connecting the external power source correctly, verifying electrical compatibility, and following specific guidelines for powerplant start-up to avoid electrical system overload. Pilots must ensure that the external power is disconnected safely after the engine starts.

[PH.II.C.K2; FAA-H-8083-21]

9. **What safety precautions should be taken when using external power for starting a helicopter?**

Safety precautions include ensuring proper grounding of the external power unit, verifying correct voltage and amperage, and having a clear communication line with the ground crew handling the external power source.

[PH.II.C.K2; FAA-H-8083-21]

10. **Are there any specific considerations for starting a turbine-powered helicopter as opposed to a piston-powered one?**

Starting a turbine-powered helicopter involves monitoring gas producer RPM and exhaust gas temperature more closely during the start sequence to avoid hot starts or over-temp conditions. The procedure may also involve different throttle settings compared to piston-powered helicopters.

[PH.II.C.K2; FAA-H-8083-21]

11. What are the limitations on the number of start attempts that can be made in a row on a helicopter?

Most helicopter manufacturers specify a limit on the number of consecutive start attempts to prevent overheating of the starter motor and battery drain. Typically, after a certain number of attempts (often three), a cooling-off period is required before further attempts can be made.

[PH.II.C.K3; FAA-H-8083-21]

12. How do temperature conditions affect starting limitations in helicopters?

Temperature conditions significantly impact starting limitations. In cold weather, additional time may be required for engine oil to reach proper operating temperature. In contrast, hot weather can lead to increased engine temperatures more quickly, potentially leading to limitations on start attempt duration and frequency.

[PH.II.C.K3; FAA-H-8083-21]

13. What limitations should be considered when using an auxiliary power unit (APU) for starting a helicopter?

When using an APU, limitations include ensuring compatibility with the helicopter's electrical system, adhering to maximum permissible power output, and monitoring for overheating. Pilots should follow specific guidelines provided by both the helicopter and APU manufacturers.

[PH.II.C.K3; FAA-H-8083-21]

14. Are there any limitations on rotor engagement speed during helicopter starting?

Yes, limitations on rotor engagement speed during starting include ensuring that rotor RPM builds up smoothly and stays within specified limits to avoid damaging the rotor system. Sudden or rapid engagement can cause excessive stress on rotor components.

[PH.II.C.K3; FAA-H-8083-21]

15. What are the limitations regarding engine warm-up time after starting a helicopter?

After starting, helicopters typically have limitations on minimum engine warm-up time to ensure all engine components reach a stable operating temperature. This period varies based on the engine type and ambient temperature, with manufacturers providing specific guidance in the operating handbook.

[PH.II.C.K3; FAA-H-8083-21]

16. How should a pilot adjust flight control frictions before takeoff?

Before takeoff, a pilot should adjust the flight control frictions to a level that allows smooth and controlled operation of the cyclic and collective, without being too loose to cause inadvertent movement or too tight to impede necessary control inputs. This ensures precise control of the helicopter during all phases of flight.

[PH.II.C.K3; FAA-H-8083-21]

17. When is it appropriate for a pilot to use increased flight control frictions?

Increased flight control frictions are appropriate in situations where the pilot anticipates removing their hands from the controls, such as during map reading or attending to other cockpit duties. The increased friction helps maintain the set control positions, aiding in the helicopter's stability.

[PH.II.C.K3; FAA-H-8083-21]

18. What are the risks of improperly set flight control frictions during flight?

Improperly set flight control frictions can lead to difficulty in controlling the helicopter, increased pilot workload, and potential safety hazards. If set too tight, they can hinder necessary control inputs, while too loose settings can lead to unintended control movements, especially in turbulent air. Correct adjustment is crucial for safe and efficient helicopter operation.

[PH.II.C.K3; FAA-H-8083-21]

19. **What are common conditions that may lead a pilot to abort a helicopter engine start?**

    Common conditions include abnormal engine sounds, failure to achieve necessary RPMs, unexpected vibrations, warning lights or abnormal gauge readings, and any signs of a fuel or oil leak. Additionally, if the engine doesn't start within the prescribed time or if there is an indication of a hot start, particularly in turbine engines, an abort is necessary.

    [PH.II.C.K4; FAA-H-8083-21]

20. **What immediate actions should a pilot take upon deciding to abort a helicopter engine start?**

    Upon deciding to abort a start, the pilot should immediately disengage the starter to prevent damage to the starter motor and engine. Follow the specific helicopter's checklist or POH/RFM for aborted start.

    [PH.II.C.K4; FAA-H-8083-21]

21. **What should a pilot check or inspect after an aborted helicopter start before attempting another start?**

    After an aborted start, the pilot should inspect the helicopter for signs of leaks, damage, or other abnormalities. Checking the engine compartment, especially in the case of a suspected hot start, is crucial. Reviewing engine and rotor system parameters to identify any discrepancies from normal values is also important. The pilot may need to consult maintenance personnel if any issues are detected.

    [PH.II.C.K4; FAA-H-8083-21]

22. **What are the primary risks associated with rotor engagement in helicopters?**

    Primary risks include rotor overspeed or underspeed, excessive vibration, and mechanical failure. There is also the risk of personnel or objects being struck by the rotor blades if the area around the helicopter is not clear.

    [PH.II.C.R1; FAA-H-8083-21]

23. What measures can a pilot take to mitigate risks during rotor engagement?

To mitigate risks, a pilot should follow the manufacturer's recommended procedures for rotor engagement, including the correct throttle and collective settings. Maintaining situational awareness, monitoring rotor RPM, and being prepared to abort the engagement if necessary are also crucial. Clear communication with ground personnel, if present, is important for safety.

[PH.II.C.R1; FAA-H-8083-21]

24. Why is completing appropriate checklists important for helicopter pilots?

Completing checklists ensures all helicopter systems function correctly and the aircraft is safe for operation. They help verify critical items systematically, reducing human error and enhancing safety.

[PH.II.C.R1; FAA-H-8083-25]

25. How should pilots manage checklist completion in high-workload situations?

In high-workload situations, prioritize checklists based on flight phase and task urgency, using abbreviated checklists for efficiency while ensuring critical items are checked. Focus and methodical approach are key, avoiding rushing.

[PH.II.C.R1; FAA-H-8083-25]

26. What are the risks of not following checklists in helicopter operations?

Skipping checklists can lead to operational oversights, such as incorrect engine settings or unchecked system issues, potentially causing emergencies or accidents. It is crucial for flight safety to follow checklists thoroughly.

[PH.II.C.R1; FAA-H-8083-25]

27. Is it advisable for pilots to rely on memory for routine procedures?

Pilots should not rely solely on memory for routine procedures to avoid complacency and missed steps. Consistent use of checklists ensures no critical item is overlooked, enhancing safe practices.

[PH.II.C.R1; FAA-H-8083-25]

28. What are the potential risks associated with using an auxiliary power unit (APU) in helicopters?

Risks include potential engine and APU overheating, fire hazards if the APU malfunctions or if there are leaks nearby, exhaust hazards, and electrical system damage if the APU is not compatible with the helicopter's systems. Incorrect operation can lead to premature wear or failure of the APU or helicopter systems.

[PH.II.C.R2; FAA-H-8083-21]

29. What steps can a pilot take to mitigate risks when using an APU?

To mitigate risks, the pilot should follow the manufacturer's operating procedures for starting, operating, and shutting down the APU. Regularly monitoring the APU's performance indicators during operation, such as temperature and oil pressure gauges, is important. Ensuring proper ventilation to avoid carbon monoxide buildup is also crucial.

[PH.II.C.R2; FAA-H-8083-21]

30. What are the best practices for positioning an APU in relation to the helicopter?

The APU should be positioned in a well-ventilated area, away from any fuel spill risk, and clear of the helicopter's rotor and exhaust path. Ensuring stable positioning to avoid vibration or movement during operation is important. The APU's exhaust should be directed away from the helicopter and personnel.

[PH.II.C.R2; FAA-H-8083-21]

31. What are common limitations a pilot should be aware of during the engine starting process of a helicopter?

Common limitations include the maximum number of consecutive start attempts to avoid overheating the starter or draining the battery, time restrictions on each start attempt to prevent engine damage, and environmental limitations such as extreme temperatures that can affect engine starting.

[PH.II.C.R3; FAA-H-8083-21]

32. How can a pilot assess the risk of a hot start in turbine helicopters and take steps to mitigate it?

A pilot can assess the risk of a hot start by closely monitoring engine temperature gauges during the start-up process. To mitigate the risk, it is important to follow the manufacturer's starting procedure precisely, ensure proper fuel-to-air mixture, and be prepared to abort the start quickly if temperatures rise unexpectedly.

[PH.II.C.R3; FAA-H-8083-21]

33. What risk management strategies should a pilot employ when starting a helicopter in cold weather?

In cold weather, risk management includes allowing extra time for engine oil to reach operating temperature, considering the use of preheating equipment if necessary, and being vigilant for signs of battery or starter motor strain due to the cold. Pilots should adhere to manufacturer's guidelines for cold starts.

[PH.II.C.R3; FAA-H-8083-21]

34. How does a pilot manage the risks associated with starting a helicopter on uneven terrain?

When starting a helicopter on uneven terrain, the pilot should ensure the helicopter is as level as possible to avoid imbalances during rotor start-up. Extra caution is needed to maintain stability and prevent any side or forward loading of the rotor system during start-up.

[PH.II.C.R3; FAA-H-8083-21]

35. What are the best practices for mitigating risks associated with overpriming during engine start in piston helicopters?

To mitigate risks associated with overpriming, the pilot should follow the manufacturer's recommended priming procedure, which often includes limiting the amount of fuel introduced into the engine before starting. Being attentive to engine sounds and behavior during the start-up sequence can also prevent flooding and reduce fire risk.

[PH.II.C.R3; FAA-H-8083-21

Skills to be demonstrated:

- Position the helicopter properly considering structures, surface conditions, other aircraft, wind, and the safety of nearby persons and property.

- Use flight control frictions, if required.

- Complete the appropriate checklist(s).

- Engage and manage the rotor system, as appropriate.

D. Before Takeoff Check

1. Why is completing the before takeoff checklist crucial in helicopter operations?

The before takeoff checklist ensures all systems are functioning correctly and the helicopter is configured for a safe takeoff. It includes verifying engine settings, control system integrity, and navigation equipment, crucial for preventing preventable in-flight emergencies.

[PH.II.D.K1a; FAA-H-8083-25]

2. How does verifying navigation and communication equipment before takeoff enhance flight safety?

Verifying navigation and communication equipment ensures the pilot can navigate accurately and maintain contact with air traffic control, which is vital for situational awareness and avoiding airspace conflicts.

[PH.II.D.K1a; FAA-H-8083-25]

3. **What is the purpose of checking the helicopter's flight control system during pre-takeoff checks?**

Checking the flight control system ensures that the cyclic, collective, and pedals are functioning correctly, providing the necessary control responsiveness for safe takeoff and flight operations.

[PH.II.D.K1a; FAA-H-8083-25]

4. **How does a pilot demonstrate proficiency in using checklists during various phases of flight?**

Proficiency is demonstrated by methodically following the checklist for each phase of flight, ensuring no item is overlooked. The pilot should adapt to different situations, such as emergency scenarios, where quick and accurate checklist completion is critical.

[PH.II.D.K1a; FAA-H-8083-25]

5. **What techniques can a pilot use to ensure complete and accurate checklist usage?**

Techniques include using a challenge-response method, where one item is read out (challenged) and its completion confirmed (response). Pilots can also cross-reference with electronic checklist systems if available and double-check critical items for accuracy.

[PH.II.D.K1a; FAA-H-8083-25]

6. **How does a pilot prioritize checklist items during high-workload situations?**

In high-workload situations, pilots should prioritize checklists based on safety-critical items first, followed by operational necessity. Time-sensitive items should be addressed promptly, and if needed, checklists can be paused and resumed once immediate tasks are managed.

[PH.II.D.K1a; FAA-H-8083-25]

7. What does effectively dividing attention inside and outside the helicopter entail for a pilot?

• Effectively dividing attention requires a pilot to simultaneously monitor and manage the helicopter's internal instruments and controls, while also keeping aware of external factors like terrain, other aircraft, and weather conditions. This skill ensures safe navigation and operational awareness.

[PH.II.D.K1a; FAA-H-8083-25]

8. Why is it crucial for a helicopter pilot to divide attention inside and outside the aircraft?

This skill is crucial for maintaining overall situational awareness, ensuring safe flight operations. It helps in detecting potential hazards, managing the flight path, and responding effectively to changing flight conditions or ATC instructions.

[PH.II.D.K1a; FAA-H-8083-25]

9. What is the role of the before takeoff checklist in detecting malfunctions in a helicopter?

The before takeoff checklist is designed to identify any malfunctions or issues in the helicopter's systems, such as engine irregularities, faulty controls, or navigation system errors, before leaving the ground. This early detection is key to preventing in-flight emergencies.

[PH.II.D.K1b; FAA-H-8083-25]

10. How can the before takeoff checklist help in identifying engine malfunctions?

The checklist includes inspecting engine instruments and gauges, listening for unusual noises, and observing abnormal engine behavior or warning lights, which can indicate potential engine problems requiring attention before takeoff.

[PH.II.D.K1b; FAA-H-8083-25]

11. Why is checking avionics part of the before takeoff checklist important for malfunction detection?

Checking avionics ensures that communication and navigation systems are working correctly. This step helps detect any electronic or signal issues that could affect flight safety and communication capabilities.

[PH.II.D.K1b; FAA-H-8083-25]

12. How does verifying flight control responsiveness help in malfunction detection?

Verifying flight control responsiveness, including the cyclic, collective, and pedals, ensures that they are operating smoothly and effectively. Any stiffness, unresponsiveness, or unusual feedback could indicate a mechanical issue needing resolution.

[PH.II.D.K1b; FAA-H-8083-25]

13. What malfunction indicators should a pilot look for during the fuel system check in the before takeoff checklist?

During the fuel system check, the pilot should look for correct fuel quantity readings, signs of fuel contamination, and proper functioning of fuel pumps and lines. Any discrepancies could signal a malfunction that needs to be addressed.

[PH.II.D.K1b; FAA-H-8083-25]

14. What skills are essential for reviewing takeoff performance in helicopter operations?

Reviewing takeoff performance requires a pilot to understand and apply performance data from the helicopter's operating handbook, including power settings, rotor RPM, and weight considerations. The pilot must also factor in environmental conditions like altitude, temperature, and wind, ensuring the helicopter has adequate power and lift for a safe takeoff.

[PH.II.D.K1b; FAA-H-8083-25]

15. How does a pilot effectively review emergency procedures before takeoff?

Effective review of emergency procedures involves a thorough understanding of the helicopter's systems and potential failure scenarios. The pilot should mentally rehearse emergency actions, ensuring familiarity with procedures for engine failure, fire, or system malfunctions during or immediately after takeoff.

[PH.II.D.K1b; FAA-H-8083-25]

16. What role does situational awareness play in reviewing takeoff performance and emergency procedures?

Situational awareness is crucial for understanding the current flight environment and how it may affect takeoff performance and potential emergencies. It includes assessing factors like terrain, nearby obstacles, and traffic, which influence the selection and review of emergency procedures.

[PH.II.D.K1b; FAA-H-8083-25]

17. Why is configuring the helicopter as recommended by the manufacturer important during the before takeoff checklist?

Configuring the helicopter as recommended by the manufacturer ensures that it is set up for optimal performance and safety according to specific design and operational parameters. This includes correct settings for engine controls, flight instruments, and navigation systems, aligning with the manufacturer's guidelines for safe takeoff and flight.

[PH.II.D.K1c; FAA-H-8083-21]

18. What items should be configured as per the manufacturer's recommendations in the before takeoff checklist?

Key items include engine throttle and mixture settings, flight control adjustments, avionics configurations, and any specific systems unique to the helicopter model. Proper configuration ensures the helicopter's readiness for the flight conditions expected.

[PH.II.D.K1c; FAA-H-8083-21]

19. What is involved in verifying that powerplant temperatures and pressures are suitable for takeoff in helicopter operations?

Verifying powerplant temperatures and pressures involves checking engine gauges against acceptable ranges outlined in the helicopter's operating manual. This includes monitoring oil temperature and pressure, coolant temperature (if applicable), and turbine inlet temperature to ensure they are within specified limits, indicating the engine is ready for the demands of takeoff.

[PH.II.D.K1c; FAA-H-8083-21]

20. How can a pilot ensure that powerplant temperature and pressure checks are consistently accurate?

Consistent accuracy in checks can be ensured by following a systematic approach using the checklist, regularly calibrating instruments, and being familiar with normal operating ranges for the specific helicopter model. Pilots should also be vigilant for any unusual readings or changes in engine behavior.

[PH.II.D.K1c; FAA-H-8083-21]

21. Why is it important to keep engine RPM and N_r speed within specified limits?

Keeping engine RPM and N_r speed within specified limits is essential for ensuring sufficient lift and thrust, preventing rotor stall, and avoiding excessive stress on the helicopter's mechanical components. Deviations can lead to decreased performance, increased wear and tear, or potentially hazardous flight conditions.

[PH.II.D.K1c; FAA-H-8083-21]

22. How does division of attention during before takeoff checks pose a risk in helicopter operations?

Division of attention during before takeoff checks can lead to missed items or incomplete assessments, as the pilot's focus is split between the checklist and other tasks or distractions. This can increase the risk of overlooking critical issues, potentially leading to unsafe flight conditions.

[PH.II.D.R1; FAA-H-8083-25]

23. What strategies can a pilot use to manage the division of attention effectively while conducting before takeoff checks?

To manage division of attention, a pilot can prioritize checklist completion before addressing other tasks, use a methodical approach to ensure no item is overlooked, and limit cockpit distractions during the process. Breaking down the checklist into manageable segments can also help maintain focus.

[PH.II.D.R1; FAA-H-8083-25]

24. How can a pilot assess the risk associated with dividing attention during before takeoff checks?

A pilot can assess this risk by considering the complexity of the checklist, the current environment (e.g., cockpit distractions, weather conditions), and personal factors like fatigue or stress. Recognizing these factors helps in determining when additional focus is required.

[PH.II.D.R1; FAA-H-8083-25]

25. How does receiving unexpected or unclear clearances from ATC pose a risk in helicopter operations?

Unexpected or unclear clearances can lead to confusion, miscommunication, and potentially incorrect actions by the pilot. This can increase the risk of airspace incursions, conflicts with other aircraft, or deviation from safe flight procedures, impacting flight safety.

[PH.II.D.R2; FAA-H-8083-25]

26. How can a pilot mitigate risks associated with unclear ATC clearances during flight?

To mitigate risks, the pilot should seek clarification from ATC if any clearance is not understood or seems unsafe. Maintaining situational awareness and being prepared to follow standard procedures or emergency protocols, if necessary, can also help mitigate risks.

[PH.II.D.R2; FAA-H-8083-25]

27. **Why is it important for pilots to maintain situational awareness when dealing with ATC clearances?**

    Maintaining situational awareness helps pilots understand their position, the positions of other aircraft, and the overall context of ATC clearances. This awareness is crucial for making informed decisions, especially when clearances are unexpected or unclear, ensuring the pilot's actions maintain safety.

    [PH.II.D.R2; FAA-H-8083-25]

Skills to be demonstrated:

- Complete the appropriate checklist(s).

- Review takeoff performance and emergency procedures.

- Verify that the powerplant temperature(s) and pressure(s) are suitable for takeoff.

- Maintain engine and rotor RPM within normal limits.

- Divide attention inside and outside the helicopter.

Airport and Heliport Operations

3

A. Runway/Taxiway/Heliport/Helipad Signs, Markings, and Lighting

1. What knowledge should a pilot have regarding airport runway and helipad markings?

A pilot should understand the significance of various runway and helipad markings, including runway designators, centerlines, touchdown zones, and helipad boundary markings. This knowledge is crucial for identifying the correct areas for takeoff, landing, and maneuvering on the ground.

[PH.III.A.K1; FAA-H-8083-25]

2. How should a pilot interpret taxiway signs and markings at airports and heliports?

Taxiway signs and markings provide direction, location, and information about taxi routes and adjacent areas. Pilots must be able to interpret these signs and markings to navigate safely and accurately on the ground, avoiding unauthorized areas and potential conflicts with other aircraft.

[PH.III.A.K1; FAA-H-8083-25]

3. Why is it important for a pilot to understand airport and heliport lighting systems?

Understanding airport and heliport lighting systems, including runway edge lights, taxiway lights, and helipad lighting, is essential for safe operations, especially during low visibility conditions such as night or fog. These lights provide critical guidance for positioning, alignment, and safe movement.

[PH.III.A.K1; FAA-H-8083-25]

4. What are the different types of markings a pilot might encounter on a helipad?

On helipads, pilots might encounter boundary markings, touchdown and lift-off area (TLOF) markings, final approach and takeoff area (FATO) markings, and safety area markings. Each type of marking provides specific guidance related to the safe use of the helipad.

[PH.III.A.K1; FAA-H-8083-21]

5. How does a pilot's understanding of signs, markings, and lighting contribute to airport and heliport safety?

A pilot's understanding of these elements contributes to operational safety by ensuring correct navigation on airfields, preventing runway incursions, and facilitating efficient, conflict-free movement in complex environments. It aids in maintaining situational awareness and complying with ATC instructions.

[PH.III.A.K1; FAA-H-8083-25]

6. What is the significance of understanding displaced thresholds on runways for helicopter pilots?

Understanding displaced thresholds is important for helicopter pilots as it indicates areas of the runway where landings and takeoffs are not allowed, often due to obstacles or noise abatement procedures. Recognizing these areas helps in planning safe approach and departure paths.

[PH.III.A.K1; FAA-H-8083-21]

7. How can a pilot distinguish between taxiway and runway lights at night or in low visibility?

Taxiway lights are typically blue, while runway edge lights are white or yellow (for displaced thresholds). Understanding these lighting color codes is essential for navigating airfields safely during night operations or in low-visibility conditions.

[PH.III.A.K1; FAA-H-8083-25]

8. What do yellow demarcation bars on taxiways with double dashed lines on one side and solid lines on the other side signify, and why are they important for helicopter pilots?

Yellow demarcation bars on taxiways indicate a runway holding position on a taxiway and are critical to prevent inadvertent entry into active runways. Helicopter pilots must recognize and adhere to these markers for safe ground operations and to avoid runway incursions.

[PH.III.A.K1; FAA-H-8083-25]

9. **Why is knowledge of visual glide slope indicators (VGSI) valuable for helicopter pilots during approach?**

VGSI, such as PAPI or VASI systems, provide visual cues to maintain the correct glide path during an approach to a runway. For helicopter pilots, understanding these indicators helps ensure a stabilized approach, especially in unfamiliar or challenging environments.

[PH.III.A.K1; FAA-H-8083-25]

10. **What is the purpose of chevron markings on runways, and how should they be interpreted by helicopter pilots?**

Chevron markings on runways identify areas unsuitable for landing or taking off, such as runway blast pads, stopways, or areas under repair. Helicopter pilots should treat these areas as non-loadbearing and avoid them during ground or hovering operations.

[PH.III.A.K1; FAA-H-8083-21]

11. **How do runway centerline markings aid helicopter pilots during takeoff and landing?**

Runway centerline markings provide a visual guide for alignment during takeoff and landing. They help helicopter pilots maintain a straight path, especially in conditions of reduced visibility, ensuring safe and precise operations on the runway.

[PH.III.A.K1; FAA-H-8083-21]

12. **What is the significance of hold short markings at airports for helicopter pilots?**

Hold short markings indicate where a pilot must stop to avoid entering a runway or critical area without clearance. Understanding these markings is essential for helicopter pilots to maintain safe separation from other aircraft and prevent runway incursions. In addition, helicopters should be cautious with their rotor downwash near active runways.

[PH.III.A.K1; FAA-H-8083-25]

13. What constitutes an airport movement area, and why is it important for helicopter pilots to understand it?

The airport movement area includes runways, taxiways, and other areas used for taxiing, takeoff, and landing of aircraft. Understanding this area is crucial for helicopter pilots to navigate safely, comply with ATC instructions, and avoid conflicts with other aircraft.

[PH.III.A.K2; FAA-H-8083-25]

14. How does knowledge of the movement area assist helicopter pilots in maintaining situational awareness?

Knowledge of the movement area helps pilots maintain situational awareness by understanding their location relative to runways, taxiways, and other aircraft. This awareness is essential for making informed decisions about routing, taxiing, and avoiding potential hazards.

[PH.III.A.K2; FAA-H-8083-25]

15. What are the responsibilities of a helicopter pilot when operating in the airport movement area?

Responsibilities include adhering to ATC clearances, observing all signage and pavement markings, maintaining vigilance for other aircraft and ground vehicles, and operating at safe speeds. Pilots must also be prepared to communicate promptly with ATC in case of any uncertainties or conflicts.

[PH.III.A.K2; FAA-H-8083-25]

16. How can misinterpreting airport signs, markings, or lighting pose a risk in helicopter operations?

Misinterpreting signs, markings, or lighting can lead to navigation errors, such as entering wrong runways or taxiways, causing potential conflicts with other aircraft and ground vehicles. It increases the risk of runway incursions and accidents, especially in complex or busy airfield environments.

[PH.III.A.R1; FAA-H-8083-25]

17. What steps should a pilot take to correctly interpret and assess airport signage and lighting?

Pilots should familiarize themselves with standard airport signage and lighting conventions as outlined in aviation handbooks and guides. Regularly reviewing these standards, especially when operating in unfamiliar airports, helps in accurate interpretation and assessment. Using airport diagrams and ATC assistance can also aid in correct navigation.

[PH.III.A.R1; FAA-H-8083-25]

18. How can a pilot mitigate risks associated with the interpretation of heliport markings?

Mitigation involves thoroughly studying heliport layout and markings before flight, staying updated with any changes or notices about heliport conditions, and maintaining vigilance while operating in these areas. Pilots should also confirm their understanding of heliport markings with ground control or ATC if unsure.

[PH.III.A.R1; FAA-H-8083-25]

19. How should a pilot assess a landing site's dimensions and limitations?

Assessment involves evaluating the site's physical dimensions, checking for obstacles like wires, trees, or structures, and considering surface conditions. Pilots should also assess wind direction and speed, and ensure the site supports the helicopter's weight and operational needs.

[PH.III.A.R2; FAA-H-8083-21]

20. What risks are associated with inadequate assessment of landing site dimensions and limitations?

Inadequate assessment can lead to selecting a landing site unsuitable for the helicopter's size or operational requirements, increasing the risk of accidents due to obstacles, insufficient space for maneuvering, or unstable surfaces. It can also compromise safety during takeoff and emergency procedures.

[PH.III.A.R2; FAA-H-8083-21]

21. How can a pilot identify potential conflict risks with other aircraft, vehicles, or persons?

Pilots can identify potential conflicts by maintaining situational awareness, regularly scanning the operational environment, and staying informed about the traffic pattern, ground movements, and pedestrian areas. Using ATC services and traffic advisory systems also aids in early conflict detection.

[PH.III.A.R3; FAA-H-8083-2]

22. What strategies can a pilot employ to assess and mitigate conflict risks?

Strategies include preflight planning to understand traffic flows, using proper communication protocols with ATC and other pilots, and adhering to standard operating procedures for taxiing, takeoff, and landing. Pilots should also be prepared to adjust plans based on observed activities and ATC advisories.

[PH.III.A.R3; FAA-H-8083-2]

23. What are the risks associated with distractions and loss of situational awareness in helicopter operations?

Distractions can lead to a loss of situational awareness, resulting in missed communications, navigational errors, or failure to respond to critical flight system indications. This can increase the risk of airspace violations, collisions, or accidents due to delayed or inappropriate responses to flight conditions.

[PH.III.A.R4; FAA-H-8083-2]

24. How can a pilot effectively assess and manage the risk of distractions and task prioritization?

Effective management involves maintaining focus on primary flight tasks, minimizing nonessential cockpit activities, especially during critical flight phases. Pilots should recognize their own cognitive load limits and use strategies like checklists and systematic workflow to ensure task prioritization.

[PH.III.A.R4; FAA-H-8083-2]

25. Why is continual self-assessment important in managing the risks of task prioritization and situational awareness?

Continual self-assessment allows pilots to monitor their mental state, workload, and situational awareness. Recognizing signs of fatigue, stress, or task saturation is crucial for taking corrective actions, such as reducing workload or seeking assistance, to maintain safe flight operations.

[PH.III.A.R4; FAA-H-8083-2]

26. What are the key risks associated with runway incursions in helicopter operations?

Runway incursions pose significant risks, including the potential for collisions with other aircraft or ground vehicles. They can lead to serious accidents, especially in busy airfields with complex layouts. Runway incursions disrupt normal airport operations and can cause delays or rerouting of other aircraft.

[PH.III.A.R5; FAA-H-8083-25]

27. How can a pilot identify and assess the risk of runway incursion before and during flight?

To identify and assess runway incursion risks, pilots should familiarize themselves with the airport layout, noting hotspot areas prone to confusion. During flight, maintaining situational awareness, listening attentively to ATC instructions, and monitoring other traffic are crucial. Before moving on the ground, reviewing taxi routes and clearances is essential.

[PH.III.A.R5; FAA-H-8083-25]

28. What strategies can a pilot employ to mitigate the risk of a runway incursion?

Strategies include adhering strictly to ATC instructions, using airport diagrams for navigation, confirming clearance before entering or crossing runways, and maintaining constant vigilance for other aircraft and vehicles. Using standardized communication protocols and ensuring comprehension of ATC instructions also helps mitigate risks.

[PH.III.A.R5; FAA-H-8083-25]

Skills to be demonstrated:

- Comply with airport/heliport/helipad signs, markings, and lighting encountered, as applicable to the helicopter provided for the practical test.

B. Communications, Light Signals, and Runway Lighting Systems

1. What is the importance of understanding how to obtain appropriate radio frequencies for helicopter operations?

Obtaining the correct radio frequencies is crucial for effective communication with air traffic control (ATC), other aircraft, and ground services. It ensures the pilot can receive vital information about traffic, weather, and airspace restrictions, and communicate intentions or emergencies, which is essential for safe flight operations.

[PH.III.B.K1; FAA-H-8083-25]

2. How can a pilot find the appropriate radio frequencies for a particular airport or airspace?

Pilots can find appropriate radio frequencies in the sectional charts, airport/facility directories, NOTAMs, or via ATC. For flight planning, frequencies are also available in electronic flight bag apps and on the FAA's website.

[PH.III.B.K1; FAA-H-8083-25]

3. What are the steps a pilot should take to ensure they have the correct frequencies before a flight?

Prior to flight, pilots should review their route and destination to note required frequencies. This includes ATIS, ground control, tower, approach/departure control, and emergency frequencies. Double-checking these frequencies during preflight planning and updating them as necessary during flight is crucial.

[PH.III.B.K1; FAA-H-8083-25]

4. Why is understanding proper radio communication procedures and ATC phraseology crucial for helicopter pilots?

Understanding proper radio communication procedures and ATC phraseology is essential for clear, efficient, and unambiguous communication. It ensures that pilots convey and receive critical information accurately, aiding in collision avoidance, airspace management, and adherence to ATC instructions, which are vital for flight safety.

[PH.III.B.K2; FAA-H-8083-25]

5. How can a pilot ensure effective use of ATC phraseology in communications?

Effective use of ATC phraseology involves familiarizing oneself with standard terms and responses as outlined in the FAA's *Aeronautical Information Manual*, practicing clear and concise communication, and using proper terminology for readbacks and acknowledgments. Regular review and training in ATC communications enhance proficiency.

[PH.III.B.K2; FAA-H-8083-25]

6. What are ATC light signals and why are they important for pilots?

ATC light signals are a series of colored light emissions used by air traffic control to communicate with aircraft when radio communication is not possible. They are important for pilots as they provide essential instructions for taxiing, takeoff, landing, and emergency responses, ensuring safe ground and air operations.

[PH.III.B.K3; FAA-H-8083-25]

7. How should a pilot respond to a steady green light signal from ATC on the ground?

A steady green light signal on the ground indicates that the pilot is cleared to taxi. The pilot should acknowledge the signal and proceed with taxiing, while maintaining vigilance for other aircraft and vehicles.

[PH.III.B.K3; FAA-H-8083-25]

8. What does a flashing green light signal mean for an aircraft in flight?

A flashing green light signal to an aircraft in flight means that the aircraft is cleared to return for landing. This signal is typically used when radio communication is lost, and the pilot needs to know they can safely proceed with the landing procedure.

[PH.III.B.K3; FAA-H-8083-25]

9. What action should a pilot take upon receiving a steady red-light signal while airborne?

A steady red-light signal while airborne means the pilot must give way to other aircraft and continue circling. The pilot should acknowledge the signal and maintain a holding pattern until further signals are received or radio communication is re-established.

[PH.III.B.K3; FAA-H-8083-25]

10. What does a flashing white light signal indicate to an aircraft on the airport surface?

A flashing white light signal directed at an aircraft on the airport surface instructs the pilot to return to the starting point on the airport. This signal is typically used to redirect an aircraft back to its point of origin for operational or safety reasons.

[PH.III.B.K3; FAA-H-8083-25]

11. How should a pilot respond to alternating red and green light signals from ATC in flight?

Alternating red and green light signals from ATC to an aircraft in flight are a general warning signal. The pilot should exercise caution and be alert to potential hazards or changes in the flight or ground environment. It is advisable to contact ATC for clarification once radio communication is established.

[PH.III.B.K3; FAA-H-8083-25]

12. What is the meaning of a flashing red light signal to an aircraft in flight?

A flashing red light signal to an aircraft in flight indicates that the airport is unsafe for landing. The pilot should not land and should maintain visual contact with the tower for further light signals or re-establish radio communication for landing instructions.

[PH.III.B.K3; FAA-H-8083-25]

13. In what situations are ATC light signals typically used in aviation?

ATC light signals are typically used when radio communication between the aircraft and control tower is not possible, such as in the event of a radio failure, or when an aircraft without a radio is operating at an airport. They provide an alternative means of conveying critical instructions.

[PH.III.B.K3; FAA-H-8083-25]

14. How should a pilot set the transponder before and during a flight?

Before flight, the pilot should set the transponder to the appropriate code given by ATC or to 1200 for VFR flight in the U.S. if no specific code is assigned. During flight, the transponder should be set to the ALT position to transmit altitude information, unless instructed otherwise by ATC.

[PH.III.B.K4; FAA-H-8083-25]

15. What are the different transponder codes a pilot might be required to use?

Common transponder codes include 1200 for standard VFR operations, 7500 for hijacking, 7600 for radio communication failure, and 7700 for emergencies. ATC may also assign specific squawk codes for individual flights to track and identify aircraft.

[PH.III.B.K4; FAA-H-8083-25]

16. How does the appropriate use of a transponder enhance safety in congested airspace?

In congested airspace, the appropriate use of a transponder enhances safety by allowing ATC to monitor the aircraft's position and altitude accurately, facilitating effective traffic separation and conflict resolution. It also aids in collision avoidance systems on board other aircraft, providing alerts to pilots about nearby traffic.

[PH.III.B.K4; FAA-H-8083-25]

17. What are the standard procedures for a pilot to follow in case of lost communication during VFR flight?

In case of lost communication during VFR flight, the pilot should attempt to reestablish communication by checking and adjusting the radio and avionics settings. If unsuccessful, squawk 7600 on the transponder, visually scan for traffic, and if in controlled airspace, follow pre-briefed or last received instructions. If near an airport, observe the traffic pattern and land while watching for light signals from the tower.

[PH.III.B.K5; FAA-H-8083-25]

18. What are the key considerations for a pilot when experiencing lost communication in controlled airspace?

When experiencing lost communication in controlled airspace, the pilot's key considerations include maintaining safe flight, avoiding collision with other aircraft, and complying with airspace rules. The pilot should follow standard lost communication procedures, keep scanning for visual traffic, and watch for ATC light signals if near an airport.

[PH.III.B.K5; FAA-H-8083-25]

19. What are common equipment issues that can lead to loss of communication in helicopter operations?

Common equipment issues include radio failure, antenna damage or disconnection, power supply problems, and headset or microphone malfunctions. Additionally, incorrect frequency selection, volume settings, or squelch adjustments can also result in communication loss. Understanding these issues helps in troubleshooting and maintaining effective communication.

[PH.III.B.K6; FAA-H-8083-25]

20. How does a pilot's understanding of the helicopter's electrical system aid in addressing communication issues?

Understanding the helicopter's electrical system aids in addressing communication issues by enabling the pilot to check circuit breakers, identify potential power supply problems, and understand the interdependence of avionics and electrical components. This knowledge is crucial for quick diagnosis and rectification of issues that may affect communication.

[PH.III.B.K6; FAA-H-8083-25]

21. What is radar assistance in aviation, and how is it beneficial to helicopter pilots?

Radar assistance refers to guidance provided by air traffic control (ATC) based on radar observations. It is beneficial for helicopter pilots in navigating through controlled airspace, avoiding other traffic, receiving vectoring for approaches or departures, and assistance during low visibility or emergency situations. Radar assistance enhances situational awareness and flight safety.

[PH.III.B.K7; FAA-H-8083-25]

22. How can a helicopter pilot effectively utilize radar assistance during flight?

A helicopter pilot can effectively utilize radar assistance by maintaining clear communication with ATC, following radar-based instructions and vectors, and using radar information for situational awareness. Pilots should inform ATC if they require assistance, especially during emergencies or challenging weather conditions.

[PH.III.B.K7; FAA-H-8083-25]

23. According to the NTSB Part 830, what are the immediate notification requirements for aircraft accidents?

Flight control system malfunction or failure; inability of any required flight crewmember to perform normal flight duties as a result of injury or illness; failure of any internal turbine engine component that results in the escape of debris other than out the exhaust path; in-flight fire; aircraft collision in flight; damage to property, estimated to exceed $25,000; where any person suffers death or serious injury, or when the aircraft receives substantial damage; a complete loss of information, excluding flickering, from more than 50 percent of an aircraft's cockpit displays; or damage to helicopter tail or main rotor blades, including ground damage, that requires major repair or replacement of the blade(s); or an aircraft is overdue and is believed to have been involved in an accident.

[PH.III.B.K8; 49 CFR 830.5]

24. How does Part 830 define an aircraft accident for reporting purposes?

An occurrence associated with the operation of an aircraft which takes place between the time any person boards the aircraft with the intention of flight and all such persons have disembarked, and in which any person suffers *death* or *serious injury*, or in which the aircraft receives *substantial damage*. For purposes of this part, the definition of "aircraft accident" includes "unmanned aircraft accident," as defined herein.

[PH.III.B.K8; 49 CFR 830.2]

25. What is the time frame for reporting an aircraft accident or incident to the NTSB according to Part 830?

According to Part 830, an aircraft accident or an incident that falls under the reportable criteria must be reported to the NTSB immediately, and by the most expeditious means available. This prompt reporting ensures that the NTSB can quickly initiate an investigation.

[PH.III.B.K8; 49 CFR 830.2]

26. What are runway status lighting systems, and why is their understanding important for pilots?

Runway status lighting systems are a set of automated red lights embedded in airport runways and taxiways to indicate when it is unsafe to enter, cross, or take off from a runway. Understanding these systems is crucial for pilots to ensure compliance with safety protocols and to prevent runway incursions, especially during periods of low visibility or high traffic.

[PH.III.B.K9; AIM 2-1-6]

27. How do runway entrance lights (REL) function in runway status lighting systems?

Runway entrance lights (REL) are a series of red lights located at taxiway/runway intersections. They illuminate to indicate that it is unsafe to enter or cross a runway. These lights are automatically controlled based on radar data and are an essential tool for pilots to make real-time decisions about entering active runways.

[PH.III.B.K9; AIM 2-1-6]

28. What is the significance of takeoff hold lights (THL) in runway status lighting systems?

Takeoff hold lights (THL) are red in-pavement lights on the runway that indicate it is not safe to take off. They illuminate when there is an aircraft on the runway or when the runway is otherwise unsafe for takeoff. Understanding and adhering to THL signals help prevent runway collisions.

[PH.III.B.K9; AIM 2-1-6]

29. What are the risks associated with ineffective communication in helicopter operations?

Ineffective communication can lead to misunderstandings or missed instructions, increasing the risk of airspace conflicts, runway incursions, and navigational errors. It may result in the failure to relay or receive critical information about flight conditions, traffic, or emergencies compromising safety.

[PH.III.B.R1; FAA-H-8083-2]

30. How can a pilot identify potential communication risks during flight operations?

Potential communication risks can be identified by monitoring the clarity and understanding of transmissions, ensuring proper frequency usage, and being alert to possible misinterpretations or missed messages, especially in high-traffic areas or challenging weather conditions. Regularly testing communication equipment also helps identify technical issues.

[PH.III.B.R1; FAA-H-8083-2]

31. **What are the key considerations in deciding when to declare an emergency in helicopter operations?**

Key considerations include the severity of the situation, potential for escalation, impact on aircraft control, and available options for resolution. Situations like engine failure, fuel shortage, or critical system malfunctions warrant an immediate emergency declaration. The decision should prioritize safety and effective resolution of the situation.

[PH.III.B.R2; FAA-H-8083-25]

32. **How can a pilot assess the risk associated with a situation to determine if an emergency should be declared?**

To assess the risk, the pilot should evaluate the immediate danger to the aircraft and occupants, considering factors like the nature of the problem, current aircraft status, weather conditions, and proximity to safe landing areas. The assessment should also include the potential consequences of not declaring an emergency.

[PH.III.B.R2; FAA-H-8083-25]

33. **What are the risks associated with the use of non-standard phraseology in helicopter communications?**

The use of non-standard phraseology can lead to misunderstandings, misinterpretations, or missed communications between pilots and air traffic control (ATC), increasing the risk of navigational errors, airspace violations, and even collisions. It can compromise the clarity and efficiency of communication, essential for safe flight operations.

[PH.III.B.R3; FAA-H-8083-25]

34. **How can a pilot assess the potential risks of using non-standard phraseology during flight operations?**

A pilot can assess risks by considering the potential for miscommunication with ATC and other aircraft, especially in complex or high-traffic airspace. The assessment should include the likelihood of ATC misinterpreting non-standard terms, leading to incorrect instructions or loss of situational awareness.

[PH.III.B.R3; FAA-H-8083-25]

35. What strategies can be employed to mitigate the risks associated with non-standard phraseology?

Strategies include adhering strictly to standard aviation phraseology as outlined in the FAA's *Aeronautical Information Manual*, regular training and familiarization with standard terms, and using clear, concise language. Pilots should also avoid colloquialisms or ambiguous terms and seek clarification if there is any doubt about communication.

[PH.III.B.R3; FAA-H-8083-25]

Skills to be demonstrated:

• Select and activate appropriate frequencies.

• Transmit using standard phraseology and procedures as specified in the *Aeronautical Information Manual* (*AIM*) and *Pilot/Controller Glossary*.

• Acknowledge radio communications and comply with ATC instructions or as directed by the evaluator.

C. Traffic Patterns

1. What is the difference in operations at towered and non-towered airports, heliports, helipads, and landing areas?

At towered facilities, operations are governed by specific instructions from air traffic control (ATC), including clearances for takeoff, landing, and taxiing. Non-towered facilities rely on standard procedures and pilot communication to ensure safe operations, with pilots making decisions based on visual cues and communication with other pilots.

[PH.III.C.K1; FAA-H-8083-25]

2. How should a pilot operate at a non-towered heliport or helipad?

At a non-towered heliport or helipad, pilots should self-announce their intentions on the common traffic advisory frequency, be vigilant for other traffic, adhere to standard traffic patterns, and coordinate with other pilots as necessary.

[PH.III.C.K1; FAA-H-8083-25]

3. **What are the key restrictions and considerations for operating in towered airport environments?**

In towered environments, pilots must adhere to ATC clearances and instructions for all aspects of flight, including taxi, takeoff, landing, and airspace transitions. It is essential to maintain clear communication with the tower, comply with all instructions, and remain aware of traffic and airspace restrictions.

[PH.III.C.K1; FAA-H-8083-25]

4. **What factors influence the determination of traffic patterns for current conditions at an airport or heliport?**

Factors influencing traffic pattern determination include wind direction and speed, type of aircraft in operation (fixed-wing or rotorcraft), runway or helipad orientation, topographical features, and any local noise abatement procedures or airspace restrictions.

[PH.III.C.K2; FAA-H-8083-25]

5. **How does a pilot identify and follow the correct traffic pattern at a non-towered airport?**

At a non-towered airport, pilots typically identify the correct traffic pattern by observing windsocks for wind direction, consulting *Chart Supplement* for pattern information, and listening to the common traffic advisory frequency for other pilots' position reports. Standard pattern entry procedures should be followed, and pilots should continuously scan for traffic and announce their position.

[PH.III.C.K2; FAA-H-8083-25]

6. **How should helicopter pilots adapt their traffic pattern in a mixed-use (fixed-wing and rotorcraft) environment?**

In mixed-use environments, helicopter pilots should be aware of fixed-wing traffic patterns and adjust their pattern accordingly to avoid conflict. This often involves flying at a lower altitude and remaining clear of the fixed-wing pattern. Coordination with ATC (if available) and other pilots is crucial for safe integration.

[PH.III.C.K2; FAA-H-8083-25]

7. Why is it important for a pilot to understand and adapt to traffic patterns based on current conditions?

Understanding and adapting to traffic patterns based on current conditions is vital for collision avoidance, efficient sequencing of aircraft, and minimizing disruptions to other traffic. It ensures safe operations, especially during takeoff and landing phases, and helps maintain orderly flow in and around the airport or heliport.

[PH.III.C.K2; FAA-H-8083-25]

8. What are the fundamental right-of-way rules in aviation for pilots?

Fundamental right-of-way rules include: an aircraft in distress has priority over all others; when converging, the aircraft to the other's right has right-of-way; when approaching head-on, both pilots alter course to the right; the faster aircraft overtaking another must pass to the right; and among different categories of aircraft (balloons, gliders, airships, powered aircraft), the less maneuverable has the right-of-way.

[PH.III.C.K3; 14 CFR 91.113]

9. How do right-of-way rules apply specifically to helicopters in mixed aircraft environments?

Helicopters must yield right-of-way to less maneuverable aircraft such as balloons, gliders, and airships. In environments with both rotorcraft and fixed-wing aircraft, helicopters should avoid the flow of fixed-wing traffic and give way when necessary, ensuring safe separation and collision avoidance.

[PH.III.C.K3; 14 CFR 91.113]

10. Why is understanding and adhering to right-of-way rules vital for aviation safety?

Understanding and adhering to right-of-way rules is essential for preventing mid-air collisions and ensuring orderly air traffic flow, especially in areas of high aircraft density or during emergency situations. It helps pilots make safe and prompt decisions to maintain safe distances from other aircraft, contributing to overall aviation safety.

[PH.III.C.K3; FAA-H-8083-25]

11. **What is the importance of using automated weather and airport/heliport information systems for pilots?**

    Automated weather systems like AWOS (Automated Weather Observing Systems) and ASOS (Automated Surface Observing Systems) provide current, site-specific weather data crucial for flight planning and in-flight decision-making. Airport/heliport information systems offer real-time data on runway conditions, traffic patterns, and other essential operational details. Utilizing these systems enhances situational awareness, safety, and efficient navigation.

    [PH.III.C.K4; FAA-H-8083-28]

12. **How can pilots access and use automated weather information for flight planning?**

    Pilots can access automated weather information via radio frequencies while in-flight, through telephone services, or online platforms before the flight. This information should be used to assess weather conditions along the route, at the destination, and at alternate sites, assisting in making informed decisions about flight routes, altitude, and the need for diversions.

    [PH.III.C.K4; FAA-H-8083-28]

13. **Why is it crucial for pilots to continuously monitor automated weather updates during flight?**

    Continuously monitoring automated weather updates is crucial due to the dynamic nature of weather conditions. It allows pilots to stay informed of any changes that could impact flight safety, such as unexpected wind shifts, visibility reductions, or the development of adverse weather phenomena. Timely weather information is key to proactive in-flight decision-making.

    [PH.III.C.K4; FAA-H-8083-28]

14. **What are the best practices for integrating automated weather and airport/heliport information into flight operations?**

Best practices include regularly checking automated weather and airport/heliport information during preflight planning, monitoring updates throughout the flight, and being prepared to adjust plans based on the latest data. Pilots should also understand how to interpret and apply this information effectively to maintain safety and efficiency in their flight operations.

[PH.III.C.K4; FAA-H-8083-28]

15. **What are common collision hazards in aviation, particularly for helicopter operations?**

Common collision hazards include other aircraft in busy airspace, terrain and obstacles (especially in low-level flight), birds and wildlife, uncrewed aerial systems (drones), and ground vehicles on airport surfaces. Helicopters, due to their operational flexibility and ability to operate at low altitudes, may face unique risks like wire strikes or collisions with structures.

[PH.III.C.R1; FAA-H-8083-2]

16. **How can a pilot effectively identify and avoid potential collision hazards?**

Effective strategies include maintaining constant vigilance through visual scanning techniques, utilizing collision avoidance systems if available, adhering to standard flight procedures, and communicating clearly with air traffic control and other aircraft. Regular training in situational awareness and hazard recognition also helps in identifying and avoiding collision risks.

[PH.III.C.R1; FAA-H-8083-2]

17. **What role does air traffic control play in helping pilots manage collision hazards?**

Air traffic control provides essential services like traffic advisories, separation guidance, and terrain avoidance assistance, particularly in controlled airspace. Controllers offer instructions to help maintain safe distances between aircraft and alert pilots to potential collision risks, contributing significantly to collision avoidance.

[PH.III.C.R1; FAA-H-8083-2]

18. **How do distractions impact a pilot's ability to safely operate an aircraft?**

    Distractions can significantly impact a pilot's ability to focus on critical tasks, leading to errors or oversights. They can range from cockpit interruptions to personal stressors and can result in missed communications, failure to adhere to flight procedures, or delayed responses to changing flight conditions. Effective management of distractions is crucial for maintaining situational awareness and ensuring flight safety.

    [PH.III.C.R2; FAA-H-8083-2]

19. **What strategies can pilots use for effective task prioritization in the cockpit?**

    Effective task prioritization involves recognizing the most critical tasks at any given moment, such as navigating, communicating, and operating the aircraft. Pilots can use strategies like the aviate, navigate, communicate hierarchy, compartmentalizing tasks, and using checklists to ensure that essential operations are not overlooked while managing less critical tasks.

    [PH.III.C.R2; FAA-H-8083-2]

20. **How can a pilot prevent loss of situational awareness, and what are the signs of its degradation?**

    To prevent loss of situational awareness, pilots should continuously monitor flight conditions, systems, and their surroundings, maintain effective communication, and avoid fixation on a single task. Signs of situational awareness degradation include confusion, fixation, missing cues, and misinterpretation of flight data. Regular training and self-awareness are key to recognizing and addressing these signs.

    [PH.III.C.R2; FAA-H-8083-2]

21. How can a pilot identify the risk of wind shear and wake turbulence?

A pilot can identify the risk of wind shear and wake turbulence by considering weather conditions, particularly during thunderstorms or strong frontal systems for wind shear, and by being aware of the presence of larger aircraft that can produce significant wake turbulence. Monitoring ATC information and pilot reports (PIREPs) also provides valuable insights into current wind and turbulence conditions.

[PH.III.C.R3; FAA-H-8083-25]

22. What strategies can a pilot use to assess the severity of wind shear or wake turbulence?

To assess the severity, pilots should consider factors like the size and proximity of the generating aircraft for wake turbulence, and the intensity of weather systems for wind shear. Using onboard weather radar and communication with ATC for real-time information can provide a clearer picture of the situation. The assessment should include potential impacts on aircraft control and flight path.

[PH.III.C.R3; FAA-H-8083-25]

23. How can pilots mitigate the risks associated with wind shear and wake turbulence?

Mitigation strategies include avoiding flying directly behind or beneath large aircraft, especially during takeoff and landing, and increasing separation distances. For wind shear, pilots should follow recommended escape procedures, adjust airspeed as appropriate, and consider delaying takeoff or landing until conditions improve. Using technology like onboard weather systems can also aid in avoiding areas of severe wind shear.

[PH.III.C.R3; FAA-H-8083-25]

24. Why is understanding aircraft performance critical in managing wind shear and wake turbulence risks?

Understanding aircraft performance is critical because it enables pilots to know how their aircraft will respond under the stress of wind shear or wake turbulence. This knowledge helps in making informed decisions about flight path adjustments, power settings, and appropriate maneuvers to safely navigate through or avoid these conditions.

[PH.III.C.R3; FAA-H-8083-25]

25. What are the best practices for a pilot to follow when operating in conditions likely to produce wind shear or wake turbulence?

Best practices include staying vigilant for signs of wind shear or wake turbulence, maintaining a heightened state of awareness during critical phases of flight, adhering to recommended airspeeds and altitudes, and being prepared to execute immediate corrective actions if encountered. Pilots should also communicate with ATC and other pilots to share and receive updates on current conditions.

[PH.III.C.R3; FAA-H-8083-25]

Skills to be demonstrated:

- Identify and interpret airport/heliport/helipad/landing area runways, taxiways, markings, signs, and lighting.

- Comply with recommended helicopter traffic pattern procedures, as appropriate.

- Correct for wind drift to maintain the proper ground track.

- Maintain orientation with the runway/landing area in use, as applicable.

- Maintain traffic pattern altitude, ±100 feet, and the appropriate airspeed, ±10 knots.

- Maintain situational awareness and proper spacing from other traffic or avoid the flow of fixed-wing traffic, as appropriate.

Hovering
Maneuvers

4

A. Vertical Takeoff and Landing

1. What are the key elements a pilot must understand for a vertical takeoff to a hover in a helicopter?

For a vertical takeoff to a hover, the pilot must understand the importance of smooth control inputs, particularly in the collective and cyclic controls, to maintain stability. The pilot should be aware of the helicopter's power requirements, wind conditions, and surrounding obstacles.

[PH.IV.A.K1; FAA-H-8083-21]

2. What considerations should a pilot keep in mind when landing a helicopter from a hover?

When landing from a hover, the pilot should consider the wind direction and speed, ensuring that the helicopter is aligned properly. The descent should be controlled and gradual, using the collective to reduce altitude while maintaining a stable hover. The pilot must also be aware of the surface condition of the landing area, and potential obstacles. Proper coordination of cyclic, collective, and antitorque pedals is essential for a smooth landing.

[PH.IV.A.K1; FAA-H-8083-21]

3. How do environmental factors affect vertical takeoff and landing in helicopter operations?

Environmental factors like wind, temperature, altitude, and air density can significantly impact helicopter performance during vertical takeoffs and landings. Wind can affect lift and rotor disc stability, while high temperatures and altitude reduce air density, affecting lift and engine performance. Pilots must adjust their techniques based on these conditions to ensure safe and efficient operations.

[PH.IV.A.K1; FAA-H-8083-21]

4. How does wind affect helicopter flight control inputs?

Wind significantly impacts helicopter flight control inputs. Winds require adjustments in cyclic control to maintain a stable hover or flight path. Wind conditions can cause the helicopter to drift, demanding constant input adjustments to compensate for these movements and maintain intended flight direction with the pedals and altitude with the collective.

[PH.IV.A.K2; FAA-H-8083-21]

5. What considerations should a pilot make regarding wind when controlling a helicopter?

Pilots should consider wind direction and speed to anticipate necessary control inputs. In strong winds, more aggressive cyclic, collective, and antitorque pedal inputs might be needed. Pilots must also be aware of potential wind gusts and changes in wind direction, which can require sudden and precise control adjustments to maintain stability and control.

[PH.IV.A.K2; FAA-H-8083-21]

6. What considerations should a pilot make regarding the center of gravity (CG) when performing a vertical takeoff?

When performing a vertical takeoff, the pilot must ensure the CG is within the allowable limits. A forward CG might result in a nose-down attitude, requiring more rearward cyclic input, while an aft CG might require forward cyclic input. An off-center CG can cause the helicopter to drift laterally. Proper CG positioning is essential for stability and control during takeoff.

[PH.IV.A.K3; FAA-H-8083-21]

7. How does weight affect a helicopter's hover performance?

The weight of the helicopter affects hover performance by influencing the power required to maintain a hover. Heavier helicopters need more power and produce more downwash, which can affect ground handling. In contrast, lighter helicopters are more responsive and require less power to hover. Pilots must adjust control inputs based on the weight to maintain a stable hover.

[PH.IV.A.K3; FAA-H-8083-21]

8. Why is understanding the effect of weight and balance on landing from a hover important?

Understanding the effect of weight and balance on landing is important for maintaining control and stability during descent. An improperly balanced helicopter may be difficult to control, especially close to the ground. Pilots need to make precise control inputs to counteract any imbalances and ensure a smooth and controlled landing.

[PH.IV.A.K3; FAA-H-8083-21]

9. What is ground effect, and how does it impact a helicopter during a vertical takeoff to a hover?

Ground effect refers to the increased lift and decreased aerodynamic drag that a helicopter experiences near the ground. During a vertical takeoff to a hover, ground effect makes the helicopter more efficient, requiring less power to hover as the rotor system benefits from the reduced vortices and increased air pressure beneath it.

[PH.IV.A.K4; FAA-H-8083-25]

10. How should a pilot account for ground effect when hovering close to the ground?

When hovering close to the ground, pilots should be aware that less power is required to maintain a hover due to ground effect. As a helicopter rises out of ground effect, more power is needed. Pilots must be prepared to adjust collective inputs smoothly to maintain the desired altitude and control the helicopter's position, especially during transitions in and out of ground effect.

[PH.IV.A.K4; FAA-H-8083-25]

11. How does ground effect vary with different surface types and conditions?

Ground effect can vary depending on the surface type and condition. Over smooth, hard surfaces like concrete, ground effect is more pronounced, whereas over rough or soft surfaces, such as water or tall grass, the effect is less significant. Pilots must consider the landing environment and adjust their technique accordingly to account for these variations.

[PH.IV.A.K4; FAA-H-8083-25]

12. How can a pilot recognize the signs of LTE during a vertical takeoff to a hover?

Signs of LTE may include unanticipated right yaw for counterclockwise main rotors, which is the helicopter's nose turning to the right without pilot input. Pilots should be alert to wind direction and speed. Prompt recognition and anticipation is key to preventing a loss of control.

13. What is dynamic rollover in helicopter operations, and how can it occur during vertical takeoffs and landings?

Dynamic rollover refers to a situation where a helicopter pivots around one of its skids or wheels and rolls over, potentially leading to a catastrophic accident. It can occur during vertical takeoffs or landings if one skid or wheel becomes snagged or if the helicopter tilts excessively to one side, surpassing the critical rollover angle. Factors such as pilot error, uneven terrain, and external forces like wind can contribute to dynamic rollover.

[PH.IV.A.R2; FAA-H-8083-21]

14. What are the best practices for a pilot to avoid dynamic rollover?

Best practices to avoid dynamic rollover include maintaining proper cyclic control to keep the helicopter level, ensuring that skids or wheels are not snagged or obstructed during takeoff and landing, and being aware of the helicopter's pivot point. Pilots should also avoid excessive lateral cyclic inputs, especially when one skid or wheel is in contact with the ground.

[PH.IV.A.R2; FAA-H-8083-21]

15. How can a pilot identify the risk of ground resonance during vertical takeoff and landing?

A pilot can identify the risk of ground resonance by being aware of factors that trigger it, such as uneven terrain, hard landings, or incorrect cyclic position during start-up. Vigilance in monitoring the helicopter's vibrations and rotor behavior during takeoff and landing can help in early identification.

[PH.IV.A.R3; FAA-H-8083-21]

16. How can pilots mitigate the risks associated with ground resonance?

Pilots can mitigate ground resonance risks by ensuring proper maintenance and alignment of rotor blades and landing gear components. Conducting smooth, controlled landings to avoid hard impacts that could trigger resonance is crucial. Pilots should also be prepared to react quickly if ground resonance signs are detected, either by lifting off again to re-stabilize the rotors or by shutting down the rotor system immediately if safe takeoff is not feasible.

[PH.IV.A.R3; FAA-H-8083-21]

17. Why is proper preflight inspection crucial in managing ground resonance risk?

Proper preflight inspection is crucial because it can detect issues like imbalanced or damaged rotor blades and malfunctioning landing gear dampers, which are potential ground resonance triggers. Ensuring that all components are in good condition and functioning correctly is a key preventive measure against ground resonance.

[PH.IV.A.R3; FAA-H-8083-21]

18. How can a pilot identify the risk of powerplant failure during a hover?

By monitoring engine performance indicators such as temperature, pressure, and RPM, any unusual noises, vibrations, or fluctuations in these readings can be early warning signs. Awareness of factors that increase the risk, such as high-density altitude, heavy loads, is also crucial for early identification.

[PH.IV.A.R4; FAA-H-8083-21]

19. What methods can a pilot use to assess the severity of powerplant failure risk during hovering maneuvers?

To assess the severity of powerplant failure risk, a pilot should consider the helicopter's current weight, environmental conditions, engine performance history, and maintenance records. Evaluating whether the helicopter is operating within safe power margins, especially in demanding conditions like high altitudes or hot temperatures, is vital in this assessment.

[PH.IV.A.R4; FAA-H-8083-21]

20. How can pilots mitigate the risks associated with powerplant failure during hovering?

Mitigating risks of powerplant failure during hovering includes conducting thorough preflight checks of the engine and fuel system, ensuring proper maintenance, and being vigilant about engine performance throughout the flight. Pilots should be proficient in hovering autorotation and maintain awareness of potential emergency landing sites when hovering. Avoiding over-stressing the engine by managing weight and power settings also helps reduce risk.

[PH.IV.A.R4; FAA-H-8083-21]

21. What are the best practices for a pilot to follow in preparation for potential powerplant failure during hovering?

Best practices include staying within the helicopter's performance limitations, especially regarding weight and balance, and avoiding operations that place excessive demand on the powerplant. Maintaining situational awareness of the surroundings during hovering for potential emergency landing sites and keeping proficient in emergency procedures are also critical. Regular maintenance checks and adhering to service intervals for the powerplant can prevent many mechanical failures.

[PH.IV.A.R4; FAA-H-8083-21]

Skills to be demonstrated:

- Complete the appropriate checklist(s).

- Comply with air traffic control (ATC) or evaluator instructions and make radio calls as appropriate.

- Maintain engine and rotor RPM within normal limits.

- Ascend to and maintain recommended hovering altitude, and descend from recommended hovering altitude in headwind, crosswind, and tailwind conditions, without drift.

- Maintain recommended hovering altitude, ±½ of that altitude within 10 feet of the surface, if above 10 feet, ±5 feet.

(continued)

- Maintain position within 4 feet of a designated point with no aft movement.

- Descend vertically to within 4 feet of the designated touchdown point.

- Maintain specified heading, ±10°.

B. Hover Taxi

1. What should a pilot understand about using the *Chart Supplement* for airport operations?

A pilot should understand that the *Chart Supplement* (formerly the *Airport/Facility Directory*) provides comprehensive data on airports, heliports, and seaplane bases. This includes information on runway dimensions, surface types, lighting, navigational aids, available services, and contact details. Familiarity with how to interpret and use this resource is essential for safe flight planning and operations.

[PH.IV.B.K1; FAA-H-8083-25]

2. How does knowledge of airport diagrams benefit a pilot?

Knowledge of airport diagrams benefits a pilot by providing a detailed layout of runways, taxiways, aprons, and important airport facilities. Understanding these diagrams aids in navigating the airport ground environment, helps in planning taxi routes, and enhances situational awareness, especially in complex or unfamiliar airports.

[PH.IV.B.K1; FAA-H-8083-25]

3. Why is it important for a pilot to be familiar with Notices to Air Missions (NOTAMs)?

Familiarity with NOTAMs is crucial as they provide timely and critical information about temporary changes or unusual conditions at an airport or in the airspace. This can include runway closures, equipment outages, construction activities, or temporary flight restrictions. Checking NOTAMs is a vital part of preflight planning for ensuring safety and compliance with current airspace rules and conditions.

[PH.IV.B.K1; FAA-H-8083-25]

4. What are the best practices for a pilot to stay updated with airport aeronautical references and information resources?

Best practices include regularly checking for the latest updates to official sources, such as the FAA's website for NOTAMs and *Chart Supplement*, and using updated electronic flight bag (EFB) applications. Pilots should also develop a habit of reviewing these references during every preflight planning session and not just relying on previous experiences, as airport conditions and regulations can change frequently.

[PH.IV.B.K1; FAA-H-8083-25]

5. What should a pilot know about hover taxi instructions and clearances?

A pilot should understand that hover taxi instructions and clearances are specific directives given by air traffic control (ATC) for maneuvering a helicopter close to the ground without leaving ground effect. These instructions include directions on the path to follow, altitude to maintain (usually not more than a few feet above ground), and any specific limitations or requirements. Compliance with hover taxi instructions is critical for safe operations, particularly in busy airfields with mixed aircraft types.

[PH.IV.B.K2; FAA-H-8083-21]

6. How does a pilot interpret and follow hover taxi clearances?

To interpret and follow hover taxi clearances, a pilot must listen carefully to ATC instructions, clarifying any uncertainties. Clearances will specify the taxi route, any areas to avoid, and sometimes specific altitudes or speeds. The pilot needs to maneuver the helicopter according to these instructions, maintaining a constant vigilance for obstacles, other aircraft, and ground personnel. Clear and concise communication with ATC is essential throughout the hover taxi process.

[PH.IV.B.K2; FAA-H-8083-21]

7. What are the limitations associated with hover taxiing a helicopter?

Limitations associated with hover taxiing include the height above ground level, typically limited to within ground effect range (one rotor diameter), and speed, which should be kept to a minimum safe level for control and safety. The pilot must also consider the helicopter's weight, wind conditions, visibility, and surrounding environment, as these factors can impact the safety and feasibility of hover taxiing. In some cases, ATC may impose additional limitations based on airport traffic and operational considerations.

[PH.IV.B.K2; FAA-H-8083-21]

8. Why is understanding hover taxi procedures important for helicopter pilots?

Proper hover taxiing helps avoid conflicts with other aircraft and ground vehicles, minimizes rotor wash impact on nearby objects, and enhances overall safety. It also demonstrates the pilot's ability to follow ATC instructions and operate the helicopter within its performance capabilities.

[PH.IV.B.K2; FAA-H-8083-21]

9. What best practices should a pilot follow when hover taxiing?

Hover taxi best practices include maintaining a steady hover height appropriate for the conditions, keeping a lookout for obstacles and other traffic, adjusting for wind and surface conditions, and being prepared to stop or change direction quickly if necessary. Pilots should use gentle control inputs to avoid abrupt movements and maintain situational awareness at all times.

[PH.IV.B.K2; FAA-H-8083-21]

10. What is the importance of understanding airport/heliport/helipad signs and markings for a pilot?

Understanding signs and markings is crucial for navigation and safety. It helps pilots identify taxiways, runways, and restricted areas, and provides essential information for safe ground operations.

[PH.IV.B.K3; FAA-H-8083-25]

11. How do lighting systems enhance safety at airports, heliports, and helipads?

Lighting systems, including runway lights, taxiway lights, and helipad beacons, provide visibility guidance, especially in low-light or poor weather conditions, aiding in safe takeoff, landing, and taxiing.

[PH.IV.B.K3; FAA-H-8083-25]

12. What are common visual indicators for wind that pilots should be aware of?

Common visual indicators include windsocks, which show wind direction and give an approximate indication of wind speed. Other indicators are smoke drift, movement of trees, water ripples, and flags.

[PH.IV.B.K4; FAA-H-8083-25]

13. How can a pilot use a windsock to determine wind conditions?

A pilot can use a windsock to determine wind direction as it points into the wind. Its degree of extension indicates wind speed: fully extended suggests high winds, while a drooping windsock indicates light winds.

[PH.IV.B.K4; FAA-H-8083-25]

14. Why is it important for pilots to understand visual wind indicators?

Understanding visual wind indicators is important for making informed decisions about takeoff, landing, and in-flight maneuvers. Correctly interpreting wind direction and strength aids in managing crosswind components and other wind-related challenges.

[PH.IV.B.K4; FAA-H-8083-25]

15. How do visual wind indicators assist in preflight planning and during flight?

Visual wind indicators assist in preflight planning by helping determine suitable runways and takeoff/landing directions. In flight, they aid in adjusting flight paths for wind changes.

[PH.IV.B.K4; FAA-H-8083-25]

16. What limitations do visual wind indicators have that pilots should consider?

Visual wind indicators cannot provide exact wind speed measurements and may not reflect conditions at higher altitudes or across the entire airport. Pilots should use them in conjunction with other wind information sources for a complete picture.

[PH.IV.B.K4; FAA-H-8083-25]

17. How do navigation lights assist in aircraft operation?

Navigation lights help determine an aircraft's orientation and direction of movement, especially during night or low-visibility conditions, assisting in collision avoidance.

[PH.IV.B.K5; FAA-H-8083-25]

18. What is the purpose of anti-collision lights on an aircraft?

Anti-collision lights, including rotating beacons and strobe lights, increase the aircraft's visibility to other aircraft and personnel, helping to prevent collisions both in the air and on the ground.

[PH.IV.B.K5; FAA-H-8083-25]

19. When should landing and taxi lights be used?

Landing lights are used during takeoffs, landings, and when flying in reduced visibility to illuminate the runway and enhance visibility. Taxi lights are used during ground movement to illuminate taxiways and during pre-takeoff checks. In addition, it is considered good pilotage to use the landing/taxi lights within the airport environment.

[PH.IV.B.K5; FAA-H-8083-25]

20. What is the sterile cockpit rule, and how does it apply during hover taxiing?

The sterile cockpit rule prohibits nonessential activities and conversations in the cockpit during critical phases of flight, including hover taxiing. This rule is implemented to ensure pilots focus solely on operating the aircraft and monitoring the environment, minimizing distractions during this high-workload phase.

[PH.IV.B.K6a; FAA-H-8083-25]

21. What are the key considerations for safe and effective taxiing?

Key considerations include understanding and adhering to taxi clearances, controlling taxi speed, using checklists for taxiing, and being prepared to stop or change directions as needed. Pilots should also consider weather conditions, such as wind and visibility.

[PH.IV.B.K6a; FAA-H-8083-25]

22. Why is it important to follow taxiway markings and signs?

Following taxiway markings and signs is important to prevent runway incursions, ensure the correct path is followed, and maintain safety on the airfield. They provide guidance for navigating complex taxiway systems and avoiding restricted areas.

[PH.IV.B.K6a; FAA-H-8083-25]

23. What role does communication play during taxiing?

Communication plays a vital role in receiving and acknowledging taxi instructions from ATC, informing ATC of any issues or requests, and coordinating with other airport users. Clear and concise communication helps prevent misunderstandings and enhances safety.

[PH.IV.B.K6a; FAA-H-8083-25]

24. What are the key procedures for hover taxiing at towered airports?

At towered airports, hover taxi procedures include following ATC instructions, maintaining a designated hover height, and adhering to the specified taxi route. Pilots must communicate effectively with ATC and remain vigilant for other aircraft and ground operations.

[PH.IV.B.K6b; FAA-H-8083-21]

25. How do hover taxi procedures differ at nontowered airports or heliports?

At nontowered airports or heliports, pilots must self-coordinate movements, communicate intentions on the common traffic advisory frequency (CTAF), and be extra vigilant for other aircraft. Pilots should hover taxi at a safe altitude, avoiding areas where rotor wash could affect other aircraft or structures.

[PH.IV.B.K6b; FAA-H-8083-21]

26. What are the safety considerations during hover taxiing?

Safety considerations include maintaining a stable hover altitude, watching for obstacles, managing rotor wash, avoiding overflight of personnel or sensitive areas, and being prepared to respond to changes in wind or operational conditions.

[PH.IV.B.K6b; FAA-H-8083-21]

27. What procedures should a pilot follow when entering or crossing runways?

Pilots should first obtain clearance from air traffic control (ATC) at towered airports. They must check both directions for traffic, be aware of runway holding position markings, and ensure no part of the aircraft crosses the hold short line until cleared. At nontowered airports, pilots should announce their intentions on the common traffic advisory frequency (CTAF) and visually scan for traffic.

[PH.IV.B.K6c; FAA-H-8083-25]

28. How does a pilot ensure it is safe to enter or cross a runway?

A pilot ensures safety by visually checking the approach paths for incoming aircraft, listening to ATC or CTAF for traffic updates, and confirming there are no conflicting aircraft on the runway or in the immediate airspace. Using landing lights and other appropriate aircraft lighting enhances visibility.

[PH.IV.B.K6c; FAA-H-8083-25]

29. What are the best practices for pilots at nontowered airports regarding runway entry and crossing?

At nontowered airports, pilots should monitor and communicate intentions on the CTAF, observe standard traffic patterns, and give way to aircraft on final approach or those already on the runway. Continuous vigilance and defensive flying practices are essential.

[PH.IV.B.K6c; FAA-H-8083-25]

30. How do runway markings and signs assist pilots in entering or crossing runways?

Runway markings and signs provide guidance on runway thresholds, holding positions, and taxi paths. Understanding these signs and markings is crucial for pilots to navigate airport surfaces correctly and safely, particularly when entering or crossing runways.

[PH.IV.B.K6c; FAA-H-8083-25]

31. What is the height/velocity (H/V) diagram and its significance for helicopter pilots?

The height/velocity (H/V) diagram illustrates safe and unsafe combinations of altitude and airspeed for a helicopter. It is significant for identifying flight conditions where a successful autorotation may or may not be feasible in the event of a power failure.

[PH.IV.B.K7; FAA-H-8083-21]

32. How should pilots use the H/V diagram in flight planning and operations?

Pilots should use the H/V diagram to plan flights in a way that avoids the combinations of height and velocity that fall within the cautionary areas, especially during takeoffs and landings. Staying within the safe zones of the diagram reduces the risk in case of an engine failure.

[PH.IV.B.K7; FAA-H-8083-21]

33. Why are H/V considerations important during low-altitude operations?

H/V considerations are particularly important during low-altitude operations because this is when the helicopter is most vulnerable to the consequences of engine failure. Adhering to safe height and velocity parameters ensures enough altitude and airspeed are available for a successful autorotation landing if needed.

[PH.IV.B.K7; FAA-H-8083-21]

34. How can a pilot stay within the safe zones of the H/V diagram during flight?

A pilot can stay within the safe zones by being aware of the current H/V limitations for their specific helicopter, avoiding low altitude and low airspeed combinations, and planning approaches and departures to minimize time spent in vulnerable flight regimes. Regular review of the H/V diagram for the specific helicopter model is also essential.

[PH.IV.B.K7; FAA-H-8083-21]

35. How does density altitude affect a helicopter's H/V curve?

Density altitude affects a helicopter's H/V curve by changing the aircraft's lift and power efficiency. Higher density altitudes can diminish performance, leading to a more restrictive H/V envelope. Pilots need to adjust their operational limits accordingly to maintain safety.

[PH.IV.B.K7; FAA-H-8083-21]

36. How should a pilot account for wind when considering H/V limitations?

Wind conditions can affect the H/V curve, particularly in terms of airspeed. Tailwinds can reduce effective airspeed, while headwinds can increase it. Pilots should adjust their flight parameters accordingly to maintain safe airspeed and altitude combinations as per the H/V diagram.

[PH.IV.B.K7; FAA-H-8083-21]

37. What are aircraft operating limitations and why are they important?

Aircraft operating limitations are specific parameters within which an aircraft is designed to operate safely. These include speed limits, weight and balance constraints, altitude limits, and engine performance criteria. Understanding these limitations is crucial for maintaining the structural integrity of the aircraft and ensuring safe flight operations.

[PH.IV.B.K8; FAA-H-8083-25]

38. How can a pilot find detailed operating limitations for their aircraft?

Detailed operating limitations for an aircraft can be found in the aircraft's pilot operating handbook (POH) or rotorcraft flight manual (RFM). These documents provide comprehensive information on all operational constraints and recommended procedures.

[PH.IV.B.K8; FAA-H-8083-25]

39. Why is adherence to weight and balance limitations vital?

Adherence to weight and balance limitations is vital as it affects the aircraft's stability, performance, and controllability. Overloading an aircraft or improper weight distribution can lead to hazardous flight conditions and potential loss of control.

[PH.IV.B.K8; FAA-H-8083-25]

40. How do environmental factors impact an aircraft's operating limitations?

Environmental factors like temperature, altitude, and wind can significantly impact an aircraft's performance. High density altitudes, for instance, can reduce engine power and lift. Pilots must adjust their operations according to these factors to stay within safe operating limits.

[PH.IV.B.K8; FAA-H-8083-25]

41. What role does a pilot play in ensuring compliance with operating limitations?

The pilot's role in ensuring compliance with operating limitations includes thoroughly understanding and adhering to the limitations set forth in the POH/RFM, regularly reviewing aircraft performance data, and making informed decisions to modify flight plans as needed based on current and anticipated conditions.

[PH.IV.B.K8; FAA-H-8083-25]

42. How can a pilot identify risks associated with distractions during flight?

A pilot can identify risks associated with distractions by being aware of anything that diverts attention from flying duties, such as nonessential cockpit activities, conversations, or electronic devices. Remember the saying, "Aviate, navigate, communicate," in that order.

[PH.IV.B.R1; FAA-H-8083-2]

43. What strategies can a pilot use to assess the impact of task prioritization on flight safety?

To assess the impact of task prioritization, a pilot should evaluate the urgency and importance of tasks, considering factors like flight phase, weather conditions, and aircraft status. Proper assessment helps in prioritizing tasks that are critical for safety over less urgent ones.

[PH.IV.B.R1; FAA-H-8083-2]

44. How can pilots mitigate the risks of losing situational awareness?

Mitigating the risk of losing situational awareness involves continuously monitoring flight instruments, navigation aids, and external cues. Regular training in situational awareness, effective workload management.

[PH.IV.B.R1; FAA-H-8083-2]

45. Why is understanding and managing disorientation crucial for pilots?

It can lead to a loss of control or spatial disorientation, especially under visual flight rules (VFR) in poor visibility conditions. Pilots should be trained to recognize and recover from disorientation using instrument references and adhering to instrument flight rules (IFR) when necessary.

[PH.IV.B.R1; FAA-H-8083-2]

46. What are best practices for a pilot to avoid distractions and maintain focus?

Best practices include establishing a sterile cockpit environment during critical phases of flight, planning and organizing cockpit tasks efficiently, and minimizing nonessential cockpit activities. Maintaining physical and mental fitness for flying also helps in avoiding distractions and maintaining focus.

[PH.IV.B.R1; FAA-H-8083-2]

47. How can a pilot identify risks associated with reduced visibility during taxi operations?

Risks in reduced visibility can be identified by difficulty in seeing airport markings, signs, other aircraft, and ground vehicles. Pilots should also be aware of weather conditions that can lead to reduced visibility, like fog, heavy rain, or snow.

[PH.IV.B.R2; FAA-H-8083-25]

48. What methods can a pilot use to assess risk during night taxi operations?

Risk assessment during night taxi operations includes evaluating lighting conditions, familiarity with the airport layout, and the effectiveness of the aircraft's lights. Pilots should also consider their night vision capabilities and the presence of other aircraft or vehicles.

[PH.IV.B.R2; FAA-H-8083-25]

49. How can pilots mitigate risks associated with reduced visibility or night taxi?

To mitigate these risks, pilots should use all available lighting aids, both on the aircraft and at the airport, taxi at slower speeds, and follow ATC instructions meticulously. Increasing the use of external cues like airport diagrams and GPS taxiway maps is also beneficial.

[PH.IV.B.R2; FAA-H-8083-25]

50. Why is careful pre-taxi planning important in low visibility conditions?

Careful pre-taxi planning in low visibility conditions is important to familiarize yourself with the taxi route, identify potential hazards, and establish alternate plans. Knowing the airport layout and having a clear taxi plan helps in navigating safely when visibility is compromised.

[PH.IV.B.R2; FAA-H-8083-25]

51. What best practices should pilots follow during reduced visibility or night taxi operations?

Best practices include maintaining a heightened awareness, using airport diagrams for navigation, keeping communications clear with ATC, using appropriate lighting, and being prepared to stop if unsure of position or direction. Regular practice and training in these conditions are also recommended.

[PH.IV.B.R2; FAA-H-8083-25]

52. How can a pilot identify risks of runway incursion?

Risks of runway incursion can be identified by understanding complex taxiway and runway layouts, recognizing confusing signage or markings, and staying alert to ATC instructions. Awareness of other aircraft and vehicles on the taxiways and runways is also crucial.

[PH.IV.B.R3; FAA-H-8083-25]

53. How can pilots mitigate the risk of runway incursion?

Pilots can mitigate runway incursion risk by thoroughly planning taxi routes, understanding and complying with ATC instructions, using airport diagrams, and maintaining situational awareness. Clear communication with ATC and regular review of standard taxi procedures also help reduce risk.

[PH.IV.B.R3; FAA-H-8083-25]

54. Why is proper communication critical in preventing runway incursions?

Proper communication is critical as it ensures the pilot understands and correctly follows ATC instructions. Clarifying any doubts or uncertainties with ATC can prevent misunderstandings and ensure the correct use of runways and taxiways.

[PH.IV.B.R3; FAA-H-8083-25]

55. How can a pilot identify risks associated with other aircraft, vehicles, and persons?

Risks can be identified by monitoring movement areas for traffic, being aware of blind spots, and listening to ATC or common traffic advisory frequency (CTAF) communications. Recognizing areas with high traffic density, such as near hangars or fuel stations, is also important.

[PH.IV.B.R4; FAA-H-8083-2]

56. What methods can a pilot use to assess risk from ground hazards?

Risk assessment involves evaluating the proximity and movement of ground vehicles, personnel, and other aircraft, especially in areas like taxiways and ramps. Pilots should also consider environmental conditions like lighting and weather that can affect visibility.

[PH.IV.B.R4; FAA-H-8083-2]

57. How can pilots mitigate risks from other aircraft and ground traffic?

To mitigate these risks, pilots should maintain vigilance during taxi, takeoff, and landing phases, use appropriate lighting and markings, communicate intentions clearly, and follow standard operating procedures. Coordination with ground crew and adherence to taxiway and runway procedures are essential.

[PH.IV.B.R4; FAA-H-8083-2]

58. Why is situational awareness key in managing risks from ground operations?

Situational awareness is key to anticipating and reacting to movements of other aircraft, vehicles, and persons. It helps pilots to avoid collisions, manage traffic flow, and respond effectively to unexpected situations.

[PH.IV.B.R4; FAA-H-8083-2]

59. How can a pilot identify the hazardous effects of downwash?

A pilot can identify hazardous downwash effects by being aware of the strong airflows generated by their rotor blades, especially during takeoff, landing, and low-altitude hovering. Noticing the impact of these airflows on nearby objects, surfaces, and personnel helps in recognizing downwash risks.

[PH.IV.B.R5; FAA-H-8083-21]

60. What methods can a pilot use to assess downwash risk?

To assess downwash risk, a pilot should consider the helicopter's size and power, current load, wind conditions, and proximity to objects or people. The type of surface (like loose gravel or water) and the presence of nearby light aircraft or unsecured items are also factors to consider.

[PH.IV.B.R5; FAA-H-8083-21]

61. How can pilots mitigate the risks associated with rotor downwash?

Pilots can mitigate downwash risks by choosing appropriate takeoff and landing areas away from people, vehicles, and loose objects. Adjusting hover heights and approach/departure paths to minimize downwash effects on the surrounding environment is also effective.

[PH.IV.B.R5; FAA-H-8083-21]

62. How can a pilot identify risks associated with main rotor, tail rotor, and tail strikes?

Risks can be identified by being aware of rotor blade clearance from obstacles, terrain, and operational surfaces. Monitoring tail rotor clearance during maneuvers, especially in confined areas or near obstacles, is crucial. Recognizing situations where tail strikes may occur, like steep approaches or departures, also helps in risk identification.

[PH.IV.B.R6; FAA-H-8083-21]

63. What methods can a pilot use to assess these risks?

Assessing these risks involves considering the helicopter's dimensions, understanding the environment where operations are being conducted, and being aware of the helicopter's limitations in various flight conditions. Regularly reviewing the aircraft's performance data and conducting thorough preflight planning are essential for accurate risk assessment.

[PH.IV.B.R6; FAA-H-8083-21]

64. How can pilots mitigate risks associated with rotor and tail strikes?

Pilots can mitigate these risks by maintaining a safe distance from obstacles, using caution in confined spaces, and being vigilant during takeoffs, landings, and low-level flight. Adhering to recommended approach and departure profiles and conducting regular inspections for rotor blade integrity are also key mitigation strategies.

[PH.IV.B.R6; FAA-H-8083-21]

65. What best practices should pilots follow to avoid rotor and tail strike hazards?

Best practices include maintaining awareness of rotor clearances at all times, using proper landing and takeoff techniques, especially in uneven terrain or confined areas, and regularly training for operations in various environments. Communicating intentions and maintaining situational awareness, particularly in busy or complex operational areas, are also important.

[PH.IV.B.R6; FAA-H-8083-21]

66. How can a pilot identify risks associated with height/velocity (H/V) considerations?

A pilot can identify H/V risks by understanding their specific helicopter's H/V diagram, which illustrates safe and unsafe flight conditions based on altitude and airspeed. Recognizing flight situations that fall into the cautionary areas of the diagram.

[PH.IV.B.R7; FAA-H-8083-21]

67. What methods can a pilot use to assess H/V risk?

Assessing H/V risk involves evaluating the current flight profile against the H/V diagram, considering factors like weight, altitude, weather conditions, and the helicopter's performance capabilities. Pilots should regularly review the H/V diagram for their aircraft and adapt their flight plan accordingly.

[PH.IV.B.R7; FAA-H-8083-21]

68. How can pilots mitigate risks associated with the H/V curve?

Pilots can mitigate H/V risks by planning flights to avoid operating in the unsafe zones of the H/V diagram, especially during critical phases like takeoff and landing. This may involve adjusting flight paths, airspeed, and altitude to ensure sufficient safety margins for autorotation in the event of an engine failure.

[PH.IV.B.R7; FAA-H-8083-21]

69. How can a pilot identify risks associated with confirmation or expectation bias in taxi instructions?

Risks can be identified by being aware of any preconceived notions about usual taxi routes or patterns and actively questioning whether ATC instructions align with these expectations. Pilots should be alert for any inconsistencies or surprises in received instructions that might contradict their expectations.

[PH.IV.B.R8; FAA-H-8083-2]

70. What methods can a pilot use to assess risk related to confirmation bias during taxiing?

To assess this risk, pilots should consider the clarity and specificity of taxi instructions received and cross-check them with airport diagrams. They should also evaluate their own level of familiarity with the airport and susceptibility to assuming routine instructions.

[PH.IV.B.R8; FAA-H-8083-2]

71. How can pilots mitigate risks associated with expectation bias in taxi instructions?

Mitigation strategies include actively listening to each ATC instruction as if it is new, regardless of familiarity with the airport, and cross-referencing with airport diagrams. Pilots should confirm instructions back to ATC and avoid making assumptions based on routine or previous experiences.

[PH.IV.B.R8; FAA-H-8083-2]

72. Why is understanding confirmation and expectation bias important for safe taxi operations?

Understanding these biases is crucial as they can lead to incorrect assumptions and actions during taxi, potentially resulting in wrong runway incursions or conflicts with other aircraft. Being aware of these biases helps pilots remain vigilant and responsive to actual instructions.

[PH.IV.B.R8; FAA-H-8083-2]

73. What best practices should pilots follow to counteract confirmation and expectation bias?

Best practices include maintaining situational awareness, using airport diagrams for all movements, verifying and reading back all ATC instructions, and being prepared to question and clarify any instruction that seems unclear or unexpected. Continuous learning and awareness of cognitive biases are also key.

[PH.IV.B.R8; FAA-H-8083-2]

Skills to be demonstrated:

- Complete the appropriate checklist(s).

- Receive and correctly read back clearances/instructions, if applicable.

- Use an airport diagram or taxi chart during taxi, if published, and maintain situational awareness.

- Comply with airport/heliport taxiway markings, signals, and signs.

- Maintain engine and rotor RPM within normal limits.

- Maintain a straight ground track within ±4 feet of a designated ground track.

- Maintain recommended hovering altitude, ±½ of that altitude within 10 feet of the surface, if above 10 feet, ±5 feet.

- Hover taxi over specified ground references, demonstrating forward, sideward, and rearward hovering and hovering turns.

- Maintain a constant rate of turn at pivot points.

- Maintain a position within 4 feet of each pivot point during turns.

- Make a 360° pivoting turn, left and right, stopping within 10° of a specified heading.

- Make smooth, timely, and correct control application during the maneuver.

C. Air Taxi

1. How does the *Chart Supplement* aid in understanding air taxi operations?

The *Chart Supplement* provides vital information for air taxi operations, including detailed descriptions of airport facilities, services, runway characteristics, and traffic procedures for the local airport.

2. What is the significance of an airport diagram in air taxi operations?

An airport diagram is crucial for air taxi operations as it clearly outlines the airport layout, showing runways, taxiways, aprons, and key landmarks. It helps pilots to plan and execute safe air taxi routes, ensuring compliance with ground traffic patterns and avoiding areas of potential conflict.

3. In what way do these aeronautical references impact decision-making during air taxi?

They enhance situational awareness and help pilots make informed decisions in real-time during air taxi operations.

4. What are air taxi instructions and how do they relate to air taxi operations?

Air taxi instructions are specific directives given by air traffic control (ATC) regarding the route and/or altitude and/or speed a helicopter should maintain while air taxiing. These instructions ensure safe navigation within the airport environment, avoiding conflicts with other aircraft and ground vehicles.

[PH.IV.C.K2; FAA-H-8083-21]

5. How should a pilot handle clearances during an air taxi?

During air taxi, a pilot must clearly understand and follow all ATC clearances. This includes adhering to specified routes, altitudes, and any restrictions. Pilots should always confirm clearances, and if uncertain, they must seek clarification from ATC.

[PH.IV.C.K2; FAA-H-8083-21]

6. What limitations are typically associated with air taxi operations?

Limitations in air taxi operations can include restrictions on altitude (often below 100 feet), speed, and designated areas for air taxiing, especially in busy or complex airport environments. These limitations are designed to mitigate risks, such as collisions or rotor wash effects on surrounding objects and personnel.

[PH.IV.C.K2; FAA-H-8083-21]

7. How do airport/heliport/helipad signs and markings impact air taxi operations?

Airport, heliport, and helipad signs and markings provide crucial information for safe navigation during air taxi. They indicate taxi routes, designated landing areas, and potential hazards. Understanding these signs and markings helps pilots to maneuver safely and comply with local ground traffic regulations.

[PH.IV.C.K3; FAA-H-8083-25]

8. What role does lighting play in air taxi operations at airports and heliports?

Lighting plays a vital role in air taxi operations, especially during low visibility conditions like night or bad weather. Lights on runways, taxiways, and helipads guide pilots in navigating and orienting themselves, enhancing safety and reducing the risk of disorientation or accidents.

[PH.IV.C.K3; FAA-H-8083-25]

9. Why is understanding landing area markings important for air taxi?

Understanding landing area markings is important for identifying safe and designated areas for takeoffs and landings during air taxi operations. These markings inform pilots about suitable landing spots, wind direction, and potential obstacles, ensuring safe and efficient ground operations.

[PH.IV.C.K3; FAA-H-8083-21]

10. What are visual indicators for wind at nontowered airports?

Visual indicators for wind include windsocks, smoke plumes, water ripples, and movement of vegetation. These indicators help pilots assess wind direction and strength, which is crucial in air taxi operations for maintaining control, determining the best approach and departure paths, and managing rotor effects like downwash and tail rotor efficiency.

[PH.IV.C.K4; FAA-H-8083-25]

11. How should pilots use windsocks during air taxi?

Pilots should use windsocks to determine wind direction and approximate wind speed at the airport or heliport. This information is vital for planning the safest approach and departure paths during air taxi, especially when maneuvering near ground obstacles or in confined areas.

[PH.IV.C.K4; FAA-H-8083-25]

12. What is the significance of aircraft lighting in air taxi operations?

Aircraft lighting, including navigation lights, anti-collision lights, and landing lights, is crucial in air taxi operations for visibility and safety. These lights help in signaling the aircraft's presence and movement to other pilots and ground personnel, especially during low visibility conditions or at night. Proper use of lighting enhances situational awareness and collision avoidance.

[PH.IV.C.K5; FAA-H-8083-25]

13. What best practices should pilots follow regarding aircraft lighting in air taxi?

Best practices include ensuring all lighting systems are operational before flight, using appropriate lights during air taxi to communicate the aircraft's position and intentions, and being mindful of the potential glare or distraction that bright lights might cause to others. Regular checks and maintenance of lighting systems are also essential for safe operations.

[PH.IV.C.K5; FAA-H-8083-21]

14. What are standard procedures for pilots during taxiing?

Standard procedures for pilots during taxiing include following the prescribed taxi routes as per ATC instructions or airport diagrams, maintaining a lookout for other aircraft and ground vehicles, and adjusting taxi speed according to conditions. Pilots should use appropriate lighting, communicate intentions clearly, and be prepared to stop or adjust the route as necessary.

[PH.IV.C.K6a; FAA-H-8083-25]

15. How should pilots manage cockpit activities during taxi?

Pilots should manage cockpit activities by ensuring all necessary navigational and communication equipment is set for the flight, minimizing distractions, and maintaining a sterile cockpit, particularly in critical areas like runways and busy taxiways. Attention should be primarily focused on safely navigating the aircraft.

[PH.IV.C.K6a; FAA-H-8083-25]

16. Why is situational awareness important during taxiing?

Situational awareness is crucial during taxiing to prevent runway incursions, collisions with other aircraft or obstacles, and to navigate the taxiway system safely. Pilots need to be aware of their surroundings, understand the airport layout, and anticipate potential hazards.

[PH.IV.C.K6a; FAA-H-8083-25]

17. What are the procedures for safe air taxi at towered airports?

At towered airports, safe air taxi procedures involve following ATC instructions precisely, maintaining clear communication, using assigned taxiways and altitudes, and adhering to the airport's traffic flow. Pilots must remain vigilant for other aircraft and ground vehicles, ensuring they comply with all clearances and avoid active runways unless cleared to cross or use them.

[PH.IV.C.K6b; FAA-H-8083-25]

18. How do procedures differ for air taxi at nontowered airports?

At nontowered airports, pilots must be more self-reliant for safe air taxi. This includes announcing intentions on the common traffic advisory frequency (CTAF), being aware of other aircraft movements, and coordinating with other pilots as necessary. Pilots should follow standard traffic patterns and be especially vigilant in looking out for other aircraft and ground hazards.

[PH.IV.C.K6b; FAA-H-8083-25]

19. What communication strategies should pilots employ during air taxi?

Effective communication strategies during air taxi include clear and concise transmissions, listening attentively to ATC or CTAF, reading back all clearances, and being proactive in seeking clarifications if instructions are unclear or seem unsafe. Good communication helps in maintaining situational awareness and preventing misunderstandings.

[PH.IV.C.K6b; FAA-H-8083-25]

20. What best practices should pilots follow for air taxi operations at both towered and nontowered airports?

Best practices for air taxi operations at both towered and nontowered airports include preflight planning, understanding current NOTAMs, using airport diagrams, maintaining a lookout for other traffic, adhering to recommended air taxi altitudes and speeds, and employing navigation lights and anti-collision lights for visibility. Regular training and familiarization with different types of airport environments are also important.

[PH.IV.C.K6b; FAA-H-8083-25]

21. What are the standard procedures for overflying runways during air taxi?

Standard procedures for overflying runways during air taxi involve obtaining specific clearance from air traffic control (ATC) at towered airports. Pilots must follow the assigned altitude and route, remain vigilant for other aircraft taking off or landing, and adhere to any ATC instructions regarding timing and speed. At nontowered airports, pilots should announce their intentions on the common traffic advisory frequency (CTAF) and ensure no conflicting traffic is present.

[PH.IV.C.K6c; FAA-H-8083-21]

22. How should a pilot approach runway overflight in air taxi operations?

When approaching a runway for overflight during an air taxi, pilots should ensure they have proper clearance, confirm no conflicting traffic is on or approaching the runway, and maintain the prescribed altitude for overflying. Continuous monitoring of ATC communications and visual scanning for traffic is essential.

[PH.IV.C.K6c; FAA-H-8083-21]

23. What considerations should be taken when overflying active runways?

When overflying active runways, considerations include ensuring clearance from ATC, maintaining an altitude that avoids interfering with other aircraft operations, and being aware of potential wake turbulence from larger aircraft. Pilots should also consider wind direction and speed, adjusting their flight path to minimize risk.

[PH.IV.C.K6c; FAA-H-8083-21]

24. How do height/velocity (H/V) considerations impact air taxi operations?

Height/velocity (H/V) considerations impact air taxi operations by defining safe operational envelopes based on altitude and airspeed. In air taxi, pilots must be mindful of the H/V diagram to avoid areas where autorotation in the event of a powerplant failure may be unsafe or ineffective.

[PH.IV.C.K7; FAA-H-8083-21]

25. What is the significance of the H/V diagram in air taxi?

The H/V diagram is significant in air taxi as it visually represents the combinations of height and airspeed where successful autorotation may or may not be possible. Pilots must understand and respect these limits to minimize risk, especially during low altitude operations common in air taxi.

[PH.IV.C.K7; FAA-H-8083-21]

26. How can a pilot identify risks associated with distractions during air taxi operations?

Risks of distractions can be identified by recognizing potential sources of attention diversion, such as cockpit activities, external noise, or complex ATC communications.

[PH.IV.C.R1; FAA-H-8083-2]

27. What methods can a pilot use to assess risks related to task prioritization while air taxiing?

To assess task prioritization risks, evaluate the complexity of the air taxi route, the level of airport activity, and the demands of cockpit management.

[PH.IV.C.R1; FAA-H-8083-2]

28. How can pilots mitigate risks of losing situational awareness during air taxi?

By continually updating their mental model of the aircraft's position, maintaining awareness of traffic patterns, and staying alert to environmental changes. Avoiding over-reliance on a single source of information and regularly scanning all available data points helps maintain situational awareness.

[PH.IV.C.R1; FAA-H-8083-2]

29. Why is it important to manage disorientation risk in air taxi?

To prevent navigation errors like incorrect taxiway usage or runway incursions. Orientation is key to safely maneuvering within the airport environment, avoiding conflicts, and efficiently following ATC instructions.

[PH.IV.C.R1; FAA-H-8083-2]

30. How can a pilot identify risks associated with reduced visibility or night operations during an air taxi?

By assessing weather conditions, visibility levels, and lighting adequacy. Pilots should be alert to challenges in identifying taxiways, runways, and other aircraft, and recognize the increased difficulty in visual navigation and spatial orientation.

[PH.IV.C.R2; FAA-H-8083-2]

31. What methods can a pilot use to assess risks in low visibility air taxi operations?

Evaluating current weather reports, understanding the limitations of the aircraft's lighting and navigation systems, and considering the pilot's own experience and comfort level with night or low visibility conditions. Familiarity with the airport layout and available visual aids is also crucial.

[PH.IV.C.R2; FAA-H-8083-2]

32. How can pilots mitigate risks during air taxi in reduced visibility or at night?

To mitigate these risks, pilots should use all available lighting systems, follow prescribed taxi routes, maintain lower taxi speeds, and enhance situational awareness using airport diagrams and ATC guidance. Pilots should also be prepared to stop if disoriented or uncertain of their position.

[PH.IV.C.R2; FAA-H-8083-2]

33. How can a pilot identify risks of runway incursion during an air taxi?

Risks of runway incursion can be identified by recognizing points where taxi paths intersect runways or other active areas. Pilots should be aware of complex taxiway layouts, high traffic volumes, and any confusing airport signage or markings that could lead to unintentional runway entry.

[PH.IV.C.R3; FAA-H-8083-2]

34. How can pilots mitigate risks associated with runway incursions during air taxi?

By adhering strictly to ATC instructions, using airport diagrams for navigation, confirming unclear directions, and maintaining heightened vigilance at taxiway intersections and holding short lines. Regularly practicing standard taxi procedures, including read-backs of all runway crossing and hold short instructions, is also crucial.

[PH.IV.C.R3; FAA-H-8083-2]

35. Why is it important to manage runway incursion risks in air taxi operations?

To prevent collisions with other aircraft and to ensure the safety of all airport users. Runway incursions can lead to serious accidents, particularly in busy or complex airport environments. Effective risk management helps maintain orderly and safe ground operations.

[PH.IV.C.R3; FAA-H-8083-2]

36. How can a pilot identify risks associated with main rotor, tail rotor, and tail strike hazards during air taxi?

By recognizing situations where rotor blades are close to obstructions, uneven terrain, or other aircraft. Awareness of the helicopter's tail position, especially in confined areas or during sharp maneuvers, is crucial to avoid tail rotor or tail strikes.

[PH.IV.C.R4; FAA-H-8083-21]

37. What methods can a pilot use to assess rotor and tail strike risks in air taxi operations?

Assessing these risks involves evaluating the operating environment for potential obstructions, considering wind conditions that may affect rotorcraft control, and understanding the helicopter's limitations. Pilots should consider the clearance needed for rotor blades and the tail during all phases of air taxi.

[PH.IV.C.R4; FAA-H-8083-21]

38. How can a pilot identify risks associated with H/V diagram performance in case of a powerplant failure during air taxi?

By understanding the height/velocity (H/V) diagram for the specific helicopter model, which indicates safe and unsafe operational zones. Pilots should recognize scenarios where flight within the unsafe zones of the H/V diagram occurs, such as low altitude and low airspeed combinations, where a safe autorotation may not be possible in the event of a powerplant failure.

[PH.IV.C.R5; FAA-H-8083-21]

39. What methods can a pilot use to assess H/V diagram risks in air taxi operations?

By analyzing the H/V diagram against the intended flight path, altitude, and airspeed during air taxi. Assessing environmental factors like wind, weight, and density altitude that may influence autorotation effectiveness is also essential. Pilots should consider how current flying conditions align with the safer zones of the H/V diagram.

[PH.IV.C.R5; FAA-H-8083-21]

40. How can pilots mitigate risks associated with the H/V diagram during air taxi?

Pilots should plan and execute air taxi maneuvers that keep the helicopter within the safe zones of the H/V diagram. This may involve adjusting altitude and airspeed to stay within the operational envelope where successful autorotation is more likely in case of a powerplant failure.

[PH.IV.C.R5; FAA-H-8083-21]

41. How can a pilot identify risks of confirmation or expectation bias in taxi instructions during air taxi?

Risks of confirmation or expectation bias can be identified by being aware of instances where a pilot might interpret taxi instructions based on what they expect to hear, rather than what is actually communicated. This bias may occur in familiar environments or under routine operations, leading to misinterpretation of ATC instructions.

[PH.IV.C.R6; FAA-H-8083-25]

42. How can pilots mitigate risks associated with bias in taxi instructions during air taxi?

To mitigate these risks, pilots should practice active listening, confirm and read back all taxi instructions, and seek clarification if there is any uncertainty or discrepancy. Remaining attentive and avoiding assumptions based on previous experiences or routines is crucial.

[PH.IV.C.R6; FAA-H-8083-25]

Skills to be demonstrated:

• Complete the appropriate checklist(s).

• Use an airport diagram or taxi chart during taxi, if published, and maintain situational awareness.

• Select a safe airspeed and altitude.

• Maintain desired track and groundspeed in headwind and crosswind conditions, avoiding conditions that might lead to loss of tail rotor/antitorque effectiveness.

• Maintain engine and rotor RPM within normal limits.

• Comply with airport/heliport/helipad/landing area markings, lights, signs, and ATC instructions.

• Maintain specified altitude, ±10 feet.

D. Taxiing with Wheel-Type Landing Gear

1. How do current airport aeronautical references assist in taxiing with wheel-type landing gear?

Chart Supplement and airport diagrams provide crucial information on runway and taxiway layouts, surface conditions, and other operational details essential for safely navigating an aircraft with wheel-type landing gear.

[PH.IV.D.K1; FAA-H-8083-25]

2. How do Notices to Air Missions (NOTAMs) impact taxi operations for aircraft with wheel-type landing gear?

NOTAMs provide critical information on temporary changes or hazards at airports, such as construction, taxiway closures, or surface conditions that may affect taxiing with wheel-type landing gear. Pilots need to review NOTAMs to adjust their taxi planning accordingly and ensure safety.

[PH.IV.D.K1; FAA-H-8083-25]

3. What is essential for understanding taxi instructions and clearances for aircraft with wheel-type landing gear?

Comprehending ATC directives regarding specific taxiways, runways, and holding positions. It requires familiarity with airport layout, ability to interpret and follow route directions, and the knowledge of standard taxi procedures and phraseology.

[PH.IV.D.K2; FAA-H-8083-25]

4. How do taxi instructions differ for aircraft with wheel-type landing gear?

Taxi instructions for aircraft with wheel-type landing gear may include specific routes suited for their maneuverability and ground handling characteristics. Unlike skid-equipped helicopters, these aircraft often taxi on designated paths and might receive different routing instructions.

[PH.IV.D.K2; FAA-H-8083-25]

5. **Why is it important to accurately interpret taxi instructions for wheel-type gear aircraft?**

   Accurate interpretation of taxi instructions is crucial to avoid runway incursions, collisions, and navigation errors. It ensures the safe and efficient movement of the aircraft within the airport environment, complying with ATC guidelines and maintaining operational safety.

   [PH.IV.D.K2; FAA-H-8083-25]

6. **What should pilots consider when receiving taxi clearances for aircraft with wheel-type landing gear?**

   Pilots should consider the taxiway width, surface conditions, turn radius limitations, and proximity to other aircraft or obstacles. Understanding ATC clearances in context with these considerations is key to safely maneuvering an aircraft with wheel-type landing gear on the ground.

   [PH.IV.D.K2; FAA-H-8083-25]

7. **How does understanding airport/heliport/helipad/landing area signage and markings aid in taxiing with wheel-type landing gear?**

   Understanding these signs and markings is crucial for safe navigation on the ground, as they provide essential information on taxiway paths, runway boundaries, and specific areas like holding positions.

   [PH.IV.D.K3; FAA-H-8083-25]

8. **What role do airport signs play in taxi operations for wheel-type gear aircraft?**

   These signs assist in making accurate navigation decisions and maintaining spatial orientation within the airport environment.

   [PH.IV.D.K3; FAA-H-8083-25]

9. How do markings on helipads or landing areas affect taxiing with wheel-type landing gear?

Markings on helipads and landing areas indicate designated spots for landing and takeoff, taxi pathways, and safety zones. For aircraft with wheel-type landing gear, these markings guide pilots in aligning the aircraft correctly, ensuring safe operations in confined or shared spaces.

[PH.IV.D.K3; FAA-H-8083-25]

10. How do visual wind indicators aid in taxiing with wheel-type landing gear?

Visual wind indicators, like windsocks or tetrahedrons, provide pilots with real-time information on wind direction and speed. This knowledge is crucial for aircraft with wheel-type landing gear to anticipate wind effects during taxi, such as increased resistance or drift, and to adjust control inputs accordingly for safe maneuvering.

[PH.IV.D.K4; FAA-H-8083-25]

11. What is the importance of understanding wind direction while taxiing with wheel-type gear?

To maintain control and stability of the aircraft. Crosswinds, for instance, can cause drifting, requiring pilots to use aileron and rudder inputs to compensate. Awareness of wind direction helps in making necessary adjustments to stay on the intended taxi path.

[PH.IV.D.K4; FAA-H-8083-25]

12. Why should pilots be aware of wind speed indicators during taxi operations?

Awareness of wind speed is crucial for gauging the potential impact on the aircraft during taxi. High wind speeds can increase the difficulty of controlling the aircraft, especially during turns or when moving across open areas. This awareness allows for proactive adjustments to control inputs.

[PH.IV.D.K4; FAA-H-8083-25]

13. How does aircraft lighting facilitate taxiing with wheel-type landing gear?

Aircraft lighting, such as taxi lights, navigation lights, and strobe lights, enhances visibility and conspicuity during taxi operations, especially in low-light conditions. Proper use of these lights helps pilots with wheel-type landing gear to see and be seen on the ground, aiding in safe navigation and collision avoidance.

[PH.IV.D.K5; FAA-H-8083-25]

14. What is the role of taxi lights in taxiing operations for wheel-type gear aircraft?

Taxi lights provide illumination of the taxiway ahead, aiding pilots in identifying taxiway markings, obstructions, and other aircraft. Their correct use is vital for safe ground navigation, particularly during night operations or in poor visibility conditions.

[PH.IV.D.K5; FAA-H-8083-25]

15. Why is it important to understand the use of navigation lights while taxiing?

Navigation lights (red for the left wing, green for the right, and white for the tail) help other pilots determine the orientation and movement direction of an aircraft during taxi. This understanding is crucial for preventing confusion and potential collisions on taxiways and runways.

[PH.IV.D.K5; FAA-H-8083-25]

16. What are the key flight deck activities prior to taxiing for aircraft with wheel-type landing gear?

Prior to taxi, pilots should engage in thorough route planning, including reviewing airport diagrams for the planned taxi route and understanding ATC taxi instructions. Identifying any potential hot spots or complex intersections on the route is essential. Pilots should also check all flight deck systems and set up navigation and communication equipment.

[PH.IV.D.K6a; FAA-H-8083-25]

17. How does route planning impact taxi operations for wheel-type gear aircraft?

Effective route planning ensures pilots are aware of their intended path, minimizing confusion and the risk of errors during taxi. It involves studying the airport layout, understanding taxi instructions, and planning for contingencies like runway changes or unexpected clearances.

[PH.IV.D.K6a; FAA-H-8083-25]

18. Why is identifying hot spots crucial before taxiing with wheel-type landing gear?

Identifying hot spots, areas on an airport surface with a history or risk of collision or runway incursion, is crucial to avoid these high-risk areas or approach them with heightened caution. Awareness of hot spots helps pilots anticipate and mitigate potential hazards during taxi.

[PH.IV.D.K6a; FAA-H-8083-25]

19. What are the key procedures for safe taxi at towered airports with wheel-type landing gear?

At towered airports, safe taxi procedures for wheel-type landing gear include adhering to ATC instructions, maintaining situational awareness, using airport diagrams to navigate, and staying alert to other traffic and runway incursions.

[PH.IV.D.K6b; FAA-H-8083-25]

20. How do taxi procedures differ at nontowered airports for aircraft with wheel-type gear?

At nontowered airports, pilots must self-coordinate with other traffic, announce intentions on the common traffic advisory frequency, and vigilantly observe for other aircraft and ground traffic. Pilots should be proactive in avoiding conflicts, especially in the absence of ATC guidance, and use standard taxi procedures and right-of-way rules.

[PH.IV.D.K6b; FAA-H-8083-25]

21. What is crucial for understanding when entering or crossing runways during taxi with wheel-type landing gear?

Proper clearance from ATC before entering or crossing any runway is crucial. Pilots must be familiar with airport signage and markings that denote runway boundaries and holding positions. It is essential to ensure there is no conflicting traffic and to be aware of visibility limitations that might affect spotting other aircraft on the runway.

[PH.IV.D.K6c; FAA-H-8083-25]

22. Why is it important to understand runway crossing procedures for aircraft with wheel-type gear?

Understanding these procedures is important to prevent runway incursions and potential collisions with other aircraft. Runway crossings involve navigating active areas where heightened caution and situational awareness are crucial for safety.

[PH.IV.D.K6c; FAA-H-8083-25]

23. How can a pilot identify risks associated with activities and distractions during taxi with wheel-type landing gear?

Risks can be identified by recognizing potential distractions such as complex ATC communications, onboard activities, or external events. Understanding the impact of these distractions on the pilot's ability to focus on taxiing, especially with the handling characteristics of wheel-type landing gear, is key.

[PH.IV.D.R1; FAA-H-8083-2]

24. How can pilots mitigate risks associated with distractions while taxiing with wheel-type gear?

Mitigating these risks involves minimizing unnecessary activities in the cockpit, maintaining a sterile cockpit environment during critical phases, staying focused on the taxi path, and ensuring clear communication with ATC. Pilots should also brief passengers about minimizing distractions during taxi.

[PH.IV.D.R1; FAA-H-8083-2]

25. Why is managing distraction risks important in taxi operations for wheel-type gear aircraft?

Managing these risks is important to prevent runway incursions, collisions with other aircraft or obstacles, and deviations from the intended taxi path. Distractions can significantly impair situational awareness and reaction times, leading to unsafe taxi operations.

[PH.IV.D.R1; FAA-H-8083-2]

26. What best practices should pilots follow to manage distractions during taxi?

Best practices include conducting thorough pre-taxi briefings, adhering to checklist procedures, maintaining situational awareness, and setting clear priorities for cockpit tasks. Pilots should also regularly train on managing distractions and develop strategies to regain focus quickly if distracted.

[PH.IV.D.R1; FAA-H-8083-2]

27. How can a pilot identify risks of confirmation or expectation bias in taxi instructions during taxi with wheel-type landing gear?

By recognizing instances where a pilot might interpret taxi instructions based on what they expect to hear, rather than what is actually communicated. This bias may occur in familiar environments or under routine operations, leading to misinterpretation of ATC instructions.

[PH.IV.D.R2; FAA-H-8083-25]

28. What methods can a pilot use to assess risks of bias in understanding taxi instructions?

Pilots can assess these risks by critically analyzing their understanding of ATC instructions, especially in complex or busy airfield environments.

[PH.IV.D.R2; FAA-H-8083-25]

29. How can pilots mitigate risks associated with bias in taxi instructions during taxi with wheel-type gear?

To mitigate these risks, pilots should practice active listening, confirm and read back all taxi instructions, and seek clarification if there is any uncertainty or discrepancy. Remaining attentive and avoiding assumptions based on previous experiences or routines is crucial.

[PH.IV.D.R2; FAA-H-8083-25]

30. Why is it important to manage bias in understanding taxi instructions in taxi operations with wheel-type gear?

Managing bias in understanding taxi instructions is important to prevent navigation errors, runway incursions, and potential collisions. Confirmation or expectation bias can lead to unsafe situations, particularly in complex taxiing scenarios or under changing airfield conditions.

[PH.IV.D.R2; FAA-H-8083-25]

31. How can a pilot identify risks of runway incursion during taxi with wheel-type landing gear?

Risks of runway incursion can be identified by recognizing complex intersections, high-traffic areas, or confusing taxiway layouts. Pilots should be aware of their exact location on the airfield and any potential areas where accidental entry onto a runway might occur.

[PH.IV.D.R3; FAA-H-8083-25]

32. How can pilots mitigate risks associated with runway incursions while taxiing with wheel-type gear?

To mitigate these risks, pilots should strictly adhere to ATC instructions, use airport diagrams for navigation, maintain situational awareness, and conduct thorough pre-taxi planning. Confirming clearances before entering or crossing runways and constant vigilance are also key.

[PH.IV.D.R3; FAA-H-8083-25]

33. Why is managing runway incursion risks important in taxi operations for wheel-type gear aircraft?

Managing runway incursion risks is crucial to prevent accidents and collisions on the airfield. Runway incursions can lead to dangerous conflicts with other aircraft and are a significant safety concern in airport ground operations.

[PH.IV.D.R3; FAA-H-8083-25]

34. What best practices should pilots follow to prevent runway incursions during taxi?

Best practices include regularly reviewing and familiarizing oneself with the layout of frequented airports, always reading back hold-short instructions, using proper lighting and markings, and remaining vigilant for any conflicting traffic or instructions. Regular training and drills on runway safety enhance a pilot's ability to avoid incursions.

[PH.IV.D.R3; FAA-H-8083-25]

35. How can a pilot identify risks associated with speed during taxi and turns with wheel-type landing gear?

Risks can be identified by noting conditions such as wet or slippery taxiways, tight turns, congested areas, and the aircraft's handling characteristics.

[PH.IV.D.R4; FAA-H-8083-21]

36. What methods can a pilot use to assess speed-related risks during taxi?

By considering factors like aircraft weight, surface conditions, visibility, traffic density, and the complexity of the taxi route. Evaluating these factors helps determine a safe taxi speed that allows adequate reaction time and maneuverability.

[PH.IV.D.R4; FAA-H-8083-21]

37. How can pilots mitigate risks associated with taxi speed and turns?

Pilots should maintain a controlled, safe taxi speed, allowing ample time for reaction and adjustments. Slowing down before turns, staying alert to changing conditions, and being prepared to stop quickly if necessary. In some helicopters using differential braking and power judiciously also helps in safe turning.

[PH.IV.D.R4; FAA-H-8083-21]

38. Why is managing speed important in taxi operations for wheel-type gear aircraft?

Managing taxi speed is crucial to maintain control, especially during turns, and to prevent runway incursions or collisions. Excessive speed can lead to loss of control, inability to stop within a safe distance, or missing critical signage and markings.

[PH.IV.D.R4; FAA-H-8083-21]

39. How can a pilot identify risks associated with thrust vector and brake use during taxi with wheel-type landing gear?

Risks can be identified by understanding the aircraft's thrust characteristics and brake responsiveness. Conditions such as wet or uneven taxiways, slopes, and aircraft weight influence thrust vector and braking efficiency. Being aware of these factors helps in anticipating the aircraft's response during taxi.

[PH.IV.D.R5; FAA-H-8083-21]

40. What methods can a pilot use to assess risks related to thrust vector and brake use?

Pilots can assess risks by considering factors like taxiway surface conditions, aircraft weight, wind direction, and slope of the taxi path. Regular brake checks and understanding the aircraft's performance characteristics under different loads and conditions are essential for accurate risk assessment.

[PH.IV.D.R5; FAA-H-8083-21]

41. How can pilots mitigate risks associated with using thrust vector and brakes during taxi?

To mitigate these risks, pilots should apply thrust gently, use brakes smoothly, and avoid sudden movements. They should be particularly cautious on slippery or sloped surfaces and during tight maneuvers.

[PH.IV.D.R5; FAA-H-8083-21]

42. How can a pilot identify risks associated with airframe and rotor clearances during taxi with wheel-type landing gear?

By assessing the aircraft's dimensions, rotor span, and tail height in relation to surrounding obstacles, aircraft, and ground vehicles. Understanding the airport environment, including taxiway widths and proximity to buildings or equipment, is crucial for ensuring adequate clearance.

[PH.IV.D.R6; FAA-H-8083-21]

43. What methods can a pilot use to assess clearance risks during taxi?

By thoroughly familiarizing themselves with the aircraft's physical dimensions and rotor disc area. Checking airport diagrams for narrow taxiways or areas with obstructions and being mindful of wingtip or rotor clearance during turns and maneuvers are essential assessment strategies.

[PH.IV.D.R6; FAA-H-8083-21]

44. How can pilots mitigate risks associated with airframe and rotor clearances during taxi?

Maintain a centered position on taxiways, give wide berth to obstacles, and be vigilant during turns. They should also use wing walkers or ground crew assistance in tight spaces and communicate effectively with ATC or ground personnel about clearance concerns.

[PH.IV.D.R6; FAA-H-8083-21]

Skills to be demonstrated:

• Complete the appropriate checklist(s).

• Use an appropriate airport/heliport diagram or taxi chart, if published.

• Properly position nosewheel/tailwheel, if applicable, locked or unlocked.

• Position the flight controls properly for the existing wind conditions, with the landing gear in contact with the surface, avoiding conditions that might lead to loss of directional control.

• Properly use cyclic, collective, and brakes as applicable to control speed while taxiing.

• Maintain engine and rotor RPM within normal limits.

• Maintain specified track within 4 feet.

• Position the helicopter relative to hold lines or a specified point.

• Receive and comply with ATC clearances/instructions, if applicable.

• Comply with airport/heliport taxiway markings, lights, and signals.

E. Slope Operations

Note: Demonstration of parallel slope operations must be conducted in accordance with the helicopter manufacturer's limitations, if published. If no slope limitations are published for the helicopter being used, parallel slope operations of approximately 5–10 degrees may be demonstrated. Landings with the helicopter facing downhill or uphill will not be tested during certification. A thorough review of the intended slope operations area must be conducted to ensure clearance from hazards.

1. What are the key elements related to slope operations that a pilot should understand?

Understanding slope operations involves knowledge of assessing the slope gradient, selecting a suitable landing site, and recognizing the limitations of the aircraft in sloped terrain. Pilots should be aware of the techniques for approach, touchdown, and departure on slopes, as well as the effects of slope on aircraft stability and control.

[PH.IV.E.K1; FAA-H-8083-21]

2. How does slope gradient affect helicopter operations?

Slope gradient impacts the helicopter's landing gear alignment and rotor clearance. Pilots must understand how to position the helicopter to ensure the uphill skid or wheel is in contact with the ground first and to maintain rotor clearance from the slope. Excessive slopes can exceed the aircraft's capabilities and lead to instability or rollover.

[PH.IV.E.K1; FAA-H-8083-21]

3. What factors should be considered when selecting an appropriate slope for helicopter operations?

When selecting a slope, consider the slope's gradient, surface condition (firmness and texture), size of the area, presence of obstructions, wind direction and strength, and the helicopter's capabilities.

[PH.IV.E.K2; FAA-H-8083-21]

4. How does the slope gradient impact helicopter operations?

The slope gradient affects the ability to maintain level attitude during touchdown and lift-off. Steeper slopes may challenge the helicopter's stability and increase the risk of dynamic rollover.

[PH.IV.E.K2; FAA-H-8083-21]

5. What role does wind direction play in selecting a slope for helicopter operations?

Pilots should select slopes that allow for operations into the wind to maximize control and lift. Crosswind or tailwind conditions can complicate slope operations and should be carefully evaluated.

[PH.IV.E.K3; FAA-H-8083-21]

6. How does wind affect slope operations in helicopter flying?

Wind significantly impacts helicopter performance during slope operations. Strong winds can alter the helicopter's approach path, affect stability during landing and takeoff, and challenge control, especially on crosswind or tailwind slopes.

[PH.IV.E.K3; FAA-H-8083-21]

7. How should pilots manage gusty or variable wind conditions during slope operations?

In gusty or variable wind conditions, pilots should be prepared for sudden changes in wind speed and direction. This requires heightened awareness and readiness to adjust control inputs promptly. Extra caution and possibly selecting an alternative site with more favorable wind conditions might be necessary.

[PH.IV.E.K3; FAA-H-8083-21]

8. What factors contribute to dynamic rollover in slope operations?

Contributing factors include slope gradient, surface traction, helicopter weight distribution, and wind conditions. Pilot inputs, such as abrupt control movements or delayed reaction to a skid lifting, can also play a significant role. Understanding these factors is crucial to identify and mitigate the risk of dynamic rollover.

[PH.IV.E.K4; FAA-H-8083-21]

9. How can pilots prevent dynamic rollover during slope operations?

Prevention techniques include careful assessment of the slope and environmental conditions, smooth and gradual control inputs, maintaining rotor RPM within recommended limits, and ensuring even weight distribution. Pilots should avoid sudden cyclic movements and be vigilant for early signs of a skid or wheel lifting off the ground.

[PH.IV.E.K4; FAA-H-8083-21]

10. What are helicopter slope limitations and why are they important for safe operations?

Helicopter slope limitations refer to the maximum degree of slope on which a helicopter can safely land and take off. These limitations are crucial for ensuring the aircraft's stability and preventing situations like dynamic rollover.

[PH.IV.E.K5; FAA-H-8083-21]

11. How are slope limitations determined for different helicopter models?

Slope limitations are determined by the helicopter's design, including the configuration of landing gear and the helicopter's center of gravity. Manufacturers provide specific slope limits in the helicopter's flight manual based on testing and the aircraft's operational capabilities. Pilots must refer to these guidelines for safe operations on sloped terrain.

[PH.IV.E.K5; FAA-H-8083-21]

12. How can a pilot identify risks associated with operations on a slope?

Risks in slope operations can be identified by assessing the slope gradient, surface conditions (like wet grass, loose gravel, or uneven terrain), wind direction and speed, and any potential obstructions. Pilots must also consider the helicopter's capabilities and limitations for operating on slopes.

[PH.IV.E.R1; FAA-H-8083-21]

13. **How can pilots mitigate risks associated with slope operations?**

To mitigate risks, pilots should conduct thorough preflight planning, practice precise control inputs, choose the least sloped area that meets safety requirements, and ensure a clear approach and departure path.

[PH.IV.E.R1; FAA-H-8083-21]

14. **How can a pilot identify risks leading to loss of tail rotor/ antitorque effectiveness specific to slope operations?**

Risks specific to slope operations include wind conditions that may disrupt airflow to the tail rotor, especially when operating on slopes with varying wind directions. The change in helicopter attitude on a slope and the potential for increased power demands also heighten the risk of tail rotor ineffectiveness.

[PH.IV.E.R2; FAA-H-8083-21]

15. **Why is it important to manage tail rotor/antitorque loss risk during slope operations?**

Managing this risk during slope operations is vital as the unique demands of these operations can exacerbate the effects of tail rotor inefficiency. Loss of tail rotor effectiveness on a slope can lead to rapid, uncontrolled yaw or drift, increasing the risk of accidents in these already challenging environments.

[PH.IV.E.R2; FAA-H-8083-21]

16. **How can a pilot identify risks associated with embarking or disembarking passengers and rotor blade hazards during slope operations?**

Risks can be identified by assessing the slope's gradient, which may affect the rotor blade clearance and stability of the helicopter. Uneven terrain can pose a hazard for passengers embarking or disembarking. Additionally, rotor blades may be closer to the ground on the downhill side, increasing the risk of contact. Pilots should ensure passengers are briefed on the specific dangers of slope operations.

[PH.IV.E.R3; FAA-H-8083-21]

17. **What methods can a pilot use to assess risks related to passenger movements and rotor blade hazards on slopes?**

    Before landing, the pilot should evaluate the slope for safety and suitability for passenger movements. The assessment should include an evaluation of the terrain for any obstacles or uneven ground that could pose a hazard.

    [PH.IV.E.R3; FAA-H-8083-21]

18. **How can pilots mitigate risks associated with embarking or disembarking passengers on slopes?**

    Pilots should ensure the helicopter is securely positioned and stable before allowing passengers to embark or disembark. Pilots should instruct passengers on safe paths to avoid rotor blades and ensure they remain in the pilot's view.

    [PH.IV.E.R3; FAA-H-8083-21]

19. **Why is it important to manage risks during passenger movements in slope operations?**

    Managing risks during passenger movements in slope operations is crucial due to the increased potential for accidents involving rotor blades or falls due to uneven terrain. Slopes can change the typical dynamics of embarking and disembarking, requiring extra caution to ensure the safety of all passengers.

    [PH.IV.E.R3; FAA-H-8083-21]

20. **How can a pilot identify risks leading to dynamic rollover specific to slope operations?**

    Pilots should be aware of the slope's gradient, surface conditions, helicopter loading, and wind effects, as these factors can influence the risk of dynamic rollover during landing and takeoff on slopes.

    [PH.IV.E.R4; FAA-H-8083-21]

21. How can pilots mitigate risks associated with dynamic rollover in slope operations?

Pilots should choose landing and takeoff areas on slopes that are within the operational limits of the helicopter. They should use gentle, controlled movements, especially when one skid or wheel contacts the slope.

[PH.IV.E.R4; FAA-H-8083-21]

22. Why is managing the risk of dynamic rollover important during slope operations?

Managing the risk of dynamic rollover during slope operations is crucial because slopes present unique challenges that can increase the likelihood of this type of accident. The uneven ground can lead to unbalanced loading of the landing gear, making the helicopter more susceptible to rolling over if not handled correctly.

[PH.IV.E.R4; FAA-H-8083-21]

23. How can a pilot identify risks associated with surface conditions during slope operations?

By assessing the terrain's firmness, texture, and stability. Slopes with loose gravel, wet grass, ice, or snow pose significant risks. The presence of hidden obstacles, such as rocks or holes, should also be considered. Pilots should evaluate the slope's surface both visually and, if possible, through a reconnaissance landing.

[PH.IV.E.R5; FAA-H-8083-21]

24. Why is managing surface condition risks important in slope operations?

Managing surface condition risks is important because unstable or unsuitable surfaces can lead to loss of control, dynamic rollover, or inability to safely land or take off. Slope operations require a stable platform for the helicopter, and adverse surface conditions can significantly compromise safety.

[PH.IV.E.R5; FAA-H-8083-21]

25. How can a pilot identify collision hazards specific to slope operations?

Collision hazards during slope operations can be identified by assessing the area for obstacles like trees, wires, or buildings, especially on the downslope side where visibility might be limited. Pilots should also be aware of the increased potential for rotor blade strikes due to uneven terrain and the proximity of the helicopter's tail to the slope.

[PH.IV.E.R6; FAA-H-8083-21]

26. What methods can a pilot use to assess collision risks on slopes?

By conducting a thorough preflight reconnaissance of the slope area, considering the helicopter's approach and departure paths, and evaluating any potential obstacles in the vicinity.

[PH.IV.E.R6; FAA-H-8083-21]

27. How can pilots mitigate collision risks during slope operations?

Mitigation strategies include choosing a slope clear of obstacles, using a spotter or ground crew to assist in identifying hazards, maintaining a high level of situational awareness, and performing slow, controlled maneuvers. Pilots should be prepared to abort the operation if an unforeseen hazard appears.

[PH.IV.E.R6; FAA-H-8083-21]

28. Why is managing collision risks important in slope operations?

Managing collision risks is vital in slope operations due to the increased complexity of the maneuver and the potential for reduced visibility and maneuvering space.

[PH.IV.E.R6; FAA-H-8083-21]

29. How can a pilot identify risks of exceeding manufacturer's slope limitations during slope operations?

By thoroughly understanding the manufacturer's slope limitations for the specific helicopter model, which are typically provided in the helicopter's flight manual. Pilots should evaluate the slope gradient, surface conditions, and helicopter loading against these limitations. Exceeding these limits can lead to loss of control or dynamic rollover.

[PH.IV.E.R7; FAA-H-8083-21]

30. How can pilots mitigate risks associated with exceeding slope limitations?

Pilots should adhere strictly to the manufacturer's specified limitations, choose landing areas within these limits, and conduct thorough preflight planning and in-flight evaluations.

[PH.IV.E.R7; FAA-H-8083-21]

31. Why is it important to manage the risk of exceeding the manufacturer's slope limitations?

Managing this risk is crucial because exceeding the manufacturer's slope limitations can significantly increase the likelihood of accidents, such as dynamic rollover, tail rotor strikes, or loss of control.

[PH.IV.E.R7; FAA-H-8083-21]

32. What best practices should pilots follow regarding manufacturer's slope limitations?

Best practices include familiarizing oneself with the helicopter's specific slope limitations, regular training in recognizing and operating within these limits, and using judgment to err on the side of caution, especially in uncertain conditions.

[PH.IV.E.R7; FAA-H-8083-21]

Skills to be demonstrated:

- Select a suitable slope.

- Complete the appropriate checklist(s).

- Properly approach the slope considering wind effect and obstacles.

- Maintain engine and rotor RPM within normal limits.

- Maintain heading and ground position and prevent movement of aircraft on slope.

- Make a smooth positive descent to touch the upslope skid or wheel(s) on the sloping surface.

- Recognize if the slope is too steep and abandon the operation prior to reaching cyclic control stops.

- Maintain positive control while lowering the downslope skid or wheel to touchdown.

- Neutralize controls after landing.

- Make a smooth transition from the slope to a stabilized hover parallel to the slope.

- Properly move away from the slope.

- Maintain a specified heading throughout the operation, ±10°.

Takeoffs, Landings, and Go-Arounds

5

A. Normal Takeoff and Climb

1. What are the effects of atmospheric conditions, including wind, on helicopter takeoff and climb performance during a normal takeoff and climb?

Atmospheric conditions significantly impact helicopter performance. Wind direction and speed can alter lift and thrust, affecting takeoff distance and climb rate. Headwinds generally enhance performance by increasing lift, while tailwinds may decrease lift and extend takeoff distance.

[PH.V.A.K1; FAA-H-8083-21]

2. How does wind direction affect a helicopter's takeoff and climb during a normal operation?

Wind direction plays a crucial role. A headwind increases airspeed, enhancing lift and allowing for a shorter takeoff distance and steeper climb. Conversely, a tailwind reduces effective lift, necessitating a longer takeoff roll and potentially a shallower climb.

[PH.V.A.K1; FAA-H-8083-21]

3. What is the impact of wind speed on a helicopter's takeoff and climb?

Wind speed affects the helicopter's performance by altering the relative airspeed over the rotor blades. Higher wind speeds, particularly headwinds, can lead to more efficient takeoffs and quicker climb rates due to increased lift. However, strong winds, especially gusts, may require additional pilot input to maintain control and stability during takeoff and climb.

[PH.V.A.K1; FAA-H-8083-21]

4. How do temperature and pressure altitude influence a helicopter's takeoff and climb performance?

Higher temperatures and higher pressure altitudes result in lower air density, which reduces engine power output and rotor efficiency. This can lead to longer takeoff distances and reduced climb performance. Pilots must account for these factors, especially in hot-and-high conditions, to ensure safe takeoff and climb operations.

[PH.V.A.K1; FAA-H-8083-21]

5. **What factors affect the profile of the height/velocity (H/V) diagram during a normal takeoff and climb?**

The profile of the height/velocity (H/V) diagram is affected by several factors, including helicopter weight, density altitude, wind conditions, and the helicopter's power and performance characteristics. The weight of the helicopter influences its ability to maneuver and achieve safe airspeeds. Density altitude affects engine and rotor performance, impacting the safe operating envelope. Wind conditions can alter the velocity component of the diagram, and the helicopter's specific design and performance capabilities define the safe operational areas within the H/V diagram.

[PH.V.A.K2; FAA-H-8083-21]

6. **How does helicopter weight influence the H/V diagram during normal takeoff and climb?**

Helicopter weight directly impacts the aircraft's performance. Heavier weights require more power for takeoff and reduce climb rates, potentially altering the safe operating areas within the H/V diagram. A heavier helicopter may have a reduced safe envelope for takeoff and climb, requiring careful consideration of airspeed and altitude to avoid areas of high risk on the H/V diagram.

[PH.V.A.K2; FAA-H-8083-21]

7. **What is the impact of density altitude on the H/V diagram during normal operations?**

Density altitude, which is altitude corrected for non-standard temperature and pressure, affects air density and therefore the performance of both the engine and rotor system. Higher density altitudes (hotter and/or higher altitude conditions) result in reduced performance, which can narrow the safe operational areas on the H/V diagram, particularly affecting the helicopter's ability to climb effectively.

[PH.V.A.K2; FAA-H-8083-21]

8. **How can a pilot identify risks associated with selecting a takeoff path based on helicopter performance and limitations, available distance, and wind?**

   Identifying risks involves evaluating the helicopter's performance capabilities and limitations in relation to the environment. This includes assessing the helicopter's weight, power available, wind direction and strength, and the available takeoff distance. Risks arise when the chosen path does not align with these factors, potentially leading to insufficient lift or obstacle clearance.

   [PH.V.A.R1; FAA-H-8083-21]

9. **What methods can a pilot use to assess risks in takeoff path selection?**

   To assess risks, pilots should analyze current weather conditions, particularly wind, and consider the helicopter's load and performance data. Assessing the terrain and any potential obstacles in the takeoff path is also crucial. Pilots should use performance charts to ensure the chosen path aligns with the helicopter's capabilities and the environmental conditions.

   [PH.V.A.R1; FAA-H-8083-21]

10. **How can pilots mitigate risks associated with takeoff path selection?**

    Mitigation strategies include thoroughly planning the takeoff considering all performance and environmental factors. Pilots should select a path that ensures the best performance given the wind direction and strength, while also considering obstacle clearance. Regularly practicing takeoffs in varying conditions and staying updated with the latest weather reports can also help mitigate risks.

    [PH.V.A.R1; FAA-H-8083-21]

11. **Why is risk management important in selecting a takeoff path for helicopters?**

    Improper selection can lead to hazardous situations, such as inability to clear obstacles, loss of control, or insufficient lift. It ensures the safest and most efficient use of the helicopter's capabilities while accounting for environmental conditions.

    [PH.V.A.R1; FAA-H-8083-21]

12. **How can a pilot identify risks associated with crosswinds during a normal takeoff and climb?**

    Risks associated with crosswinds can be identified by evaluating wind direction and speed relative to the helicopter's takeoff path. Crosswinds can affect lift and control, making it challenging to maintain the desired flight path. The pilot should assess the crosswind component against the helicopter's crosswind limitations and be alert to signs of control difficulties or drift.

    [PH.V.A.R2a; FAA-H-8083-21]

13. **How can pilots mitigate risks associated with crosswinds in normal takeoff and climb?**

    Pilots can mitigate crosswind risks by adjusting their takeoff technique, such as by using more aggressive control inputs to counteract the crosswind. The takeoff path should be aligned to minimize the crosswind component. Pilots should be prepared to abort the takeoff if the crosswind exceeds safe operational limits or if control issues arise.

    [PH.V.A.R2a; FAA-H-8083-21]

14. **How can a pilot identify risks associated with wind shear during a normal takeoff and climb?**

    Identifying risks associated with wind shear involves monitoring weather conditions for indications of sudden changes in wind speed or direction. This can include listening to weather reports, ATC advisories, and checking for visual signs like dust patterns or changes in cloud movements. Pilots should be particularly vigilant in conditions conducive to wind shear, such as thunderstorms or strong temperature gradients.

    [PH.V.A.R2b; FAA-H-8083-25]

15. **What methods can a pilot use to assess wind shear risks during takeoff and climb?**

    To assess wind shear risks, pilots should analyze weather reports for wind shear warnings, observe environmental cues indicating changing wind patterns, and consider reports from other pilots. They should also evaluate the performance capabilities of their helicopter against potential wind shear conditions, taking into account factors like weight, altitude, and available power.

    [PH.V.A.R2b; FAA-H-8083-25]

16. How can a pilot identify risks associated with tailwinds during a normal takeoff and climb?

Tailwinds reduce the effective lift and extend the distance required for takeoff, which could lead to insufficient altitude gain and difficulty in clearing obstacles. Observing wind indicators like windsocks and considering weather reports are essential in identifying these risks.

[PH.V.A.R2c; FAA-H-8083-21]

17. What methods can a pilot use to assess tailwind risks during takeoff and climb?

Pilots should assess tailwind risks by checking the latest weather reports for wind direction and speed. It is crucial to compare the wind information against the helicopter's performance data to understand how the tailwind might impact takeoff distance, climb rate, and overall control.

[PH.V.A.R2c; FAA-H-8083-21]

18. How can a pilot identify risks associated with turbulence, including wake turbulence, during a normal takeoff and climb?

Risks associated with turbulence and wake turbulence can be identified by observing weather conditions that indicate potential turbulence, such as strong winds, thunderstorms, or temperature inversions. Wake turbulence risks are higher near airports with heavy aircraft operations. Pilots should be aware of the flight paths of larger aircraft and time intervals between takeoffs and landings to gauge wake turbulence risk.

[PH.V.A.R2d; FAA-H-8083-25]

19. What methods can a pilot use to assess turbulence risks during takeoff and climb?

Pilots should assess turbulence risks by checking weather forecasts, particularly for wind shear, thermal activity, and convective conditions. For wake turbulence, pilots need to consider the size and type of nearby aircraft and their flight paths. Using ATC information and observing the movements of other aircraft can help in assessing the likelihood and severity of turbulence.

[PH.V.A.R2d; FAA-H-8083-25]

20. How can pilots mitigate risks associated with turbulence and wake turbulence in normal takeoff and climb?

To mitigate these risks, pilots should avoid areas known for significant turbulence and plan takeoff and climb paths that steer clear of the flight paths of larger aircraft to avoid wake turbulence. Increasing airspeed within safe limits can provide more control in turbulent conditions. Pilots should be prepared with techniques to maintain control and altitude in turbulent air and should communicate with ATC for information on potential turbulence areas.

[PH.V.A.R2d; FAA-H-8083-25]

21. How can a pilot identify risks associated with runway/departure point surface and condition during a normal takeoff and climb?

Risks can be identified by inspecting the takeoff surface for conditions such as uneven terrain, loose gravel, wet or icy patches, and obstacles. The surface condition can significantly affect the helicopter's performance, including traction, lift-off, and climb.

[PH.V.A.R2e; FAA-H-8083-21]

22. How can pilots mitigate risks associated with runway/departure point surface conditions?

To mitigate these risks, pilots should choose the most suitable area for takeoff, considering the surface condition. Adjusting takeoff techniques to match the surface, such as a running takeoff on rough terrain, can also be effective.

[PH.V.A.R2e; FAA-H-8083-21]

23. Why is it important to manage risks associated with runway/departure point surface and condition?

Managing these risks is important because surface conditions can drastically affect the helicopter's ability to safely take off and achieve a stable climb. Poor surface conditions can lead to control issues, reduced lift, and potential damage to the helicopter.

[PH.V.A.R2e; FAA-H-8083-21]

24. How can a pilot identify risks associated with abnormal operations and a rejected takeoff during a normal takeoff and climb?

Risks associated with abnormal operations and a rejected takeoff can be identified by evaluating factors like helicopter performance limitations, prevailing weather conditions, potential mechanical issues, and runway or departure area obstructions. Pilots should be vigilant for any indications of abnormal performance or handling issues during the takeoff roll and be prepared for immediate action.

[PH.V.A.R3a; FAA-H-8083-21]

25. What methods can a pilot use to assess the risk of a rejected takeoff?

To assess the risk of a rejected takeoff, pilots should consider the helicopter's weight, engine performance, wind conditions, and runway or departure area length. Reviewing emergency procedures and understanding the specific criteria for aborting a takeoff, such as unusual noises, warning lights, or inadequate lift, are also crucial.

[PH.V.A.R3a; FAA-H-8083-21]

26. How can pilots mitigate risks associated with planning for a rejected takeoff?

Mitigation strategies include thorough preflight planning, understanding the helicopter's emergency procedures, and having a clear plan for a rejected takeoff. Pilots should mentally rehearse the actions they would take in case of an aborted takeoff and ensure they are familiar with the helicopter's performance characteristics under current conditions.

[PH.V.A.R3a; FAA-H-8083-21]

27. How can a pilot identify risks associated with powerplant failure during the takeoff and climb phase?

Risks of powerplant failure can be identified by monitoring engine performance indicators, being aware of any unusual engine sounds or vibrations, and understanding the helicopter's powerplant reliability history.

[PH.V.A.R3b; FAA-H-8083-21]

28. What methods can a pilot use to assess the risk of powerplant failure during takeoff and climb?

By reviewing the helicopter's maintenance records, understanding the performance characteristics of the engine, and being familiar with the warning signs of engine trouble.

[PH.V.A.R3b; FAA-H-8083-21]

29. How can pilots mitigate risks associated with powerplant failure during takeoff and climb?

To mitigate these risks, pilots should be proficient in emergency procedures for powerplant failure, including autorotation and immediate landing techniques. They should ensure that all engine systems are functioning optimally before takeoff.

[PH.V.A.R3b; FAA-H-8083-21]

30. Why is risk management important for powerplant failure during the takeoff and climb phase?

Effective risk management for powerplant failure is crucial because this type of failure during takeoff and climb is a high-risk scenario that requires immediate and correct action. Being prepared and knowing how to respond can prevent accidents and ensure the safety of the flight, especially when altitude and airspeed are limited.

[PH.V.A.R3b; FAA-H-8083-21]

31. How can a pilot identify collision hazards during a normal takeoff and climb?

By maintaining a thorough lookout for other aircraft in the vicinity, observing the movement of ground vehicles and personnel near the departure area, and being aware of potential airborne obstacles like birds or drones.

[PH.V.A.R4; FAA-H-8083-25]

32. What methods can a pilot use to assess collision risk during takeoff and climb?

By constantly scanning the environment during takeoff and climb, using both visual observation and onboard collision avoidance systems if available. They should also consider the volume of traffic, visibility conditions, and any known flight path intersections with other aircraft.

[PH.V.A.R4; FAA-H-8083-25]

33. How can pilots mitigate risks associated with collision hazards during takeoff and climb?

To mitigate collision risks, pilots should adhere to standard traffic patterns, maintain clear and concise communication with ATC, and follow their instructions diligently. They should use lights and other visibility aids to enhance the helicopter's conspicuity and keep a vigilant lookout for other aircraft, especially in areas with high traffic density.

[PH.V.A.R4; FAA-H-8083-25]

34. Why is risk management important for collision hazards during the takeoff and climb phase?

Effective risk management for collision hazards is critical because the takeoff and climb phase is a busy period with high potential for conflicting traffic paths. Proper management ensures the pilot's situational awareness and readiness to react to potential collision threats, thereby maintaining flight safety.

[PH.V.A.R4; FAA-H-8083-25]

35. How can a pilot identify risks associated with distractions, task prioritization, loss of situational awareness, or disorientation during takeoff and climb?

Risks can be identified by noticing moments of excessive cockpit activity, complex ATC instructions, or environmental factors that demand high attention. Recognizing feelings of being overwhelmed or unsure about the aircraft's position or status also indicates potential risks.

[PH.V.A.R5; FAA-H-8083-2]

36. **What methods can a pilot use to assess these risks during takeoff and climb?**

    Pilots should assess these risks by evaluating the complexity of the takeoff environment, including weather conditions, traffic density, and navigational challenges. Self-assessment of mental workload and stress levels is also important.

    [PH.V.A.R5; FAA-H-8083-2]

37. **How can pilots mitigate risks associated with distractions and loss of situational awareness?**

    To mitigate these risks, pilots should establish and adhere to a structured cockpit routine, prioritize tasks based on their importance and urgency, and use effective communication techniques. Maintaining a clean and organized cockpit, using checklists, and dividing tasks among crew members, if applicable, can reduce distractions.

    [PH.V.A.R5; FAA-H-8083-2]

38. **How can a pilot identify risks associated with runway incursion during a normal takeoff and climb?**

    Risks of runway incursion can be identified by monitoring ATC communications for other aircraft clearances, observing the movement and position of other aircraft and vehicles on the ground, and being aware of the airport's layout, including taxiways and hot spots. Pilots should also look for any unclear or conflicting ATC instructions and be aware of their own position relative to runways and taxiways.

    [PH.V.A.R6; FAA-H-8083-25]

39. **How can pilots mitigate risks associated with runway incursions during takeoff and climb?**

    Mitigation strategies include thorough preflight planning with a focus on understanding the airport layout, confirming all ATC instructions before proceeding, using airport diagrams for navigation, and maintaining vigilance in observing other aircraft and ground vehicle movements.

    [PH.V.A.R6; FAA-H-8083-25]

40. Why is risk management important for preventing runway incursions during the takeoff and climb phase?

Risk management is vital in this context because runway incursions can lead to dangerous conflicts and potential collisions. Managing these risks ensures the safety of all airport users by preventing unauthorized aircraft, vehicles, or personnel from entering runways and interfering with takeoff and landing operations.

[PH.V.A.R6; FAA-H-8083-25]

Skills to be demonstrated:

• Complete the appropriate checklist(s).

• Make radio calls as appropriate.

• Verify assigned/correct runway, if at an airport.

• Determine wind direction with or without visible wind direction indicators.

• Clear the area, taxi into the takeoff position and align the helicopter on the runway centerline or with the takeoff path.

• Establish a stationary position on the surface or a stabilized hover, prior to takeoff in headwind and crosswind conditions.

• Confirm takeoff power and instrument indications prior to forward movement.

• After clearing all obstacles, transition to normal climb attitude, airspeed, ±10 knots, and power setting.

• Maintain engine and rotor RPM within normal limits.

• Maintain proper ground track with crosswind correction, as needed.

• Comply with noise abatement procedures, as applicable.

• Use runway incursion avoidance procedures, if applicable.

B. Normal Approach and Landing

1. What should a pilot understand about the effects of wind on normal approach and landing performance?

A pilot should understand that wind direction and speed significantly affect approach and landing. Headwinds increase performance by reducing groundspeed, making landings more controlled, while tailwinds decrease performance by increasing groundspeed, potentially leading to overshooting the landing area.

[PH.V.B.K1; FAA-H-8083-21]

2. How are approach paths adjusted based on wind conditions?

The approach path is adjusted by changing the helicopter's descent rate and speed to compensate for the wind's effect on ground speed and trajectory. Pilots must continuously assess wind conditions and make adjustments throughout the approach to maintain the correct flight path and ensure a safe landing.

[PH.V.B.K2; FAA-H-8083-21]

3. What techniques are used for crosswind correction during the final approach and landing?

In crosswind conditions, pilots should use the crab method during the initial approach to maintain the desired track by pointing the helicopter slightly into the wind. As they approach the landing zone, transitioning to a sideslip by aligning the helicopter's nose with the landing path and applying opposite cyclic control is essential to counteract the crosswind.

[PH.V.B.K2; FAA-H-8083-21]

4. What should a pilot understand about landing surfaces for normal approach and landing?

Pilots need to understand the types of surfaces suitable for landing, such as paved runways, grass fields, or helipads, and how different surfaces can affect helicopter performance. Surface conditions should be assessed for potential hazards like loose debris, slippery or uneven areas, and to ensure the surface can support the helicopter's weight.

[PH.V.B.K3; FAA-H-8083-21]

5. What factors should be considered in selecting a suitable touchdown point?

When selecting a touchdown point, pilots should consider factors like wind direction and speed, helicopter performance capabilities, available landing area size, and any emergency procedures needed.

[PH.V.B.K3; FAA-H-8083-21]

6. What factors influence the profile of the height/velocity (H/V) diagram during normal approach and landing?

The profile of the H/V diagram is influenced by factors such as helicopter weight, wind conditions, air density (affected by altitude and temperature), and helicopter performance characteristics. Understanding how these factors affect the safe operational envelope is crucial for pilots, as they dictate the ideal altitude and airspeed combinations for safe operations during approach and landing phases.

[PH.V.B.K4; FAA-H-8083-21]

7. How can a pilot identify risks associated with the selection of approach path and landing based on aircraft performance and limitations, and wind?

Risks can be identified by assessing the helicopter's current performance capabilities, including weight and balance, power availability, and any mechanical limitations. Understanding how wind conditions, such as speed and direction, will affect the approach and landing is also crucial.

[PH.V.B.R1; FAA-H-8083-21]

8. What methods can a pilot use to assess crosswind risks during approach and landing?

To assess crosswind risks, pilots should consider the wind's strength and angle relative to the runway or landing path, the helicopter's crosswind limitations as specified in the flight manual, and their own proficiency in handling crosswinds. The assessment should also include the potential for gusts and changes in wind direction, which can further complicate the approach and landing phases.

[PH.V.B.R2a; FAA-H-8083-21]

9. How can a pilot identify risks associated with wind shear during a normal approach and landing?

Risks associated with wind shear can be identified by monitoring weather reports and ATC communications for wind shear warnings, observing sudden changes in wind direction and speed, and noting unexpected aircraft performance changes such as rapid airspeed fluctuations or uncommanded altitude changes. Pilots should also be vigilant in areas where wind shear is commonly encountered, like near large buildings, mountains, or during thunderstorms.

[PH.V.B.R2b; FAA-H-8083-21]

10. How can a pilot identify risks associated with tailwind effects during a normal approach and landing?

A pilot can identify tailwind risks by checking wind direction and speed reports, observing windsocks or other wind indicators, and noting increased ground speed during approach. A tailwind condition can be inferred from longer than expected glide paths, reduced descent rates, and difficulties in reducing speed for landing.

[PH.V.B.R2c; FAA-H-8083-25]

11. How can a pilot identify risks associated with turbulence and wake turbulence during a normal approach and landing?

A pilot can identify these risks by monitoring weather conditions known to cause turbulence, such as strong winds or storm fronts, and by being aware of traffic patterns to anticipate wake turbulence from larger aircraft. Signs of turbulence include erratic changes in airspeed, altitude, and uncommanded aircraft movements. For wake turbulence, pilots should be particularly cautious when operating behind larger aircraft, especially during takeoffs and landings.

[PH.V.B.R2d; FAA-H-8083-25]

12. How can a pilot identify risks associated with vortex ring state (VRS) during a normal approach and landing?

Risks associated with VRS can be identified by recognizing conditions conducive to its development, such as decelerating below ETL (16-24kts) with a vertical descent greater than 300 fpm descent rate while using more than 20% power. Warning signs include a rapid increase in descent rate and vibrations, despite increasing collective pitch. Pilots should be vigilant when descending at low forward speeds or during steep approaches, as these are common scenarios for VRS.

[PH.V.B.R2e; FAA-H-8083-21]

13. How can pilots mitigate risks associated with touchdown surface and condition?

To mitigate these risks, pilots should choose landing sites that are suitable for the helicopter's capabilities and avoid surfaces that may be hazardous. They should use appropriate approach techniques for different surfaces, such as a higher hover on loose surfaces to avoid debris. Additionally, pilots should be prepared to abort the landing and go around if the surface condition appears to be unsafe as they get closer.

[PH.V.B.R2f; FAA-H-8083-21]

14. How can a pilot identify risks associated with a go-around/rejected landing during a normal approach and landing?

Risks can be identified by monitoring for situations like unstable approaches, excessive airspeed or descent rate, misalignment with the landing area, unexpected obstacles, or sudden changes in wind conditions. Pilots should also be aware of their own proficiency and comfort level with the approach and be ready to initiate a go-around if conditions are not ideal for a safe landing.

[PH.V.B.R3; FAA-H-8083-21]

15. What methods can a pilot use to assess these risks during approach and landing?

Pilots should assess collision risks by evaluating the density of air traffic, visibility conditions, and the complexity of the airspace. They should also consider their proficiency in traffic pattern operations and collision avoidance maneuvers. Assessing the adequacy of communication with ATC and other pilots in the area, especially in non-towered airports, is also important.

[PH.V.B.R4; FAA-H-8083-25]

16. How can a pilot identify risks associated with distractions, task prioritization, loss of situational awareness, or disorientation during a normal approach and landing?

Risks can be identified by monitoring for signs of excessive workload or stress, such as missing radio calls, fixating on a single task, or feeling rushed. Recognizing when one is deviating from standard procedures or experiencing confusion about current flight status and location also indicates a risk. Being aware of potential in-flight distractions, such as complex ATC instructions or unexpected system alerts, is key.

[PH.V.B.R5; FAA-H-8083-25]

17. What methods can a pilot use to assess LTE risks during approach and landing?

Pilots should assess LTE risks by considering factors like wind direction and speed relative to the helicopter's flight path, the helicopter's weight and center of gravity, and the current power setting. Evaluating the flight environment, such as operating near obstacles or in turbulent air, and understanding the specific LTE characteristics of their helicopter model are also critical.

[PH.V.B.R6; FAA-H-8083-21]

Skills to be demonstrated:

• Complete the appropriate checklist(s).

• Make radio calls as appropriate.

• Determine wind direction with or without visible wind direction indicators.

• Align the helicopter with the correct/assigned runway or touchdown point.

• Scan the landing area/touchdown point and adjoining area for traffic and obstructions.

• Maintain proper ground track with crosswind correction, if necessary.

• Establish and maintain a normal approach angle and rate of closure.

• Maintain engine and rotor RPM within normal limits.

• Arrive at the termination point, on the surface or at a stabilized hover, ±4 feet.

• Use runway incursion avoidance procedures, if applicable.

C. Maximum Performance Takeoff and Climb

1. What situations necessitate a maximum performance takeoff and climb in helicopter operations?

A maximum performance takeoff and climb are typically required in situations where obstacle clearance is critical, such as in confined areas or urban environments with tall structures. It is also appropriate when operating in high-density altitude conditions where helicopter performance is reduced, or when taking off from hot and high environments that demand maximum lift capability.

[PH.V.C.K1; FAA-H-8083-21]

2. How do atmospheric conditions like wind and temperature affect maximum performance takeoff and climb in helicopter operations?

High temperatures and high-density altitudes can decrease air density, reducing rotor efficiency and engine power, thereby limiting the helicopter's climb performance. Headwinds can enhance climb performance by increasing airspeed and lift.

[PH.V.C.K2; FAA-H-8083-21]

3. In what ways do environmental conditions like terrain and obstacles affect the H/V diagram during maximum performance takeoff and climb?

Operating in mountainous terrain or areas with significant obstacles requires careful consideration of the H/V diagram to ensure safe obstacle clearance. These conditions might demand steeper climb angles and higher climb rates, influencing the safe operational zones on the H/V diagram. Pilots need to be adept at interpreting and adjusting their flight path based on these environmental factors to maintain safety while adhering to the H/V diagram's constraints where possible.

[PH.V.C.K3; FAA-H-8083-21]

4. How can a pilot identify risks associated with the selection of takeoff path for maximum performance takeoff and climb?

Pilots must consider factors like wind direction and speed, which can greatly affect performance during takeoff. Assessing the environment for obstacles or terrain that may influence the takeoff path is also crucial.

[PH.V.C.R1; FAA-H-8083-21]

5. How can pilots mitigate risks associated with crosswinds during maximum performance takeoff and climb?

Pilots should plan the takeoff path to minimize crosswind effects, possibly by choosing a different takeoff direction if possible. Being prepared to adjust the takeoff technique based on actual wind conditions are key. Continuous monitoring of wind changes during takeoff is also essential for timely response to crosswind effects.

[PH.V.C.R2a; FAA-H-8083-21]

6. How can pilots mitigate risks associated with wind shear during maximum performance takeoff and climb?

By avoiding takeoff or climb in known or forecasted wind shear conditions whenever possible. If wind shear is encountered during takeoff, applying appropriate power and control inputs to maintain airspeed and climb performance is crucial. Pilots should also be prepared for rapid changes in flight path and maintain extra vigilance to react promptly.

[PH.V.C.R2b; FAA-H-8083-21]

7. How can pilots mitigate risks associated with tailwinds during maximum performance takeoff and climb?

To mitigate tailwind risks, pilots should, if possible, adjust the takeoff direction to minimize tailwind effects or wait for more favorable wind conditions. While taking off with a tailwind is not recommended, pilots should be prepared for longer takeoff distances and reduced climb rates, and ensure they have adequate clearance over obstacles.

[PH.V.C.R2c; FAA-H-8083-21]

8. How can pilots mitigate risks associated with turbulence, including wake turbulence, during maximum performance takeoff and climb?

To mitigate turbulence risks, pilots should alter their flight path to avoid areas of known turbulence or wake turbulence, such as altering takeoff direction or timing to avoid the path of larger aircraft.

[PH.V.C.R2d; FAA-H-8083-21]

9. How can pilots mitigate risks associated with surface conditions during maximum performance takeoff and climb?

To mitigate surface condition risks, pilots should choose the most suitable takeoff area considering the current surface conditions. Adjusting takeoff techniques to account for reduced traction or increased rolling resistance is important. Pilots should also consider delaying takeoff until conditions improve or relocating to a more suitable takeoff point if feasible.

[PH.V.C.R2e; FAA-H-8083-21]

10. How can pilots mitigate risks associated with rejected takeoffs during maximum performance takeoff and climb?

To mitigate these risks, pilots should have a clear plan for handling emergencies, including rejected takeoffs. This involves knowing the specific procedures for their helicopter, maintaining situational awareness, and being prepared to take immediate action if a problem arises. Have a plan!

[PH.V.C.R3a; FAA-H-8083-21]

11. How can a pilot identify risks associated with powerplant failure during the takeoff/climb phase in maximum performance takeoff and climb?

Risks of powerplant failure can be identified by monitoring engine performance indicators, like temperature, pressure, and RPM, for abnormalities. Pilots should be alert to any unusual engine sounds or vibrations and changes in helicopter performance, such as unexpected loss of lift or thrust. Additionally pilots must have a plan for where to go in the event of an engine failure.

[PH.V.C.R3b; FAA-H-8083-21]

12. Why is risk management important for handling collision hazards during maximum performance takeoff and climb?

Effective risk management in avoiding collision hazards is critical as the takeoff and climb phases are vulnerable to conflicts with other aircraft, especially near airports and in controlled airspace. Proper risk management ensures the pilot remains alert to potential hazards, enabling timely and appropriate actions to avoid collisions and maintain safety throughout the flight.

[PH.V.C.R4; FAA-H-8083-21]

13. How can pilots mitigate risks associated with low rotor RPM during maximum performance takeoff and climb?

Mitigating risks of low rotor RPM involves ensuring the helicopter is not overloaded and adhering to recommended power settings and operational limits. Pilots should continuously monitor rotor RPM during takeoff and climb, ready to adjust throttle or collective as needed to maintain optimal RPM.

[PH.V.C.R5; FAA-H-8083-21]

14. How can pilots mitigate risks associated with distractions and loss of situational awareness during maximum performance takeoff and climb?

To mitigate these risks, pilots should establish a systematic workflow and adhere to standard operating procedures, including the use of checklists. Maintaining a sterile cockpit during critical phases of flight, where nonessential communications are minimized, can help reduce distractions.

[PH.V.C.R6; FAA-H-8083-21]

Skills to be demonstrated:

- Complete the appropriate checklist(s).

- Make radio calls as appropriate.

- Use control inputs to initiate lift-off from the takeoff position using a forward climb attitude to fly the departure profile.

- Maintain engine and rotor RPM within normal limits.

- Use required takeoff power, or power as specified by the evaluator.

- After clearing all obstacles, transition to normal climb attitude, airspeed, ±5 knots, and power setting.

- Maintain directional control, ground track, and proper wind-drift correction throughout the maneuver.

D. Steep Approach

1. What is a stabilized steep approach and what are its key characteristics?

A steep approach is used primarily when there are obstacles in the approach path that are too high to allow a normal approach. A steep approach permits entry into most confined areas and is sometimes used to avoid areas of turbulence around a pinnacle. An approach angle of approximately 13° to 15° is considered a steep approach.

[PH.V.D.K1; FAA-H-8083-21]

2. How should a pilot perform a steep approach?

During a steep approach, maintain alignment with the wind as much as possible at the recommended approach airspeed. Lower the collective to initiate descent and deceleration, adjusting the antitorque pedal for trim. As the approach angle is steeper, reduce the collective more than in a normal approach, decelerate with slight aft cyclic, and smoothly lower the collective to maintain the approach angle.

[PH.V.D.K2; FAA-H-8083-21]

3. What are the techniques for steep approaches and when are they applicable?

These techniques are applicable in situations where obstacle clearance is necessary, in confined areas, or when operating in environments where minimizing noise impact is required. Pilots must carefully manage airspeed, descent rate, and rotor RPM, and be prepared for increased power demand as they transition to hover. It is crucial to maintain a constant angle of descent and avoid high rates of closure with the landing area. Precision and control are key in steep approaches to ensure a safe landing.

[PH.V.D.K2; FAA-H-8083-21]

4. How does performance data and the height/velocity (H/V) diagram relate to conducting a steep approach?

The H/V diagram shows safe combinations of altitude and airspeed for a particular helicopter, especially in single-engine operations. When planning a steep approach, pilots must consider these parameters to ensure they remain within the safe operating envelope of the helicopter where possible. This involves analyzing data like power available, power required, wind conditions, and weight to determine if the helicopter can perform the steep approach without entering areas of high risk for vortex ring state or low rotor RPM.

[PH.V.D.K3; FAA-H-8083-21]

5. What are the effects of atmospheric conditions on approach and landing performance in steep approaches?

Atmospheric conditions significantly impact the performance of a helicopter during steep approaches. Factors such as wind speed and direction can affect the approach path and descent rate. Tailwinds can lead to a steeper approach angle with higher ground speeds, while headwinds may cause a shallower approach and slower groundspeed. Crosswinds require careful control to maintain alignment with the landing area. Temperature and altitude also influence helicopter performance, as higher temperatures and altitudes reduce air density, potentially leading to decreased lift and engine performance.

[PH.V.D.K4; FAA-H-8083-21]

6. What are the wind correction techniques relevant to conducting a steep approach?

Pilots must adjust the approach path based on the wind direction and speed. Throughout the approach, pilots should continuously adjust their inputs to maintain a stable descent path, compensating for any wind drift and ensuring a controlled and precise touchdown.

[PH.V.D.K5; FAA-H-8083-21]

7. How do aircraft performance and limitations affect conducting a steep approach?

The aircraft's performance data, including maximum allowable descent rates, power availability, and rotor RPM limits, dictate how steep an approach can be executed. Limitations like maximum wind conditions for operation, weight restrictions, and power margins must be considered to ensure the helicopter can maintain control and stability during the steep descent. Pilots must be aware of their specific aircraft's capabilities and adhere to these parameters to avoid scenarios such as rotor RPM decay, vortex ring state, or loss of tail rotor effectiveness, which can compromise safety during a steep approach.

[PH.V.D.K6; FAA-H-8083-21]

8. What should a pilot be aware of regarding the loss of effective translational lift during steep approaches?

Be aware that the loss of effective translational lift occurs at a higher altitude during a steep approach. An increase in collective is needed to prevent settling, along with additional forward cyclic to achieve the proper rate of closure, allowing the helicopter to halt at a hover altitude of 3 feet over the intended landing point with minimal additional power required.

[PH.V.D.K6; FAA-H-8083-21]

9. What methods are used to assess risks in selecting approach paths for steep approaches in varying wind conditions?

Assessing risks involves a thorough evaluation of current weather reports and forecasts, understanding the helicopter's limitations in the specific wind conditions, and considering alternate approaches or landing sites if necessary. Pilots should use performance charts to determine the helicopter's capabilities in the given conditions, taking into account factors like weight, temperature, and altitude. Practicing situational awareness and being prepared to adjust the approach or abort if conditions deteriorate is also key in risk assessment.

[PH.V.D.R1; FAA-H-8083-21]

10. What methods are used to assess risks related to wind direction in steep approaches?

Risk assessment includes analyzing current and forecasted wind conditions, understanding how wind direction affects rotorcraft performance and stability during a steep approach, and considering the helicopter's limitations. Pilots should use performance charts and calculations to determine the impact of wind on descent path and airspeed control. Additionally, continuous monitoring of wind changes during the approach is essential for a real-time assessment.

[PH.V.D.R2a; FAA-H-8083-21]

11. Why is it important for pilots to manage the risks associated with wind shear during steep approaches?

Wind shear can cause abrupt changes in flight dynamics, potentially leading to loss of control or unintentional altitude changes. By understanding and preparing for the possibility of wind shear, pilots can maintain better control over the helicopter, ensuring a safe approach and landing. Effective risk management also involves being ready to abort the approach and execute a go-around if wind shear conditions become too severe for a safe landing.

[PH.V.D.R2b; FAA-H-8083-21]

12. What mitigation strategies can be employed for turbulence and wake turbulence during steep approaches?

To mitigate risks associated with turbulence during steep approaches, pilots should adjust their approach path to avoid known turbulence areas or wake vortices. This might involve increasing separation behind large aircraft or altering the flight path to stay clear of their wake. Pilots should also be prepared to adjust airspeed, power, and control inputs to maintain stability in turbulent air.

[PH.V.D.R2c; FAA-H-8083-21]

13. What factors should a pilot assess when considering a rejected landing or go-around in a steep approach?

When considering a rejected landing or go-around, a pilot should assess factors such as the current altitude and airspeed, the helicopter's performance capabilities, wind conditions, and the presence of obstacles. It is important to evaluate whether it is safer to continue the approach or to execute a go-around. The pilot should also consider fuel reserves and the availability of alternative landing areas.

[PH.V.D.R3a; FAA-H-8083-21]

14. What are effective strategies to mitigate the risks associated with powerplant failure during steep approaches?

Pilots should maintain proficiency in autorotation and emergency landing procedures. Regularly practicing emergency procedures under various conditions can prepare pilots for such events. Additionally, pilots should always have a plan for emergency landing areas throughout the approach phase and be ready to initiate autorotation if needed. Keeping altitude and airspeed within safe parameters for potential autorotation is also vital.

[PH.V.D.R3b; FAA-H-8083-21]

15. What factors should a pilot assess to evaluate the risk of collision during a steep approach?

A pilot should assess various factors to evaluate the risk of collision during a steep approach. These include the density of air traffic in the area, visibility conditions, the complexity of the airspace, and the proximity to other aircraft or obstacles. The pilot should also consider the helicopter's speed and trajectory, as these can affect the time available to react to a potential collision.

[PH.V.D.R4; FAA-H-8083-21]

16. What are effective mitigation strategies for VRS during steep approaches?

To mitigate VRS during steep approaches, pilots should avoid combinations of high descent rates and low forward airspeed. Maintaining an appropriate airspeed above the VRS threshold is vital. If VRS symptoms are detected, the recommended recovery procedure is to lower the collective slightly to reduce the descent rate, and simultaneously apply forward cyclic to gain airspeed.

[PH.V.D.R5; FAA-H-8083-21]

17. What factors should a pilot consider regarding the landing surface during steep approaches?

When considering the landing surface during steep approaches, a pilot should evaluate the size of the area, its slope, and the presence of any obstructions. The type of surface, whether it is solid, soft, or uneven, will affect the helicopter's landing gear and stability.

[PH.V.D.R6; FAA-H-8083-21]

18. **What are effective strategies for mitigating risks related to aircraft limitations in steep approaches?**

Effective strategies for mitigating risks related to aircraft limitations in steep approaches include thorough preflight planning and a comprehensive understanding of the helicopter's capabilities. Pilots should plan approaches within the safe operational envelope, considering factors like weight, temperature, and altitude. Staying within prescribed airspeeds and descent rates, and practicing steep approach maneuvers under varying conditions, can also help mitigate risks.

[PH.V.D.R7; FAA-H-8083-21]

19. **What factors should a pilot consider regarding task prioritization during steep approaches?**

In steep approaches, a pilot should consider factors such as the complexity of the maneuver, environmental conditions, helicopter performance, and traffic density. Prioritizing tasks that are critical for the safe execution of the approach, such as maintaining proper airspeed, descent rate, and alignment with the landing area, is essential. Nonessential tasks should be deferred or minimized during this critical phase of flight.

[PH.V.D.R8; FAA-H-8083-21]

20. **What strategies can a pilot employ to mitigate the risk of LTE during steep approaches?**

To mitigate the risk of LTE during steep approaches, pilots should avoid conditions that can lead to LTE, such as tailwinds, pedal turns at low speeds, and out-of-ground effect hover. They should maintain awareness of wind direction and speed and adjust their approach accordingly.

[PH.V.D.R9; FAA-H-8083-21]

21. **What factors should a pilot consider regarding DVE and flat light conditions during steep approaches?**

During steep approaches, pilots should consider factors like the current weather conditions, time of day, geographical location, and terrain. DVE and flat light conditions are more prevalent in areas with uniform terrain, such as snow-covered landscapes or deserts, and during times of low sun angle. The pilot must also consider the limitations of their own vision and how their helmet visor or cockpit glass may affect visibility.

[PH.V.D.R10; FAA-H-8083-21]

Skills to be demonstrated:

- Complete the appropriate checklist(s).

- Make radio calls as appropriate.

- Consider the wind direction and conditions, landing surface, and obstacles.

- Select a suitable termination point.

- Establish and maintain a steep approach angle, (15° maximum) and proper rate of closure.

- Maintain proper ground track with crosswind correction, if necessary.

- Maintain engine and rotor RPM within normal limits.

- Arrive at the termination point, on the surface or at a stabilized hover, ±4 feet.

- Use runway incursion avoidance procedures, if applicable.

E. Go-Around

1. How does a pilot determine when to execute a go-around during an approach?

A pilot determines when to execute a go-around by continuously assessing the approach's stability, including alignment with the landing area, descent rate, airspeed, and altitude. If at any point the approach becomes unstable, or if there is any doubt about the ability to land safely, the pilot should immediately initiate a go-around.

[PH.V.E.K1; FAA-H-8083-21]

2. What are the key considerations when executing a go-around in a helicopter?

Important considerations include immediate recognition and initiation of the maneuver, smooth power application to climb, adjusting pitch to maintain control, configuring the helicopter for the go-around, maintaining awareness to avoid obstacles, and communicating with ATC.

[PH.V.E.K1; FAA-H-8083-21]

3. How can a pilot prepare for a possible go-around during approach planning?

Preparation involves reviewing go-around procedures for the helicopter, identifying potential hazards near the landing area, understanding local traffic patterns and ATC procedures, briefing passengers, and mentally rehearsing the go-around steps.

[PH.V.E.K1; FAA-H-8083-21]

4. What are the consequences of delaying or failing to execute a go-around when needed?

Delaying or failing to execute a go-around can lead to collision risks, unstable approaches, potential accidents from persisting under worsening conditions, and increased chances of runway overshoots or hard landings. Prompt action is crucial to avoid these outcomes.

[PH.V.E.K1; FAA-H-8083-21]

5. What are the effects of atmospheric conditions on a go-around maneuver?

Atmospheric conditions such as wind, temperature, and humidity can significantly affect a go-around maneuver. High winds, especially crosswinds, can impact directional control. Hot and humid conditions can decrease helicopter performance, reducing climb rate and power availability.

[PH.V.E.K2; FAA-H-8083-21]

6. How do wind conditions affect a helicopter's performance during a go-around?

Wind conditions, especially strong or gusty winds, can significantly impact a helicopter's performance during a go-around by altering its airspeed, climb rate, and trajectory. Pilots must adjust their control inputs to compensate for wind effects, ensuring a stable climb out and repositioning for another approach if necessary.

[PH.V.E.K2; FAA-H-8083-21]

7. How does atmospheric density affect a go-around?

Atmospheric density, influenced by altitude, temperature, and humidity, affects engine performance and rotor efficiency. In high-density altitude conditions, the helicopter may have reduced climb performance, requiring pilots to anticipate the need for greater power settings and possibly a more gradual climb during a go-around.

[PH.V.E.K2; FAA-H-8083-21]

8. What role does turbulence play during a go-around maneuver?

Turbulence can complicate a go-around by making it more challenging to control the helicopter and maintain a steady climb path. Pilots must be prepared to counteract the turbulence effects with appropriate control inputs and may need to adjust the go-around procedure to ensure safety, such as initiating the maneuver at a higher altitude or speed to maintain control.

[PH.V.E.K2; FAA-H-8083-21]

9. How does a timely decision to go-around contribute to flight safety?

A timely decision to go-around contributes to flight safety by preventing situations that could lead to accidents or incidents, such as runway overruns or collisions. By deciding early, the pilot has more control and space to execute the go-around safely, ensuring enough altitude and airspeed are available for a stable climb. Delaying the decision can lead to rushed maneuvers and potential loss of control, especially in helicopters where power and climb performance are critical.

[PH.V.E.K3; FAA-H-8083-21]

10. What situations may necessitate a go-around during helicopter operations?

Situations that may require a go-around include Unexpected obstacles on the landing area, sudden changes in wind conditions, traffic conflicts, and any scenario where continuing the approach or landing could compromise safety. The pilot must remain vigilant and ready to initiate a go-around if the approach does not meet safety criteria.

[PH.V.E.K3; FAA-H-8083-21]

11. How can a pilot effectively assess the situation for a potential go-around?

Effective assessment for a potential go-around involves monitoring the approach parameters continuously, such as airspeed, altitude, descent rate, and helicopter alignment with the intended landing path. Pilots should also be vigilant for changes in wind or weather conditions, traffic conflicts, or any indications of mechanical issues. Regular training and practicing go-arounds under various conditions can enhance a pilot's ability to assess and react appropriately.

[PH.V.E.R1; FAA-H-8083-21]

12. What risk management strategies should a pilot use when applying power and flight control inputs during a go-around?

Effective risk management during a go-around involves smooth and coordinated application of power and flight controls. The pilot should gradually increase power to avoid over-torquing the engine and ensure rotor RPM is within safe limits. Flight control inputs must be adjusted to maintain desired climb attitude and airspeed. Pilots should be aware of the helicopter's performance characteristics and avoid abrupt maneuvers that could lead to loss of control.

[PH.V.E.R2; FAA-H-8083-21]

13. How can a pilot identify and assess collision hazards during a go-around?

By maintaining vigilant situational awareness. This involves constantly scanning the airspace for other aircraft, especially in busy traffic patterns. Pilots should also be aware of ground hazards, such as buildings or terrain, particularly when operating in confined areas or near obstacles. Using onboard collision avoidance systems and listening to ATC communications can further assist in identifying potential hazards.

[PH.V.E.R3; FAA-H-8083-21]

14. What strategies can a pilot use to mitigate risks of task prioritization issues during a go-around?

To mitigate risks of task prioritization issues during a go-around, a pilot should follow the aviate, navigate, communicate principle, ensuring that flying the helicopter remains the top priority. This involves maintaining proper flight attitude, airspeed, and altitude before addressing other tasks. Using checklists and standard operating procedures can help in managing tasks efficiently and minimizing workload.

[PH.V.E.R4; FAA-H-8083-21]

15. What are effective strategies to mitigate runway incursion risks during a go-around?

To mitigate runway incursion risks during a go-around, a pilot should maintain clear communication with ATC, declaring intentions and confirming received instructions. Staying vigilant about the assigned flight path and avoiding assumptions about clearances are important. Pilots should also be familiar with airport signage, markings, and lighting to navigate safely and avoid accidental runway entry.

[PH.V.E.R5; FAA-H-8083-21]

Skills to be demonstrated:

- Make a timely decision to discontinue the approach or at the direction of the evaluator.

- Maintain engine and rotor RPM within normal limits while applying proper control input to stop descent and initiate climb.

- Transition to a positive rate of climb and appropriate airspeed of ±10 knots.

- Maintain directional control, ground track, and proper wind-drift correction throughout the maneuver.

- Notify/coordinate with air traffic control (ATC) or evaluator instructions as required.

- Complete the appropriate checklist(s).

- Use single-pilot resource management (SRM) or crew resource management (CRM), as appropriate.

- Use runway incursion avoidance procedures, if applicable.

F. Confined Area Operations

1. How does wind direction and speed affect helicopter operations in confined areas?

Wind direction and speed can significantly impact a helicopter's ability to perform confined area operations. Tailwinds can reduce performance during takeoff and landing, while crosswinds can challenge pilot control. Proper assessment and adjustment for wind conditions are crucial for safe operations, including selecting an approach path that minimizes wind-related risks.

[PH.V.F.K1; FAA-H-8083-21]

2. What considerations should a pilot make regarding helicopter weight during confined area operations?

The weight of the helicopter affects its performance capabilities, including takeoff, climb, and maneuverability within a confined area. Pilots must ensure the helicopter is within its weight and balance limits to maintain control and performance, especially in environments where maneuvering space is limited. Preflight planning should include weight management strategies to optimize performance for the expected conditions.

[PH.V.F.K1; FAA-H-8083-21]

3. In what ways does temperature impact helicopter operations in confined areas?

Higher temperatures can decrease air density, resulting in reduced lift and engine performance. This can significantly impact a helicopter's ability to perform in confined areas, where precise control and adequate power margins are essential. Pilots need to account for the effects of temperature on helicopter performance and may need to adjust their approach and departure techniques accordingly.

[PH.V.F.K1; FAA-H-8083-21]

4. What is the impact of density altitude on helicopter performance in confined areas?

Density altitude, a function of atmospheric pressure, temperature, and humidity, significantly impacts helicopter performance in confined areas. Higher density altitudes, indicative of thinner air, can reduce lift, engine power, and rotor efficiency. This impacts the helicopter's ability to maneuver effectively in confined spaces, making it essential for pilots to understand and anticipate these effects for safe operation.

[PH.V.F.K1; FAA-H-8083-21]

5. What strategies can pilots employ to mitigate the risks associated with wind, weight, temperature, and density altitude during confined area operations?

Pilots can mitigate risks by conducting thorough preflight planning that includes evaluating the current and forecasted weather conditions, accurately calculating weight and balance, and understanding the effects of temperature and density altitude on performance. Choosing the optimal time of day for operations, when conditions are most favorable, and having alternate plans in case conditions deteriorate are also key strategies. Continuous training and proficiency in confined area operations under various conditions enhance a pilot's ability to safely manage these risks.

[PH.V.F.K1; FAA-H-8083-21]

6. **What are the typical situations where a confined area approach and landing is recommended?**

   A confined area approach and landing is typically recommended in situations where the available landing space is limited by obstacles like buildings, trees, or terrain. It is also used in emergency scenarios, such as medical evacuations or rescue operations, where the only available landing area is restricted. Pilots must carefully assess the environment, considering factors like approach paths, potential hazards, and escape routes.

   [PH.V.F.K2; FAA-H-8083-21]

7. **What are the key factors that necessitate a confined area approach and landing?**

   Confined area approaches and landings are recommended when operating in areas with limited space due to natural or man-made obstacles, such as in mountainous terrain, between buildings, or in heavily forested areas. Such operations require careful planning to ensure safety, considering the helicopter's performance, wind conditions, and potential escape routes in case of an aborted landing.

   [PH.V.F.K2; FAA-H-8083-21]

8. **What role does the height/velocity (H/V) diagram play in planning confined area operations?**

   The H/V diagram is crucial in planning confined area operations as it identifies safe operating speeds and altitudes for takeoffs and landings. It helps pilots avoid conditions where an engine failure would severely limit safe autorotation options. Understanding and adhering to the H/V diagram's recommendations is vital, especially in confined areas where maneuverability is limited and the margin for error is small.

   [PH.V.F.K2; FAA-H-8083-21]

9. **What are the best practices for conducting a confined area approach and landing?**

   Best practices for conducting a confined area approach and landing include conducting a thorough reconnaissance of the area to identify obstacles, wind conditions, and potential landing zones. Pilots should use an approach path that allows for a gradual descent, maintaining a safe altitude above obstacles and ensuring that the helicopter's performance capabilities are not exceeded. It is also important to have a clear plan for aborting the landing if necessary and to continuously assess conditions throughout the approach to make timely decisions.

[PH.V.F.K2; FAA-H-8083-21]

10. What is the purpose of high reconnaissance in confined area operations?

The purpose of high reconnaissance is to obtain an overall assessment of the landing area from a higher altitude. This allows the pilot to identify wind direction and speed, potential hazards, suitable approach and departure paths, and any obstacles that could affect the operation. High reconnaissance also helps in evaluating forced landing areas in case of an emergency.

[PH.V.F.K3; FAA-H-8083-21]

11. How does low reconnaissance complement high reconnaissance during confined area operations?

Low reconnaissance is conducted at a lower altitude and provides a closer inspection of the landing area, verifying details observed during high reconnaissance and identifying any additional hazards not visible from higher altitudes, such as wires, poles, and small ground features. It allows the pilot to make a final assessment of the landing site's suitability before committing to the approach and landing.

[PH.V.F.K3; FAA-H-8083-21]

12. What factors should be considered when planning takeoff and departure from a confined area?

Factors to consider include wind conditions, available power versus power required, obstacle clearance, and the best use of available space for takeoff to ensure a safe climb out. Pilots must also consider the helicopter's performance capabilities under the current conditions and plan a departure path that allows for an obstacle-free climb to cruising altitude.

[PH.V.F.K3; FAA-H-8083-21]

13. How can pilots use the H/V diagram in planning confined area operations?

Pilots can use the height/velocity (H/V) diagram to understand the safest airspeeds and altitudes for takeoff and landing in confined areas. The diagram helps identify operational zones where an engine failure could be safely managed through autorotation and zones where such an event would pose significant risks. Planning takeoffs and landings outside of the critical areas indicated on the H/V diagram enhances safety.

[PH.V.F.K3; FAA-H-8083-21]

14. What are best practices for a confined area approach and landing in terms of reconnaissance and planning?

Best practices include conducting thorough high and low reconnaissance to assess all aspects of the landing area, including environmental conditions, obstacles, and suitable emergency areas. Pilots should plan their approach and departure paths to minimize risks, considering wind direction and speed for optimal performance. It is also crucial to maintain situational awareness and be prepared to abort the landing if conditions change or hazards are identified during the final approach.

[PH.V.F.K3; FAA-H-8083-21]

15. What are the implications of operating a helicopter near its maximum power limit during confined area operations?

Operating near the maximum power limit reduces the safety margin, increases the risk of over-stressing the engine, and leaves less power available for emergency maneuvers. It requires careful monitoring of engine instruments and precise handling to avoid power overloads.

[PH.V.F.K4; FAA-H-8083-21]

16. What considerations must be made regarding power requirements versus power available when planning a departure from a confined area?

Pilots must consider the maximum power the helicopter's engine can produce under the current environmental conditions (power available) against the power required to safely complete the departure, including clearing any obstacles. Factors such as weight, altitude, temperature, and wind play significant roles in affecting both the power required and the power available. Ensuring that there is sufficient power available to meet or exceed the power required is essential for a safe departure.

[PH.V.F.K4; FAA-H-8083-21]

17. How can wind direction and speed influence the power dynamics during confined area operations?

Wind direction and speed can significantly influence the power required for operations in confined areas. Headwinds can assist in lift generation, potentially reducing the power required for takeoff or landing. Tailwinds, conversely, can increase the power required by reducing the effective lift. Crosswinds can also complicate control, requiring careful power management. Pilots must assess wind conditions to ensure safe and efficient use of power.

[PH.V.F.K4; FAA-H-8083-21]

18. Explain how a pilot should assess the risk associated with the selection of an approach path for a helicopter.

First, the aircraft's performance and limitations must be reviewed to ensure it can safely execute the approach under the current conditions. This includes understanding the helicopter's capabilities in terms of maneuverability, maximum and minimum speeds, and power requirements. Wind conditions, including speed and direction, should be evaluated as they can significantly affect the helicopter's performance during the approach. The pilot should also be aware of the availability of alternate landing sites in case the primary site becomes unsuitable or if an emergency arises during the approach. Additionally, environmental factors, such as terrain, obstacles, and airspace restrictions, should be considered to avoid potential hazards.

[PH.V.F.R1; FAA-H-8083-21]

19. What is the primary concern regarding wind direction when operating a helicopter in confined areas?

The primary concern with wind direction in confined area operations is the potential for turbulence and wind shear, which can affect the helicopter's performance and controllability. In confined spaces, obstacles can cause the wind to funnel or change direction unexpectedly, leading to challenging flight conditions. Pilots must be vigilant in assessing and mitigating these risks. Prior to confined area operations, a pilot should conduct a thorough assessment of wind conditions.

[PH.V.F.R2a; FAA-H-8083-21]

20. What are the risks associated with wind shear during confined area operations, and how can pilots mitigate these risks?

Wind shear, the sudden change in wind speed and/or direction, can pose significant risks during confined area operations by causing unexpected changes in airspeed, lift, and altitude. Pilots can mitigate these risks by conducting thorough preflight weather briefings to identify potential wind shear conditions, maintaining higher airspeeds for added performance margins, and being prepared to abort the approach or departure if wind shear is encountered. Constant vigilance and readiness to adjust controls to compensate for the effects of wind shear are essential.

[PH.V.F.R2a; FAA-H-8083-21]

21. How should pilots adjust their confined area operation techniques in response to varying wind conditions?

Pilots should adjust their operation techniques by considering the wind's effect on helicopter performance, including alterations to approach angles, airspeeds, and the use of power. In strong or gusty wind conditions, pilots may need to allow for additional space to maneuver, anticipate the need for greater power application, and remain flexible in their approach and departure paths to account for shifting wind directions. Tailoring techniques to the current wind conditions is key to maintaining control and safety.

[PH.V.F.R2a; FAA-H-8083-21]

22. In what ways can pilots use environmental cues to assess wind direction and strength when operating in confined areas?

Pilots can use environmental cues such as smoke, water ripples, tree movement, and flags to assess wind direction and strength in confined areas. Observing these cues during high and low reconnaissance can help pilots plan their approaches and departures more effectively. Additionally, understanding local topography and how it may influence wind patterns is crucial for anticipating changes in wind conditions that might not be immediately apparent.

[PH.V.F.R2a; FAA-H-8083-21]

23. How does turbulence affect helicopter performance and handling in confined areas?

Turbulence can lead to variations in rotor RPM, fluctuations in altitude and airspeed, and unexpected changes in aircraft attitude. It demands greater pilot attention and skill to maintain stable flight, especially in confined areas where there is less room for error and more potential obstacles.

[PH.V.F.R2c; FAA-H-8083-21]

24. How can pilots mitigate the risks associated with the height/velocity diagram during confined area operations?

To mitigate risks, pilots should:

- Avoid flying in the unsafe zones of the height/velocity diagram as much as possible.
- Maintain situational awareness and be prepared for immediate autorotation.
- Regularly train for autorotation procedures and emergency scenarios.
- Continuously monitor helicopter performance and environmental conditions during flight.

[PH.V.F.R3; FAA-H-8083-21]

25. How should a pilot interpret the shaded areas on an H/V diagram during confined area operations?

The shaded areas on an H/V diagram represent the combinations of height and velocity where, in the event of an engine failure, a safe autorotation may not be achievable, leading to an increased risk of damage upon landing. Pilots should plan their approaches and departures to stay clear of these zones whenever possible, especially when operating in or out of confined areas.

[PH.V.F.R3; FAA-H-8083-21]

26. Can the H/V diagram vary between different helicopter models, and how does this affect operations in confined areas?

Yes, the H/V diagram can vary significantly between different helicopter models due to differences in aerodynamics, engine performance, and rotor systems. Pilots must be familiar with the specific H/V diagram for their helicopter model to effectively plan and conduct safe operations in confined areas, taking into account the unique performance limitations and safe operational envelopes of their aircraft.

[PH.V.F.R3; FAA-H-8083-21]

27. What factors should a pilot consider when applying H/V diagram information to confined area operations under varying environmental conditions?

Pilots should consider factors such as wind direction and speed, temperature, density altitude, and helicopter weight, as these can affect both the power available and the power required for operations. These factors can also influence the helicopter's ability to remain within the safe zones of the H/V diagram under varying environmental conditions. Pilots must adjust their flight plans accordingly to maintain safety margins when operating in confined areas.

[PH.V.F.R3; FAA-H-8083-21]

28. What procedures should a pilot follow to safely execute a go-around in a confined area?

To safely execute a go-around in a confined area, a pilot should:

- *Initiate early*—Decide to go around at the earliest sign of an unstabilized approach or any safety concerns.

- *Apply power smoothly*—Increase power smoothly and gradually to avoid over-torquing the engine and losing tail rotor effectiveness.

- *Maintain positive control*—Ensure positive aircraft control, maintaining a safe airspeed and avoiding abrupt control inputs.

- *Use optimal climb profile*—Establish an optimal climb profile that balances altitude gain with forward airspeed to clear obstacles.

- *Monitor systems*—Continuously monitor engine and rotor RPM, and other critical flight instruments.

- *Communicate intentions*—Use radio communications to inform any other nearby aircraft or personnel on the ground of the go-around.

[PH.V.F.R4; FAA-H-8083-21]

29. How can a pilot mitigate the risks associated with performing a forced landing in a confined area?

Risk mitigation strategies include regular practice of autorotation and emergency procedures, thorough preflight planning with consideration of potential emergency landing zones along the route, and maintaining situational awareness to quickly identify suitable landing areas in case of an emergency.

[PH.V.F.R5; FAA-H-8083-21]

30. How does the type of landing surface impact the risk assessment for confined area operations?

The type of landing surface (e.g., grass, dirt, gravel, or concrete) affects the helicopter's landing and takeoff performance due to different friction levels and potential for debris. Pilots must assess the surface type to anticipate changes in helicopter behavior, such as reduced braking effectiveness or the risk of foreign object damage, and adjust their approach and departure techniques accordingly.

[PH.V.F.R6; FAA-H-8083-21]

31. What considerations should a pilot make regarding landing surface conditions in confined areas?

Pilots should consider surface conditions such as uneven terrain, slopes, loose debris, and potential obstacles. Assessing these factors during the planning phase and high/low reconnaissance allows pilots to identify safe landing zones, anticipate the need for power adjustments, and develop contingency plans for unexpected surface conditions.

[PH.V.F.R6; FAA-H-8083-21]

32. What strategies can pilots employ to mitigate risks associated with uncertain landing surface conditions in confined areas?

To mitigate risks associated with uncertain landing surface conditions, pilots can conduct thorough preflight planning, including reviewing satellite imagery and maps for preliminary assessment. During flight, performing detailed reconnaissance allows for real-time assessment of the landing area. Choosing an approach path that allows for a go-around if the surface is deemed unsuitable and being prepared to abort the landing are key strategies.

[PH.V.F.R6; FAA-H-8083-21]

33. How can a pilot effectively assess the risk of dynamic rollover before performing a confined area operation?

Risk assessment for dynamic rollover in confined area operations involves evaluating several factors. These include assessing the landing zone for uneven terrain, obstacles that could interfere with skids or wheels, and wind conditions that could affect control. The pilot should also consider the helicopter's weight and balance, as an improperly loaded helicopter can be more susceptible to dynamic rollover.

[PH.V.F.R7; FAA-H-8083-21]

34. What factors contribute to dynamic rollover occurrence during confined area operations?

Factors contributing to its occurrence include pilot error, uneven landing surfaces, obstructions, and environmental conditions like wind. Proper training, vigilance, and preflight planning are essential to recognize and avoid conditions that may lead to dynamic rollover.

[PH.V.F.R7; FAA-H-8083-21]

35. What are the key strategies for mitigating the risk of dynamic rollover in confined area operations?

Key strategies include thorough preflight planning to understand the terrain and wind conditions, conducting high and low reconnaissance of the landing area, maintaining a vigilant attitude during takeoff and landing to ensure the helicopter remains level, avoiding abrupt control inputs, and being prepared to execute a go-around if the landing area becomes untenable.

[PH.V.F.R7; FAA-H-8083-21]

36. What is ground resonance, and under what conditions is it likely to occur during confined area operations?

Ground resonance is a dangerous vibration phenomenon that can occur in helicopters with fully articulated rotor systems when one or more of the rotor blades become out of phase with the others. It is most likely to occur when a helicopter with such a rotor system touches down unevenly, if one skid contacts the ground before the other, or during operations on uneven surfaces often found in confined areas. Pilots must ensure even ground contact and monitor for early signs of ground resonance to initiate immediate corrective actions.

[PH.V.F.R8; FAA-H-8083-21]

37. How can pilot actions contribute to the onset or prevention of ground resonance in confined area operations?

Pilot actions can significantly influence the onset or prevention of ground resonance. Careful handling during touchdown and takeoff, ensuring even contact with the ground, and maintaining rotor RPM within specified limits are critical to preventing ground resonance. If signs of ground resonance are detected, the pilot must apply corrective actions promptly, such as lifting off immediately if conditions permit, to prevent the resonance from escalating.

[PH.V.F.R8; FAA-H-8083-21]

38. In the context of confined area operations, how should pilots plan their approach and landing to minimize the risk of encountering ground resonance?

Pilots should plan their approach and landing in confined areas by conducting thorough reconnaissance of the landing site to identify the flattest possible area for touchdown. Approaches should be stabilized, and landings should be executed with minimal lateral or longitudinal movement at touchdown to ensure even loading on the landing gear. Continuous monitoring of rotor RPM and immediate corrective actions if anomalies are detected are also crucial parts of planning to minimize the risk of ground resonance.

[PH.V.F.R8; FAA-H-8083-21]

39. What are the signs of impending low rotor RPM a pilot should monitor for during confined area operations?

Signs of impending low rotor RPM include the activation of the low-RPM warning system (audio and/or visual alerts), a noticeable decrease in control responsiveness, and an unusual vibration or noise from the rotor system. Pilots should remain vigilant for these signs, especially during critical phases of flight like takeoff and landing in confined areas, where power management is crucial.

[PH.V.F.R9; FAA-H-8083-21]

40. How can pilots mitigate the risk of encountering low rotor RPM during confined area operations?

Pilots can mitigate the risk of low rotor RPM by conducting thorough preflight performance calculations to ensure the helicopter's weight and environmental conditions are within safe operating limits. Proper planning, including consideration of wind conditions and density altitude, can help maintain adequate power margins. Regular training on power management and emergency procedures for low rotor RPM situations is also crucial for preparedness.

[PH.V.F.R9; FAA-H-8083-21]

41. What is loss of tail rotor effectiveness (LTE), and how can it impact helicopter operations in confined areas?

Loss of tail rotor effectiveness (LTE) is a condition where the helicopter's tail rotor loses its ability to provide adequate yaw control, leading to an uncommanded and rapid yaw movement. In confined areas, LTE can be particularly dangerous due to the proximity of obstacles and limited space for recovery maneuvers. Pilots must recognize the onset of LTE and respond promptly to regain control.

[PH.V.F.R10; FAA-H-8083-21]

42. What are the primary factors that contribute to LTE, and how can they be managed during confined area operations?

The primary factors contributing to LTE include high gross weight, high density altitude, low airspeed, and wind conditions such as tailwinds, crosswinds, or out-of-ground-effect (OGE) operations. Pilots can manage these factors by carefully planning their approach and departure paths, maintaining adequate airspeed, and being vigilant about wind conditions and their helicopter's performance capabilities.

[PH.V.F.R10; FAA-H-8083-21]

43. How does wind direction and speed affect the likelihood of experiencing LTE in confined area operations?

Wind direction and speed can significantly increase the likelihood of LTE, especially with tailwinds or strong crosswinds that reduce the effectiveness of the tail rotor. Pilots should approach and depart from confined areas into the wind whenever possible to maximize tail rotor effectiveness and minimize the risk of LTE.).

[PH.V.F.R10; FAA-H-8083-21]

44. How can pilots prepare and train to handle LTE situations, especially in confined areas?

Pilots can prepare for LTE situations by thoroughly understanding their helicopter's flight manual, especially sections related to LTE. Understanding what wind azimuths are conducive to LTE situations and how best to plan approaches with those in mind. Additionally, preflight planning to assess wind conditions and choosing landing sites that minimize LTE risk are crucial steps in preparation.

[PH.V.F.R10; FAA-H-8083-21]

45. What preflight preparations are crucial for mitigating collision hazards in confined area operations?

Preflight preparations should include a detailed briefing on the confined area, studying maps or satellite imagery of the location, understanding local weather patterns, and pre-planning entry and exit routes with a high/low recon. It is also essential to check the helicopter's performance capabilities under the expected conditions with the manufacturer's recommendations.

[PH.V.F.R11; FAA-H-8083-21]

46. How can environmental factors exacerbate the risk of VRS during confined area operations?

Environmental factors such as high density altitude, hot temperatures, and heavy helicopter weight can exacerbate the risk of VRS by reducing the performance margins of the helicopter. Wind conditions, particularly downdrafts or tailwinds, can also increase the likelihood of entering VRS during descent. Pilots must consider these factors during preflight planning and when executing operations in confined areas.

[PH.V.F.R12; FAA-H-8083-21]

47. What immediate actions should a pilot take if encountering VRS in a confined area?

If encountering VRS, the pilot should immediately take actions to exit the condition by applying forward cyclic to gain airspeed and exit the downwash area, while cautiously managing the collective to prevent an excessive descent rate or loss of rotor RPM. Exiting the vortex ring state requires moving the helicopter to an area of undisturbed air, which might be challenging in confined spaces but is necessary for recovery.

[PH.V.F.R12; FAA-H-8083-21]

48. What strategies can pilots employ to mitigate the risk of VRS when planning and conducting confined area operations?

To mitigate the risk of VRS, pilots should plan approaches and descents that minimize the need for steep or prolonged vertical descents where VRS is more likely to occur. Maintaining a higher forward airspeed and a shallower descent angle can help avoid the condition. Additionally, conducting thorough reconnaissance of the landing area to understand the environmental conditions and potential wind patterns is vital for safe operations. Continuous training on VRS recognition and recovery techniques is also crucial for pilot preparedness.

[PH.V.F.R12; FAA-H-8083-21]

49. What are the key factors a pilot should consider when assessing aircraft limitations for confined area operations?

When assessing aircraft limitations for confined area operations, a pilot should consider factors such as the performance capabilities of the helicopter, including maximum takeoff weight, power available versus power required, wind conditions, density altitude, and the effects of obstacles in the vicinity. Additionally, the pilot must account for the helicopter's maneuverability, tail rotor effectiveness, and the potential for vortex ring state.

[PH.V.F.R13; FAA-H-8083-21]

50. In what ways do environmental factors such as wind, temperature, and altitude affect helicopter limitations in confined area operations?

Environmental factors like wind, temperature, and altitude significantly affect helicopter performance by altering the density altitude and thus the power available from the engine and the efficiency of the rotor system. High temperatures and altitudes can decrease engine performance and rotor lift, while wind can affect the helicopter's ability to hover and maneuver. Pilots must assess these factors and adjust their operational plans to ensure that limitations are not exceeded.

[PH.V.F.R13; FAA-H-8083-21]

51. What are the primary risks associated with distractions during confined area operations in helicopters?

Distractions can lead to a loss of situational awareness, delayed reactions to changing conditions, and missed communications or critical cues about the environment or aircraft performance. In confined area operations, where precision and attention to detail are paramount, distractions can significantly increase the risk of an incident or accident.

[PH.V.F.R14; FAA-H-8083-21]

52. How can pilots effectively manage task prioritization to prevent loss of situational awareness in confined areas?

Effective task prioritization involves identifying critical tasks that require immediate attention and distinguishing them from less critical tasks that can be managed later. Utilizing checklists, maintaining a clean cockpit to minimize physical distractions, and employing effective cockpit resource management techniques can help pilots stay focused on essential tasks, particularly in the demanding environment of confined area operations. Remember to aviate, navigate, and communicate.

[PH.V.F.R14; FAA-H-8083-21]

53. How does the complexity of confined area operations contribute to the risk of losing situational awareness, and what can be done to mitigate this risk?

The complexity of confined area operations can overload a pilot's cognitive resources, leading to tunnel vision or fixation on a single task. Pilots can mitigate this risk by thorough preflight planning, including a detailed analysis of the operational environment, weather, and potential hazards. In flight, maintaining a disciplined approach to cockpit management and decision-making helps ensure that attention is distributed appropriately across all critical areas.

[PH.V.F.R14; FAA-H-8083-21]

54. How does understanding the power required versus power available relationship assist in confined area operations?

Understanding the relationship between power required and power available is critical in confined area operations to ensure that the helicopter has sufficient lift and maneuverability. This knowledge allows pilots to assess whether the helicopter can safely take off, hover, and land in the confined area given the current conditions. It also helps in making informed decisions about load adjustments and the necessity of performing operations at cooler times of the day or at lower gross weights to increase power margins.

[PH.V.F.R15; FAA-H-8083-21]

55. What factors increase the power required for helicopter operations in confined areas?

Factors that increase the power required for helicopter operations in confined areas include high AUW, high density altitude conditions (caused by high altitude, high temperature, or both), and operations out of ground effect (OGE). Wind conditions, such as tailwinds or crosswinds, can also affect the power required by influencing the helicopter's performance during takeoff and landing.

[PH.V.F.R15; FAA-H-8083-21]

56. What factors should a pilot consider when assessing power requirements for a confined area departure?

When assessing power requirements for a confined area departure, a pilot should consider factors such as helicopter weight, density altitude, wind direction and speed, obstacle clearance, and the power margin available. The pilot must ensure that the power required does not exceed the power available, taking into account the environmental conditions and helicopter performance limitations.

[PH.V.F.R15; FAA-H-8083-21]

Skills to be demonstrated:

- Complete the appropriate checklist(s).

- Make radio calls as appropriate.

- Confirm power available meets or exceeds the power required for the selected arrival or departure profile(s).

- Determine wind direction with or without visible wind direction indicators.

- Accomplish a proper high and low reconnaissance of the confined landing area.

- Select a suitable approach path, termination point, and departure path.

- Track the selected approach path at an acceptable approach angle and rate of closure to the termination point.

- Continually evaluate the suitability of the confined landing area and termination point.

- Maintain engine and rotor RPM within normal limits.

- Accomplish a proper ground reconnaissance.

- Terminate in a hover or on the surface, as appropriate.

- Select a suitable takeoff point, consider factors affecting takeoff and climb performance under various conditions.

- Use single-pilot resource management (SRM) or crew resource management (CRM), as appropriate.

G. Pinnacle Operations

1. What are the key considerations a pilot must take into account when planning a pinnacle or platform operation?

The pilot must consider the helicopter's performance capabilities, wind direction and speed, temperature, altitude, weight, and center of gravity limits. Additionally, the pilot should assess the size and slope of the pinnacle or platform, potential obstructions, approach and departure paths, and emergency landing areas.

[PH.V.G.K1; FAA-H-8083-21]

2. How does high altitude affect the performance of a helicopter during pinnacle or platform operations?

High altitude can significantly impact helicopter performance due to thinner air. This leads to reduced lift, engine power, and rotor efficiency, requiring careful calculation of performance data to ensure the helicopter can safely operate in these conditions.

[PH.V.G.K1; FAA-H-8083-21]

3. Describe the appropriate approach and departure techniques for a pinnacle operation.

The approach to a pinnacle should be done into the wind, allowing for better performance and control. The pilot must maintain a constant angle of approach, ensuring clear visibility of the landing area. The departure should be planned considering wind direction, ensuring that any loss of performance or tail rotor effectiveness can be safely managed.

[PH.V.G.K1; FAA-H-8083-21]

4. How does wind direction and speed impact helicopter operations during pinnacle landings?

Wind direction and speed significantly impact helicopter operations during pinnacle landings by affecting the approach path, landing stability, and power required for a safe operation. Tailwinds can reduce lift and increase the descent rate, while strong crosswinds or gusts may challenge the pilot's ability to maintain control. Pilots must assess and utilize wind conditions to their advantage, ensuring approaches are made into the wind whenever possible to maximize performance and safety.

[PH.V.G.K2; FAA-H-8083-21]

5. What are the considerations for weight management in helicopter pinnacle operations?

Weight management is crucial in pinnacle operations due to the performance limitations at high altitudes and confined spaces. Heavier weights increase the power required for takeoff and landing, potentially pushing the helicopter's capabilities to its limits. Pilots must carefully calculate weight, considering fuel, passengers, and cargo, to ensure it does not exceed the helicopter's maximum performance capabilities, especially under conditions of high density altitude.

[PH.V.G.K2; FAA-H-8083-21]

6. Why is temperature an important consideration during pinnacle/platform operations, and what effect does it have?

Temperature affects air density, which in turn impacts helicopter performance. Warmer temperatures result in lower air density, reducing the rotor system's lift capacity. This can lead to reduced hover ceiling, climb rate, and overall performance. Pilots must be aware of the temperature to ensure the helicopter's performance capabilities meet the demands of pinnacle or platform operations, especially in hot and high conditions.

[PH.V.G.K2; FAA-H-8083-21]

7. In what ways can pilots mitigate the risks associated with density altitude in pinnacle operations?

Pilots can mitigate risks associated with high density altitude by conducting operations during cooler parts of the day, reducing weight to lower the power required for takeoff and landing, and thoroughly preflight planning to understand the environmental conditions. Additionally, pilots should always have an alternate plan in case conditions change or the operation exceeds the safety margins of the helicopter's performance capabilities.

[PH.V.G.K2; FAA-H-8083-21]

8. What are the key considerations for selecting a suitable takeoff point and departure flight path during pinnacle/ platform operations?

- *Wind direction and speed*—Choose a takeoff point that allows for takeoff into the wind to maximize lift and control.

- *Obstacle clearance*—Ensure adequate clearance from obstacles in the flight path during climb.

- *Helicopter performance*—Consider the helicopter's performance capabilities, especially at high altitudes or in hot temperatures which can affect lift and engine performance.

- *Emergency procedures*—Ensure the takeoff point allows for a safe area to execute emergency procedures if needed.

[PH.V.G.K3; FAA-H-8083-21]

9. What are the key considerations for deciding to perform a pinnacle or platform operation?

Key considerations include assessing the necessity of the operation based on mission requirements, evaluating the helicopter's performance capabilities in relation to the environmental conditions (wind, weight, temperature, and density altitude), and ensuring the pilot's proficiency and experience are adequate for the operation's complexity. The decision should also factor in the availability of alternative landing sites and emergency procedures specific to the operation.

[PH.V.G.K4; FAA-H-8083-21]

10. How does high altitude affect helicopter performance during pinnacle or platform operations?

High altitude can significantly impact helicopter performance during pinnacle or platform operations. As altitude increases, air density decreases, which can reduce rotor efficiency and engine power output. This leads to a decrease in lift and thrust capabilities, requiring the pilot to be aware of the helicopter's weight and balance, power available, and power required for these operations. Additionally, the helicopter's hover ceiling, both in and out of ground effect, may be reduced at higher altitudes, affecting the ability to perform safe landings and takeoffs on pinnacles or platforms.

[PH.V.G.K4; FAA-H-8083-21]

11. What strategies can be employed to ensure a safe takeoff and landing during pinnacle/platform operations?

Strategies include conducting detailed preflight planning with an emphasis on environmental assessment, performing reconnaissance of the landing area to identify hazards and assess wind conditions, and employing a conservative approach to weight and fuel management. Additionally, practicing pinnacle/platform approaches and departures under various conditions enhances pilot proficiency and preparedness for these challenging operations.

[PH.V.G.K4; FAA-H-8083-21]

12. Why is it important for a pilot to perform both high and low reconnaissance during pinnacle operations?

Performing both high and low reconnaissance is crucial for ensuring the safety and success of pinnacle operations. High reconnaissance allows the pilot to get an initial broad overview of the area, identify major hazards, and plan the general approach. Low reconnaissance provides a detailed, close-up assessment, confirming the initial observations, and ensuring no small hazards are overlooked. This two-tiered approach ensures a comprehensive evaluation of the landing site, considering all possible risks and challenges.

[PH.V.G.K5; FAA-H-8083-21]

13. How does low reconnaissance complement high reconnaissance in preparing for pinnacle operations?

Low reconnaissance complements high reconnaissance by allowing the pilot to inspect the landing area and its immediate surroundings at a closer range, typically at altitudes of 300 to 500 feet above the surface. This closer inspection helps in identifying finer details such as surface conditions, smaller obstacles, and precise wind effects, enabling more accurate planning of the approach, landing, and departure phases.

[PH.V.G.K5; FAA-H-8083-21]

14. **How do pilots determine the most suitable approach path for pinnacle operations considering aircraft performance and environmental conditions?**

    Pilots determine the most suitable approach path by evaluating aircraft performance capabilities against environmental conditions such as wind direction, speed, temperature, and density altitude. This assessment involves analyzing how these factors affect lift, power availability, and maneuverability, ensuring the selected approach path allows for a safe operation within the aircraft's performance limitations. Pilots must also consider obstacle clearance and potential escape routes in case the approach needs to be aborted.

    [PH.V.G.R1; FAA-H-8083-21]

15. **What factors influence the selection of a termination point during pinnacle operations, and how is it related to aircraft performance?**

    The selection of a termination point is influenced by factors including the need for sufficient space to maneuver, the ability to maintain visual contact with the landing area, and the requirement for a clear path for departure. Aircraft performance considerations such as maximum allowable weight, power available versus power required, and wind effects are crucial in determining a safe termination point. The chosen point must allow the aircraft to hover or land without exceeding its performance capabilities, especially in variable wind conditions and high-density altitudes.

    [PH.V.G.R1; FAA-H-8083-21]

16. **How should wind considerations affect the planning of departure paths in pinnacle operations?**

    Wind considerations affect the planning of departure paths by dictating the most advantageous direction for takeoff to maximize lift and control. Pilots should plan to take off into the wind whenever possible to reduce ground speed and increase aerodynamic performance. Crosswind and tailwind components require careful consideration, as they can adversely affect the helicopter's ability to climb out safely from a pinnacle location. Adjustments to the departure path may be necessary to account for changing wind conditions and to ensure obstacle clearance.

    [PH.V.G.R1; FAA-H-8083-21]

17. **What are the key risk mitigation strategies for managing aircraft performance limitations during pinnacle operations?**

    Key risk mitigation strategies include thorough preflight planning with detailed analysis of aircraft performance charts, consideration of environmental factors such as wind, temperature, and density altitude, and careful weight management to ensure the operation stays within safe limits. Pilots should also conduct reconnaissance flights when possible to gather real-time information about the operational area and adjust plans accordingly. Continuous monitoring of aircraft performance and environmental conditions during the operation is essential for timely decision-making and risk mitigation.

    [PH.V.G.R1; FAA-H-8083-21]

18. **How can wind direction and speed impact the approach and departure paths in pinnacle operations?**

    Wind direction and speed can significantly affect helicopter performance, particularly in pinnacle operations. The pilot must consider the wind to maintain effective control of the helicopter, avoid tailwind conditions, and ensure adequate performance during approach and departure.

    [PH.V.G.R2a; FAA-H-8083-21]

19. **What strategies can a pilot employ to mitigate risks associated with changing wind conditions during pinnacle operations?**

    To mitigate risks, the pilot can continuously monitor wind conditions, be prepared to adjust the approach and departure paths as necessary, and have an alternative plan in case of sudden changes in wind that may affect the safety of the operation.

    [PH.V.G.R2b; FAA-H-8083-21]

20. **How should a pilot prepare for potential turbulence when planning for a pinnacle operation?**

    A pilot should conduct a thorough preflight weather check focusing on wind speed, direction, and potential for turbulence. Terrain analysis is crucial as turbulence can be exacerbated by local topography. The pilot should also review the helicopter's performance data under expected conditions and plan the approach and departure paths to minimize exposure to turbulence.

[PH.V.G.R2c; FAA-H-8083-21]

21. What are the primary risks associated with operating outside of the recommended zones in the H/V diagram during pinnacle operations?

Operating outside of the recommended zones in the H/V diagram poses significant risks, including decreased chances of successfully performing an autorotation in case of engine failure, increased likelihood of catastrophic outcomes due to inadequate altitude or airspeed for recovery, and generally less margin for error in emergency response. These risks underscore the importance of adhering to the diagram's guidelines, especially in the challenging environments of pinnacle operations.

[PH.V.G.R3; FAA-H-8083-21]

22. What strategies should pilots employ when planning and executing pinnacle operations to ensure adherence to the H/V diagram's safe zones?

Pilots should employ strategies such as detailed preflight planning that considers current and forecasted environmental conditions, weight management to ensure optimal performance, and continuous monitoring of aircraft performance relative to the H/V diagram during flight. Additionally, choosing approach and departure paths that allow for maintaining airspeed and altitude within the safe zones, even in the event of an engine failure, is crucial for mitigating risks associated with pinnacle operations.

[PH.V.G.R3; FAA-H-8083-21]

23. In what scenarios should a pilot consider a go-around during pinnacle operations?

Scenarios include encountering unexpected obstacles or wind changes, being unable to maintain a stable approach, mechanical issues, or indications that the landing zone is unsuitable. A go-around should also be considered if the pilot feels uncertain about any aspect of the landing. Once the go-around decision has been made, the pilot should immediately initiate a go-around procedure.

[PH.V.G.R4; FAA-H-8083-21]

24. What are the key considerations for selecting an emergency landing site during a powerplant failure in pinnacle operations?

Key considerations include the size of the area (sufficient for safe landing), surface type (preferably level and free of obstructions), wind direction (for optimal approach and touchdown), and any environmental factors (such as altitude or temperature) that might affect helicopter performance during autorotation.

[PH.V.G.R5; FAA-H-8083-21]

25. What are the primary collision hazards a pilot should be aware of during pinnacle operations?

Primary collision hazards include terrain features, such as cliffs or trees, other aircraft operating in the vicinity, wildlife, and man-made structures like antennas or power lines. Due to the often confined nature of pinnacle sites, pilots must also be vigilant about rotor clearance and tail rotor strikes.

[PH.V.G.R6; FAA-H-8083-21]

26. What are effective strategies for a pilot to avoid vortex ring state during pinnacle operations?

To avoid VRS, pilots should approach pinnacle sites with a forward airspeed, avoiding steep descent angles and high power settings. Maintaining an airspeed above the effective translational lift (ETL) speed until the final phase of landing can help prevent entering VRS. Continuous monitoring of descent rate and vertical speed is also vital.

[PH.V.G.R7; FAA-H-8083-21]

27. How can a pilot mitigate risks associated with uncertain or unstable landing surfaces in pinnacle operations?

Risk mitigation strategies include conducting a high reconnaissance to assess the landing area, using a low hover to visually inspect and test the surface, and employing a cautious approach with readiness to abort if the surface appears unstable. Additionally, pilots should approach with the minimum necessary airspeed and use gentle control inputs to avoid destabilizing the surface.

[PH.V.G.R8; FAA-H-8083-21]

28. How does a pilot handle a situation where the landing surface condition changes unexpectedly during pinnacle operations?

If the landing surface condition changes (e.g., surface becomes loose or shifts), the pilot should be prepared to immediately abort the landing, applying power to climb and stabilize the helicopter. The pilot should reassess the situation, considering alternate landing sites or waiting for conditions to improve, and communicate any changes or delays to relevant parties.

[PH.V.G.R8) FAA-H-8083-21]

29. What are effective strategies for a pilot to prevent low rotor RPM during pinnacle operations?

Effective strategies include proper preflight planning to understand power requirements, continuous monitoring of the rotor RPM gauge during flight, avoiding abrupt or excessive collective inputs, and managing the collective and throttle carefully, especially during high-power demand maneuvers. Pilots should also be familiar with the helicopter's power limitations under various environmental conditions.

[PH.V.G.R9; FAA-H-8083-21]

30. What techniques should a pilot use to mitigate the risk of dynamic rollover in pinnacle operations?

To mitigate the risk, pilots should approach the landing zone with caution, ensuring that both skids or wheels touch down simultaneously. They should avoid excessive side loads, maintain proper cyclic control to keep the helicopter level, and be prepared to abort the landing if the helicopter becomes unstable. Pilots should also avoid rapid or large collective inputs, especially when one skid or wheel is in contact with the ground.

[PH.V.G.R10; FAA-H-8083-21]

31. What are effective strategies for a pilot to prevent ground resonance during pinnacle operations?

To prevent ground resonance, pilots should ensure a smooth, even touchdown, with both skids contacting the ground simultaneously. Maintaining proper rotor RPM is crucial, as low RPM can contribute to the condition. Pilots should also conduct regular maintenance checks to ensure the rotor system is properly balanced and dampers are functioning correctly.

[PH.V.G.R11; FAA-H-8083-21]

32. What strategies should a pilot use to prevent LTE during pinnacle operations?

To prevent LTE, pilots should be aware of wind direction and speed, avoiding tailwind conditions, especially during low-speed flight. Careful power management and avoiding high-pitch attitudes are also important. Pilots should be vigilant when operating in high-risk LTE wind azimuths and ensure that tail rotor inputs are smooth and coordinated.

[PH.V.G.R12; FAA-H-8083-21]

33. How can a pilot effectively assess the impact of aircraft limitations on a planned pinnacle operation?

The pilot can assess the impact by reviewing the helicopter's performance charts for power available versus power required, considering factors such as altitude, temperature, and weight. It is also important to evaluate the landing zone's altitude, size, slope, and wind conditions to ensure they are within the helicopter's operational capabilities.

[PH.V.G.R13; FAA-H-8083-21]

34. What strategies should a pilot employ to ensure proper task prioritization during pinnacle operations?

The pilot should employ the aviate, navigate, communicate hierarchy to prioritize tasks. This means focusing first on controlling the helicopter, then on navigation and maintaining orientation, and finally on communications. Preflight planning and setting clear priorities for each phase of the operation can help manage workload and prevent task saturation.

[PH.V.G.R14; FAA-H-8083-21]

35. How can a pilot effectively communicate and ensure passenger safety regarding main and tail rotor hazards during pinnacle operations?

Effective communication includes conducting a thorough preflight safety briefing for all passengers, emphasizing the importance of avoiding rotor areas and following specific paths for boarding and disembarking. The pilot should clearly explain the dangers of rotor blades and rotor wash. Visual aids, such as diagrams showing safe areas, can also be helpful.

[PH.V.G.R15; FAA-H-8083-21]

36. What are the primary factors a pilot must consider when assessing the risk of a forced landing during pinnacle operations?

Primary factors include the condition and suitability of potential emergency landing sites within the pinnacle area, current helicopter load and fuel state, weather conditions, and any nearby obstacles. The pilot must also consider the helicopter's current altitude and airspeed, which can affect the glide distance and maneuverability during a forced landing.

[PH.V.G.R16; FAA-H-8083-21]

Skills to be demonstrated:

- Complete the appropriate checklist(s).

- Confirm power available meets or exceeds the power required for the selected arrival or departure profile(s).

- Make radio calls as appropriate.

- Accomplish high and low reconnaissance.

- Determine wind direction with or without visible wind direction indicators.

- Select a suitable approach path, termination point, and departure path.

- Select an approach path considering wind direction.

(continued)

- Track the selected approach path at an acceptable approach angle and rate of closure to the termination point.

- Maintain engine and rotor RPM within normal limits.

- Accomplish a proper ground reconnaissance.

- Terminate in a hover or on the surface, as appropriate.

- Select a suitable takeoff point, and consider factors affecting takeoff and climb performance under various conditions.

H. Shallow Approach and Running/ Roll-On Landing

1. When is it appropriate for a pilot to use a shallow approach and running/roll-on landing during helicopter operations?

A shallow approach and running/roll-on landing are appropriate in situations where a helicopter cannot perform a vertical descent and hover due to high gross weight, high density altitude, or insufficient power. This technique is also used when landing on surfaces where a hover could be hazardous, such as on loose gravel, snow, or in high wind conditions.

[PH.V.H.K1; FAA-H-8083-21]

2. What are the key aircraft limitations that pilots must consider when performing a shallow approach and running/roll-on landing?

Key aircraft limitations include the maximum allowable forward speed for landing, the weight and balance limitations of the helicopter, and the rotor system's lift capabilities under current environmental conditions. Pilots must also consider the helicopter's skid or wheel configuration and ensure that the aircraft's structure can withstand the forces associated with a running landing.

[PH.V.H.K1; FAA-H-8083-21]

3. **How should a pilot assess and prepare for the effect of the landing surface texture when planning a shallow approach and running/roll-on landing?**

The pilot should assess the landing surface for firmness, slope, and potential for obstacles or debris. Soft or uneven surfaces can affect the helicopter's stability during the roll-on phase. Preparation involves choosing a landing path that is as level and clear of debris as possible and considering the possibility of surface damage from rotor wash or skids. Pilots should also anticipate the helicopter's response to different surface textures, such as skidding or bouncing, and adjust their technique accordingly.

[PH.V.H.K1; FAA-H-8083-21]

4. **How does wind affect the execution of a shallow approach and running/roll-on landing in helicopter operations?**

Wind affects the helicopter's performance and control during a shallow approach and running/roll-on landing. Headwinds can provide additional lift and allow for a slower ground speed on touchdown, whereas tailwinds can reduce lift and require a higher ground speed, increasing the distance needed for landing. Crosswinds can cause drift and require careful cyclic control to maintain the desired ground track. Pilots must adjust their approach and landing technique based on wind conditions to ensure a safe and controlled landing.

[PH.V.H.K2; FAA-H-8083-21]

5. **What impact does weight have on a helicopter's performance during a shallow approach and running/roll-on landing?**

Increased weight reduces the helicopter's performance by lowering the available power margin. This can lead to a higher descent rate and faster ground speed at touchdown, making the running/roll-on landing more challenging. Pilots must carefully manage the collective and cyclic to control the rate of descent and forward speed, especially when operating near maximum gross weight.

[PH.V.H.K2; FAA-H-8083-21]

6. **How do temperature and density altitude affect a helicopter's shallow approach and running/roll-on landing?**

High temperatures and high density altitudes decrease air density, which reduces rotor efficiency and engine performance. This can lead to decreased lift and increased power requirements, making it harder to control the descent rate and ground speed during landing. Pilots must be aware of these limitations and may need to adjust their approach angle, descent rate, and touchdown speed to compensate for the reduced performance.

[PH.V.H.K2; FAA-H-8083-21]

7. **How should a pilot select the approach path for a shallow approach and running/roll-on landing considering aircraft performance and limitations?**

The pilot should select the approach path based on the helicopter's performance charts, considering factors such as weight, altitude, temperature, and wind conditions. The path should allow for a gradual descent at a controlled rate, avoiding maneuvers that exceed the aircraft's limitations. The pilot must ensure that the approach path is free of obstacles and provides sufficient space for the running/roll-on landing.

[PH.V.H.R1; FAA-H-8083-21]

8. **How does wind direction impact the planning and execution of a shallow approach and running/roll-on landing in helicopter operations?**

Wind direction significantly affects the helicopter's performance during a shallow approach and running/roll-on landing. A headwind increases lift and reduces the ground speed required for landing, allowing for a more controlled and shorter landing roll. A tailwind reduces lift and increases ground speed, potentially leading to a longer landing roll and reduced control. Crosswinds can cause drift and require careful cyclic control to maintain the desired ground track. Pilots must adjust their approach technique based on the wind direction to ensure a safe landing.

[PH.V.H.R2a; FAA-H-8083-21]

9. **What emergency procedures should be in place in case of sudden wind changes during a shallow approach and running/roll-on landing?**

Emergency procedures include being prepared to conduct a go-around if wind conditions change suddenly and adversely affect the approach or landing. The pilot should have a clear plan for quickly applying power and adjusting the flight path to regain altitude and stabilize the helicopter. In the event of a wind shear or gust front, the pilot should be ready to counteract sudden losses of lift or increases in descent rate. Effective communication with air traffic control or ground crew for updated wind information is also crucial.

[PH.V.H.R2b; FAA-H-8083-21]

10. **How can a pilot mitigate the risks associated with turbulence during a shallow approach and running/roll-on landing?**

To mitigate turbulence risks, pilots should increase their situational awareness, particularly in windy or gusty conditions. It's advisable to approach at a slightly higher airspeed to maintain better control. Pilots should also ensure adequate separation from other aircraft to avoid wake turbulence. Adjustments to the flight path might be necessary to maintain stability. In extreme cases, choosing an alternate landing site or delaying the operation may be prudent.

[PH.V.H.R2c; FAA-H-8083-21]

11. **How can a pilot assess the helicopter's capability to perform a running/roll-on landing in the event of a powerplant failure?**

The pilot can assess this capability by reviewing the helicopter's flight manual for procedures and limitations related to autorotation and emergency landings. This includes understanding the glide distance at various altitudes and airspeeds, rotor RPM management during autorotation, and the specific techniques for transitioning from autorotation to a running/roll-on landing.

[PH.V.H.R3a; FAA-H-8083-21]

12. **What techniques should a pilot employ to mitigate collision risks during a shallow approach and running/ roll-on landing?**

To mitigate collision risks, the pilot should maintain a vigilant lookout throughout the approach and landing, using both visual scanning and any available onboard collision-avoidance systems. Approach paths should be planned to maximize visibility and minimize exposure to potential hazards. The pilot should also communicate intentions clearly with any ground personnel, and if operating in a controlled airspace, with air traffic control. Controlled and stabilized approaches help in maintaining situational awareness and readiness to react to unexpected obstacles.

[PH.V.H.R4; FAA-H-8083-21]

13. **What are the implications of different types of landing surfaces (e.g., grass, gravel, paved) for a shallow approach and running/roll-on landing?**

Different landing surfaces have varied implications for a shallow approach and running/roll-on landing. Grass surfaces may be soft and uneven, posing a risk of bogging down. Gravel surfaces can create debris hazards due to rotor wash. Paved surfaces are generally the most stable but can be slippery, especially when wet. The pilot must consider these factors in planning the approach, touchdown point, and rollout.

[PH.V.H.R5; FAA-H-8083-21]

14. **What factors contribute to dynamic rollover, and how can they be identified during a shallow approach and running/roll-on landing?**

Contributing factors to dynamic rollover include uneven landing surfaces, pilot inattention to lateral cyclic control, high wind conditions, and excessive lateral cyclic input. During a shallow approach and running/roll-on landing, pilots should be vigilant for these factors, particularly when one skid contacts the ground before the other or when making corrections for wind. In addition pilots should use the pedals to maintain directional heading, if the pilot does not maintain proper directional control with the pedals there is a potential for dynamic rollover during the ground run.

[PH.V.H.R6; FAA-H-8083-21]

15. What steps can a pilot take to mitigate the risk of ground resonance during a shallow approach and running/roll-on landing?

To mitigate the risk of ground resonance, pilots should aim for a smooth and controlled touchdown, avoiding hard landings that can initiate the vibration. Maintaining proper rotor RPM is crucial, as low RPM can contribute to the condition. Additionally, pilots should ensure that the helicopter's landing gear and rotor system are well-maintained and that dampers are functioning correctly. During landing, quick reaction to any signs of ground resonance is essential, including applying power to become airborne again if safe to do so.

[PH.V.H.R6; FAA-H-8083-21]

16. What strategies can a pilot employ to mitigate the risks associated with aircraft limitations during a shallow approach and running/roll-on landing?

To mitigate risks, the pilot should perform thorough preflight planning, considering the current weight, center of gravity, and environmental factors, and ensure that the operation stays within the helicopter's performance envelope. During the approach and landing, the pilot should continuously monitor aircraft performance, be ready to adjust the approach path or abort the landing if performance issues are noted, and maintain awareness of the helicopter's handling characteristics under the current conditions.

[PH.V.H.R8; FAA-H-8083-21]

17. What strategies should a pilot use to effectively prioritize tasks during the critical phases of a shallow approach and running/roll-on landing?

Pilots should adhere to the aviate, navigate, communicate hierarchy, ensuring that flying the helicopter safely is always the primary focus. Preplanning the approach and being familiar with the landing zone can reduce workload. Pilots should also sequence tasks in a way that critical actions are completed first, and nonessential tasks are deferred until the helicopter is safely on the ground and has come to a complete stop.

[PH.V.H.R9; FAA-H-8083-21]

Skills to be demonstrated:

- Complete the appropriate checklist(s).

- Make radio calls as appropriate.

- Maintain engine and rotor RPM within normal limits.

- Establish and maintain the recommended approach angle, and proper rate of closure.

- Determine wind direction and maintain ground track with crosswind correction.

- Maintain effective translational lift during surface contact with landing gear parallel to the ground track.

- Make smooth, timely, and correct control inputs after surface contact to maintain directional control.

- Use runway incursion avoidance procedures, if applicable.

I. Rolling Takeoff (Wheel-Type Landing Gear)

1. What are the key considerations for a pilot when conducting a rolling takeoff with a helicopter equipped with wheel-type landing gear?

Key considerations include assessing runway or takeoff path length and surface conditions, understanding the helicopter's weight and balance, and knowing the performance capabilities of the helicopter under current conditions. The pilot must also consider wind direction and strength, as well as any obstacles in the takeoff path. It is essential to ensure that the rotor RPM is within the required range and that the helicopter is properly configured for the takeoff.

[PH.V.I.K1; FAA-H-8083-21]

2. **How does the pilot adjust the takeoff technique in a wheeled helicopter based on varying environmental conditions like wind, temperature, and altitude?**

The takeoff technique in a wheeled helicopter must be adjusted based on environmental conditions to ensure safety and optimal performance. In strong wind conditions, the pilot might need to initiate the takeoff roll into the wind to maximize lift and control. In high-temperature or high-altitude conditions, where the air density is lower, the helicopter's performance may be reduced, requiring a longer takeoff roll and careful management of collective and cyclic to achieve the necessary lift. The pilot must be aware of these variations and plan the takeoff accordingly, potentially requiring adjustments in takeoff speed and rotor RPM management.

[PH.V.I.K2; FAA-H-8083-21]

3. **What are the typical situations in which a rolling takeoff is recommended for a helicopter with wheel-type landing gear?**

A rolling takeoff is recommended in situations where the helicopter is near its maximum gross weight, in high-density altitude conditions, or when operating from a confined area where a vertical takeoff is not feasible. It is also preferred when the surface conditions are such that a hover could cause damage or be hazardous, such as on loose gravel or snow-covered surfaces. Additionally, a rolling takeoff may be utilized to conserve power and reduce rotor wear in normal operations.

[PH.V.I.K3; FAA-H-8083-21]

4. **At what point during a rolling takeoff does translational lift typically occur, and what are the signs that a pilot should look for?**

Translational lift typically occurs when the helicopter reaches a forward airspeed of approximately 16–24 knots. Signs that translational lift is occurring include a noticeable increase in lift, a reduction in power required to maintain altitude, and an improvement in the helicopter's overall stability and controllability. The pilot may also observe a decrease in the rate of descent if initially descending or an increase in the rate of climb.

[PH.V.I.K4; FAA-H-8083-21]

5. What are the key factors that can affect the onset and effectiveness of translational lift during a rolling takeoff?

Key factors affecting translational lift include wind speed and direction, helicopter weight, air density (affected by altitude and temperature), and rotor system design. A headwind can enhance translational lift by increasing the relative airflow over the rotor blades. Heavier helicopter weight and higher density altitude (lower air density) can delay the onset of translational lift, requiring higher forward speed to achieve it.

[PH.V.I.K4; FAA-H-8083-21]

6. How should a pilot select an appropriate takeoff path for a rolling takeoff considering the helicopter's performance and limitations?

The pilot should select a takeoff path based on the helicopter's performance capabilities as detailed in the flight manual, taking into account factors such as weight, balance, power available, and any performance limitations specific to the helicopter model. This includes assessing the power required for takeoff under the current load and environmental conditions, and ensuring the path selected allows for a safe and controlled acceleration to the required airspeed within the available distance.

[PH.V.I.R1; FAA-H-8083-21]

7. What factors related to available distance must be considered when planning a rolling takeoff with wheel-type landing gear?

Factors related to available distance include the length and condition of the takeoff surface, any obstacles that may affect the takeoff path, and the surface's ability to support the helicopter without causing damage or sinking. The pilot must calculate the required takeoff distance based on current weight, environmental conditions, and helicopter performance, ensuring there is adequate room to accelerate to the necessary airspeed and become airborne safely.

[PH.V.I.R1; FAA-H-8083-21]

8. **How does wind affect the planning and execution of a rolling takeoff in a helicopter with wheel-type landing gear?**

   Wind direction and strength play a significant role in the planning and execution of a rolling takeoff. A headwind can decrease the required takeoff distance by increasing the relative airflow over the rotor blades, enhancing lift. Conversely, a tailwind can increase the required takeoff distance and reduce climb performance. Crosswinds require careful control to maintain the desired takeoff path. The pilot must adjust the takeoff technique to accommodate wind conditions, ensuring control and stability throughout the takeoff roll.

   [PH.V.I.R1; FAA-H-8083-21]

9. **How does wind direction affect the performance of a helicopter during a rolling takeoff with wheel-type landing gear?**

   Wind direction significantly influences helicopter performance during a rolling takeoff. A headwind increases lift and allows the helicopter to achieve necessary airspeed and lift-off more efficiently, potentially reducing the takeoff roll distance. Conversely, a tailwind can reduce lift and increase the required takeoff distance. Crosswinds can affect directional control, requiring careful management of cyclic inputs to maintain the desired takeoff path.

   [PH.V.I.R2a; FAA-H-8083-21]

10. **What emergency procedures should be in place in case of unexpected wind changes during a rolling takeoff?**

    In case of unexpected wind changes, such as sudden wind shear or gusts, the pilot should have a plan to abort the takeoff if conditions become unsafe. This involves reducing the collective to settle the helicopter back on its wheels and applying brakes if necessary while maintaining directional control. If the helicopter has already achieved sufficient airspeed and lift, the pilot may need to perform an immediate transition to forward flight, adjusting the climb profile to manage the effects of the wind change.

    [PH.V.I.R2b; FAA-H-8083-21]

11. **What emergency procedures should be in place in case of severe turbulence or wake turbulence encounter during a rolling takeoff?**

In case of severe turbulence or wake turbulence encounter, the pilot should be prepared to abort the takeoff if it compromises control or safety. This involves reducing the collective to bring the helicopter back down onto its wheels and applying brakes as necessary. If already airborne and unable to safely continue the takeoff, the pilot should focus on regaining control of the helicopter, potentially executing an emergency landing if needed. After encountering significant turbulence, a postflight inspection of the helicopter for potential damage is advisable.

[PH.V.I.R2c; FAA-H-8083-21]

12. **What strategies should a pilot employ to mitigate risks associated with the H/V curve during a rolling takeoff?**

The pilot should aim to accelerate quickly to a safe airspeed that allows for an effective autorotation in case of an engine failure. This might involve a longer takeoff roll or a steeper initial climb, depending on the helicopter's performance and the environment. The pilot should also be vigilant in monitoring engine performance and be prepared to react promptly in the event of an engine failure.

[PH.V.I.R3a; FAA-H-8083-21]

13. **What are the key risks associated with a rejected takeoff in a wheeled helicopter, and how can they be mitigated?**

Key risks associated with a rejected takeoff include loss of control, overrunning the available surface, and potential mechanical stress or failure. To mitigate these risks, pilots should have a clear understanding of their helicopter's performance limits and ensure all maintenance is up to date. Practicing rejected takeoffs in a safe environment can also help prepare pilots for such situations. Pre-takeoff briefings should include the criteria for rejecting a takeoff and the procedures to follow.

[PH.V.I.R3b; FAA-H-8083-21]

14. **What are the critical considerations for a pilot when planning for the possibility of powerplant failure during the takeoff/climb phase in a helicopter with wheel-type landing gear?**

Critical considerations include understanding the performance characteristics of the helicopter under various weight and environmental conditions, knowing the emergency procedures for powerplant failure, and being familiar with the helicopter's glide and autorotation capabilities. The pilot should also consider the takeoff environment, including available landing areas in the event of a powerplant failure, and the effects of wind and temperature on aircraft performance.

[PH.V.I.R3c; FAA-H-8083-21]

15. **How can a pilot mitigate the risks associated with collision hazards specific to the environment where the rolling takeoff is being conducted?**

To mitigate collision risks, the pilot should be familiar with the specific environment, including any unique hazards it presents. This might include understanding typical wildlife patterns, being aware of common areas where ground vehicles operate, and knowing the usual flight paths of other aircraft. Adjusting the takeoff plan based on these factors, such as selecting a time of day with less wildlife activity or avoiding busy air traffic periods, can reduce collision risks.

[PH.V.I.R4; FAA-H-8083-21]

16. **What are the risks associated with various takeoff surfaces, and how can a pilot mitigate these risks during a rolling takeoff?**

Risks associated with various takeoff surfaces include reduced traction on wet or icy surfaces, potential for foreign object damage on loose surfaces like gravel or dirt, and uneven lift-off on uneven or sloped surfaces. To mitigate these risks, the pilot should adjust the takeoff technique, such as increasing the takeoff distance to compensate for reduced traction or avoiding areas with loose debris.

[PH.V.I.R5; FAA-H-8083-21]

17. How can a pilot assess the condition and functionality of the landing gear before initiating a rolling takeoff?

Prior to takeoff, the pilot should conduct a thorough preflight inspection of the landing gear, checking for any signs of wear, damage, or malfunction. This includes inspecting tires for proper inflation and condition, checking wheel bearings and brakes (if equipped), and ensuring that all components of the landing gear are secure and functioning correctly. Any anomalies should be addressed before proceeding with the takeoff.

[PH.V.I.R6; FAA-H-8083-21]

18. How can a pilot identify and manage potential distractions during a rolling takeoff with wheel-type landing gear?

To manage potential distractions, a pilot should first identify sources of distraction such as cockpit activities, external environment, or communication requirements. Effective management involves minimizing nonessential cockpit activities, maintaining a clean and organized cockpit, and prioritizing tasks. Clear communication with co-pilots or ground crew and allocating specific times for certain tasks can also help in minimizing distractions.

[PH.V.I.R7; FAA-H-8083-21]

19. What are the signs of loss of situational awareness or disorientation a pilot should be aware of during a rolling takeoff?

Signs of loss of situational awareness or disorientation include missing checklist items, failure to respond to air traffic control communications, deviation from the planned takeoff path, and unexpected changes in airspeed or altitude. A pilot might also experience tunnel vision, fixation on a single task, or confusion about the helicopter's location or status. Recognizing these signs early is key to taking corrective action.

[PH.V.I.R7; FAA-H-8083-21]

Skills to be demonstrated:

- Complete the appropriate checklist(s).

- Make radio calls as appropriate.

- Determine wind direction with or without visible wind direction indicators.

- Verify assigned/correct takeoff path.

- Maintain engine and rotor RPM within normal limits.

- Use control inputs that initiate the takeoff roll.

- Maintain proper ground track with crosswind correction, while accelerating.

- Transition to a normal climb airspeed, ±10 knots, and set appropriate power.

- Maintain proper ground track with crosswind correction after liftoff.

- Use runway incursion avoidance procedures, if applicable.

Performance
Maneuvers

6

A. Rapid Deceleration/Quick Stop

1. What is the primary purpose of performing a rapid deceleration or quick stop maneuver in a helicopter?

The primary purpose of a rapid deceleration or quick stop maneuver in a helicopter is to reduce airspeed quickly while maintaining control and preparing for either an immediate landing or transition to hover. This maneuver is particularly useful in situations where the pilot needs to stop the helicopter quickly due to unexpected obstacles, sudden changes in traffic patterns, or to avoid collisions.

[PH.VI.A.K1; FAA-H-8083-21]

2. What are the key skills a pilot must demonstrate during a rapid deceleration or quick stop maneuver?

Key skills include precise control of the collective to manage altitude, smooth and coordinated use of the cyclic to control pitch and maintain a safe airspeed, and effective use of the antitorque pedals to maintain directional control. The pilot must also exhibit good judgment in deciding when to initiate and terminate the maneuver and must maintain spatial awareness and vigilance for potential hazards during the maneuver.

[PH.VI.A.K1; FAA-H-8083-21]

3. How does mastering the rapid deceleration or quick stop maneuver contribute to a pilot's overall flying proficiency?

Mastering the rapid deceleration or quick stop maneuver contributes to a pilot's overall flying proficiency by enhancing their ability to react quickly and effectively to changing situations, improving their control of the helicopter under various flight conditions, and increasing their confidence in handling emergency situations. This maneuver also develops the pilot's coordination, judgment, and situational awareness, all of which are critical skills for safe and efficient helicopter operation.

[PH.VI.A.K1; FAA-H-8083-21]

4. What impact does air density have on a helicopter's ability to perform a rapid deceleration or quick stop?

Air density, affected by altitude, temperature, and humidity, impacts the amount of lift generated by the rotor blades and the overall performance of the helicopter. In lower air density conditions, such as high altitudes or hot temperatures, the helicopter may experience reduced lift and power, potentially making a rapid deceleration or quick stop less effective and requiring greater distance to slow down. The pilot may need to compensate for these variations to maintain control and achieve the desired rate of deceleration.

[PH.VI.A.K2; FAA-H-8083-21]

5. How do varying wind conditions affect a helicopter's performance during a rapid deceleration or quick stop maneuver?

Varying wind conditions, particularly headwinds or tailwinds, can significantly affect a helicopter's performance during a rapid deceleration or quick stop. A headwind can assist in deceleration, making the maneuver more effective, while a tailwind can increase the distance and time required to decelerate. Crosswinds can also challenge directional control during the maneuver, requiring careful use of antitorque pedals to maintain heading.

[PH.VI.A.K3; FAA-H-8083-21]

6. What factors should a pilot consider to help recognize the need for a rapid deceleration or quick stop maneuver?

A pilot should consider factors such as unexpected obstacles or hazards in the flight path, sudden changes in air traffic or ATC instructions, weather conditions like gusting winds or reduced visibility, and any indications of mechanical issues with the helicopter. Additionally, the pilot should be alert to changes in the operational environment, such as the appearance of ground vehicles or personnel in the intended landing area.

[PH.VI.A.R1; FAA-H-8083-21]

7. **How can a pilot assess the risk associated with performing a rapid deceleration or quick stop under different flight conditions?**

   To assess the risk, the pilot should evaluate the current flight conditions, including airspeed, altitude, wind direction and speed, helicopter weight, and center of gravity. The pilot should also consider the helicopter's performance capabilities and limitations, as well as the surrounding environment for potential hazards or obstacles that could affect the maneuver.

   [PH.VI.A.R1; FAA-H-8083-21]

8. **What are the potential hazards of improper powerplant and rotor management during a quick stop maneuver?**

   Potential hazards include rotor RPM decay, which could lead to a loss of lift and control, and rotor overspeed, which can cause structural damage to the rotor system. Improper management could also lead to excessive airspeed or descent rate, making the maneuver unsafe or leading to a hard landing. Engine over-torque or over-temp conditions are also risks if the powerplant is not managed correctly.

   [PH.VI.A.R2; FAA-H-8083-21]

9. **How can a pilot mitigate risks associated with powerplant and rotor management during a rapid deceleration?**

   Risk mitigation involves maintaining proficiency in rapid deceleration maneuvers, understanding the specific response characteristics of the helicopter's powerplant and rotor system, and using smooth, controlled inputs to manage the collective and cyclic. Pilots should practice anticipating and compensating for inertia and rotor lag. Regularly reviewing emergency procedures for powerplant or rotor system failures is also important.

   [PH.VI.A.R2; FAA-H-8083-21]

10. **If a helicopter enters vortex ring state (VRS) during a rapid deceleration, what immediate actions should the pilot take to recover?**

If a helicopter enters VRS, the pilot should immediately apply forward cyclic to gain airspeed and exit the downwash area. Simultaneously, the pilot should avoid increasing collective rapidly, as this can worsen the situation. Instead, a slight reduction in collective may be necessary before applying power to arrest the descent once translational lift is regained. The pilot must act quickly and decisively to prevent a rapid descent.

[PH.VI.A.R3; FAA-H-8083-21]

11. **What techniques should a pilot use to mitigate the risk of collision during a rapid deceleration?**

To mitigate collision risks, the pilot should choose an area for the maneuver that is clear of obstacles and away from dense air traffic. Maintaining a high level of vigilance and readiness to adjust the maneuver based on the dynamic environment is crucial. The pilot should also communicate intentions clearly with any crew members and air traffic control and be prepared to abort the maneuver if an unexpected obstacle or aircraft enters the path.

[PH.VI.A.R4; FAA-H-8083-21]

12. **What strategies can a pilot employ to manage distractions during a rapid deceleration or quick stop maneuver?**

To manage distractions, a pilot should maintain a clear and focused mindset, prioritizing the immediate tasks required for the maneuver. Preflight planning should include a review of the rapid deceleration procedure to minimize the need for reference during flight. Limiting unnecessary cockpit conversation and muting nonessential communications can help maintain focus. The pilot should also establish a clean and organized cockpit environment to reduce physical distractions.

[PH.VI.A.R5; FAA-H-8083-21]

13. How can a pilot mitigate the risks of disorientation or loss of situational awareness during a rapid deceleration or quick stop?

To mitigate these risks, the pilot should maintain a high level of vigilance and continuously monitor the helicopter's flight instruments and external environment. Regular training and practice in rapid deceleration maneuvers under various conditions can improve proficiency and confidence. The pilot should also be mentally prepared for the maneuver, anticipating the required actions and potential challenges. If disorientation occurs, the pilot should slow down the maneuver, if possible, to regroup and reestablish situational awareness.

[PH.VI.A.R5; FAA-H-8083-21]

Skills to be demonstrated:

• Complete the appropriate checklist(s).

• Maintain engine and rotor RPM within normal limits.

• Coordinate all controls throughout the execution of the maneuver to terminate in a hover at an appropriate hover height.

• Maintain an altitude that permits safe clearance between the tail boom and the surface.

• Maintain heading throughout the maneuver, ±10°.

B. Straight-In Autorotation in a Single-Engine Helicopter

Note: The minimum entry altitude must be at least 500 feet AGL or a suitable higher entry altitude in strong wind conditions. Initiating a go-around because of an applicant's inability to complete this Task within the tolerances specified in the skill elements is considered unsatisfactory. Landing area safety concerns beyond the control of the applicant or evaluator that necessitate a go-around would not be considered unsatisfactory. The applicant and evaluator must not sacrifice the safety of flight and force a landing to complete this Task.

1. How does wind direction and speed affect the performance of a helicopter during a straight-in autorotation?

Wind direction and speed significantly affect autorotation performance. Headwinds can increase rotor efficiency by providing additional airflow through the rotor system, potentially extending glide distance. Tailwinds can reduce rotor efficiency and glide distance, making it more challenging to reach the intended landing spot. Crosswinds can cause drift and require corrective cyclic inputs to maintain the desired glide path.

[PH.VI.B.K1; FAA-H-8083-21]

2. In what ways does the weight of the helicopter impact its behavior during a straight-in autorotation?

The weight of the helicopter influences its descent rate and forward airspeed during autorotation. Heavier helicopters generally have a higher rate of descent and may require a steeper glide angle to maintain optimal rotor RPM. The pilot must adjust the autorotative descent to accommodate the weight, ensuring sufficient airspeed and rotor RPM are maintained for effective control and a safe landing.

[PH.VI.B.K1; FAA-H-8083-21]

3. How do temperature variations influence autorotation in a single-engine helicopter?

Temperature variations affect the density of the air, which in turn impacts rotor system efficiency and engine performance. In warmer temperatures, the air is less dense, potentially leading to reduced rotor efficiency and a higher descent rate during autorotation. The pilot may need to adjust autorotation techniques, such as flattening the glide path, to compensate for these effects.

[PH.VI.B.K1; FAA-H-8083-21]

4. What is the impact of density altitude on the performance of a helicopter during straight-in autorotation?

Density altitude refers to the altitude relative to the standard atmospheric conditions. At higher density altitudes, the air is less dense, which can reduce the lift produced by the rotor blades and decrease engine power, if applicable. This results in a higher descent rate and possibly a lower forward airspeed during autorotation. Pilots must be aware of these changes and may need to adjust their autorotation technique accordingly, such as initiating autorotation at a higher altitude.

[PH.VI.B.K1; FAA-H-8083-21]

5. Why is maintaining optimal main rotor speed (N_r) speed critical during a straight-in autorotation in a single-engine helicopter?

Maintaining optimal main rotor speed (N_r) speed is critical during autorotation because it ensures sufficient rotor RPM to generate the necessary lift and control for a safe descent and landing. If N_r is too low, the rotor system may not produce enough lift, leading to a high rate of descent. If N_r is too high, it can cause excessive stress on the rotor system and may lead to rotor overspeed. Optimal N_r allows for effective control of the helicopter during the descent and landing phase of autorotation.

[PH.VI.B.K2; FAA-H-8083-21]

6. **How can a pilot effectively manage main rotor speed (N_r) speed during a straight-in autorotation in a single-engine helicopter?**

   Effective management of main rotor speed (N_r) speed during autorotation involves using the collective to control rotor RPM. Lowering the collective decreases blade pitch, reducing drag, and preventing N_r decay. Raising the collective increases blade pitch, increasing drag, and preventing N_r overspeed. The pilot must continuously monitor the N_r and make smooth, timely collective adjustments to maintain it within the recommended range. Understanding the relationship between collective position, airspeed, and N_r is key to effective management.

   [PH.VI.B.K2; FAA-H-8083-21]

7. **What are the consequences of allowing main rotor speed (N_r) to drop below the recommended range during autorotation?**

   Allowing the main rotor speed (N_r) to drop below the recommended range during autorotation can have serious consequences. Low N_r results in reduced rotor efficiency, significantly increasing the rate of descent and reducing the pilot's ability to control the helicopter's glide path and flare during landing. This can lead to a hard landing, potentially causing injury to occupants and damage to the helicopter. In extreme cases, very low N_r may lead to a loss of aircraft control, making a controlled landing impossible.

   [PH.VI.B.K2; FAA-H-8083-21]

8. **What is the significance of energy management in the context of a straight-in autorotation in a single-engine helicopter?**

   Energy management during a straight-in autorotation is crucial as it involves managing the potential and kinetic energy of the helicopter to ensure a safe landing. This includes controlling the descent rate (potential energy) and forward airspeed (potential energy) to maintain optimal rotor RPM (kinetic energy) and ensure enough energy is stored in the rotor system for effective flare and cushioning during the landing. Proper energy management allows the pilot to control the helicopter's glide path and touchdown point effectively.

[PH.VI.B.K3; FAA-H-8083-21]

9. How does a pilot manage the helicopter's kinetic and potential energy during the descent phase of a straight-in autorotation?

During the descent phase, kinetic energy in the rotor system is managed by controlling the helicopter's forward airspeed, and by controlling the rate of descent. The pilot adjusts the collective to maintain optimal rotor RPM and uses the cyclic to control airspeed. The balance between descent rate and forward airspeed is key to ensuring sufficient energy is available for the flare and landing phase. The pilot must continually monitor and adjust the flight controls to maintain this balance.

[PH.VI.B.K3; FAA-H-8083-21]

10. In what ways does the pilot need to adjust energy management during the flare phase of a straight-in autorotation?

During the flare phase, the pilot uses cyclic inputs to increase the pitch attitude of the helicopter, reducing forward speed and converting the potential energy into kinetic energy. This action increases/maintains the rotor RPM and decreases descent rate. The timing and degree of flare are critical; too early or aggressive a flare can dissipate energy too quickly, while a late or insufficient flare may not provide enough lift to cushion the landing. The pilot must judge the flare based on altitude, airspeed, and rotor RPM.

[PH.VI.B.K3; FAA-H-8083-21]

11. What are the primary causes of high descent rates during a straight-in autorotation in a single-engine helicopter?

The primary causes of high descent rates in autorotation include any of the following or a combination of the following, excessively low forward airspeed, high helicopter weight, inappropriate collective pitch setting, low rotor RPM, and environmental factors like high density altitude or strong tailwinds. Mismanagement of the cyclic and or collective control can also contribute to an increased descent rate by not maintaining an optimal airspeed/rotor RPM for autorotation.

[PH.VI.B.K4; FAA-H-8083-21]

12. How does a high descent rate affect the safety and outcome of a straight-in autorotation maneuver?

A high descent rate during autorotation can significantly reduce the pilot's ability to control the helicopter's descent and landing. It can lead to a harder landing, increasing the risk of injury to occupants and damage to the helicopter. High descent rates also reduce the time and altitude available for the pilot to correctly execute the flare and landing phases of autorotation, making it challenging to achieve a safe touchdown.

[PH.VI.B.K4; FAA-H-8083-21]

13. What are the potential risks associated with not correcting a high descent rate promptly during autorotation?

Failing to correct a high descent rate promptly can lead to several risks, including the inability to reach the intended landing spot due to a rapid loss of altitude. It also increases the likelihood of a hard or uncontrolled landing, potentially resulting in structural damage to the helicopter or injury to its occupants. Additionally, it limits the pilot's ability to execute an effective flare, crucial for a smooth touchdown.

[PH.VI.B.K4; FAA-H-8083-21]

14. How do varying bank angles affect a helicopter's glide path and descent rate during a straight-in autorotation?

Varying bank angles during a straight-in autorotation can significantly affect the helicopter's glide path and descent rate. Increased bank angles can lead to a steeper glide path and higher descent rate due to the loss of vertical lift component. Steeper bank angles also result in a reduction of effective rotor disk area, which can diminish lift. The pilot must carefully manage bank angles to maintain an optimal glide path and descent rate for a safe autorotation landing.

[PH.VI.B.K5; FAA-H-8083-21]

15. What is the impact of airspeed variation on rotor RPM and autorotation performance in a single-engine helicopter?

Airspeed variation directly impacts rotor RPM and autorotation performance. Higher forward air speeds generally increase rotor RPM due to increased airflow through the rotor system, enhancing autorotative lift and extending glide distance. Conversely, lower airspeeds can lead to a reduction in rotor RPM, potentially decreasing lift and shortening the glide distance. The pilot must maintain an airspeed that optimizes rotor RPM and autorotation efficiency.

[PH.VI.B.K5; FAA-H-8083-21]

16. How does rotor RPM influence autorotation characteristics such as glide distance and rate of descent?

Rotor RPM is a critical factor in autorotation, influencing both glide distance and rate of descent. Optimal rotor RPM provides the best compromise between lift and drag, maximizing glide distance and minimizing descent rate. If rotor RPM is too low, the rotor system becomes less efficient, increasing the rate of descent. Conversely, excessively high rotor RPM can lead to rotor overspeed, posing a risk of structural damage. Maintaining appropriate rotor RPM is essential for a controlled descent and successful autorotation landing.

[PH.VI.B.K5; FAA-H-8083-21]

17. What are the risks associated with initiating a straight-in autorotation at a low entry altitude in a single-engine helicopter?

Initiating a straight-in autorotation at a low entry altitude poses several risks. The primary risk is the limited time and altitude available for the pilot to establish an effective autorotative descent and prepare for landing. This can lead to insufficient rotor RPM, inadequate airspeed management, and a reduced ability to effectively flare and cushion the landing. Additionally, low entry altitudes offer limited options for choosing a safe landing area, increasing the risk of an uncontrolled or hard landing, or increasing the risk of a longer ground run depending on airspeed at time of entry.

[PH.VI.B.R1; FAA-H-8083-21]

18. What strategies can a pilot use to mitigate the risks associated with low entry altitudes during straight-in autorotations?

To mitigate these risks, the pilot should maintain proficiency in autorotation procedures and be familiar with the helicopter's performance limits. Following the guidelines of the specific helicopters height/velocity diagram is crucial. Practicing autorotations from various altitudes can help the pilot develop quick decision-making skills and efficient control techniques. During an actual low-altitude autorotation, the pilot should focus on maintaining optimal rotor RPM and controlling the descent path to maximize the glide distance. Quick and precise control inputs are essential for managing airspeed and rotor RPM effectively.

[PH.VI.B.R1; FAA-H-8083-21]

19. What are the critical flight control inputs a pilot must manage during a straight-in autorotation in a single-engine helicopter?

The critical flight control inputs during a straight-in autorotation include collective pitch, cyclic control, and antitorque pedals. The collective is used to manage rotor RPM and descent rate, the cyclic controls the helicopter's attitude and airspeed, and the antitorque pedals are used to maintain directional control. Proper coordination of these controls is essential for a controlled descent and safe landing.

[PH.VI.B.R2; FAA-H-8083-21]

20. How can inappropriate collective pitch inputs during autorotation impact helicopter performance and safety?

Inappropriate collective pitch inputs can significantly impact helicopter performance and safety during autorotation. Raising the collective too much can lead to a loss of rotor RPM, reducing lift and increasing the descent rate. If RPMs are lowered too far the helicopter's main rotor blades will stall leading to a critical loss of lift and potentially catastrophic outcome. Lowering the collective excessively can cause the rotor RPM to increase beyond safe limits, risking rotor overspeed and potential structural damage. Maintaining optimal collective pitch is crucial to ensure sufficient rotor RPM for controlled descent and landing.

[PH.VI.B.R2; FAA-H-8083-21]

21. What are the potential risks of improper cyclic control during a straight-in autorotation, and how can they be mitigated?

Improper cyclic control during autorotation can lead to loss of airspeed control, resulting in either too high or too low airspeed. Excessively high airspeed can lead to increased descent rate and difficulty in flaring for landing. Too low airspeed can reduce rotor efficiency and glide distance and potentially not enough cushion for a safe landing. To mitigate these risks, the pilot should maintain the recommended autorotation airspeed by adjusting the cyclic for an optimal descent path and preparing for an effective flare at the end of the autorotation.

[PH.VI.B.R2; FAA-H-8083-21]

22. How does the management of antitorque pedals during autorotation affect the outcome of the maneuver?

Management of antitorque pedals during autorotation affects the helicopter's yaw control and directional stability. Ineffective use of pedals can result in yaw oscillations or drift, reducing the pilot's ability to maintain a straight descent path toward the intended landing area. Proper pedal input is necessary to counteract any yawing motion and keep the helicopter aligned with the wind and glide path, especially important during the flare and touchdown phases.

[PH.VI.B.R2; FAA-H-8083-21]

23. What are the potential risks associated with encountering turbulence during a straight-in autorotation in a single-engine helicopter?

Encountering turbulence during a straight-in autorotation can lead to sudden changes in airspeed and rotor RPM, making it challenging to maintain control and optimal descent conditions. Turbulence can cause erratic helicopter movements, increasing the risk of loss of control. It also complicates the management of the autorotation descent path and can disrupt the pilot's ability to execute a smooth flare and landing.

[PH.VI.B.R3; FAA-H-8083-21]

24. How can wake turbulence from other aircraft impact a helicopter performing a straight-in autorotation?

Wake turbulence from other aircraft can significantly impact a helicopter during autorotation. It can induce sudden and unexpected changes in helicopter attitude and altitude. If encountered during descent or flare, wake turbulence can disrupt the pilot's control inputs and lead to instability or loss of control. The helicopter might enter a wake vortex at a critical phase, potentially causing a rapid descent or uncontrolled movements.

[PH.VI.B.R3; FAA-H-8083-21]

25. What strategies can a pilot employ to assess and avoid turbulence and wake turbulence during autorotation?

To assess and avoid turbulence and wake turbulence, the pilot should be aware of current weather conditions and wind patterns that might indicate the presence of turbulence. Monitoring communications for reports of turbulence from other aircraft and paying attention to ATC advisories on wake turbulence are essential. The pilot should also plan the autorotation descent path to avoid known turbulence areas and flight paths of larger aircraft. Keeping a safe distance from large aircraft and adjusting the flight path based on their position and movement can help avoid wake turbulence.

[PH.VI.B.R3; FAA-H-8083-21]

26. What is wind shear and how can it impact a straight-in autorotation in a single-engine helicopter?

Wind shear refers to a sudden change in wind speed and/or direction over a short distance, either horizontally or vertically. During a straight-in autorotation, wind shear can significantly affect the helicopter's glide path, airspeed, and rotor RPM. It can cause unexpected changes in descent rate and direction, making it challenging to maintain a controlled autorotative descent and accurately judge the landing point. Sudden loss of airspeed due to wind shear can also reduce rotor efficiency, affecting the helicopter's ability to flare and land safely.

[PH.VI.B.R4; FAA-H-8083-21]

27. What are the key strategies for a pilot to mitigate wind shear effects during a straight-in autorotation?

To mitigate wind shear effects, the pilot should maintain a flexible approach to the autorotation, being ready to adjust flight controls as necessary to respond to changing wind conditions. This includes adjusting the cyclic to maintain desired airspeed and using the collective to control rotor RPM. Keeping a higher airspeed during descent can provide additional energy to compensate for sudden wind speed reductions. The pilot should also plan the autorotation trajectory with potential wind shear in mind, choosing a landing area that allows for flexibility in approach and touchdown point.

[PH.VI.B.R4; FAA-H-8083-21]

28. What is energy management in the context of a straight-in autorotation in a single-engine helicopter, and why is it important?

Energy management in autorotation refers to the control of kinetic and potential energy to ensure a safe and controlled descent and landing. It is crucial because the pilot must use the helicopter's altitude and forward airspeed to maintain rotor RPM and ensure enough energy is stored in the rotor system for effective flare and cushioning during the landing. Proper energy management allows for a controlled descent, accurate landing spot targeting, and minimizes the risk of hard landing or loss of control.

[PH.VI.B.R5; FAA-H-8083-21]

29. **In what ways does the pilot need to adjust energy management during the flare phase of a straight-in autorotation?**

During the flare phase, the pilot uses cyclic inputs to increase the pitch attitude of the helicopter, reducing forward speed and converting potential energy into kinetic energy. This action increases rotor RPM and decreases descent rate. The timing and degree of flare are critical; too early or aggressive a flare can dissipate energy too quickly, while a late or insufficient flare may not provide enough lift to cushion the landing. The pilot must judge the flare based on altitude, airspeed, and rotor RPM.

[PH.VI.B.R5; FAA-H-8083-21]

30. **Why is maintaining optimal main rotor speed (N_r) crucial during a straight-in autorotation in a single-engine helicopter?**

Maintaining optimal main rotor speed (N_r) is crucial during autorotation because it ensures sufficient rotor RPM to generate the necessary lift and control for a safe descent and landing. If N_r is too low, the rotor system may not produce enough lift, leading to a high rate of descent. If N_r is too high, it can cause excessive stress on the rotor system and may lead to rotor overspeed. Optimal N_r allows for effective control of the helicopter during the descent and landing phase of autorotation.

[PH.VI.B.R6; FAA-H-8083-21]

31. **What factors can influence main rotor speed (N_r) behavior during a straight-in autorotation, and how should they be managed?**

Factors influencing main rotor speed (N_r) behavior include airspeed, collective pitch, helicopter weight, and atmospheric conditions like air density. The pilot must manage airspeed within the recommended autorotation range, as it directly affects the N_r. Changes in collective pitch should be made smoothly to maintain optimal N_r. Heavier helicopter weight can lead to a higher descent rate, requiring careful N_r management. Atmospheric conditions such as high-density altitude can also affect N_r, necessitating adjustments to collective inputs.

[PH.VI.B.R6; FAA-H-8083-21]

32. What are the risks of low rotor RPM during a straight-in autorotation in a single-engine helicopter?

Low rotor RPM during a straight-in autorotation can significantly reduce the rotor system's ability to generate lift and control, leading to a higher rate of descent and decreased maneuverability. This can compromise the pilot's ability to effectively flare and cushion the helicopter during the landing phase, potentially resulting in a hard landing or total loss of control. Low rotor RPM also limits the energy available in the rotor system, which is crucial for a successful autorotation landing.

[PH.VI.B.R7; FAA-H-8083-21]

33. What immediate actions should a pilot take if low rotor RPM or rotor stall is detected during autorotation?

If low rotor RPM or rotor stall is detected, the pilot should immediately lower the collective to reduce blade pitch and decrease drag on the rotor system, helping to increase or recover rotor RPM. The pilot should make smooth and coordinated adjustments to prevent exacerbating the situation. The pilot should also adjust the cyclic as necessary to maintain optimal airspeed, further aiding in rotor RPM recovery.

[PH.VI.B.R7; FAA-H-8083-21]

34. What are the potential risks associated with main rotor overspeed (N_r overspeed) during a straight-in autorotation in a single-engine helicopter?

N_r overspeed during a straight-in autorotation can lead to excessive stresses on the rotor system, potentially causing structural damage to the rotor blades and hub. It can also result in a loss of rotor control, making it difficult to effectively manage the descent and landing phases of the autorotation. In extreme cases, N_r overspeed can lead to catastrophic rotor failure. Maintaining rotor RPM within the specified limits is crucial for the safety of the flight.

[PH.VI.B.R8; FAA-H-8083-21]

35. What immediate actions should a pilot take upon detecting N$_r$ overspeed during an autorotation?

Upon detecting main rotor (N$_r$) overspeed, the pilot should promptly but smoothly raise the collective to increase blade pitch and create more drag on the rotor system, thereby reducing RPM. It is important to avoid abrupt collective movements that could lead to a sudden loss of rotor efficiency or an excessive decrease in RPM. The pilot should also adjust the cyclic as necessary to maintain a stable descent path and airspeed.

[PH.VI.B.R8; FAA-H-8083-21]

36. What are the main risks associated with an excessive rate of descent during a straight-in autorotation in a single-engine helicopter?

An excessive rate of descent during a straight-in autorotation can significantly increase the risk of a hard or uncontrolled landing, potentially leading to aircraft damage and injury to occupants. It can compromise the pilot's ability to effectively execute the flare and touchdown phases, resulting in insufficient energy dissipation and a high-impact landing. Additionally, a high descent rate can limit the pilot's options for choosing a safe landing spot and reduce the margin for error in managing the autorotation.

[PH.VI.B.R9; FAA-H-8083-21]

37. What immediate actions should a pilot take if an excessive rate of descent is detected during autorotation?

If an excessive rate of descent is detected, the pilot should immediately take corrective action by adjusting the cyclic to increase forward airspeed, which can help decrease the descent rate. The collective should be adjusted carefully to maintain optimal rotor RPM, as sudden changes can exacerbate the descent rate. The pilot must balance these controls to stabilize the descent and prepare for an effective flare and touchdown. Continuous monitoring of descent rate and rotor RPM is key to making timely adjustments.

[PH.VI.B.R9; FAA-H-8083-21]

38. **What are the primary risks associated with a powerplant failure during a straight-in autorotation in a single-engine helicopter?**

The primary risks of a powerplant failure during a straight-in autorotation include the inability to execute a go-around, limited options for selecting a landing site, and the challenge of maintaining rotor RPM without engine power. This situation demands immediate initiation of autorotation procedures to maintain rotor speed and control descent, ensuring a safe landing. The pilot must also quickly identify a suitable landing area within the helicopter's glide distance.

[PH.VI.B.R10; FAA-H-8083-21]

39. **How can a pilot mitigate the risk of a hard landing or loss of control following a powerplant failure during an autorotation?**

To mitigate the risk of a hard landing or loss of control, the pilot should maintain proper airspeed and rotor RPM to ensure adequate control and lift during the descent. Practicing autorotation procedures regularly helps develop the skills needed for a controlled descent and landing. During the final phase of autorotation, the pilot should execute a proper flare to reduce descent rate and forward speed, followed by a gentle collective pull for cushioning just before touchdown.

[PH.VI.B.R10; FAA-H-8083-21]

40. **What types of collision hazards are most pertinent during a straight-in autorotation in a single-engine helicopter?**

The most pertinent collision hazards during a straight-in autorotation include ground obstacles like trees, buildings, power lines, and terrain, as well as the risk of colliding with other aircraft. Additionally, the emergency nature of an autorotation may lead to landing in unprepared or populated areas, increasing the risk of collision with vehicles, people, or other structures.

[PH.VI.B.R11; FAA-H-8083-21]

41. What are the critical considerations for a pilot when terminating an autorotation in a single-engine helicopter?

Critical considerations for terminating an autorotation include assessing the landing area for suitability, managing rotor RPM for optimal energy, timing the flare precisely to reduce descent rate and forward speed, and ensuring a smooth transition from the flare to the touchdown. The pilot must also be prepared to make last-minute adjustments based on changes in wind conditions or unexpected obstacles in the landing area.

[PH.VI.B.R12; FAA-H-8083-21]

42. How should a pilot assess the landing area during the final approach of a straight-in autorotation?

During the final approach of a practice straight-in autorotation, the pilot should assess the landing area for size, surface conditions, slope, and the presence of obstacles. This includes evaluating the wind direction and speed to approach into the wind when possible. The pilot should also be aware of any changes in the landing area conditions that may have occurred since the autorotation was initiated. If any issues arise during a practice autorotation the maneuver should be terminated, and the pilot should recover smoothly with power.

[PH.VI.B.R12; FAA-H-8083-21]

43. What are the key factors a pilot must consider when deciding to initiate a power recovery or go-around during a straight-in autorotation?

Key factors in deciding to initiate a power recovery or go-around include the helicopter's altitude, airspeed, and position relative to the landing area, as well as the rotor RPM. The pilot must also consider wind conditions, potential obstacles in the flight path, and the remaining available power. The decision should be based on whether the helicopter has sufficient altitude and energy to safely transition to powered flight and whether the landing area is no longer suitable or safe for touchdown.

[PH.VI.B.R13; FAA-H-8083-21]

44. How can a pilot effectively manage the transition from autorotation to powered flight during a go-around?

To effectively manage the transition from autorotation to powered flight, the pilot should smoothly and progressively apply power while adjusting the collective to increase lift. Cyclic and pedal inputs may be needed to maintain directional control and desired flight path. The pilot should monitor rotor RPM closely to ensure it remains within safe limits during the transition. It is important to anticipate changes in helicopter behavior as engine power is applied and to adjust controls accordingly.

[PH.VI.B.R13; FAA-H-8083-21]

45. What are the risks associated with delayed or improper execution of a power recovery or go-around during an autorotation?

Delayed or improper execution of a power recovery or go-around can lead to several risks, including vortex ring state, loss of rotor RPM, and insufficient altitude to complete the maneuver safely. There is also a risk of losing control due to abrupt or excessive control inputs. If the decision to go around is made too late, the helicopter may not have enough altitude or airspeed to recover safely, leading to a hard or crash landing.

[PH.VI.B.R13; FAA-H-8083-21]

46. What strategies can a pilot employ to manage distractions during a straight-in autorotation in a single-engine helicopter?

Strategies to manage distractions include establishing a clear mental checklist and prioritizing tasks, maintaining focus on critical flight parameters like rotor RPM, airspeed, and altitude, and minimizing unnecessary cockpit activities. The pilot should also communicate effectively with any passengers or crew to ensure they understand the need for minimal interruptions during the critical phases of autorotation. Using well-practiced procedures can help maintain focus during high-workload situations.

[PH.VI.B.R14; FAA-H-8083-21]

47. What are the risks of task saturation during a straight-in autorotation, and how can a pilot effectively prioritize tasks?

Task saturation during a straight-in autorotation can lead to missed critical steps, incorrect control inputs, or delayed reactions, increasing the risk of an unsafe landing. To effectively prioritize tasks, the pilot should focus on the most critical aspects of flight first, such as maintaining rotor RPM, controlling descent path, and identifying a suitable landing area. Training and experience can help a pilot quickly identify and focus on the most urgent tasks.

[PH.VI.B.R14; FAA-H-8083-21]

48. How does a pilot deal with the potential for disorientation during a straight-in autorotation, especially in challenging environments?

To deal with disorientation, the pilot should rely on flight instruments to provide accurate information about the helicopter's attitude and altitude, especially in environments where visual cues are limited. Practicing autorotations in various conditions, including simulators, can help a pilot become accustomed to different scenarios and learn how to stay oriented. Keeping head movements to a minimum and maintaining a steady visual scan can also help prevent disorientation.

[PH.VI.B.R14; FAA-H-8083-21]

49. What role does regular training and simulation play in helping a pilot manage distractions, maintain situational awareness, and prioritize tasks during an autorotation?

Regular training and simulation play a crucial role in helping a pilot manage distractions, maintain situational awareness, and prioritize tasks by providing a safe environment to practice and develop these skills. Simulations can mimic a wide range of scenarios and emergency situations, allowing the pilot to experience and learn how to handle various distractions and high-pressure situations. This training helps build confidence and competence, which are key to managing complex situations like a straight-in autorotation.

[PH.VI.B.R14; FAA-H-8083-21]

Skills to be demonstrated:

- Complete the appropriate checklist(s).

- Make radio calls as appropriate.

- Select a suitable landing area.

- Clear the area.

- Select an appropriate entry altitude.

- Initiate the maneuver at the proper point.

- Establish power-off glide with the helicopter trimmed and autorotation airspeed, ±10 knots.

- Maintain main rotor speed (N_r) within normal limits.

- Maneuver to avoid undershooting or overshooting the selected landing area.

- Use proper deceleration and collective pitch application that permits safe clearance between the aircraft tail boom and the surface.

- Initiate proper power recovery.

- Terminate autorotation to a stabilized hover, within 200 feet of a designated point.

C. Autorotation with Turns in a Single-Engine Helicopter

Note: The minimum entry altitude must be above 500 feet AGL or a suitable higher entry altitude in strong wind conditions. At least two 90-degree turns in the same direction or one continuous 180-degree turn must be performed. If the applicant does not roll out of the turn by 300 feet AGL then the evaluator must direct the applicant to perform a power recovery and initiate a go-around, and the Task is considered unsatisfactory.

1. **How do wind direction and speed affect autorotations with turns in a single-engine helicopter?**

   Wind direction and speed significantly affect autorotations with turns. Headwinds can increase the rate of descent and reduce ground speed, requiring adjustment in glide path and flare timing. Tailwinds can lead to a decreased rate of descent but increase ground speed, potentially leading to overshooting the intended landing spot. Crosswinds require careful management to maintain a proper flight path and can complicate the control of the helicopter during the flare and touchdown. Pilots must adjust their autorotation technique based on wind conditions to ensure a safe landing.

   [PH.VI.C.K1; FAA-H-8083-21]

2. **What is the impact of helicopter weight on autorotations with turns?**

   Helicopter weight directly affects autorotation performance. A heavier helicopter typically has a higher rate of descent and less glide distance due to increased gravitational forces. This requires the pilot to initiate the autorotation at a higher altitude and may necessitate a steeper glide angle or more aggressive flare. Conversely, a lighter helicopter may have a lower rate of descent and longer glide distance, allowing for more flexibility in choosing a landing spot and executing the autorotation.

   [PH.VI.C.K1; FAA-H-8083-21]

3. How do temperature and density altitude influence autorotations with turns in a single-engine helicopter?

Temperature and density altitude significantly influence the performance of a helicopter during autorotations with turns. Higher temperatures and higher density altitudes result in thinner air, reducing the efficiency of the rotor blades and decreasing lift. This can lead to a higher rate of descent and a reduced glide distance. Pilots must be aware of these effects, especially in hot and high-altitude environments, and may need to adjust their autorotation technique accordingly.

[PH.VI.C.K1; FAA-H-8083-21]

4. Why is maintaining optimal main rotor speed (N_r) critical during autorotations with turns in a single-engine helicopter?

Maintaining optimal main rotor speed (N_r) is critical during autorotations with turns because it ensures sufficient rotor RPM to generate the necessary lift and control for a safe descent and landing. In turns, centrifugal force can affect rotor RPM; if N_r is too low, the rotor system may not produce enough lift, leading to a high rate of descent and reduced control effectiveness. Conversely, if the N_r is too high, it can cause excessive stress on the rotor system. Optimal N_r allows for effective control of the helicopter throughout the autorotation, particularly during turns.

[PH.VI.C.K2; FAA-H-8083-21]

5. What are the potential consequences of allowing main rotor speed (N_r) to deviate from the recommended range during autorotations with turns?

Allowing the main rotor speed (N_r) to deviate from the recommended range during autorotations with turns can lead to serious consequences. If the N_r drops too low, the rotor may not produce sufficient lift, resulting in an increased rate of descent and reduced maneuverability, which could lead to an unsafe landing. If the N_r becomes too high, the rotor system could be subjected to excessive stress, risking structural damage or failure. Maintaining the N_r within the proper range is essential for safe autorotation and effective control during turns.

[PH.VI.C.K2; FAA-H-8083-21]

6. **What is the importance of energy management in autorotations with turns for a single-engine helicopter?**

Energy management is crucial in autorotations with turns because it involves maintaining the right balance of kinetic and potential energy for a safe landing. This includes managing airspeed, rotor RPM, and descent rate to ensure that the helicopter has sufficient energy to execute the flare and touchdown effectively. Proper energy management helps in maintaining control during the autorotation and ensures that the helicopter has enough inertia in the rotor system to cushion the landing.

[PH.VI.C.K3; FAA-H-8083-21]

7. **How does turning during an autorotation affect the helicopter's energy state, and how should a pilot compensate?**

Turning during an autorotation affects the helicopter's energy state by altering airspeed and rotor RPM, which in turn affects the kinetic and potential energy of the helicopter. When turning, there is a tendency for the descent rate to increase and airspeed to decrease along with an increase in main rotor RPM, which can lead to a potential loss of energy. The pilot should compensate by carefully adjusting the cyclic for level turns while maintaining optimal airspeed and the collective to maintain optimal rotor RPM, thus preserving the energy needed for a controlled landing.

[PH.VI.C.K3; FAA-H-8083-21]

8. **What are the primary causes of high descent rates during autorotations with turns in a single-engine helicopter?**

The primary causes of high descent rates during autorotations with turns in a single-engine helicopter include inappropriate airspeed, incorrect rotor RPM management, steep turn angles, and failure to properly adjust for wind conditions. A descent rate that is too high can occur if the airspeed is either too slow or too fast, if rotor RPM is not adequately maintained within the optimal range, or if turns are executed too steeply, leading to loss of lift. Additionally, wind conditions like tailwinds during the descent can increase the descent rate if not appropriately compensated for.

[PH.VI.C.K4; FAA-H-8083-21]

9. **What techniques should a pilot employ to correct a high descent rate during autorotation with turns?**

   To correct a high descent rate during autorotation with turns, the pilot should first ensure the rotor RPM is within the recommended range by adjusting the collective, as necessary. Managing airspeed is also crucial; slightly increasing forward airspeed can help reduce the descent rate. The pilot should avoid steep turns and instead use shallower bank angles to maintain lift and control. Continuous monitoring of descent rate and rotor RPM, combined with timely adjustments, is key to managing the descent effectively.

   [PH.VI.C.K4; FAA-H-8083-21]

10. **How do varying bank angles during an autorotation with turns affect the helicopter's performance in a single-engine helicopter?**

    Varying bank angles during an autorotation with turns can significantly affect a helicopter's performance. Steeper bank angles increase the load factor, which can lead to a higher descent rate and increased rotor RPM. Shallower bank angles generally allow for better control of descent rate and rotor RPM. Pilots must find a balance in bank angle that maintains sufficient rotor energy and control for a safe autorotation descent and landing.

    [PH.VI.C.K5; FAA-H-8083-21]

11. **What impact does airspeed have on autorotations with turns in a single-engine helicopter?**

    Airspeed plays a critical role in autorotations with turns. Too high an airspeed can lead to an increased descent rate and reduced rotor RPM, while too low an airspeed may not provide enough airflow through the rotor system to sustain lift and control. Optimal airspeed allows for an effective glide ratio and rotor RPM, enabling the pilot to manage the descent rate appropriately and prepare for the flare and touchdown.

    [PH.VI.C.K5; FAA-H-8083-21]

12. How does rotor RPM (N$_r$) need to be managed during autorotations with turns in a single-engine helicopter?

Effective management of rotor RPM (N$_r$) is essential during autorotations with turns. The pilot must maintain N$_r$ within the recommended range to ensure sufficient lift and control. Turning maneuvers can affect N$_r$ due to changes in aerodynamic loads. The pilot needs to adjust the collective as necessary during turns to prevent rotor RPM from decaying (which reduces lift) or increasing excessively (which can cause rotor damage). Keeping N$_r$ within the optimal range ensures that enough energy is available for the flare and landing phase.

[PH.VI.C.K5; FAA-H-8083-21]

13. What are the risks associated with improper management of bank angle, airspeed, and rotor RPM during autorotations with turns?

Improper management of bank angle, airspeed, and rotor RPM during autorotations can lead to several risks. Excessive bank angles can increase the descent rate and reduce rotor RPM, compromising the helicopter's ability to flare effectively. Inappropriate airspeed can also affect the descent rate and glide distance, potentially leading to an uncontrolled landing. Inadequate rotor RPM management may result in insufficient lift and rotor control, which can cause a hard landing or loss of control during the flare and touchdown.

[PH.VI.C.K5; FAA-H-8083-21]

14. What are the primary risks associated with initiating an autorotation with turns at low entry altitudes in a single-engine helicopter?

The primary risks associated with low entry altitudes in autorotations with turns include insufficient altitude to properly manage the descent, limited time for correcting errors or adjusting for wind changes, and reduced options for selecting a suitable landing area. Low entry altitudes also provide less margin for error in managing rotor RPM and airspeed, increasing the risk of a hard landing or loss of control during the autorotation.

[PH.VI.C.R1; FAA-H-8083-21]

15. **How can a pilot effectively assess and mitigate the risks of low entry altitudes during autorotations with turns?**

    To effectively mitigate risks at low entry altitudes, the pilot should continuously assess the altitude and be prepared for immediate and decisive action. This includes promptly establishing the optimal autorotation airspeed and rotor RPM and making quick but smooth adjustments to control inputs. The pilot should also have a clear plan for the intended landing area and be ready to adapt to changing circumstances.

    [PH.VI.C.R1; FAA-H-8083-21]

16. **What techniques should a pilot employ to manage rotor RPM and airspeed during a low-altitude autorotation with turns?**

    During a low-altitude autorotation with turns, managing rotor RPM and airspeed is crucial. The pilot should quickly establish and maintain the optimal autorotation airspeed to ensure adequate rotor RPM and control. This involves smooth collective adjustments to maintain RPM within the desired range. The pilot should avoid steep turns and excessive bank angles, as they can rapidly increase descent rate and affect rotor RPM. Any turns should be made as efficiently as possible to conserve altitude and energy.

    [PH.VI.C.R1; FAA-H-8083-21]

17. **What are the key flight control inputs a pilot must manage during an autorotation with turns in a single-engine helicopter?**

    During an autorotation with turns in a single-engine helicopter, the key flight control inputs include collective, cyclic, and pedal controls. The collective is used to maintain optimal rotor RPM, the cyclic to control airspeed and direction, and the pedals to manage yaw and coordinate turns. Effective management of these controls is crucial to maintain a controlled descent and prepare for a safe landing.

    [PH.VI.C.R2; FAA-H-8083-21]

18. What risks are associated with over-controlling or under-controlling the helicopter during autorotation with turns, and how can these be mitigated?

Over-controlling the helicopter during autorotation with turns can lead to oscillations, increased descent rate, and difficulty in maintaining a stable approach and landing. Under-controlling can result in delayed responses, inadequate correction for wind drift, and potential loss of control. To mitigate these risks, the pilot should use smooth, coordinated control inputs, anticipate the helicopter's response, and continuously monitor flight parameters. Regular practice and training in autorotation procedures are essential for developing precise control techniques.

[PH.VI.C.R2; FAA-H-8083-21]

19. What are the key considerations for a pilot when encountering turbulence during autorotation with turns in a single-engine helicopter?

During autorotation with turns in a single-engine helicopter, encountering turbulence requires the pilot to consider the effects on rotor RPM, descent rate, and helicopter control. The pilot must be prepared to make prompt and smooth adjustments to the collective and cyclic to maintain desired rotor RPM and flight path. It is also important to anticipate changes in airspeed and altitude caused by turbulence and to adjust the flight controls accordingly to ensure a safe and controlled descent.

[PH.VI.C.R3; FAA-H-8083-21]

20. How does wake turbulence impact auto rotation with turns, and what strategies should a pilot employ to mitigate its effects?

Wake turbulence can significantly impact the stability and control of a helicopter during autorotation with turns. It can cause abrupt changes in altitude and attitude, potentially leading to loss of control. To mitigate the effects of wake turbulence, the pilot should avoid the flight path of larger aircraft and remain vigilant for signs of turbulence. If wake turbulence is encountered, the pilot should focus on maintaining rotor RPM and control of the helicopter using smooth and decisive control inputs. Avoiding areas where wake turbulence is likely, such as behind large aircraft on approach or departure paths, is also crucial.

[PH.VI.C.R3; FAA-H-8083-21]

21. What risks does turbulence pose during the flare and touchdown phase of an autorotation with turns, and how can they be managed?

Turbulence during the flare and touchdown phase of an autorotation with turns can cause erratic movements, making it challenging to execute a smooth flare and controlled landing. The pilot must be prepared to adjust the flare timing and intensity based on the turbulence's effects. Keeping a higher airspeed and rotor RPM margin can provide more control and flexibility during the flare. Additionally, being ready to make quick cyclic and collective adjustments to compensate for sudden altitude and attitude changes is crucial for a safe touchdown.

[PH.VI.C.R3; FAA-H-8083-21]

22. What are the specific risks associated with encountering wind shear during an autorotation with turns in a single-engine helicopter?

Encountering wind shear during an autorotation with turns in a single-engine helicopter can pose significant risks such as sudden changes in airspeed, altitude, and flight path. This can lead to a loss of rotor RPM, increased descent rate, and reduced control effectiveness. Wind shear can also disrupt the pilot's planned approach path and landing area, increasing the difficulty of executing a safe autorotation and landing.

[PH.VI.C.R4; FAA-H-8083-21]

23. What strategies should a pilot employ to mitigate the effects of wind shear during autorotation with turns?

The pilot should be prepared for quick and smooth control inputs to adjust to the changing wind conditions, while continuously reassessing the landing approach ready to adjust the flight path as needed. Avoiding areas where wind shear is likely, such as near large buildings or terrain features, can also help reduce risk.

[PH.VI.C.R4; FAA-H-8083-21]

24. **What techniques should a pilot employ to effectively manage energy during autorotations with turns?**

    To effectively manage energy during autorotations with turns, a pilot should focus on maintaining the recommended autorotation airspeed and rotor RPM. This involves adjusting the collective to control rotor RPM and using the cyclic to maintain the desired airspeed and flight path. Anticipating the need for adjustments during turns and maintaining situational awareness regarding altitude and descent rate are also important. Additionally, avoiding overly steep turns can help conserve energy for the flare and landing.

    [PH.VI.C.R5; FAA-H-8083-21]

25. **How can a pilot mitigate the risk of energy loss during autorotations with turns in different wind conditions?**

    To mitigate the risk of energy loss in different wind conditions, a pilot must be adept at adjusting flight controls based on the wind's direction and strength. In a headwind, the pilot may need to decrease the rate of descent by adjusting the collective, while in a tailwind, the pilot may need to increase forward airspeed to maintain rotor RPM. Crosswinds require careful coordination of cyclic and pedal inputs to maintain the desired flight path.

    [PH.VI.C.R5; FAA-H-8083-21]

26. **What is the importance of maintaining appropriate main rotor speed (N_r) during autorotations with turns in a single-engine helicopter?**

    Maintaining appropriate main rotor speed (N_r) during autorotations with turns is crucial for ensuring sufficient lift and control responsiveness. Proper N_r ensures that the rotor system generates enough lift to control the descent and execute the flare for landing. Inadequate N_r can lead to a high rate of descent and reduced control effectiveness if N_r is too low catastrophic loss to the helicopter is possible. Excessive N_r can cause structural stress on the rotor system.

    [PH.VI.C.R6; FAA-H-8083-21]

27. What training practices can help a pilot develop proficiency in managing main rotor speed (N$_r$) during autorotations with turns?

Training practices that can help a pilot develop proficiency in managing main rotor speed (N$_r$) during autorotations with turns include practicing autorotations under various conditions, such as different wind conditions and aircraft weights, to understand how these factors affect N$_r$. Flight simulators can also provide valuable experience in managing N$_r$ in a controlled environment. Regular practice and thorough understanding of rotor dynamics are key to developing the skill to manage N$_r$ effectively during autorotations with turns.

[PH.VI.C.R6; FAA-H-8083-21]

28. What are the primary risks associated with low rotor RPM during autorotations with turns in a single-engine helicopter?

The primary risks associated with low rotor RPM during autorotations with turns include a significant loss of lift and rotor control, leading to an increased rate of descent and reduced maneuverability. Low rotor RPM can compromise the pilot's ability to effectively execute the flare and landing, increasing the risk of a hard or uncontrolled landing. Additionally, rotor stall can occur if the RPM drops too low, resulting in a catastrophic loss.

[PH.VI.C.R7; FAA-H-8083-21]

29. What are the key indicators a pilot should watch for to identify the onset of low rotor RPM or rotor stall during an autorotation?

Key indicators of low rotor RPM or rotor stall during an autorotation include a noticeable drop in the rotor RPM gauge, an unexpected increase in descent rate, changes in the helicopter's sound and vibration patterns, and reduced responsiveness of flight controls. If these signs are noticed, immediate corrective action is required, typically involving a reduction in collective pitch to increase rotor RPM.

[PH.VI.C.R7; FAA-H-8083-21]

30. What are the primary factors that can lead to an excessive rate of descent during autorotations with turns in a single-engine helicopter?

The primary factors leading to an excessive rate of descent during autorotations with turns include inappropriate airspeed, improper rotor RPM management, steep or aggressive turning maneuvers, and inadequate reaction to changing wind conditions. A high rate of descent can also result from delayed or insufficient collective inputs. Maintaining control over these factors is crucial to manage the descent rate effectively.

[PH.VI.C.R9; FAA-H-8083-21]

31. What corrective actions should a pilot take if an excessive rate of descent is identified during autorotation with turns?

If an excessive rate of descent is identified during autorotation with turns, the pilot should take corrective actions by adjusting the collective to manage rotor RPM and using the cyclic to attain the appropriate autorotation airspeed. If the descent rate is still too high, the pilot may need to flatten the turn or reduce the bank angle to decrease the descent rate. These adjustments must be made smoothly to maintain control and rotor RPM within safe limits.

[PH.VI.C.R9; FAA-H-8083-21]

32. What are the key considerations for a pilot when experiencing a powerplant failure during autorotation with turns in a single-engine helicopter?

During a powerplant failure in a single-engine helicopter, the pilot's key considerations should include immediately entering autorotation, maintaining optimal rotor RPM, choosing a suitable landing area, and managing airspeed and descent rate. The pilot must also be prepared to adjust the autorotation technique based on altitude, wind conditions, and available landing spots, ensuring a safe touchdown despite the loss of engine power.

[PH.VI.C.R10; FAA-H-8083-21]

33. How can abrupt or improper rolling out of a turn impact the autorotation maneuver in a single-engine helicopter?

Abrupt or improper rolling out of a turn can lead to a sudden change in descent rate, loss of rotor RPM, and potential loss of control. It can cause disorientation, increase the rate of descent, and lead to difficulty in aligning with the landing area. Smooth and controlled rolling out is essential to maintain rotor efficiency and ensure a stable flight path during autorotation.

[PH.VI.C.R11; FAA-H-8083-21]

34. How can a pilot assess and mitigate the risk of altitude loss during the roll-out phase of a turn in autorotation?

To mitigate altitude loss during the roll-out phase, the pilot should start the roll-out at an altitude that provides sufficient height above the ground for maneuvering and recovery. Monitoring the vertical speed indicator and maintaining an appropriate airspeed are key to managing altitude. If altitude loss is greater than expected, the pilot should adjust the cyclic and collective to stabilize the descent rate and prepare for the landing phase.

[PH.VI.C.R11; FAA-H-8083-21]

35. What are the key factors a pilot must consider to help avoid collision hazards during autorotation with turns in a single-engine helicopter?

During autorotation with turns in a single-engine helicopter, key factors to avoid collision hazards include maintaining situational awareness, choosing a clear and safe area for the autorotation, and being vigilant of other air traffic, terrain, and obstacles. The pilot must continuously scan the environment, particularly when executing turns, and be prepared to adjust the flight path if necessary to maintain a safe distance from potential hazards.

[PH.VI.C.R12; FAA-H-8083-21]

36. What are the key considerations a pilot must account for when terminating an autorotation with turns in a single-engine helicopter?

Key considerations when terminating an autorotation with turns include managing rotor RPM, controlling descent rate, aligning with the intended landing area, and timing the flare correctly. The pilot must ensure that rotor RPM is within optimal limits for effective energy management during the flare and touchdown. Additionally, the approach should be adjusted to maintain a safe glide path and prepare for the transition to a hover or run-on landing, depending on the helicopter's capabilities and the situation.

[PH.VI.C.R13; FAA-H-8083-21]

37. What are the key considerations for a pilot when executing power recovery and go-around during autorotations with turns in a single-engine helicopter?

Timing the initiation of power application, ensuring sufficient rotor RPM is maintained, and managing the helicopter's airspeed and flight path. The pilot must smoothly apply power to transition from the autorotation to powered flight while maintaining control and situational awareness. Altitude and airspeed must be monitored to ensure a safe transition and avoid vortex ring state or over-speeding.

[PH.VI.C.R14; FAA-H-8083-21]

38. What risks are associated with improper power application during a go-around from an autorotation with turns?

Improper power application during a go-around from an autorotation with turns can lead to several risks, including loss of rotor RPM, vortex ring state, and loss of control. If power is applied too abruptly, it can cause a rapid change in airspeed and pitch attitude, leading to disorientation and potentially a loss of control. Inadequate power application may result in insufficient altitude gain or an extended period in a vulnerable flight state.

[PH.VI.C.R14; FAA-H-8083-21]

39. What strategies should a pilot employ to manage distractions during autorotation with turns in a single-engine helicopter?

A pilot should maintain a high level of focus on the primary task of safely executing the autorotation. This includes adhering to a well-practiced routine, using checklists where appropriate, and minimizing nonessential cockpit activities. The pilot should also establish clear communication protocols with any crew or passengers to ensure that interactions do not interfere with critical flight tasks.

[PH.VI.C.R15; FAA-H-8083-21]

40. How does effective task prioritization contribute to safe execution of autorotations with turns in a single-engine helicopter?

Effective task prioritization is crucial for the safe execution of autorotations with turns as it ensures that the pilot focuses on the most critical aspects of flight at the right time. This involves continuously assessing the situation and deciding which tasks require immediate attention, such as maintaining rotor RPM, controlling descent rate, and selecting a suitable landing area. Prioritizing these key tasks helps prevent workload overload and ensures that the pilot remains in control throughout the autorotation.

[PH.VI.C.R15; FAA-H-8083-21]

Skills to be demonstrated:

• Complete the appropriate checklist(s).

• Make radio calls as appropriate.

• Select a suitable landing area.

• Clear the area.

• Select an appropriate entry altitude.

• Initiate the maneuver at the proper point.

• Establish power-off glide with the helicopter trimmed and autorotation airspeed, ±10 knots .

• Maintain main rotor speed (N_r) within normal limits.

• Maneuver to avoid undershooting or overshooting the selected landing area.

• Roll out no lower than 300 feet above ground level (AGL) along the flight path to the selected landing area.

• Use proper deceleration and collective pitch application that permits safe clearance between the aircraft tail boom and the surface.

• Initiate proper power recovery.

• Terminate autorotation to a stabilized hover, within 200 feet of a designated point.

Navigation 7

A. Pilotage and Dead Reckoning

1. What is pilotage, and how is it applied in helicopter navigation?

Pilotage in helicopter navigation refers to the technique of determining the helicopter's position and course by visually comparing landmarks on the ground with those on a map. It involves recognizing terrain features, roads, rivers, and other significant landmarks, and using them to navigate from one point to another. Pilots use pilotage to maintain orientation, especially during VFR (visual flight rules) flights.

[PH.VII.A.K1; FAA-H-8083-25]

2. How does dead reckoning complement pilotage in helicopter navigation?

Dead reckoning complements pilotage by providing a method to navigate when visual references are limited or not available. It involves calculating the helicopter's position based on a known starting point, time, speed, and heading. Dead reckoning uses the helicopter's airspeed, compass heading, wind correction, and elapsed time to estimate the current position. It serves as a backup to pilotage and is especially useful in poor visibility or over featureless terrain.

[PH.VII.A.K1; FAA-H-8083-25]

3. What are the key elements a pilot needs to consider when using dead reckoning for helicopter navigation?

Key elements in dead reckoning for helicopter navigation include accurate heading and speed control, precise timekeeping, and correction for wind drift. The pilot must accurately know the helicopter's airspeed and heading, monitor the time elapsed from a known position, and adjust for any wind effects. Regular cross-checks with visual landmarks (if available) and navigation aids can help verify the dead reckoning calculations.

[PH.VII.A.K1; FAA-H-8083-25]

4. In what situations is pilotage preferred over dead reckoning in helicopter navigation, and why?

Pilotage is preferred over dead reckoning in situations where visual reference to the ground is clear, such as in good weather conditions and over well-defined terrain. It is more straightforward and reliable when landmarks are easily identifiable. Pilotage allows for real-time navigation adjustments based on visible terrain features, making it ideal for low-level flying, obstacle avoidance, and VFR flight in familiar areas.

[PH.VII.A.K1; FAA-H-8083-25]

5. How can a pilot effectively combine pilotage and dead reckoning techniques during a helicopter flight?

To effectively combine pilotage and dead reckoning, a pilot should use landmarks and terrain features for pilotage while simultaneously tracking the flight's progress using dead reckoning. This involves regularly updating the helicopter's estimated position based on time, speed, and heading, and cross-referencing this with visual references and map data. The integration of both methods provides a more comprehensive and accurate navigation approach, ensuring redundancy and increasing safety.

[PH.VII.A.K1; FAA-H-8083-25]

6. What are the common types of magnetic compass errors encountered in helicopter navigation?

Common types of magnetic compass errors in helicopter navigation include variation, deviation, oscillation, dip errors, and acceleration and turning errors.

- *Variation* is the difference between true north and magnetic north.
- *Deviation* is caused by magnetic fields within the helicopter.
- *Oscillation* is the erratic movement of the compass needle due to turbulence or helicopter vibration.
- *Dip errors* occur because the compass tries to align with the magnetic field of the Earth, which varies with latitude.
- *Acceleration and turning errors* are specific to aircraft movement, particularly noticeable when accelerating, decelerating, or turning.

[PH.VII.A.K2; FAA-H-8083-25]

7. **How does topography influence flight planning and route selection in helicopter navigation?**

   Topography influences flight planning and route selection by dictating safe flying altitudes, identifying viable routes, and highlighting areas to avoid due to terrain obstacles or challenging weather conditions. Pilots must consider elevation changes, mountainous areas, valleys, and water bodies to ensure a safe and efficient flight path, particularly in areas with significant terrain variation. Topography also plays a role in determining emergency landing spots and alternate routes.

   [PH.VII.A.K3; FAA-H-8083-25]

8. **What are the key topographic features a helicopter pilot should be able to recognize and interpret on a map for effective navigation?**

   Key topographic features a helicopter pilot should recognize and interpret include mountains, valleys, rivers, lakes, forests, urban areas, and coastlines. The pilot should be able to understand contour lines indicating elevation changes, recognize significant landmarks, and interpret symbols representing various terrain and structures. This knowledge assists in visual navigation and situational awareness.

   [PH.VII.A.K3; FAA-H-8083-25]

9. **What factors should be considered when selecting an appropriate route for helicopter navigation?**

   When selecting an appropriate route for helicopter navigation, factors to consider include terrain and topography, weather conditions, airspace restrictions, availability of landing zones, proximity to navigational aids, and potential hazards such as high-tension lines or tall structures. The route should also be planned considering fuel requirements, helicopter performance capabilities, and alternate routes in case of emergencies.

   [PH.VII.A.K4a; FAA-H-8083-25]

10. **How can a pilot incorporate emergency considerations into route selection for helicopter navigation?**

    Incorporating emergency considerations into route selection involves planning for potential contingencies and ensuring access to safe landing areas or alternate airports. Pilots should identify suitable areas along the route for precautionary or emergency landings, such as open fields, helipads, or airports. Additionally, factors like fuel reserves, helicopter performance under various emergency conditions, and proximity to rescue or medical facilities should be considered in route planning.

    [PH.VII.A.K4a; FAA-H-8083-25]

11. **What factors should a helicopter pilot consider when selecting the appropriate cruising altitude for a flight?**

    When selecting the appropriate cruising altitude for a helicopter flight, a pilot should consider factors such as terrain elevation, weather conditions, airspace restrictions, obstacle clearance, helicopter performance capabilities, and efficiency. Altitude must be sufficient to ensure obstacle clearance, including buildings and terrain, while also considering factors like wind direction and speed, temperature, and density altitude for optimal performance and fuel efficiency. Additionally, compliance with VFR cruising altitude rules based on magnetic course is important above 3,000 feet.

    [PH.VII.A.K4b; FAA-H-8083-25]

12. **Why is altitude selection important in congested areas, and what should pilots consider in such environments?**

    Altitude selection is crucial in congested areas to ensure safe separation from buildings, other aircraft, and structures like towers and cranes. Pilots should consider noise abatement procedures, local air traffic patterns, helicopter performance, and the potential need for quick maneuvering or emergency landings. Higher altitudes may offer safer options for emergency landings and better visibility, but they must be balanced with considerations for noise sensitivity and local airspace restrictions.

    [PH.VII.A.K4b; FAA-H-8083-25]

13. **What characteristics make a feature a good checkpoint for navigation in helicopter flight?**

A good checkpoint for navigation in helicopter flight should be easily identifiable from the air, distinctive from surrounding features, and marked on aeronautical charts. Ideal checkpoints include large, unique landmarks such as lakes, rivers, bridges, large buildings, or intersections of major highways. The checkpoint should be located at a reasonable interval along the flight path and remain visible under various weather conditions.

[PH.VII.A.K4c; FAA-H-8083-25]

14. **How does a helicopter pilot determine the heading to maintain along a plotted course?**

A helicopter pilot determines the heading to maintain along a plotted course by first calculating the true course from the aeronautical chart. The pilot then adjusts this true course for magnetic variation to find the magnetic course. Further adjustments are made for wind correction angle, considering wind direction and speed, to compute the heading to fly. This heading accounts for wind drift to ensure the helicopter remains on the intended course.

[PH.VII.A.K5a; FAA-H-8083-25]

15. **What is the significance of calculating ground speed in course plotting, and how is it accomplished?**

Calculating ground speed in course plotting is significant as it determines the actual speed over the ground, affecting estimated time en route and fuel consumption. Ground speed can be calculated using flight computer tools or electronic flight planning software. The pilot needs to consider the helicopter's airspeed and adjust it for wind speed and direction. Accurate calculation of ground speed is essential for effective flight planning and timely arrivals at destinations or checkpoints along with fuel burn calculations.

[PH.VII.A.K5a; FAA-H-8083-25]

16. What are the key considerations a helicopter pilot must make when determining the course, heading, and speed for a flight?

Key considerations for a helicopter pilot when determining the course, heading, and speed for a flight include the desired route and destination, magnetic variation, wind speed and direction, helicopter performance characteristics, terrain, airspace restrictions, and weather conditions. The pilot must calculate the true course, adjust for magnetic variation to find the magnetic course, determine wind correction angle for wind drift, and calculate the ground speed to estimate time en route and fuel requirements. Safety considerations, such as alternate routes and emergency landing areas, should also be factored into the planning.

[PH.VII.A.K5a; FAA-H-8083-25]

17. What is the wind correction angle (WCA), and why is it important in helicopter navigation?

The wind correction angle (WCA) is the angle between the intended course over the ground and the actual heading of the helicopter to counteract the effect of the wind. It is important in helicopter navigation because it ensures that the helicopter stays on the desired ground track despite the lateral drift caused by crosswinds. Correctly calculating and applying WCA is essential for accurate navigation and reaching the intended destination along the planned route.

[PH.VII.A.K5b; FAA-H-8083-25]

18. How does a pilot calculate the wind correction angle for a helicopter flight?

To calculate the wind correction angle for a helicopter flight, the pilot needs to know the helicopter's intended ground track (true course), true airspeed, wind direction, and wind speed. This information is used to determine how much the wind will push the helicopter off course. The calculation can be done using a flight computer, E6B flight calculator, or electronic flight planning tools. The result is the angle that the helicopter must head into the wind to maintain the desired ground track.

[PH.VII.A.K5b; FAA-H-8083-25]

19. How can a pilot verify and adjust the wind correction angle during a helicopter flight?

A pilot can verify and adjust the wind correction angle during flight by observing ground landmarks and the helicopter's progress along the intended track. If the helicopter drifts off course, the pilot can adjust the heading to compensate. GPS navigation systems and avionics can provide real-time feedback on track made good and cross-track error, helping the pilot to fine-tune the wind correction angle as needed. Regular cross-checking with visual references or navigation aids ensures accuracy in maintaining the planned route.

[PH.VII.A.K5b; FAA-H-8083-25]

20. How does a helicopter pilot estimate the time required for a flight segment during course plotting?

A helicopter pilot estimates the time required for a flight segment by calculating the distance to be covered and dividing it by the expected ground speed. The distance can be measured on an aeronautical chart using a plotter and then converted to nautical miles or kilometers. The ground speed is estimated based on the helicopter's airspeed and adjusted for wind effects. The resulting time estimate helps in planning fuel requirements, scheduling, and maintaining adherence to flight plans.

[PH.VII.A.K5c; FAA-H-8083-25]

21. Why is it important for helicopter pilots to accurately estimate time, speed, and distance, and how does it impact flight operations?

Accurately estimating time, speed, and distance is critical for helicopter pilots to ensure effective flight planning, fuel management, compliance with airspace and ATC requirements, and timely arrivals at destinations. It impacts flight operations by influencing decisions on route selection, altitude, and timing for reaching checkpoints or destinations. Accurate estimations are also vital for emergency planning, such as identifying potential landing sites or alternates in case of unforeseen circumstances.

[PH.VII.A.K5c; FAA-H-8083-25]

22. What is true airspeed in helicopter navigation, and how is it different from indicated airspeed?

True airspeed (TAS) in helicopter navigation is the actual speed of the helicopter through the air, which takes into account the effect of altitude and temperature on air density. It differs from indicated airspeed (IAS), which is the speed shown on the airspeed indicator and does not account for these environmental factors. TAS is higher than IAS at high altitudes or in warmer temperatures due to lower air density. Accurate calculation of TAS is essential for precise navigation, especially over long distances.

[PH.VII.A.K5d; FAA-H-8083-25]

23. What is density altitude, and why is it important for helicopter pilots to consider when planning a flight?

Density altitude is the altitude relative to the standard atmosphere conditions at which the air density would be equal to the current air density. It is a critical performance factor for helicopters as it directly affects engine power, rotor efficiency, lift, and overall aircraft performance. Higher density altitudes, typically found in hot or high-altitude conditions, result in reduced performance. Helicopter pilots must consider density altitude in flight planning to ensure the helicopter can safely operate within its performance limitations.

[PH.VII.A.K5d; FAA-H-8083-25]

24. How does altitude affect the power setting selection in helicopter navigation?

Altitude affects power setting selection in helicopter navigation because as altitude increases, air density decreases. This reduction in air density means that the helicopter's engine and rotor system become less efficient, requiring adjustments in power settings to achieve the desired performance. At higher altitudes, more power may be required to maintain the same level of lift and airspeed as at lower altitudes. Pilots must be aware of the helicopter's performance capabilities at various altitudes to select the appropriate power settings.

[PH.VII.A.K6; FAA-H-8083-21]

25. **What role does the helicopter's flight manual play in determining appropriate power settings for navigation?**

The helicopter's flight manual plays a crucial role in determining appropriate power settings for navigation as it provides specific guidelines and limitations for engine operation and performance parameters. The manual includes power setting charts and tables that consider various factors such as altitude, temperature, weight, and flight conditions. Pilots must refer to these guidelines to select power settings that ensure the helicopter operates within safe and efficient operational limits, thus enabling accurate and effective navigation.

[PH.VII.A.K6; FAA-H-8083-21]

26. **Why is it important for a helicopter pilot to compare planned calculations with actual flight results during navigation?**

It is important for a helicopter pilot to compare planned calculations with actual flight results during navigation to ensure the accuracy and safety of the flight. This comparison helps identify deviations from the planned course, speed, altitude, and time estimates, which may be caused by factors such as unexpected wind changes, air traffic control (ATC) instructions, or helicopter performance differences. By recognizing these deviations, a pilot can make timely corrections to stay on course, maintain schedule, and ensure efficient fuel usage.

[PH.VII.A.K7; FAA-H-8083-25]

27. **What common factors might lead to discrepancies between planned calculations and actual results in helicopter navigation?**

Common factors that might lead to discrepancies between planned calculations and actual results in helicopter navigation include unexpected wind speed and direction changes, air traffic reroutes, variations in helicopter performance, and differences in air temperature or pressure from forecasted values. Pilots might also encounter navigational errors, unanticipated airspace restrictions, or differences in ATC instructions. These factors can affect ground speed, course accuracy, fuel consumption, and time en route.

[PH.VII.A.K7; FAA-H-8083-25]

28. **What are effective measures for a helicopter pilot to mitigate the risk of collision during navigation?**

Effective measures to mitigate the risk of collision during helicopter navigation include maintaining a thorough and consistent visual lookout, using proper communication protocols with ATC and other aircraft, and adhering to established flight rules and procedures. Pilots should also utilize any available collision avoidance technologies and be proactive in adjusting their flight path to ensure safe separation from other aircraft, terrain, and obstacles. Regular training in collision avoidance techniques and emergency procedures is also crucial for mitigating collision risks.

[PH.VII.A.R1; FAA-H-8083-25]

29. **What techniques can a helicopter pilot use to manage distractions and maintain focus during navigation?**

A helicopter pilot can use cockpit resource management techniques such as setting priorities for tasks, dividing tasks between crew members if applicable, and minimizing nonessential activities during critical phases of flight. Implementing a sterile cockpit rule during high-workload periods, such as takeoff and landing, can help reduce distractions. Additionally, preparing and organizing navigational materials in advance and using checklists can aid in maintaining focus on essential tasks.

[PH.VII.A.R2; FAA-H-8083-25]

30. **How can a helicopter pilot effectively prioritize tasks during complex navigation scenarios?**

In complex navigation scenarios, a helicopter pilot can effectively prioritize tasks by using the aviate, navigate, communicate principle. This means the pilot's first priority is always to control the helicopter (aviate), then to ensure they are following the correct course (navigate), and finally to communicate with ATC or other relevant parties. Setting clear objectives before the flight and recognizing which tasks are critical and which can be delayed or delegated helps in managing workload and maintaining situational awareness.

[PH.VII.A.R2; FAA-H-8083-25]

31. What factors should a helicopter pilot consider to help assess risks associated with unplanned fuel/energy consumption during navigation?

A pilot should consider factors such as flight duration, route distance, weather conditions, potential for headwinds or tailwinds, altitude, helicopter weight, and any possible deviations or delays that could extend flight time. Additionally, understanding the helicopter's fuel burn rate under various operating conditions and incorporating a buffer for contingencies is essential for accurate fuel planning.

[PH.VII.A.R3; FAA-H-8083-25]

32. What measures can a helicopter pilot take to mitigate the risk of running out of fuel due to unplanned consumption?

Plan the flight with conservative fuel estimates, including reserves for unexpected events like diversions, delays, or adverse weather. Pilots should also continuously monitor fuel levels and consumption rates throughout the flight and be prepared to adjust the flight plan, such as changing the route, altitude, or even landing for refueling if necessary.

[PH.VII.A.R3; FAA-H-8083-25]

Skills to be demonstrated:

- Prepare and use a flight log.

- Navigate by pilotage.

- Navigate by means of precomputed headings, groundspeeds, elapsed time, and reference to landmarks or checkpoints.

- Use the magnetic direction indicator in navigation, including turns to headings.

- Verify position within three nautical miles of the flight-planned route.

- Correct for and record the differences between preflight fuel, groundspeed, and heading calculations and those determined en route.

- Arrive at the en route checkpoints within five minutes of the initial or revised estimated time of arrival (ETA) and provide a destination estimate.

- Maintain the selected altitude, ±200 feet and heading, ±15°.

B. Navigation Systems and Radar Services

1. What are the key components of ground-based navigation systems used in helicopter flying, and how do they assist in orientation and course determination?

Key components of ground-based navigation systems used in helicopter flying include VOR (VHF Omnidirectional Range), NDB (Non-Directional Beacon), and DME (Distance Measuring Equipment).

- *VOR* provides azimuth information, allowing pilots to determine their bearing to or from the station.
- *NDB* transmits signals that a helicopter's ADF (Automatic Direction Finder) uses for orientation towards the beacon.
- *DME* measures the slant range distance from the aircraft to the ground station.

These systems assist pilots in determining their position, orientation, and course relative to specific ground stations.

[PH.VII.B.K1; FAA-H-8083-25]

2. How should a pilot test and verify the proper functioning of ground-based navigation equipment before and during a flight?

A pilot should test and verify the proper functioning of ground-based navigation equipment before a flight by performing preflight checks as outlined in the helicopter's flight manual. This includes checking the operational status of VOR, ADF, and DME systems and verifying the accuracy of the instruments by using ground test signals or known reference points. During flight, pilots should continuously monitor the performance of the navigation systems, cross-checking with other navigational aids, and ensuring signal integrity and accuracy.

[PH.VII.B.K1; FAA-H-8083-25]

3. What regulations govern the use of ground-based navigation aids in helicopter navigation?

Regulations governing the use of ground-based navigation aids in helicopter navigation include FAA regulations, which specify the requirements for equipment maintenance, pilot proficiency, and operational procedures. Pilots must adhere to the regulations outlined in 14 CFR Part 91 and Part 97 for the proper use of navigation aids like VOR, NDB, and DME. These regulations cover aspects such as airspace restrictions, minimum equipment requirements, and procedures for instrument flight rules (IFR) operations.

[PH.VII.B.K1; FAA-H-8083-25]

4. How can interference affect ground-based navigation signals, and what steps can pilots take to mitigate its impact?

Interference can affect ground-based navigation signals by causing signal degradation, distortion, or loss, leading to inaccurate readings or signal dropout. Sources of interference include terrain obstructions, atmospheric conditions, and electronic interference from other aircraft systems or external sources. Pilots can mitigate its impact by regularly cross-checking navigation data with other aids, such as GPS, using redundant systems, maintaining situational awareness, and being prepared to switch to alternate navigation methods if necessary. Reporting any suspected signal interference to ATC is also important for safety and system maintenance.

[PH.VII.B.K1; FAA-H-8083-25]

5. Why is understanding signal integrity crucial for pilots using ground-based navigation, and how can they ensure appropriate use of navigation data?

Understanding signal integrity is crucial for pilots using ground-based navigation because it ensures the reliability and accuracy of the navigational information being used for flight decisions. Signal integrity issues can lead to navigation errors, potentially compromising flight safety. Pilots can ensure appropriate use of navigation data by regularly validating the accuracy of navigation aids, being aware of the limitations of each navigation system, and cross-checking with other sources of navigation data, such as GPS or visual landmarks. Staying informed about NOTAMs (Notices to Air Missions) that may affect navigation aid functionality is also essential.

[PH.VII.B.K1; FAA-H-8083-25]

6. What are the key components of satellite-based navigation systems used in helicopter flying, and how do they enhance navigation?

The key components of satellite-based navigation systems, such as the Global Positioning System (GPS), include space-based satellites, ground control stations, and onboard GPS receivers. These systems provide accurate position, velocity, and time information to the helicopter, enhancing navigation by offering precise real-time data for global positioning. GPS systems are crucial for route planning, enroute navigation, approach, and departure procedures, particularly in areas where ground-based navigational aids are limited or unavailable.

[PH.VII.B.K2; FAA-H-8083-25]

7. How is receiver autonomous integrity monitoring (RAIM) used in helicopter navigation, and why is it significant?

Receiver autonomous integrity monitoring (RAIM) is a technology used in GPS receivers to assess the integrity of GPS signals and ensure their accuracy. It checks the consistency of GPS satellite data to detect any anomalies or malfunctions that could affect positioning information. RAIM is significant because it provides a warning to the pilot if the GPS accuracy degrades below a certain threshold, ensuring the reliability of satellite-based navigation, particularly during critical phases of flight like approach and landing.

[PH.VII.B.K2; FAA-H-8083-25]

8. **What should a pilot consider when using satellite-based navigation databases in helicopter operations?**

When using satellite-based navigation databases in helicopter operations, a pilot should consider the currency and certification of the database, ensuring it is up to date with the latest navigational information, including waypoints, airways, and approach procedures. The pilot should be familiar with the database update procedures and check for any NOTAMs that may affect the navigation data. It is also essential to understand the limitations of the database and the navigation system, especially in areas with limited satellite coverage or signal interference.

[PH.VII.B.K2; FAA-H-8083-25]

9. **What is radar assistance for visual flight rules (VFR) aircraft, and how can helicopter pilots utilize this service?**

Radar assistance for VFR aircraft refers to the use of radar by air traffic control (ATC) to provide navigational guidance, traffic advisories, and other assistance to pilots flying under VFR. Helicopter pilots can utilize this service by requesting radar services from ATC, which can include flight following, where ATC provides regular updates on nearby traffic, navigation assistance, and information on weather conditions along the route. This service enhances situational awareness and flight safety, especially in congested airspace or during long-distance flights.

[PH.VII.B.K3; FAA-H-8083-25]

10. **Under what circumstances can a VFR helicopter pilot request radar assistance, and what information should they provide to ATC?**

A VFR helicopter pilot can request radar assistance in various circumstances, such as for flight following on cross-country flights, navigating through complex airspace, or when needing assistance due to disorientation or unexpected weather conditions. When requesting radar assistance, the pilot should provide ATC with their current position, altitude, flight intentions (destination, route, and altitude), and any specific assistance needed. The pilot should also inform ATC about the helicopter's type and any relevant flight plan details.

[PH.VII.B.K3; FAA-H-8083-25]

11. What are the differences between Transponder Mode A, C, and S, and how do they function in helicopter navigation?

Transponder Mode A provides an identification code (squawk code) assigned by air traffic control (ATC) for radar identification. Mode C includes the Mode A function and adds automatic reporting of the helicopter's altitude from a pressure altitude sensor. Mode S (Selective) transponders provide the same functions as Mode A and C but also include data-link capabilities, allowing selective interrogation by radar (secondary surveillance radar) and transmission of more detailed aircraft information, such as identification and flight data. These modes enhance situational awareness and traffic management in controlled airspace.

[PH.VII.B.K4; AIM 4-1-20]

12. How does ADS-B technology enhance helicopter navigation and what are its key components?

Automatic Dependent Surveillance-Broadcast (ADS-B) technology enhances helicopter navigation by providing real-time precision tracking of aircraft. The key components of ADS-B include an ADS-B Out transmitter, which broadcasts the helicopter's GPS position, altitude, velocity, and other data, and an ADS-B In receiver, which allows the pilot to receive and display traffic and weather information from other ADS-B equipped aircraft and ground stations. This technology improves situational awareness, collision avoidance, and efficient airspace utilization.

[PH.VII.B.K4; AIM 4-1-20]

13. What are the regulatory requirements for helicopters to be equipped with transponders and ADS-B systems?

The regulatory requirements for helicopters to be equipped with transponders and ADS-B systems are outlined in 14 CFR §91.225 and §91.227. Generally, helicopters operating in controlled airspace, above certain altitudes, or near busy airports are required to have a transponder with at least Mode C capabilities. As of January 1, 2020, helicopters operating in most controlled airspace must also be equipped with ADS-B Out technology, which broadcasts the helicopter's position to ATC and other nearby aircraft. Compliance with these regulations enhances safety and airspace management.

[PH.VII.B.K4; AIM 4-1-20]

14. What are the common risks associated with over-reliance on automated navigation and auto flight systems in helicopters, and how can pilots mitigate these risks?

Loss of situational awareness, degradation of manual flying skills, and inability to quickly take over control in case of system failure. To mitigate these risks, pilots should maintain proficiency in manual flying and navigation skills, regularly practice flying without reliance on automation, and thoroughly understand the capabilities and limitations of the auto flight systems. They should also regularly monitor and cross-check the automated systems to ensure accuracy and proper functioning.

[PH.VII.B.R1; FAA-H-8083-25]

15. What strategies should a pilot employ to maintain situational awareness while using automated systems for navigation in a helicopter?

To maintain situational awareness while using automated systems, a pilot should continuously monitor flight progress against the flight plan, regularly cross-check the automated system's indications with visual references and other navigational aids, and stay informed of weather and traffic conditions. Actively managing the flight by verifying system inputs and outputs, rather than passively monitoring, helps maintain awareness. The pilot should also listen to ATC communications and be aware of the helicopter's position relative to terrain, obstacles, and other aircraft. Regular training in the use of automated systems and understanding their limitations is essential.

[PH.VII.B.R1; FAA-H-8083-25]

16. **What strategies can helicopter pilots employ to manage distractions and maintain focus while using navigation systems and radar services?**

    Helicopter pilots can manage distractions and maintain focus by preflight planning to familiarize with the route and navigation systems, using checklists for systematic task completion, implementing a sterile cockpit rule during critical flight phases to limit nonessential communication, delegating tasks to other crew members to distribute workload, and regularly practicing emergency and abnormal scenarios to stay prepared for unexpected situations.

    [PH.VII.B.R2; FAA-H-8083-25]

17. **How can helicopter pilots prioritize tasks effectively when using complex navigation systems and interacting with radar services?**

    To effectively prioritize tasks, pilots can adhere to the aviate, navigate, communicate priority rule, break down tasks into smaller steps and complete them by importance, plan flights in detail including contingencies, use automation for routine tasks to focus on critical decisions, and continuously assess the situation for any required task reprioritization.

    [PH.VII.B.R2; FAA-H-8083-25]

18. **What are the potential risks of disorientation when using navigation systems and radar services in helicopters, and how can these be mitigated?**

    The risks include reliance on incorrect or misinterpreted information leading to errors, and spatial disorientation from conflicting visual and instrument cues, especially in poor visibility. Mitigation strategies include regularly cross-checking navigational data with multiple sources, maintaining proficiency in both visual and instrument navigation, understanding the interpretation and use of navigation and radar information, and training in spatial disorientation recognition and recovery techniques.

    [PH.VII.B.R2; FAA-H-8083-25]

19. What are common limitations in helicopter navigation systems that pilots should be aware of?

Common limitations in helicopter navigation systems that pilots should be aware of include:

- Signal reception issues, especially in areas with obstructions like tall buildings or mountainous terrain.
- Limitations in the accuracy and update rate of GPS systems.
- Potential errors or outdated information in navigation databases.
- Limitations in adverse weather conditions affecting certain types of equipment, like radar.
- System-specific features and operational constraints that may affect performance under certain flight conditions.

[PH.VII.B.R3; FAA-H-8083-25]

20. How can pilots mitigate the risks associated with navigation system limitations during flight operations?

Pilots can mitigate the risks by:

- Maintaining proficiency in manual navigation techniques to compensate for potential system failures or inaccuracies.
- Regularly updating navigation system software and databases to ensure the most current and accurate information is available.
- Using redundancy in navigation systems, where possible, to provide backup in case of a failure.
- Staying informed about NOTAMs and weather reports that may affect navigation system performance.
- Maintaining situational awareness and being ready to switch to alternative navigation methods if necessary.

[PH.VII.B.R3; FAA-H-8083-25]

21. What are the primary risks associated with the loss of a navigation signal in helicopter operations, and how can pilots prepare for this scenario?

The primary risks associated with the loss of a navigation signal in helicopter operations include disorientation, loss of situational awareness, and the potential for navigational errors that could lead to airspace violations or unsafe conditions.

[PH.VII.B.R4; FAA-H-8083-25]

22. What steps can pilots take to mitigate the impact of navigation signal loss on helicopter flight safety?

Pilots can mitigate the impact of navigation signal loss on helicopter flight safety by:

- Conducting thorough preflight planning, including alternative plans for navigation.
- Regularly practicing manual and traditional navigation skills.
- Keeping navigation databases and system software up to date.
- Having redundancy in navigation systems to provide backup options.
- Staying aware of the helicopter's position at all times to facilitate transition to manual navigation if needed.

[PH.VII.B.R4; FAA-H-8083-25]

23. What are the potential risks associated with the reliance on electronic flight bags (EFBs) for navigation in helicopters, and how can these risks be mitigated?

The potential risks associated with reliance on EFBs for navigation in helicopters include technical malfunctions, outdated or incorrect data, over-reliance leading to reduced situational awareness, and distraction from flight tasks.

[PH.VII.B.R5; FAA-H-8083-25]

24. How should a pilot assess the functionality and reliability of an EFB before and during flight operations?

A pilot should assess the functionality and reliability of an EFB by:

- Performing preflight checks to ensure the EFB is functioning correctly and the software is up-to-date.
- Confirming that all necessary documents, charts, and data are loaded and accessible.
- Testing the responsiveness and accuracy of the EFB's features, such as charts and navigational aids.
- Monitoring the EFB's performance throughout the flight, ensuring it remains consistent and reliable.
- Being prepared to switch to alternative navigation methods if the EFB shows signs of malfunction.

[PH.VII.B.R5; FAA-H-8083-25

Skills to be demonstrated:

- Use an airborne electronic navigation system.

- Determine the aircraft's position using the navigation system.

- Intercept and track a given course, radial, or bearing.

- Recognize and describe the indication of station or waypoint passage.

- Recognize loss of navigational signal and take appropriate action.

- Use proper communication procedures when utilizing radar services.

- Maintain the selected altitude, ±200 feet and headings, ±15°.

C. Diversion

1. What factors should a helicopter pilot consider when selecting an alternate destination due to unforeseen circumstances during a flight?

A helicopter pilot should consider factors such as weather conditions at the alternate destination, distance and fuel requirements, availability of landing zones or helipads, terrain and obstacles, air traffic control requirements, and the helicopter's performance capabilities under the current load and weather conditions. It is also important to consider any specific aircraft limitations and emergency procedures outlined in the pilot's operating handbook or rotorcraft flight manual for the helicopter being operated.

[PH.VII.C.K1; FAA-H-8083-25]

2. How should a helicopter pilot assess the availability of landing zones or helipads when selecting an alternate destination?

The pilot should assess the availability of landing zones or helipads by considering their proximity to the flight route, size, surface condition, and any associated restrictions or requirements. Verify that the landing zone can safely accommodate the helicopter's size and weight. Information about helipads can often be found in aeronautical charts, NOTAMs, and the *Pilot/Controller Glossary*. The pilot should also be prepared for off-airport landings if a suitable helipad is not available.

[PH.VII.C.K1; FAA-H-8083-21]

3. **What are the primary reasons a helicopter pilot might need to deviate from the flight plan and divert to an alternate location?**

A helicopter pilot may need to deviate from the flight plan due to unforeseen circumstances such as sudden changes in weather, mechanical issues, medical emergencies onboard, air traffic control (ATC) advisories, or restricted airspace activation. The pilot must assess the situation and decide on a diversion that ensures the safety of the flight.

[PH.VII.C.K2; FAA-H-8083-25]

4. **In what situations might a helicopter pilot need to deviate from ATC instructions during a flight?**

A helicopter pilot might need to deviate from ATC instructions due to reasons like avoiding unexpected weather conditions (e.g., thunderstorms, strong winds), collision avoidance, responding to a traffic collision avoidance system (TCAS) resolution advisory, or dealing with an onboard emergency (e.g., medical, fire). The pilot is responsible for the safety of the flight and must take appropriate action while keeping ATC informed.

[PH.VII.C.K2; FAA-H-8083-25]

5. **How should a helicopter pilot communicate with ATC when an unplanned diversion is necessary?**

When a diversion is necessary, the helicopter pilot should promptly inform ATC, providing the reason for the diversion, the new intended destination, and any assistance required. The pilot should use standard radio communication procedures, be clear and concise, and follow any instructions or clearances provided by ATC to ensure a safe transition to the new course.

[PH.VII.C.K2; FAA-H-8083-25]

6. What are key strategies for a helicopter pilot to identify potential collision hazards during a diversion?

A helicopter pilot should maintain a high level of situational awareness, continuously scan for other aircraft, use available navigation and communication systems to identify nearby traffic, and listen attentively to ATC communications for traffic advisories. Additionally, the use of onboard collision avoidance systems, if available, can help in identifying potential hazards.

[PH.VII.C.R1; FAA-H-8083-25]

7. What are the key considerations for a helicopter pilot when planning and executing a diversion to avoid areas with high potential for air traffic conflicts?

When planning and executing a diversion, the pilot should avoid areas known for high air traffic density, such as major airports, popular VFR routes, and military operation areas. The pilot should also consider the altitude and routes that are less likely to intersect with fixed-wing traffic and be mindful of temporary flight restrictions (TFRs) and other NOTAMs that might indicate increased activity in certain areas.

[PH.VII.C.R1; FAA-H-8083-25]

8. How can a helicopter pilot identify and mitigate the risks of distractions during a diversion?

A helicopter pilot can identify risks of distractions by recognizing activities or situations that draw attention away from flying tasks, such as complex navigation, communication with ATC, or managing cabin issues. To mitigate these risks, the pilot should use effective cockpit resource management, delegate tasks to crew members if available, and utilize available automation systems to maintain a focus on critical flight tasks. Maintaining a sterile cockpit during critical phases of flight is also important.

[PH.VII.C.R2; FAA-H-8083-25]

9. How can a helicopter pilot effectively manage the workload during a diversion to prevent task saturation and maintain safety?

Effective workload management during a diversion involves anticipating and planning for increased workload, breaking down tasks into manageable steps, and using available technology and automation to reduce pilot workload. Prioritizing tasks based on safety and importance, using a systematic approach to decision-making, and, if possible, sharing responsibilities with other crew members can help manage workload and prevent task saturation.

[PH.VII.C.R2; FAA-H-8083-25]

10. What are the common circumstances that necessitate a diversion in helicopter flight operations?

Circumstances that may necessitate a diversion in helicopter operations include:

- Adverse Weather conditions (like fog, storms, or high winds)
- Unexpected airspace restrictions
- Medical emergencies onboard
- Mechanical or technical issues
- Fuel shortages
- Sudden changes in mission requirements

A prudent pilot must recognize these situations early and decide on a diversion to ensure flight safety.

[PH.VII.C.R3; FAA-H-8083-25]

11. How should a helicopter pilot assess the need for a diversion in response to deteriorating weather conditions?

A pilot should assess the need for a diversion due to deteriorating weather by continuously monitoring weather updates, observing changing weather patterns, understanding the helicopter's limitations in various weather conditions, and maintaining awareness of nearby alternate destinations. If weather conditions are likely to compromise safety or exceed the operational limits of the helicopter, a diversion should be strongly considered.

[PH.VII.C.R3; FAA-H-8083-25]

12. What risk assessment measures should a helicopter pilot take when considering a diversion due to mechanical issues?

When considering a diversion due to mechanical issues, the pilot should assess the severity and impact of the issue on helicopter performance and safety, determine the helicopter's ability to reach an alternate destination, consult the aircraft's emergency procedures or checklist, and communicate with maintenance personnel or ATC for advice and assistance. The pilot should consider the nearest suitable landing area for safety if the mechanical issue is critical.

[PH.VII.C.R3; FAA-H-8083-25]

13. How can a helicopter pilot mitigate the risks associated with an unplanned diversion due to a medical emergency onboard?

To mitigate risks during a diversion for a medical emergency, the pilot should quickly assess the severity of the emergency, identify the nearest suitable landing area with medical facilities, communicate the situation to ATC for priority handling and assistance, and maintain a calm and focused approach to flying the helicopter. The pilot should also be familiar with basic first aid and the location of medical kits onboard.

[PH.VII.C.R3; FAA-H-8083-25]

14. What are the key factors a helicopter pilot should consider when selecting an airport, heliport, or helipad for diversion?

A helicopter pilot should consider factors such as the distance to the diversion point, fuel requirements to reach the destination, current weather conditions at the site, the size and condition of the landing area, availability of emergency and maintenance services, air traffic and airspace considerations, and any specific limitations of the helicopter, such as weight and performance capabilities.

[PH.VII.C.R4; FAA-H-8083-25]

15. How can a pilot effectively use available resources to determine the best diversion option among airports, heliports, or helipads?

A pilot can effectively use resources such as onboard navigation systems, aviation charts, ATC communication, and flight planning tools to identify potential diversion points. The pilot should consider the real-time information available, such as weather updates, NOTAMs, and the current traffic situation from ATC, to make an informed decision.

[PH.VII.C.R4; FAA-H-8083-25]

16. How can a helicopter pilot effectively use automation systems during a diversion to enhance safety and reduce workload?

A helicopter pilot can use automation systems such as autopilot, flight management systems, and GPS navigation to maintain stable flight, accurately follow a revised flight path, and monitor flight parameters. These systems help reduce the pilot's workload, allowing more focus on assessing the diversion situation and making strategic decisions. The pilot should be familiar with the capabilities and limitations of the automation systems and be prepared to take manual control if necessary.

[PH.VII.C.R5; FAA-H-8083-25]

17. In what ways can flight deck planning aids, such as electronic flight bags (EFBs), be utilized during a helicopter diversion?

Flight deck planning aids like EFBs can be utilized during a diversion to access real-time information, including weather updates, alternate airport data, approach plates, and navigational charts. These tools can assist in quickly determining the best alternate destinations, understanding airspace restrictions, and planning the most efficient route to the diversion point. They can also provide access to emergency checklists and performance calculators, aiding in critical decision-making.

[PH.VII.C.R5; FAA-H-8083-25]

Skills to be demonstrated:

• Select a suitable airport/heliport/helipad, as applicable, and route for diversion.

• Make a reasonable estimate of heading, groundspeed, arrival time, and fuel required to the divert to destination.

• Promptly divert toward the airport/heliport/helipad.

• Maintain the selected altitude, ±200 feet and headings, ±15°.

• Update/interpret weather in flight.

• Use displays of digital weather and aeronautical information, as applicable to maintain situational awareness.

D. Lost Procedures

1. What techniques should a helicopter pilot use for visual position determination when traditional navigation aids are unavailable?

When traditional navigation aids are unavailable, a helicopter pilot should use visual flight rules (VFR) techniques such as pilotage, which involves navigating using visible landmarks (rivers, roads, cities, distinctive terrain features), and dead reckoning, which involves calculating the current position based on previously known positions, elapsed time, speed, and heading. These techniques require a good understanding of topographical features and the ability to read and interpret aeronautical charts accurately.

[PH.VII.D.K1; FAA-H-8083-25]

2. What are the primary methods a helicopter pilot can use to determine their position if they become disoriented or lost?

A helicopter pilot can determine their position by using a combination of visual landmarks, navigational aids (like VORs, NDBs, and GPS), referencing aeronautical charts, utilizing onboard navigation systems (such as moving map displays or flight management systems), and employing pilotage and dead reckoning techniques. In cases where visual references are limited, reliance on radio navigation and GPS becomes crucial.

[PH.VII.D.K1; FAA-H-8083-25]

3. **What is the role of air traffic control (ATC) in assisting a helicopter pilot with lost procedures?**

   ATC can play a crucial role in assisting a helicopter pilot during lost procedures. The pilot can contact ATC to declare uncertainty or disorientation. ATC can provide assistance by identifying the helicopter's position using radar, offering directional guidance, suggesting navigational aids to use, and providing information about nearby landmarks, airports, or other identifiable features.

   [PH.VII.D.K1; FAA-H-8083-25]

4. **What types of radar services can ATC provide to a helicopter pilot who is lost?**

   ATC can provide radar services such as radar vectors to guide a lost helicopter pilot to a known location or the nearest suitable airport. ATC can also use radar to identify the helicopter's current position and provide information on nearby navigational aids, terrain, obstacles, and other air traffic. In some cases, ATC may offer radar monitoring to ensure safe transit through controlled airspace.

   [PH.VII.D.K2; FAA-H-8083-25]

5. **What are the appropriate communication procedures for a helicopter pilot to declare being lost in an area without radar coverage?**

   In an area without radar coverage, the helicopter pilot should use the emergency frequency (121.5 MHz) to declare being lost, clearly stating their situation, helicopter identification, last known position, current altitude, and fuel status. The pilot should also attempt to contact other aircraft in the vicinity for assistance. If equipped with an emergency locator transmitter (ELT), the pilot should know how to activate it. Broadcasting on the common traffic advisory frequency (CTAF) of nearby airports may also help in establishing contact with someone who can assist.

   [PH.VII.D.K2; FAA-H-8083-25]

6. **How can a pilot use transponders and ADS-B (Automatic Dependent Surveillance-Broadcast) effectively when lost?**

   When lost, a pilot can use the transponder by squawking 7700, the universal code for emergencies, which will alert ATC to the helicopter's distress situation. If the helicopter is equipped with ADS-B, it can provide ATC with real-time location data, making it easier for them to provide assistance and vector the pilot to safety. The pilot should also be familiar with the transponder and ADS-B system operations and limitations.

   [PH.VII.D.K2; FAA-H-8083-25]

7. **What steps should a helicopter pilot take upon encountering rapidly deteriorating weather while already disoriented or lost?**

   Upon encountering rapidly deteriorating weather, a helicopter pilot should first aim to maintain control of the aircraft, often by transitioning to instrument flight if visual references are lost. The pilot should communicate with ATC immediately, informing them about the situation and requesting assistance, such as vectors to the nearest suitable airport or advice on exiting the weather. Remember the saying, "climb, confess, and comply." If possible, the pilot should use onboard weather radar or other technology to avoid severe weather and find a safe area for landing or holding. The pilot should also consider landing in a safe area if continuing the flight is unsafe.

   [PH.VII.D.K3; FAA-H-8083-25]

8. **How can a helicopter pilot manage the risk of fuel exhaustion when lost or disoriented?**

   To manage the risk of fuel exhaustion, the pilot should first assess the remaining fuel and calculate the endurance considering current conditions. The pilot should then communicate with ATC, declaring the situation and requesting priority handling to the nearest suitable landing site. While seeking a landing site, the pilot should minimize fuel consumption by flying at optimal airspeed for fuel efficiency. If fuel exhaustion is imminent, the pilot should prepare for an emergency landing in the safest possible area.

   [PH.VII.D.K3; FAA-H-8083-25]

9. **What techniques should a helicopter pilot use to avoid collision hazards while operating in a disoriented or lost state?**

   To avoid collision hazards, a helicopter pilot should maintain a high level of situational awareness and use a systematic scan technique to continually monitor for other aircraft. The pilot should also utilize any available collision avoidance systems like TCAS (traffic collision avoidance system) or ADS-B (automatic dependent surveillance-broadcast). Communication with ATC for traffic advisories should be maintained and standard altitude and airspeed regulations followed to reduce the risk of collisions.

   [PH.VII.D.R1; FAA-H-8083-25]

10. **What strategies can a helicopter pilot employ to manage distractions and maintain focus during lost procedures?**

    A helicopter pilot can manage distractions by using a disciplined approach to cockpit management, ensuring that all nonessential activities are minimized or deferred until after resolving the lost situation. The pilot should use a checklist to stay on track and allocate specific times for tasks like communication and navigation. Prioritizing tasks based on their importance to safety and using available automation wisely to reduce workload are also key strategies.

    [PH.VII.D.R2; FAA-H-8083-25]

11. **What role does effective cockpit resource management play in preventing task saturation during lost procedures in a helicopter?**

    Effective cockpit resource management plays a crucial role in preventing task saturation by ensuring that all available resources, including crew members, instruments, and navigation aids, are used efficiently. The pilot should delegate tasks where possible, communicate clearly with crew members, and avoid fixating on a single problem. Managing workload effectively through planning, anticipation of future needs, and staying ahead of the helicopter are key elements of effective cockpit resource management.

    [PH.VII.D.R2; FAA-H-8083-25]

12. **Why is it important for a helicopter pilot to record times over waypoints, especially during lost procedures?**

    Recording times over waypoints is important as it allows a helicopter pilot to track the progress of the flight against the planned route, which is crucial if disorientation or deviation occurs. This information helps in retracing the flight path and determining the current position more accurately. It is particularly vital during lost procedures as it provides a reference point for starting search procedures or for communicating with ATC about the last known position.

    [PH.VII.D.R3; FAA-H-8083-25]

13. **What are the best practices for a helicopter pilot to accurately record times over waypoints, and how can this practice aid in risk mitigation during lost procedures?**

    Best practices for recording times over waypoints include using a consistent method to record the time at each waypoint, such as a cockpit timer or a chronometer on the instrument panel. The pilot should note the time immediately upon passing each waypoint to ensure accuracy. This practice aids in risk mitigation by providing reliable data that can be used to determine the helicopter's position and progress, which is essential if the pilot needs to communicate their last known position to ATC or initiate a search pattern.

    [PH.VII.D.R3; FAA-H-8083-25]

14. **What indicators should a helicopter pilot recognize as cues to seek assistance or declare an emergency during lost procedures?**

    A helicopter pilot should recognize indicators such as inability to determine current position, rapidly deteriorating weather conditions, diminishing fuel reserves, approaching darkness (if not equipped or qualified for night flight), and any signs of helicopter system malfunctions. Other cues include increased pilot workload leading to high stress levels, and the inability to safely reach a known location or landing area. These indicators signal the need for immediate assistance or declaration of an emergency.

    [PH.VII.D.R4; FAA-H-8083-25]

15. In a lost procedure scenario, how should a helicopter pilot determine the timing of declaring an emergency?

The timing of declaring an emergency in a lost procedure scenario should be determined based on the urgency of the situation. If the pilot believes that the safety of the flight is compromised and immediate assistance is required, an emergency should be declared without delay.

[PH.VII.D.R4; FAA-H-8083-25]

16. What are the implications of declaring an emergency for a helicopter pilot, and how does this action assist in managing a lost situation?

Declaring an emergency alerts ATC and other authorities to the seriousness of the situation, prompting them to provide immediate assistance and prioritize the helicopter's needs. This action may include providing radar vectors, clearing airspace, expediting landing clearances, and mobilizing search and rescue if needed. Declaring an emergency also gives the pilot legal latitude to deviate from standard flight rules if necessary to maintain safety. It is a critical step in managing a lost situation as it mobilizes all available resources to assist the pilot in resolving the situation safely.

[PH.VII.D.R4; FAA-H-8083-25]

Skills to be demonstrated:

- Select an appropriate course of action.

- Use an appropriate method to determine position.

- Maintain an appropriate heading and climb, as necessary.

- Identify prominent landmarks.

- Use navigation systems/facilities or contact an ATC facility for assistance.

Emergency
Operations

8

A. Powerplant Failure in a Hover in a Single-Engine Helicopter

1. What immediate actions should a pilot take in the event of a powerplant failure while hovering in a single-engine helicopter?

Upon experiencing a powerplant failure in a hover, the pilot should immediately enter a hovering autorotation by applying pedal to maintain the helicopter's heading, as necessary. Allow the helicopter to settle closer to the ground then raise the collective to cushion the landing as needed.

[PH.VIII.A.K1; FAA-H-8083-21]

2. What are the key considerations for a pilot when selecting emergency landing area after a powerplant failure in a hover?

When selecting an emergency landing area after a powerplant failure in a hover, key considerations include the size of the area (it should be large enough to accommodate the helicopter safely), the nature of the surface (looking for a level, solid surface to minimize the risk of rollover), and the absence of obstacles that could interfere with the landing. Due to the low altitude in hover, the pilot often has limited options and must make a rapid decision based on immediate surroundings.

[PH.VIII.A.K1; FAA-H-8083-21]

3. How does wind affect a helicopter's performance and pilot's response during a powerplant failure in a hover?

A headwind can help maintain the helicopter's heading into the wind. Conversely, a tailwind can increase the directional stability of the helicopter making a hovering autorotation more challenging. A pilot must adjust the autorotative descent accordingly, considering the wind direction and speed to optimize control during the descent and cushioning.

[PH.VIII.A.K2; FAA-H-8083-21]

4. **How do temperature and density altitude impact a helicopter's performance in the event of a powerplant failure during a hover?**

   High temperatures and high-density altitudes reduce the air density, which in turn decreases rotor system efficiency and the helicopter's overall performance. In the event of a powerplant failure during a hover at high density altitudes, the helicopter will have a higher descent rate in autorotation, and the pilot will have less margin for controlling rotor RPM. The helicopter's ability to cushion the landing using collective pitch will also be diminished, requiring more precise control inputs from the pilot.

   [PH.VIII.A.K2; FAA-H-8083-21]

5. **What is the difference between high and low inertia rotor systems in helicopters, particularly in the context of powerplant failure during a hover?**

   High inertia rotor systems have more mass in the rotor blades and/or hub, which allows them to store more kinetic energy. This results in a slower rate of rotor RPM decay during a powerplant failure. Low inertia rotor systems, on the other hand, have less mass and therefore store less kinetic energy, leading to a quicker loss of rotor RPM in the event of a powerplant failure.

   [PH.VIII.A.K3; FAA-H-8083-21]

6. **What are the key considerations for a hovering autorotation in a powerplant failure scenario with a low inertia rotor system?**

   In a powerplant failure scenario with a low inertia rotor system, key considerations for autorotation include:

   • Quick and decisive actions due to the faster decay of rotor energy.

   • Smooth and efficient handling of the controls to maximize energy conservation in the rotor system.

   • Practicing autorotation procedures specific to low inertia systems to enhance muscle memory and response time.

   [PH.VIII.A.K3; FAA-H-8083-21]

7. What aerodynamic effect is most significant during a powerplant failure in a hover for a single-engine helicopter?

During a powerplant failure in a hover, the most significant aerodynamic effect is the loss of rotor RPM due to the absence of engine power. This loss of RPM reduces lift, making it crucial for the pilot to immediately respond to maintain rotor RPM to cushion the fast-approaching landing. In addition, the pilot must maintain directional control with the pedals during the large power change from the loss of the engine.

[PH.VIII.A.K4; FAA-H-8083-21]

8. What is the importance of proper orientation during a powerplant failure in a hover?

Proper orientation during a powerplant failure in a hover is crucial for situational awareness and safe recovery. It involves maintaining an awareness of the helicopter's position relative to the ground, potential obstacles, and wind direction. This orientation helps the pilot to quickly assess the situation and make informed decisions for a safe autorotative descent and landing.

[PH.VIII.A.K5; FAA-H-8083-21]

9. What are the key aspects of proper planning for a powerplant failure during a hover?

Key aspects of proper planning for a powerplant failure during a hover include preflight preparation such as familiarization with emergency procedures, identifying potential emergency landing areas, and mentally rehearsing the autorotation procedure. During flight, maintaining awareness of the surroundings and being prepared to execute emergency procedures at any moment are essential.

[PH.VIII.A.K5; FAA-H-8083-21]

10. **How can a pilot identify potential risks before experiencing a powerplant failure in a hover?**

    A pilot can identify potential risks before experiencing a powerplant failure in a hover by conducting a thorough preflight inspection, being aware of the helicopter's maintenance history, understanding the current weather conditions, and being familiar with the helicopter's performance capabilities. Additionally, the pilot should assess the environment around the hover area for potential hazards like obstacles or unsuitable terrain.

    [PH.VIII.A.R1; FAA-H-8083-21]

11. **What are effective strategies for mitigating risk during a powerplant failure in a hover?**

    Effective strategies for mitigating risk during a powerplant failure in a hover include maintaining proficiency in autorotation procedures, ensuring a constant awareness of suitable emergency landing areas while hovering, and being vigilant about the helicopter's performance and any indications of potential powerplant issues. Regular training and practicing emergency procedures are also crucial for risk mitigation.

    [PH.VIII.A.R1; FAA-H-8083-21]

12. **What initial flight control inputs should a pilot make immediately after identifying a powerplant failure in a hover?**

    If in a high hover, lowering the collective to maintain rotor RPM and initiate autorotation. The pilot should immediately make the control input of maintaining desired heading with the pedals, keeping the desired track over the ground with the cyclic. This action is crucial to prevent a rapid descent and to manage the helicopter's energy for a controlled landing. If in a normal to low hover, the pilot should maintain directional control of the helicopter with the pedals, and the desired ground track with the cyclic and allow the helicopter to settle, then cushion the landing with any remaining collective.

    [PH.VIII.A.R2; FAA-H-8083-21]

13. What key helicopter movements should a pilot be prepared to manage during a powerplant failure in a hover?

During a powerplant failure in a hover, the pilot should be prepared to manage helicopter movements such as a rapid descent and potential drift due to loss of lift and thrust. The pilot needs to control the helicopter's attitude to facilitate an autorotative descent, adjust for wind drift, and aim for the safest possible landing area.

[PH.VIII.A.R3; FAA-H-8083-21]

14. How can a pilot mitigate the risks of helicopter movement during a powerplant failure in a hover?

A pilot can mitigate the risks of helicopter movement during a powerplant failure in a hover by maintaining proficiency in autorotation and emergency procedures, ensuring thorough preflight planning with consideration of emergency landing areas, and practicing quick and precise control inputs to maintain control of the helicopter during the descent. Constant situational awareness and readiness to react are key to mitigating these risks.

[PH.VIII.A.R3; FAA-H-8083-21]

15. What is dynamic rollover and how can it occur during a powerplant failure in a hover?

Dynamic rollover is a condition in helicopter flight where the helicopter rolls about its pivot point (usually one of the landing skids or wheels) if the pilot applies cyclic input in an attempt to counteract a lateral rolling tendency. During a powerplant failure in a hover, dynamic rollover can occur if the pilot over-controls the cyclic while trying to maintain lateral balance, especially when one skid or wheel is in contact with the ground.

[PH.VIII.A.R4; FAA-H-8083-21]

16. **How can a pilot mitigate the risk of dynamic rollover when experiencing a powerplant failure in a hover?**

    A pilot should maintain proper hovering techniques with minimal lateral cyclic inputs and be prepared to execute a controlled autorotation landing. Training and proficiency in recognizing and responding to powerplant failures and understanding the helicopter's roll-over characteristics are crucial. Additionally, choosing flat and obstacle-free areas for hovering can reduce the likelihood of dynamic rollover.

    [PH.VIII.A.R4; FAA-H-8083-21]

17. **What strategies should a pilot employ to prioritize tasks during a powerplant failure in a hover?**

    During a powerplant failure in a hover, a pilot should employ strategies like the aviate, navigate, communicate principle to prioritize tasks. First, aviate by maintaining control of the helicopter and initiating autorotation. Next, navigate by selecting an appropriate landing area. Finally, communicate the situation to any passengers and, if possible, to air traffic control or nearby aircraft. This prioritization ensures that the most critical tasks for safety are addressed first.

    [PH.VIII.A.R5; FAA-H-8083-25]

18. **In what ways can loss of situational awareness impact a pilot during a powerplant failure in a hover?**

    Loss of situational awareness during a powerplant failure in a hover can lead to the pilot being unaware of critical factors such as altitude, descent rate, and nearby obstacles. This lack of awareness can result in inadequate response to the emergency, potentially leading to an uncontrolled descent and collision with terrain or obstacles.

    [PH.VIII.A.R5; FAA-H-8083-25]

Skills to be demonstrated:

- Complete the appropriate checklist(s).

- Make radio calls as appropriate.

- Clear the area.

- Select a suitable landing area.

- Establish a stationary or forward hover into the wind.

- Simulate powerplant failure.

- Maintain a heading, ±10°, throughout the maneuver.

- Touchdown with minimum sideward movement and no rearward movement.

- Use appropriate flight control inputs to cushion the touchdown.

- After touchdown, lower collective and neutralize flight controls.

B. Powerplant Failure at Altitude in a Single-Engine Helicopter

Note: The altitude, airspeed, and location must be considered so the helicopter is in a position to achieve a safe landing if an actual power-plant failure occurs. The minimum altitude to initiate a power failure must be at least 1,000 feet AGL with a power recovery completed by at least 500 feet AGL.

1. What are the immediate physical signs of a powerplant failure in a single-engine helicopter while at altitude?

The immediate physical signs of a powerplant failure in a single-engine helicopter at altitude include a sudden reduction or loss of engine noise, a decrease in rotor RPM (indicated by the rotor tachometer), and a loss of thrust. The helicopter may also experience a change in pitch and yaw due to the loss of engine power and torque.

[PH.VIII.B.K1; FAA-H-8083-21]

2. **How does wind affect autorotation and emergency landing procedures during a powerplant failure at altitude in a single-engine helicopter?**

Wind significantly affects autorotation and emergency landing procedures during a powerplant failure at altitude in a single-engine helicopter. Headwinds can decrease glide distance and reduce the rate of descent, while tailwinds can extend the glide distance and increase the rate of descent. Crosswinds can cause drift, requiring the pilot to adjust the autorotation path to compensate. The pilot should plan the emergency landing final approach and landing into the wind to maximize control and minimize ground speed at touchdown where possible.

[PH.VIII.B.K2; FAA-H-8083-21]

3. **In what way does the weight of a single-engine helicopter impact its autorotation characteristics during a powerplant failure at altitude?**

The weight of a single-engine helicopter directly impacts its autorotation characteristics during a powerplant failure at altitude. Heavier helicopters have a higher rate of descent and require collective adjustments to maintain optimal rotor RPM. This increased weight reduces the glide distance and can lead to a steeper approach angle during the emergency landing. The pilot must manage the collective and cyclic controls carefully to maintain rotor efficiency and ensure a controlled descent and landing.

[PH.VIII.B.K2; FAA-H-8083-21]

4. **How does ambient temperature influence the performance of a single-engine helicopter during autorotation after a powerplant failure?**

Ambient temperature influences the performance of a single-engine helicopter during autorotation after a powerplant failure. Higher temperatures, which correspond to lower air density, can reduce the lift generated by the rotor blades, leading to a higher rate of descent during autorotation. The pilot may need to adjust autorotation airspeed and rotor RPM to compensate for the decreased lift in warmer conditions.

[PH.VIII.B.K2; FAA-H-8083-21]

5. What is the effect of density altitude on autorotation in a single-engine helicopter experiencing a powerplant failure at altitude?

Density altitude has a significant effect on autorotation in a single-engine helicopter experiencing a powerplant failure at altitude. Higher density altitude, associated with higher elevations, hotter temperatures, or lower atmospheric pressure, results in thinner air and reduced rotor blade efficiency. This can lead to a higher descent rate and reduced glide distance during autorotation. The pilot must be aware of these changes and adjust the autorotation technique accordingly to ensure a safe emergency landing.

[PH.VIII.B.K2; FAA-H-8083-21]

6. What is the significance of maintaining optimal main rotor speed (N_r) during a powerplant failure at altitude in a single-engine helicopter?

Maintaining optimal main rotor speed (N_r) during a powerplant failure at altitude in a single-engine helicopter is critical for sustaining sufficient lift and control during autorotation. The N_r determines the rotor blades' ability to generate lift and thrust as they auto rotate through the air. If the N_r falls below the optimal range, the rotor system may not produce enough lift to support a controlled descent and landing. Conversely, excessively high N_r speed can lead to structural stresses on the rotor system.

[PH.VIII.B.K3; FAA-H-8083-21]

7. What should a pilot monitor and adjust during the final phase of autorotation to ensure optimal main rotor speed (N_r) is maintained for landing?

During the final phase of autorotation, the pilot should continuously monitor the main rotor speed (N_r) indicator to ensure the rotor speed remains within the optimal range for landing. As the helicopter descends and approaches the landing site, the pilot should use the collective to control descent rate and N_r, preparing for the flare maneuver. During the flare, N_r typically increases, and the pilot must adjust the collective accordingly to prevent overspeeding while simultaneously slowing the helicopter's forward and downward motion for a controlled touchdown.

[PH.VIII.B.K3; FAA-H-8083-21]

8. How does energy management relate to a powerplant failure in a single-engine helicopter at altitude?

Energy management during a powerplant failure in a single-engine helicopter at altitude involves efficiently using the helicopter's kinetic and potential energy to ensure a controlled and safe descent and landing. When the engine fails, the helicopter loses its primary power source, and the pilot must manage the rotor's rotational energy (kinetic) and the altitude (potential energy) to maintain sufficient rotor RPM for autorotation and to control the descent rate for landing. As the helicopter approaches the ground the additional airspeed (potential energy) is bled off to maintain rotor RPM and simultaneously slow the helicopter. Once the helicopter is slowed both vertically and horizontally the last of the kinetic energy stored in the rotor's RPM is used to cushion the landing.

[PH.VIII.B.K4; FAA-H-8083-21]

9. How should a pilot manage collective and cyclic inputs to optimize energy use during autorotation in a powerplant failure?

To optimize energy use during autorotation following a powerplant failure, a pilot should manage collective and cyclic inputs effectively. The collective should be initially lowered to maintain rotor RPM and prevent excessive loss of energy. The cyclic is used to control the helicopter's attitude and airspeed, which directly affects the rate of descent and the distance covered during the glide. The pilot must balance these controls to maintain the appropriate descent profile and prepare for the flare and touchdown.

[PH.VIII.B.K4; FAA-H-8083-21]

10. What are the common causes of high descent rates during autorotation following a powerplant failure at altitude in a single-engine helicopter?

Not maintaining optimal autorotation airspeed (too fast or too slow), improper collective management leading to low rotor RPM, and excessively steep glide angles. Additionally, external factors such as high-density altitude, heavy helicopter weight, and adverse wind conditions (like tailwinds) can also contribute to a higher-than-normal descent rate.

[PH.VIII.B.K5; FAA-H-8083-21]

11. **What are the potential consequences of a high descent rate during autorotation in a single-engine helicopter?**

    The potential consequences of a high descent rate during autorotation in a single-engine helicopter include increased difficulty in controlling the helicopter during the final approach and landing, higher impact forces at touchdown, which can lead to a hard landing or potential damage to the helicopter, and reduced ability to execute a successful flare maneuver to slow down the helicopter before landing. In extreme cases, it can also result in injury to occupants.

    [PH.VIII.B.K5; FAA-H-8083-21]

12. **How do varying bank angles affect autorotation performance during a powerplant failure at altitude in a single-engine helicopter?**

    Moderate bank angles can aid in controlling the helicopter's descent path and can be used to manage the glide distance towards the intended landing area. However, steep bank angles can increase the descent rate and reduce rotor RPM, which may compromise the rotor system's ability to generate sufficient lift for a controlled landing. Maintaining an optimal bank angle is crucial for effective autorotation and a safe landing.

    [PH.VIII.B.K6; FAA-H-8083-21]

13. **What is the significance of managing airspeed during autorotation after a powerplant failure in a single-engine helicopter?**

    The appropriate airspeed enables the rotor system to generate the necessary lift and control for autorotation. Too low an airspeed can lead to potentially insufficient lift and a high rate of descent, while too high an airspeed can lead to excessive rotor disk loading and potential loss of control. The pilot must maintain the manufacturer-recommended airspeed to optimize autorotative descent and landing. There are some techniques in specific scenarios that would justify a slower than normal indicated airspeed, for example adjusting a glide to safely land a helicopter in a tight spot. Pilots should regularly practice autorotations with a qualified flight instructor to help identify and practice adjusting the auto for those specific scenarios.

    [PH.VIII.B.K6; FAA-H-8083-21]

14. How does rotor RPM (N$_r$) influence the autorotative descent in a single-engine helicopter experiencing a powerplant failure?

Optimal rotor RPM ensures that the rotor system has enough inertia to maintain lift and control during the descent. If N$_r$ is too low, the helicopter may not have enough lift to slow the descent rate for a controlled landing. If N$_r$ is too high, it could lead to structural stress on the rotor system. The pilot must manage the collective to maintain the N$_r$ within the recommended range for effective autorotation.

[PH.VIII.B.K6; FAA-H-8083-21]

15. What are the unique risks associated with a powerplant failure at a low entry altitude in a single-engine helicopter?

The unique risks associated with a powerplant failure at a low entry altitude in a single-engine helicopter include limited time and altitude to establish an effective autorotation, reduced options for selecting a suitable emergency landing area, and increased difficulty in executing the autorotation maneuver successfully. These factors can lead to a higher likelihood of a hard landing or an inability to reach a safe landing zone.

[PH.VIII.B.R1; FAA-H-8083-21]

16. What are the key factors in effectively managing autorotation following a powerplant failure at a low entry altitude?

Promptly lowering the collective to maintain rotor RPM, selecting the best possible landing area within glide distance, and controlling the helicopter's airspeed and descent rate. The pilot must balance the need to reach a suitable landing spot with the need to control descent speed and prepare for landing. Quick, precise control inputs are essential due to the limited altitude available.

[PH.VIII.B.R1; FAA-H-8083-21]

17. **What factors should a pilot consider when selecting a landing area following a powerplant failure at altitude in a single-engine helicopter?**

When selecting a landing area following a powerplant failure at altitude in a single-engine helicopter, the pilot should consider factors such as the size and suitability of the area for landing, terrain type and condition, obstacles like trees or power lines, wind direction and speed, and accessibility for rescue or emergency services. The landing area should be as flat and clear of obstacles as possible to minimize the risk during touchdown.

[PH.VIII.B.R2; FAA-H-8083-21]

18. **How can a pilot mitigate risks associated with landing area selection when experiencing a powerplant failure at altitude?**

A pilot should maintain situational awareness throughout the flight, pre-identify potential landing areas along the flight path, and be prepared to make quick decisions. Training in emergency procedures and practicing autorotations enhance the pilot's ability to evaluate and choose suitable landing areas under pressure. The pilot should constantly update this mental map of emergency landing sites as the flight progresses. Know where to go!

[PH.VIII.B.R2; FAA-H-8083-21]

19. **What immediate flight control inputs are critical for a pilot to make following a powerplant failure at altitude in a single-engine helicopter?**

The pilot must immediately lower the collective to preserve rotor RPM and initiate autorotation. This action helps maintain sufficient rotor speed for controlled descent. The cyclic should be used to maintain proper airspeed, attitude and heading, while the pedals are adjusted to maintain directional control.

[PH.VIII.B.R3; FAA-H-8083-21]

20. What risks are associated with improper flight control inputs during autorotation following a powerplant failure?

Improper flight control inputs during autorotation following a powerplant failure can lead to several risks, including a loss of rotor RPM (if the collective is not lowered promptly), resulting in insufficient lift for a controlled descent. Incorrect cyclic inputs can cause inappropriate airspeed, affecting the glide distance and descent rate. Poor pedal use can lead to loss of directional control. These risks may result in an uncontrolled descent and hard landing, jeopardizing the safety of the pilot and passengers.

[PH.VIII.B.R3; FAA-H-8083-21]

21. What are the key considerations for a pilot when encountering turbulence during autorotation following a powerplant failure at altitude in a single-engine helicopter?

Key considerations when encountering turbulence include maintaining control of the helicopter, adjusting flight control inputs to counteract the effects of turbulence, and ensuring rotor RPM remains within the optimal range. The pilot must also be vigilant about maintaining the intended descent path and airspeed, as turbulence can cause fluctuations in both. Over-controlling the helicopter in response to turbulence must be avoided as it can lead to further instability.

[PH.VIII.B.R4; FAA-H-8083-21]

22. How should a pilot modify autorotation and landing techniques in response to turbulence during a powerplant failure in a single-engine helicopter?

The pilot should use smooth and coordinated control inputs to maintain the desired flight path and rotor RPM. Anticipating the effects of turbulence and making timely adjustments is key. The pilot may need to choose a landing site that offers more open space and less exposure to turbulence. During the flare and landing, the pilot should be prepared for sudden changes in descent rate and airspeed and adjust controls accordingly to achieve a safe touchdown.

[PH.VIII.B.R4; FAA-H-8083-21]

23. What causes low rotor RPM or rotor stall during autorotation in a single-engine helicopter after a powerplant failure?

Low rotor RPM or rotor stall during autorotation in a single-engine helicopter after a powerplant failure can be caused by improper collective management, where the collective is not lowered sufficiently or quickly enough after the engine failure. This leads to insufficient aerodynamic force to keep the rotor blades spinning at the required speed. Additionally, excessive pitch or inappropriate airspeed can also contribute to low rotor RPM or stall.

[PH.VIII.B.R5; FAA-H-8083-21]

24. What immediate actions should a pilot take to correct low rotor RPM or prevent rotor stall during a powerplant failure?

The pilot should immediately lower the collective to reduce the pitch angle of the rotor blades, decreasing drag and allowing the rotor system to regain RPM. The cyclic should be adjusted to maintain the recommended autorotation airspeed, as too low an airspeed can contribute to low RPM in certain situations. Quick and decisive action is crucial to prevent a rotor stall and maintain rotor efficiency for a controlled descent.

[PH.VIII.B.R5; FAA-H-8083-21]

25. What is wind shear and how can it affect a single-engine helicopter during autorotation following a powerplant failure at altitude?

Wind shear refers to a sudden change in wind speed and/or direction over a short distance. It can significantly affect a single-engine helicopter during autorotation following a powerplant failure at altitude by unexpectedly altering the helicopter's flight path, airspeed, and descent rate. Wind shear can cause sudden increases or decreases in airspeed, impacting the pilot's ability to control the helicopter and maintain optimal rotor RPM for a controlled descent and landing.

[PH.VIII.B.R5; FAA-H-8083-25]

26. **What immediate actions should a pilot take if encountering wind shear during autorotation in a powerplant failure situation?**

If encountering wind shear during autorotation in a powerplant failure situation, the pilot should immediately adjust the cyclic and collective to maintain control of the helicopter and keep the rotor RPM within the optimal range. This may involve increasing airspeed if encountering a headwind shear or reducing airspeed in a tailwind shear. The pilot must also be prepared to adjust the autorotation descent path to compensate for the changes in wind conditions and ensure a safe landing approach.

[PH.VIII.B.R5; FAA-H-8083-25]

27. **How can a pilot effectively scan for and identify potential collision hazards during an autorotation descent?**

To effectively scan for and identify potential collision hazards during an autorotation descent, the pilot should maintain a thorough and systematic visual lookout. This includes continuously scanning the glide path and the intended landing area for obstacles and other hazards. The pilot should also use peripheral vision and occasionally check instrument readings. Being vigilant about the surroundings and not fixating on a single point is essential for early detection of potential collision hazards.

[PH.VIII.B.R6; FAA-H-8083-21]

28. **What immediate actions should a pilot take upon identifying a potential collision hazard during an autorotation descent due to a powerplant failure?**

Upon identifying a potential collision hazard during an autorotation descent due to a powerplant failure, the pilot should immediately take corrective actions to avoid the hazard. This may involve adjusting the autorotation glide path using cyclic inputs, changing the planned landing area if the hazard is in the original target zone, and communicating with air traffic control, if possible, for assistance and to alert other aircraft in the vicinity. Quick decision-making and maneuvering are crucial in such situations.

[PH.VIII.B.R6; FAA-H-8083-21]

29. What is the significance of the power-off never-exceed speed (V$_{NE}$) limitation during autorotation in a powerplant failure situation?

Exceeding this speed can lead to structural damage to the helicopter or loss of control. V$_{NE}$ is the maximum speed at which the helicopter can be safely flown; exceeding this speed, especially during the low power conditions of autorotation, increases aerodynamic stresses on the rotor system and airframe, potentially leading to catastrophic failure. Staying below V$_{NE}$ is essential for maintaining helicopter integrity and control during emergency descent.

[PH.VIII.B.R7; FAA-H-8083-21]

30. What training and preparation can help pilots maintain safe airspeeds within V$_{NE}$ limitations during autorotation in emergency scenarios?

Regular practice of autorotation procedures under various conditions, thorough knowledge of the helicopter's flight manual and its limitations, and training in flight simulator scenarios that replicate emergency situations. Understanding the aerodynamics of autorotation and the factors that influence airspeed is crucial. Pilots should also be trained to remain calm and focused during emergencies, enabling them to make precise and controlled inputs to maintain safe airspeeds. Keep your eyes moving, keep scanning!

[PH.VIII.B.R7; FAA-H-8083-21]

31. What is the importance of maintaining proper helicopter trim during autorotation following a powerplant failure at altitude?

Maintaining proper helicopter trim during autorotation following a powerplant failure at altitude is crucial for ensuring stable flight and optimal aerodynamic efficiency. Proper trim minimizes drag and allows for a more controlled descent, which is essential when the engine power is not available. It ensures that the helicopter remains aligned with the relative wind, maximizing rotor efficiency and enabling better control and maneuverability during the autorotation descent and landing phase.

[PH.VIII.B.R8; FAA-H-8083-21]

32. **How can a pilot quickly assess and adjust trim during autorotation in a single-engine helicopter after a powerplant failure?**

A pilot can quickly assess and adjust trim during autorotation in a single-engine helicopter after a powerplant failure by monitoring the helicopter's response and control pressures. The pilot should check for any unusual control inputs or attitudes and use cyclic and pedal inputs to maintain a balanced and coordinated flight attitude. Keeping the helicopter aligned with the relative wind and maintaining the recommended autorotation airspeed are key to achieving proper trim. Additionally, the pilot should be aware of any changes in wind conditions or helicopter performance that might affect trim.

[PH.VIII.B.R8; FAA-H-8083-21]

33. **What strategies should a pilot use to manage distractions during autorotation following a powerplant failure at altitude in a single-engine helicopter?**

The pilot should prioritize tasks based on their immediate impact on safety. This includes focusing first on controlling the helicopter, establishing autorotation, and selecting a landing site. It is crucial that the pilot memorizes the correct action items for each emergency maneuver. Effective cockpit management, such as minimizing unnecessary communications and simplifying tasks, is also essential to reduce distractions.

[PH.VIII.B.R9; FAA-H-8083-25]

34. **How can a pilot prioritize tasks effectively during an emergency descent to manage workload and maintain control?**

The pilot should follow the aviation adage "aviate, navigate, communicate." This means the first priority is flying the helicopter, including establishing autorotation and maintaining control. The second priority is navigation, which involves choosing the best possible landing site. Lastly, communication with air traffic control or other aircraft should occur once immediate control and navigation tasks are under control. Using checklists, if time and workload permit, can also aid in task prioritization.

[PH.VIII.B.R9; FAA-H-8083-25]

35. How can a pilot maintain situational awareness during a powerplant failure in autorotation to avoid disorientation?

A pilot should continuously monitor the helicopter's altitude, airspeed, and rotor RPM, as well as external cues like wind direction and potential landing areas. Maintaining a mental picture of the helicopter's position and the surrounding environment is crucial. Regular training in emergency procedures, including simulator sessions, can help a pilot stay oriented under stress. Staying calm and methodically working through the problem can also prevent disorientation.

[PH.VIII.B.R9; FAA-H-8083-25]

Skills to be demonstrated:

- Establish an autorotation.

- Establish power-off glide with the helicopter trimmed and autorotation airspeed, ±10 knots.

- Maintain main rotor speed (N_r) within normal limits.

- Select a suitable landing area considering altitude, wind, terrain, and obstructions.

- Maneuver to avoid undershooting or overshooting the selected landing area.

- Make radio calls as appropriate.

- Terminate approach with a power recovery at a safe altitude as directed by the evaluator.

C. Approach and Landing with One Engine Inoperative (OEI) (Simulated) (Multi-Engine Helicopter Only)

Note: The evaluator must include this Task on the practical test for an applicant who provides a multi-engine helicopter. The minimum altitude to initiate this Task must be at least 1000 feet AGL for this maneuver. The evaluator must conduct a preflight briefing with the applicant regarding the expectations of any simulated powerplant failure. See Appendix 2 of the ACS.

1. **What are the key flight control adjustments a pilot must make during an OEI approach in a multi-engine helicopter?**

   During an OEI approach in a multi-engine helicopter, key flight control adjustments include maintaining the appropriate airspeed for single-engine operation, adjusting the collective to manage rotor RPM and descent rate, and using the cyclic and pedals to ensure proper alignment and approach path. The pilot must also balance the workload between managing the remaining engine's power setting and controlling the helicopter's flight path. These adjustments are critical to compensate for the reduced power availability and asymmetric thrust.

   [PH.VIII.C.K1; FAA-H-8083-21]

2. **What are the critical aspects to consider when selecting a landing site during an OEI approach in a multi-engine helicopter?**

   When selecting a landing site during an OEI approach in a multi-engine helicopter, critical aspects to consider include the size and suitability of the site for a safe landing, the presence of obstacles or hazards, wind direction and speed, and the helicopter's glide capabilities under OEI conditions. The pilot should choose a site that allows for a straight-in approach if possible and provides enough space for the landing maneuver, considering the reduced power and maneuverability with one engine inoperative. Accessibility for emergency services should also be considered.

   [PH.VIII.C.K1; FAA-H-8083-21]

3. **What considerations should a pilot make regarding atmospheric conditions when planning an emergency approach with OEI?**

When planning an emergency approach with OEI, a pilot should consider atmospheric conditions such as wind direction and speed, temperature, humidity, and visibility. Understanding how these factors impact helicopter performance and handling is crucial. The pilot should plan the approach path to take advantage of favorable winds, if possible, and be mindful of potential performance degradation due to high density altitude. Additionally, poor visibility conditions might require a more conservative approach strategy to ensure the landing area is clearly visible and avoid spatial disorientation.

[PH.VIII.C.K2; FAA-H-8083-21]

4. **What constitutes a stabilized approach in the context of an OEI situation in a multi-engine helicopter?**

A stabilized approach in an OEI situation in a multi-engine helicopter is characterized by a consistent descent path and airspeed, proper alignment with the landing area, controlled descent rate, and appropriate power management with the operative engine. The helicopter should be in the correct landing configuration, with no excessive deviations in pitch, roll, or yaw. The approach should be smooth with minimal corrections, and the pilot should be prepared for a go-around if the approach becomes unstable.

[PH.VIII.C.K3; FAA-H-8083-21]

5. **How can a pilot effectively manage airspeed and descent rate during a stabilized OEI approach?**

The pilot should use the collective to control the descent rate and the cyclic to maintain the desired airspeed. Adjustments should be smooth and coordinated to avoid abrupt changes. The airspeed indicator and vertical speed indicator must be monitored closely and small corrections made as needed. The pilot should also be aware of any changes in wind conditions that might affect the approach and adjust accordingly.

[PH.VIII.C.K3; FAA-H-8083-21]

6. **What are the key elements of the approach profile for an OEI landing in a multi-engine helicopter?**

   The key elements of the approach profile for an OEI landing in a multi-engine helicopter include establishing a glide path that allows for a safe and controlled descent to the landing area, maintaining an airspeed that optimizes lift and rotor RPM, and ensuring a gradual reduction in altitude and airspeed as the helicopter approaches the landing area. The approach should be planned to minimize altitude loss and maximize glide distance, considering the reduced power available. It is important to maintain a constant angle of descent and avoid steep or abrupt maneuvers.

   [PH.VIII.C.K4; FAA-H-8083-21]

7. **How does the OEI approach and landing profile differ from a standard approach in a multi-engine helicopter?**

   In the need to manage the reduced power available more efficiently. The glide path may be shallower to maximize the distance covered, and the approach may be flown at a slightly higher airspeed to maintain better control and ensure adequate rotor RPM. The pilot must be more vigilant in monitoring aircraft performance and be prepared for a more demanding landing maneuver, as the available power for adjustments is limited. The emphasis is on energy management and control to ensure a safe landing.

   [PH.VIII.C.K4; FAA-H-8083-21]

8. **What strategies should be employed to mitigate risks associated with wind conditions during an OEI approach?**

   The pilot should be aware of the wind direction and speed and use this information to plan the approach. A headwind is generally preferable as it can reduce ground speed and increase lift, allowing for a more controlled descent. The pilot should also be prepared to adjust the approach path to compensate for crosswinds or tailwinds, which can affect the glide path and landing approach. Additionally, awareness of potential wind shear or gusty conditions is important for making timely corrections to maintain stability and control.

   [PH.VIII.C.R1; FAA-H-8083-21]

9. **How does terrain and the presence of obstructions influence the approach and landing strategy in an OEI situation?**

The pilot must choose a landing path that avoids terrain features and obstructions like buildings, trees, or power lines. This may require selecting an alternate landing site or adjusting the glide path and approach angle. Terrain considerations also include assessing the suitability of the landing surface, such as its slope, texture, and firmness. The pilot must be prepared to execute maneuvers to navigate around obstacles while maintaining control of the helicopter under OEI conditions.

[PH.VIII.C.R1; FAA-H-8083-21]

10. **What factors should be considered when assessing the available landing area during an OEI approach?**

Factors to consider include the size of the area, its proximity, surface condition, and any potential hazards or obstacles. The landing area should be large enough to accommodate the helicopter's landing footprint and allow for some margin of error. The surface should be firm and level to prevent rollover or damage upon touchdown. Proximity to the current flight path is important for ensuring the helicopter can reach the area with the available altitude and glide capability. The pilot should also consider accessibility for emergency services if needed.

[PH.VIII.C.R1; FAA-H-8083-21]

11. **What factors should be considered when planning a flightpath to the selected landing area during an OEI situation in a multi-engine helicopter?**

Factors to consider include the glide distance of the helicopter under OEI conditions, the altitude available for the approach, wind direction and speed, terrain features and obstacles along the flightpath, and the size and suitability of the landing area. The pilot should also consider potential hazards such as power lines, buildings, or populated areas and plan a flight path that minimizes risk to both the helicopter and people on the ground.

[PH.VIII.C.R2; FAA-H-8083-21]

12. How can a pilot assess the feasibility of reaching a selected landing area during an OEI approach?

The pilot should consider the helicopter's current altitude and airspeed, the distance to the landing area, and the glide performance of the helicopter with one engine inoperative. The pilot should use visual cues and onboard navigational instruments to estimate the glide ratio and trajectory. Additionally, the pilot must factor in wind conditions and any obstacles that might affect the approach. If the selected area is not reachable, the pilot should quickly identify an alternative.

[PH.VIII.C.R2; FAA-H-8083-21]

13. What techniques should a pilot use to identify potential collision hazards during an OEI approach in a multi-engine helicopter?

A pilot should employ vigilant scanning techniques to identify potential collision hazards. This includes a thorough visual scan of the approach path and landing area for obstacles such as terrain features, buildings, power lines, and other aircraft. The use of onboard navigation and collision avoidance systems, if available, can also aid in detecting hazards. The pilot should continuously assess the environment, adjusting the flight path as necessary to avoid potential collisions.

[PH.VIII.C.R3; FAA-H-8083-21]

14. What strategies can a pilot employ to manage distractions during an OEI approach in a multi-engine helicopter?

A pilot should focus on prioritizing tasks based on their criticality to safety. This involves following the mantra "aviate, navigate, communicate"—first ensuring the helicopter is under control, then navigating to the landing area, and finally communicating with air traffic control or other crew members. Utilizing checklists to ensure all necessary procedures are followed can help in managing workload. Additionally, minimizing unnecessary cockpit conversations and delegating tasks to other crew members, if available, can reduce distractions.

[PH.VIII.C.R4; FAA-H-8083-21]

15. What are the risks of losing situational awareness during an OEI approach, and how can they be mitigated?

The risks of losing situational awareness during an OEI approach include the potential for controlled flight into terrain, deviation from the planned flight path, inability to effectively manage airspeed and descent rate, and missing critical cues for safe landing. These risks can be mitigated by thorough preflight planning, understanding the helicopter's capabilities and limitations under OEI conditions, and regularly practicing OEI procedures in various scenarios. Maintaining a calm and methodical approach to the situation, and avoiding fixation on a single task, are also crucial for preserving situational awareness.

[PH.VIII.C.R4; FAA-H-8083-21]

Skills to be demonstrated:

- Maintain the operating powerplant within OEI limits.

- Maintain, prior to beginning the final approach segment, the recommended flight profile with altitude ±200 feet, airspeed, ±20 knots, heading ±10°, and maintain track.

- Make radio calls as appropriate.

- Plan and follow a flightpath to the selected landing area considering altitude, wind, terrain, and obstructions.

- Complete the appropriate checklist(s).

- Maintain directional control and appropriate crosswind correction throughout the approach and landing.

- Use single-pilot resource management (SRM) or crew resource management (CRM), as appropriate.

D. Systems and Equipment Malfunctions

1. What are common causes of partial power loss in piston-engine helicopters?

Common causes of partial power loss in piston-engine helicopters include fuel contamination, carburetor icing, spark plug fouling, and issues with the fuel delivery system like clogged fuel filters or fuel lines. Incorrect fuel mixture settings can also lead to partial power loss. These issues can prevent the engine from receiving the correct air-fuel mixture or spark, resulting in reduced engine performance. Regular maintenance and preflight inspections are essential to identify and mitigate these risks.

[PH.VIII.D.K1; FAA-H-8083-21]

2. How can a turbine engine in a helicopter experience a complete power loss, and what are the typical causes?

Complete power loss in a turbine engine helicopter can occur due to fuel starvation, mechanical failure, compressor stall, or severe damage to the engine components such as turbine blades. Fuel starvation can be caused by empty tanks, contaminated fuel, or blockages in the fuel system. Mechanical failures may arise from wear and tear or defective parts. Compressor stalls occur due to disrupted airflow in the engine, often caused by foreign object damage, icing, or operating outside the engine's designed parameters. Regular maintenance and adherence to operational limitations are crucial to prevent these issues.

[PH.VIII.D.K1; FAA-H-8083-21]

3. What indicators should a pilot monitor to identify early signs of powerplant malfunctions in helicopters?

Pilots should monitor indicators such as the engine temperature gauges, oil pressure and temperature gauges, fuel pressure indicators, and power output readings (like torque or gas producer RPM) to identify early signs of powerplant malfunctions in helicopters. Unusual noises, vibrations, or changes in engine performance are also key indicators. Prompt attention to any discrepancies in these readings can allow early detection of potential issues before they lead to a power loss.

[PH.VIII.D.K1; FAA-H-8083-21]

4. What emergency procedures should a pilot be familiar with in the event of a powerplant malfunction in a helicopter?

In the event of a powerplant malfunction in a helicopter, a pilot should be familiar with emergency procedures such as autorotation, engine restart procedures, and emergency landing techniques. Autorotation allows the pilot to descend and land safely without engine power. Engine restart procedures vary based on the type of engine and the specific malfunction but generally involve steps to reestablish fuel flow and ignition. In cases where a restart is not possible or practical, the pilot must be prepared to perform an immediate emergency landing, selecting a suitable site, and maneuvering the helicopter to land safely. Familiarity with the specific helicopter's emergency procedures, as outlined in the pilot's operating handbook (POH) or rotorcraft flight manual (RFM), is essential.

[PH.VIII.D.K1; FAA-H-8083-21]

5. What are common signs of an electrical malfunction in a helicopter?

Common signs of an electrical malfunction in a helicopter include flickering or dimming lights, unresponsive or erratic instrument readings, failure of electrical systems such as radios or navigation equipment, and warning lights or alarms indicating electrical system issues. A sudden loss of power to avionics or other electrical components is also a key indicator. The pilot should be vigilant in monitoring the helicopter's electrical system indicators, such as the ammeter and voltage meter, for any abnormal readings.

[PH.VIII.D.K2a; FAA-H-8083-21]

6. How can a pilot identify and respond to a failing alternator or generator in a helicopter?

A pilot can identify a failing alternator or generator in a helicopter by observing the ammeter and voltage meter for indications of charging system irregularities, such as low voltage or fluctuating readings. Warning lights or annunciators specific to the charging system may also activate. In response, the pilot should follow the emergency checklist procedures, which typically involve reducing electrical load by turning off nonessential electrical equipment and attempting a reset or restart of the alternator or generator. If the issue persists, the pilot should prepare for the possibility of a complete electrical failure and proceed accordingly.

[PH.VIII.D.K2a; FAA-H-8083-21]

7. What steps should a pilot take if experiencing a complete electrical failure in a helicopter?

If experiencing a complete electrical failure in a helicopter, the pilot should first ensure that the helicopter remains in stable flight. The immediate priority is to fly the helicopter safely. The pilot should then attempt to identify and rectify the cause of the failure, such as checking circuit breakers or switching to an alternate power source if available. Essential flight information may need to be obtained from backup instruments or mechanical gauges. The pilot should consider the need to land as soon as practical, especially if navigation and communication systems are compromised, and follow visual flight rules (VFR) if in visual meteorological conditions (VMC).

[PH.VIII.D.K2a; FAA-H-8083-21]

8. How can electrical system redundancy be used to mitigate the impact of electrical malfunctions in helicopters?

Electrical system redundancy in helicopters mitigates the impact of electrical malfunctions by providing backup systems or components, such as dual alternators/generators, batteries, and independent electrical circuits for critical systems. This redundancy ensures that if one component fails, another can take over, reducing the risk of complete system failure. Pilots should be familiar with their helicopter's redundant electrical systems and know how to switch to backup systems when necessary. Regular testing and maintenance of these systems are also crucial to ensure their reliability.

[PH.VIII.D.K2a; FAA-H-8083-21]

9. What are the potential hazards of an electrical fire in a helicopter, and how should a pilot handle such a situation?

An electrical fire in a helicopter poses significant hazards, including the risk of damage to critical flight systems, reduced visibility due to smoke, and the potential for injury to occupants. If an electrical fire is suspected or detected, the pilot should follow emergency procedures, which typically involve shutting down the electrical system to cut off the fire's power source and using a fire extinguisher if available and safe to do so. The pilot should also ventilate the cockpit to remove smoke and prepare for an emergency landing. Quick and decisive action is essential to minimize the risks associated with an electrical fire.

[PH.VIII.D.K2a; FAA-H-8083-21]

10. How can a pilot identify a malfunction in the helicopter's attitude indicator?

A pilot can identify a malfunction in the helicopter's attitude indicator by noting any unusual or erratic movements, a failure to respond to changes in the helicopter's pitch or bank, or a tumbling of the gyroscope beyond its normal limits of operation. The attitude indicator may also freeze or show an incorrect attitude. Cross-checking with other flight instruments, such as the altimeter, airspeed indicator, and turn coordinator, can help confirm a suspected malfunction in the attitude indicator.

[PH.VIII.D.K2b; FAA-H-8083-25]

11. What should a pilot do if the helicopter's altimeter fails during flight?

If a helicopter's altimeter fails during flight, the pilot should rely on other available instruments and navigation aids to maintain altitude awareness. This includes using the vertical speed indicator (VSI) to monitor climb or descent rates and GPS altitude readings if available. The pilot should also increase visual scanning outside the cockpit to maintain terrain clearance, especially in hilly or mountainous areas. Communication with air traffic control (ATC) is important for altitude reporting and collision avoidance, and the pilot should declare an emergency if the situation warrants.

[PH.VIII.D.K2b; FAA-H-8083-25]

12. What are the potential consequences of a malfunction in the helicopter's airspeed indicator and how should it be addressed?

A malfunction in the helicopter's airspeed indicator can lead to inaccurate readings, which can affect the pilot's ability to maintain safe airspeeds and may result in unsafe flight conditions like stalling or overspeeding. To address this, the pilot should use other cues to estimate airspeed, including engine power settings, sound, and visual references. The GPS ground speed can also serve as a rough airspeed estimate in steady-state flight.

[PH.VIII.D.K2b; FAA-H-8083-25]

13. What indications might a pilot observe if the helicopter's turn coordinator malfunctions?

If the helicopter's turn coordinator malfunctions, the pilot might observe a failure of the instrument to respond to turns or an indication of a turn while the helicopter is flying straight. The turn coordinator's ball might also become stuck or unresponsive, failing to indicate proper coordination. To manage this, the pilot should rely on the magnetic compass and other flight instruments for turn information and maintain coordinated flight using visual cues and control inputs. Cross-referencing with the heading indicator and GPS can also assist in maintaining proper flight orientation.

[PH.VIII.D.K2b; FAA-H-8083-25]

14. What actions should a pilot take if the radar altimeter in a helicopter fails during a low-altitude flight?

If the radar altimeter in a helicopter fails during a low-altitude flight, the pilot should immediately switch to using the barometric altimeter for altitude information, keeping in mind its limitations near the ground. The pilot should increase vigilance in monitoring altitude using visual references, particularly when flying over terrain with varying elevation. In situations where precise altitude information is critical, such as during landing approaches or low-altitude operations, the pilot should consider adjusting the flight plan to ensure safety.

[PH.VIII.D.K2b; FAA-H-8083-21]

15. How can a pilot manage a pitot-static system failure in flight?

To manage a pitot-static system failure in flight, a pilot should recognize the failure by identifying erratic or non-responsive airspeed, altimeter, and vertical speed indicator readings. The pilot can use alternative methods such as GPS for ground speed estimation and visual references for altitude awareness. If equipped, the pilot should try switching to an alternate static source. It is crucial to maintain visual flight rules (VFR) if possible and communicate the situation to ATC for assistance. The pilot should also follow any specific emergency procedures outlined in the helicopter's operating manual and prepare for a precautionary landing if necessary.

[PH.VIII.D.K2c; FAA-H-8083-25]

16. What are the typical indications of a pitot tube blockage in a helicopter?

Typical indications of a pitot tube blockage in a helicopter include a stagnant or erroneous airspeed indicator reading. If the pitot tube is completely blocked, the airspeed indicator may not show any change in speed regardless of the actual speed of the helicopter. If the blockage occurs only in the drain hole and not in the pitot port, the airspeed indicator may behave like an altimeter, increasing with altitude and decreasing with descent.

[PH.VIII.D.K2c; FAA-H-8083-25]

17. What are the potential risks associated with flying a helicopter with a malfunctioning pitot-static system?

Flying a helicopter with a malfunctioning pitot-static system poses several risks, including the inability to accurately determine altitude, airspeed, and climb or descent rates. This can lead to dangerous flight conditions such as unintentional altitude deviations, airspeed control issues, and the potential for airspace violations or terrain collisions, especially in poor visibility conditions. The misreading of instruments may also lead to disorientation and incorrect decision-making by the pilot. Such a situation should be handled with caution and appropriate emergency procedures followed.

[PH.VIII.D.K2c; FAA-H-8083-25]

18. **What are common indications of a malfunction in the electronic flight deck display of a helicopter?**

    They include flickering screens, frozen or unresponsive displays, incorrect or inconsistent data being shown, error messages, or a complete blackout of the display screens. The pilot may also notice discrepancies between the information on the electronic displays and backup analog instruments or external cues.

    [PH.VIII.D.K2d; FAA-H-8083-25]

19. **How should a pilot respond to a primary flight display (PFD) failure in a helicopter?**

    The pilot should immediately switch to using standby or backup instruments for essential flight information such as altitude, airspeed, and attitude. If available, the pilot should attempt to reset or reboot the malfunctioning display. Communication with air traffic control (ATC) is essential to report the malfunction, especially if it affects the pilot's ability to navigate or maintain situational awareness. The pilot should also refer to the helicopter's emergency procedures and consider the safest option for landing.

    [PH.VIII.D.K2d; FAA-H-8083-25]

20. **What backup systems should a pilot be familiar with in case of electronic display malfunctions in a helicopter?**

    Traditional analog instruments like the altimeter, airspeed indicator, attitude indicator, and magnetic compass. Familiarity with handheld or backup GPS units and radio navigation aids like VOR or ADF can also be crucial. Understanding the helicopter's electrical system and knowing how to isolate or reset malfunctioning displays is important. Pilots should regularly practice flying with these backup systems during training to ensure proficiency in their use during electronic failures.

    [PH.VIII.D.K2d; FAA-H-8083-25]

21. How should a pilot respond to a failure of the landing gear to extend in a wheel-equipped helicopter?

If the landing gear fails to extend in a wheel-equipped helicopter, the pilot should first attempt to troubleshoot the issue using the emergency gear extension procedures outlined in the helicopter's operating manual. This may include manual gear extension methods or cycling the landing gear control. The pilot should also inform air traffic control (ATC) of the situation and prepare for a potential emergency landing. If the gear cannot be extended, the pilot must plan for a gear-up landing, choosing an appropriate surface and preparing the helicopter and passengers for the landing. Safety measures such as securing loose items and briefing passengers are important.

[PH.VIII.D.K2e; FAA-H-8083-21]

22. What emergency procedures should be executed in the event of a landing gear indication failure?

In the event of a landing gear indication failure, where the gear's position cannot be confirmed by the cockpit indicators, the pilot should follow emergency checklists which might involve using an alternate method to verify gear position, such as a visual inspection or seeking confirmation from ground personnel or ATC. If the gear position remains uncertain, the pilot should treat the situation as a potential gear malfunction and prepare for an emergency landing accordingly. This includes selecting an appropriate landing site, securing the cabin, and briefing passengers on emergency procedures.

[PH.VIII.D.K2e; FAA-H-8083-21]

23. What are the initial signs that a helicopter's flight control system may be malfunctioning?

Initial signs of a malfunctioning flight control system in a helicopter include unresponsiveness or stiffness in the cyclic, collective, or tail rotor pedals. The helicopter may not respond as expected to pilot inputs or may exhibit abnormal flight characteristics such as drifting, pitching, or rolling unexpectedly. Additionally, unusual noises or vibrations from the control system could indicate a problem. Regular checks of control responsiveness and feedback during flight are crucial for early detection.

[PH.VIII.D.K2f; FAA-H-8083-21]

24. **How should a pilot manage a situation where the helicopter's trim system becomes inoperative?**

    The pilot should first ensure that the helicopter is in a safe and stable flight condition. The pilot must then manually maintain the desired flight attitude and heading without the assistance of the trim system. This may require more physical effort and concentration. Pilots should adjust their flight plan to reduce the duration and complexity of the flight if possible. Informing air traffic control (ATC) about the situation is important, especially if the malfunction affects the ability to adhere to assigned routes or altitudes. Continuous monitoring of helicopter performance and readiness to make manual adjustments as needed are key until a safe landing can be accomplished.

    [PH.VIII.D.K2f; FAA-H-8083-21]

25. **What are the potential consequences of flying a helicopter with an inoperative trim system?**

    Flying a helicopter with an inoperative trim system can lead to increased pilot workload and fatigue due to the need for constant manual control inputs to maintain desired flight attitudes and headings. It can also result in less precise control of the helicopter, especially in turbulent conditions or during complex maneuvers. The inability to use the trim system may affect the helicopter's performance and handling characteristics, potentially leading to control difficulties.

    [PH.VIII.D.K2f; FAA-H-8083-21]

26. **How can a pilot compensate for a malfunctioning tail rotor control in a helicopter?**

    To compensate for a malfunctioning tail rotor control in a helicopter, the pilot must manage the yaw of the helicopter using available power and cyclic inputs. In case of reduced tail rotor effectiveness, adjusting the collective pitch to reduce torque can help control yaw. If the tail rotor is completely inoperative, the pilot may need to perform an autorotation landing, as controlled flight is typically not possible. The pilot should immediately reduce power to minimize torque and prepare for an emergency landing, selecting an appropriate area and configuring the helicopter for the safest possible touchdown. Clear communication with ATC and adherence to emergency procedures are essential.

    [PH.VIII.D.K2f; FAA-H-8083-21]

27. What are the typical indications of a hydraulic system failure in a helicopter?

Typical indications of a hydraulic system failure in a helicopter include increased resistance or stiffness in the flight controls, such as the cyclic and collective. The pilot may also notice abnormal feedback or vibrations from the controls. Warning lights or annunciators specific to the hydraulic system may activate, signaling a loss of hydraulic pressure. In some helicopters, a noticeable change in control response or unusual noises from the hydraulic system can also indicate a failure.

[PH.VIII.D.K2g; FAA-H-8083-21]

28. How should a pilot manage a helicopter following a hydraulic system failure?

In the event of a hydraulic system failure, the pilot should first stabilize the helicopter and maintain control using manual force on the flight controls. The pilot should refer to the emergency procedures in the helicopter's flight manual, which typically involve reducing the helicopter's speed to minimize control forces and heading towards the nearest suitable landing area. Communication with air traffic control (ATC) is essential to declare an emergency and request assistance. The pilot should also prepare the helicopter and passengers for a precautionary landing, given the increased control forces required.

[PH.VIII.D.K2g; FAA-H-8083-21]

29. What emergency procedures are recommended for a helicopter experiencing a hydraulic failure during flight?

Emergency procedures for a hydraulic failure during flight typically include immediately reducing speed to lessen control forces and manually flying the helicopter. The pilot should follow the specific emergency checklist provided in the helicopter's flight manual, which may include isolating the failed hydraulic system if a backup system is available. The pilot should notify ATC of the situation and, if necessary, declare an emergency. Preparations should be made for a precautionary landing at the nearest suitable area, considering the increased physical effort required to operate the controls.

[PH.VIII.D.K2g; FAA-H-8083-21]

30. What are common causes of low-frequency vibrations in helicopters and which components are typically affected?

Common causes of low-frequency vibrations in helicopters often involve the main rotor system, including imbalances or damage to the rotor blades, issues with the rotor hub, or problems with the main rotor transmission and drive system. Components typically affected include the rotor blades themselves, rotor head, and associated linkages. Low-frequency vibrations can also stem from misalignment or imbalance in the main gearbox. These vibrations are usually felt throughout the airframe and can significantly affect flight control and comfort.

[PH.VIII.D.K3; FAA-H-8083-21]

31. How can a pilot identify and troubleshoot medium-frequency vibrations in a helicopter?

Medium-frequency vibrations in a helicopter are often associated with the tail rotor system or the intermediate and tail rotor gearboxes. To identify and troubleshoot these vibrations, the pilot should look for changes in vibration patterns at different flight regimes or rotor RPMs. Inspecting the tail rotor blades for damage, imbalance, or misalignment is crucial, as is checking the condition and alignment of the tail rotor gearbox and drive shaft. The pilot should also be attentive to changes in noise or feedback from the tail rotor controls, which can indicate developing issues.

[PH.VIII.D.K3; FAA-H-8083-21]

32. What are the potential sources of high-frequency vibrations in helicopters and how do they impact the aircraft?

High-frequency vibrations in helicopters are typically associated with the engine and its components, such as the compressor or turbine sections of a turbine engine, or the pistons and crankshaft in a piston engine. Other sources can include accessory gearboxes, generator or alternator imbalances, and certain types of bearing failures. These vibrations often manifest in the cockpit as a buzzing or rapid vibration felt through the controls or airframe. High-frequency vibrations can lead to accelerated wear of components, discomfort for the crew and passengers, and in severe cases, structural damage.

[PH.VIII.D.K3; FAA-H-8083-21]

33. How do vibrations from the helicopter's components affect its overall performance and structural integrity?

Vibrations from a helicopter's components can significantly affect its overall performance and structural integrity. Persistent vibrations can lead to fatigue in airframe components, loosening of fasteners, and potential failure of critical parts. They can cause wear and tear on rotor and engine components, reducing efficiency and potentially leading to malfunctions. Vibrations can also interfere with the accuracy of flight instruments and the effectiveness of control inputs. In the long term, continued exposure to vibrations can lead to structural damage and decreased reliability of the helicopter. Therefore, identifying and addressing the sources of vibrations is crucial for maintaining the safety and performance of the aircraft.

[PH.VIII.D.K3; FAA-H-8083-21]

34. What are common causes of smoke or fire in a helicopter?

Common causes of smoke or fire in a helicopter include electrical malfunctions, such as short circuits or overheated components; engine-related issues, like oil leaks igniting on hot surfaces or turbine engine malfunctions; and hydraulic fluid leaks that come into contact with hot parts. Additionally, friction or overheating in mechanical components, such as bearings or gearboxes, can cause smoke or fire. Improperly maintained or faulty equipment and combustible materials stored improperly can also lead to such emergencies.

[PH.VIII.D.K4; FAA-H-8083-21]

35. How should a pilot respond to indications of an in-flight fire in a helicopter?

In response to indications of an in-flight fire, the pilot should first confirm the presence of fire or smoke. The immediate action is to follow the emergency procedures outlined in the helicopter's flight manual, which typically include shutting down electrical systems to isolate potential sources of the fire, and if available, using onboard fire suppression systems. The pilot should divert to the nearest suitable landing area and prepare for an emergency landing.

Airspeed may be increased within safe limits to help extinguish flames. If smoke is present, the pilot should ventilate the cockpit. Communication with air traffic control to declare an emergency and request assistance is also essential.

[PH.VIII.D.K4; FAA-H-8083-21]

36. How can environmental control system malfunctions affect helicopter operations, and what are the remedial actions?

Environmental control system malfunctions in a helicopter can affect operations by impacting cabin temperature, ventilation, and, in some cases, pressurization in high-altitude flights. This can lead to discomfort, visibility issues due to windshield fogging, or, in severe cases, hypoxia or heat exhaustion. Remedial actions include manually adjusting the system if possible, using alternative ventilation methods like opening vents or windows, and altering altitude to maintain a comfortable and safe cabin environment. In cases of pressurization issues, descending to a lower altitude where supplemental oxygen is not required might be necessary.

[PH.VIII.D.K5; FAA-H-8083-21]

37. What are the steps to troubleshoot an auto-pilot system failure in a helicopter?

To troubleshoot an auto-pilot system failure in a helicopter, the pilot should first disengage the autopilot and manually control the helicopter to ensure stability and control. The pilot should then check circuit breakers and reset them if necessary. Consulting the helicopter's flight manual for specific troubleshooting procedures is important, as different models have unique systems and reset processes. If the autopilot remains non-functional, the pilot should continue the flight manually and inform air traffic control if the failure affects the flight plan or safety. Postflight, a qualified technician should inspect and repair the system.

[PH.VIII.D.K5; FAA-H-8083-21]

38. How should a pilot manage a failure in the helicopter's rotor brake system?

Managing a failure in the helicopter's rotor brake system requires ensuring that the helicopter is brought to a complete stop with the rotors fully spooled down before attempting to shut down the engine, as the rotor brake is used to stop the rotor blades from spinning after engine shutdown. The pilot should follow the specific procedures outlined in the helicopter's flight manual, which may include allowing the rotors to naturally slow down and stop. The pilot should ensure the helicopter is in a safe, clear area where the rotors can turn freely without obstruction. Caution is advised during shutdown to prevent damage to the rotor system.

[PH.VIII.D.K5; FAA-H-8083-21]

39. What is a startle response in the context of helicopter operations, and how can it impact pilot performance during a system malfunction?

A startle response in helicopter operations refers to the pilot's instinctive reaction to an unexpected event or system malfunction, such as sudden noises, warnings, or control issues. This response can impact pilot performance by causing temporary disorientation, overreaction, or a freeze response, potentially leading to inappropriate or delayed corrective actions. The startle response can impair cognitive functions and decision-making abilities, making it challenging to effectively manage the malfunction.

[PH.VIII.D.R1; FAA-H-8083-21]

40. How can pilots train to manage their startle response effectively during unexpected system malfunctions in a helicopter?

Pilots can train to manage their startle response effectively by participating in realistic simulator training that includes unexpected system malfunctions and emergency scenarios. This training helps pilots become more accustomed to handling surprising situations and develops their ability to quickly regain composure and think clearly under stress. Regular practice of emergency procedures, both in simulators and during flight training, enhances muscle memory and decision-making skills. Pilots should also learn stress management techniques and maintain a high level of situational awareness during all phases of flight.

[PH.VIII.D.R1; FAA-H-8083-21]

41. What are the key strategies a helicopter pilot can use to mitigate the impact of a startle response during an in-flight emergency?

Key strategies for mitigating the impact of a startle response during an in-flight emergency include maintaining a calm and focused demeanor, taking deep breaths to reduce stress, and consciously slowing down to think through the situation. Pilots should prioritize flying the helicopter first (aviate), then navigate, and finally communicate the situation to ATC or other crew members. Adhering to standard operating procedures and relying on training and checklists can provide a structured approach to resolving the emergency, helping to override the initial startle reaction.

[PH.VIII.D.R1; FAA-H-8083-21]

42. What is the importance of using checklists during a system or equipment malfunction in a helicopter?

The importance of using checklists during a system or equipment malfunction in a helicopter lies in ensuring a structured and thorough approach to addressing the malfunction. Checklists provide step-by-step procedures that help pilots manage complex situations methodically, reducing the likelihood of missing critical steps of making errors under stress. They serve as a memory aid, particularly in high-pressure scenarios, ensuring that all necessary actions are taken to mitigate the malfunction. Consistent checklist usage enhances safety by standardizing responses to emergencies and malfunctions.

[PH.VIII.D.R2; FAA-H-8083-25]

43. What strategies can be employed to mitigate risks associated with delayed checklist usage in a helicopter malfunction?

To mitigate risks associated with delayed checklist usage in a helicopter malfunction, pilots should prioritize maintaining control of the aircraft and navigating safely (aviate, navigate) before referring to checklists. Regular training and familiarization with common emergency procedures can reduce reliance on immediate checklist reference. Developing a habit of reviewing pertinent checklists during preflight preparation can also aid in faster recall during emergencies. In addition, having quick-reference handbooks or emergency checklists readily accessible in the cockpit can expedite their usage. Emphasizing CRM principles in multicrew helicopters ensures that one crew member can fly the aircraft while the other accesses and reads the checklist.

[PH.VIII.D.R2; FAA-H-8083-25]

44. What are the potential risks of incorrectly following a checklist during a system malfunction in a helicopter, and how can they be mitigated?

The potential risks of incorrectly following a checklist during a system malfunction in a helicopter include exacerbating the malfunction, missing critical steps that could resolve the issue, or creating additional hazards. These risks can be mitigated by regular training on checklist procedures to ensure familiarity and proficiency. Pilots should always cross-reference the checklist with the actual situation to ensure its relevance and completeness. In multi-crew operations, cross-checking and confirming actions with crew members can prevent errors. Pilots should also be trained to recognize when deviation from the checklist is necessary due to unique circumstances of the malfunction. Emphasizing a calm and methodical approach to checklist usage, even under pressure, is key to minimizing risks.

[PH.VIII.D.R2; FAA-H-8083-25]

45. How can a helicopter pilot manage distractions during a system or equipment malfunction to maintain safety?

To manage distractions during a system or equipment malfunction, a helicopter pilot should prioritize tasks using the aviate, navigate, communicate principle. This means first ensuring that the helicopter is under control, then navigating safely, and finally communicating with air traffic control or other relevant parties. The pilot should focus on essential tasks and avoid noncritical activities that can divert attention. Using checklists can help in systematically addressing the malfunction while maintaining situational awareness. Crew resource management (CRM) techniques are also effective in multicrew helicopters for distributing tasks and maintaining focus on critical issues.

[PH.VIII.D.R3; FAA-H-8083-25]

46. How can a pilot effectively prioritize tasks during an equipment malfunction in a helicopter?

Effective task prioritization during an equipment malfunction in a helicopter involves focusing first on flying the aircraft, ensuring that control and stability are maintained. The pilot should then address the most critical aspects of the malfunction based on its impact on flight safety. Reference to emergency checklists and standard operating procedures can guide the prioritization process. The pilot should also consider factors such as fuel state, weather, and proximity to suitable landing areas in determining priorities.

[PH.VIII.D.R3; FAA-H-8083-25]

47. How can a helicopter pilot prevent or overcome disorientation during an unexpected equipment malfunction?

To prevent or overcome disorientation during an unexpected equipment malfunction, a helicopter pilot should rely on training and adhere to known procedures and checklists. Focusing on basic flying skills and instrument readings can help maintain orientation, especially in low visibility or at night. In multi-crew helicopters, effective communication and task sharing can assist in managing the situation and prevent fixation on a single problem. Regular practice of emergency scenarios, including simulator training, equips pilots with the skills to handle unexpected malfunctions without becoming disoriented. Maintaining a calm demeanor and taking deep breaths can also help in staying focused and clear-headed.

[PH.VIII.D.R3; FAA-H-8083-25]

48. What defines an undesired aircraft state (UAS) in helicopter operations, and what are common triggers?

An undesired aircraft state (UAS) in helicopter operations is defined as any flight condition where the aircraft deviates or is at risk of deviating from parameters set by the pilot, flight manual, or safety guidelines. Common triggers include system failures, environmental factors such as turbulence or weather phenomena, incorrect pilot inputs, loss of situational awareness, or mechanical malfunctions. Recognizing the onset of a UAS is crucial for timely corrective action.

[PH.VIII.D.R4; FAA-H-8083-21]

49. How can helicopter pilots effectively recognize and assess a UAS caused by a system malfunction?

Helicopter pilots can effectively recognize and assess a UAS caused by a system malfunction through continuous monitoring of flight instruments, system indicators, and helicopter performance. Vigilance in detecting early signs of malfunction, such as unexpected noises, vibrations, warning lights, or changes in handling characteristics, is key. Regular training and familiarity with the specific helicopter model's systems and normal operating parameters enable pilots to quickly identify discrepancies and assess their impact on flight safety.

[PH.VIII.D.R4; FAA-H-8083-21]

50. What immediate actions should a pilot take upon identifying a UAS related to equipment malfunctions in a helicopter?

Upon identifying a UAS related to equipment malfunctions in a helicopter, the pilot's immediate actions should prioritize regaining control and stabilizing the aircraft. This includes following the aviate, navigate, communicate hierarchy: ensuring that the helicopter is flying safely, determining the best course of action or route to minimize risk, and then communicating with air traffic control (ATC) or other crew members about the situation. Consulting the relevant emergency or abnormal procedures checklist for the specific malfunction can guide the pilot in taking appropriate corrective actions.

[PH.VIII.D.R4; FAA-H-8083-21]

51. How can pilots mitigate the risks associated with a UAS due to equipment malfunctions during critical phases of flight?

Pilots can mitigate the risks associated with a UAS due to equipment malfunctions during critical phases of flight by maintaining high situational awareness, especially during takeoff, landing, and low-altitude operations. Preflight planning and briefings that include contingency plans for malfunctions at critical moments enhance preparedness. Effective use of crew resource management (CRM) techniques, where applicable, ensures that all crew members are engaged in monitoring for and responding to UAS conditions. Pilots should also practice manual flying skills to maintain proficiency in handling the helicopter without reliance on automated systems.

[PH.VIII.D.R4; FAA-H-8083-21]

Skills to be demonstrated:

• Determine appropriate action for simulated emergencies specified by the evaluator, from at least three of the elements or sub-elements listed in PH.VIII.D.K1 through PH.VIII.D.K5.

• Complete the appropriate checklist(s).

E. Vortex Ring State (VRS)

The evaluator must conduct a briefing with the applicant regarding the selection of a safe entry altitude, recognition of the onset of VRS, and recovery within the Task standards. The area must be free of obstructions should landing become necessary.

1. What is the vortex ring state in helicopter flight, and under what conditions is it most likely to occur?

The vortex ring state is a dangerous flight condition in helicopters where the aircraft descends into its own downwash, resulting in a loss of lift. It most likely occurs under conditions of low forward airspeed (less than ETL), high vertical descent rates (generally more than 300 feet per minute), and high-power settings (more than 20% of power).

[PH.VIII.E.K1; FAA-H-8083-21]

2. How can a pilot recognize the onset of the vortex ring state during flight?

A pilot can recognize the onset of the vortex ring state by observing a sudden and uncommanded increase in the rate of descent and the need for more collective to maintain altitude, despite having available power. Other indications include a loss of helicopter control effectiveness, increased vibrations, and a lack of response to control inputs or a mushy feeling in the controls. The aircraft may also experience a buffeting or oscillating sensation. Recognizing these symptoms early is crucial for taking timely corrective action.

[PH.VIII.E.K1; FAA-H-8083-21]

3. How does wind affect the likelihood of a helicopter entering a vortex ring state (VRS)?

Wind can significantly affect the likelihood of a helicopter entering VRS. Calm or tailwind conditions are more conducive to VRS because they reduce the effective airspeed over the rotor system, making it easier for the helicopter to descend into its own downwash. Conversely, a headwind can help prevent VRS by increasing the flow of undisturbed air through the rotor disc. Pilots must be particularly cautious in low-wind conditions or when descending with a tailwind, as these scenarios increase the risk of encountering VRS.

[PH.VIII.E.K2; FAA-H-8083-21]

4. How does the weight of a helicopter influence its susceptibility to VRS?

The weight of a helicopter directly influences its susceptibility to VRS. Heavier helicopters require more power to maintain a hover or slow flight, which can create a stronger rotor downwash. This increased downwash, combined with a high rate of descent, can make it easier for the helicopter to enter VRS. Pilots operating helicopters near their maximum gross weight should be especially vigilant during operations that could lead to VRS, such as hovering OGE (out of ground effect) or performing steep approaches.

[PH.VIII.E.K2; FAA-H-8083-21]

5. In what ways do temperature and density altitude affect the risk of entering VRS in helicopter flight?

Temperature and density altitude have a significant effect on the risk of entering VRS during helicopter flight. Higher temperatures and higher density altitudes result in thinner air, reducing the efficiency of the rotor system. This reduced efficiency requires the use of more power to maintain lift, especially in hovering or slow flight, which increases the downwash intensity and the potential for VRS. Pilots operating in hot and high conditions should be aware of the heightened risk of VRS and manage their descent rates and power settings accordingly.

[PH.VIII.E.K2; FAA-H-8083-21]

6. What are the primary conditions necessary for the formation of vortex ring state (VRS) in a helicopter?

The primary conditions necessary for the formation of VRS in a helicopter include a vertical or nearly vertical descent rate typically greater than 300 feet per minute, a low forward airspeed (often less than the effective translational lift speed), and the application of a power setting above 20%. These conditions can lead to the rotor system descending into its own downwash, causing disrupted airflow and a loss of lift. The combination of these factors is essential for the onset of VRS.

[PH.VIII.E.K3; FAA-H-8083-21]

7. How does the rate of descent contribute to the formation of VRS in helicopter flight?

When a helicopter descends vertically or nearly vertically at a rate typically exceeding 300 feet per minute, it can enter its own rotor downwash. This descent rate leads to a disturbed airflow pattern where the air circulates upwards around the rotor tips and downwards through the rotor disc, causing a ring-like vortex flow. This disrupted airflow pattern reduces rotor efficiency and lift, contributing to the formation of VRS.

[PH.VIII.E.K3; FAA-H-8083-21]

8. Why is low forward airspeed a critical factor in the development of VRS in helicopters?

Because it limits the amount of fresh, undisturbed air entering the rotor system. When a helicopter has little to no forward airspeed, especially during steep descents, it is more likely to descend into its own downwash. This recirculation of air through the rotor disc disrupts the normal lift-generating airflow, leading to a decrease in rotor efficiency and the potential onset of VRS. Therefore, maintaining some forward airspeed during descent is key to avoiding VRS.

[PH.VIII.E.K3; FAA-H-8083-21]

9. In what ways does the application of high-power settings influence the formation of VRS?

By increasing the amount of downwash produced by the rotor blades. When a helicopter is descending with a high power setting, especially at low airspeeds, the rotor blades generate a strong column of air moving downwards. If the helicopter's descent rate is high enough, it can cause the rotor system to descend into this column of downwash. The interaction of the rotor blades with their own downwash leads to disturbed airflow and a reduction in lift, thereby facilitating the formation of VRS.

[PH.VIII.E.K3; FAA-H-8083-21]

10. What are the key aerodynamic factors involved in the formation of vortex ring state (VRS) in helicopters?

The helicopter may descend at a rate that exceeds the normal downward induced-flow rate of the inner blade sections. As a result, the airflow of the inner blade sections is upward relative to the disk. This produces a secondary vortex ring in addition to the normal tip vortices. The secondary vortex ring is generated about the point on the blade where the airflow changes from up to down. The result is an unsteady turbulent flow over a large area of the disk. Rotor efficiency is lost even though power is still being supplied from the engine.

[PH.VIII.E.K4; FAA-H-8083-21]

11. **What are the common indications that a helicopter pilot may experience when entering VRS?**

    Common indications that a helicopter pilot may experience when entering VRS include a sudden and uncommanded increase in the rate of descent, despite applying more collective pitch. The pilot may also notice a lack of response to control inputs, increased vibrations, and a feeling of sinking or settling. In some cases, the helicopter may experience buffeting or oscillations. These symptoms indicate that the helicopter is descending into its own downwash, leading to the loss of lift and control associated with VRS.

    [PH.VIII.E.K4; FAA-H-8083-21]

12. **What flight scenario during a helicopter approach increases the risk of encountering VRS?**

    During a helicopter approach, the risk of encountering VRS increases significantly in a steep approach with a high rate of descent and low forward airspeed. This scenario can lead to the helicopter descending into its own downwash, particularly if the descent rate exceeds 300 feet per minute. Steep approaches that require high power settings, combined with minimal horizontal movement, create ideal conditions for the formation of VRS. Pilots should aim for shallower approach angles and maintain some forward airspeed to mitigate this risk.

    [PH.VIII.E.K5; FAA-H-8083-21]

13. **How can hovering operations, particularly out of ground effect (OGE), lead to VRS in a helicopter?**

    Hovering operations, especially out of ground effect (OGE), can lead to VRS in a helicopter due to the increased power required to maintain a stable hover in OGE conditions. When hovering at high altitudes or in high-density altitude environments, the helicopter may require near-maximum power, which increases the rotor downwash. If the helicopter begins to descend while hovering OGE, it can easily enter the downwash, disrupting the airflow over the rotor blades and leading to VRS. Pilots should be cautious of their altitude and descent rate while hovering OGE to prevent this scenario.

    [PH.VIII.E.K5; FAA-H-8083-21]

14. **What are the recommended recovery procedures from a vortex ring state for helicopter pilots?**

There are two techniques:

- The classical technique for escaping from VRS is to lower collective as required, simultaneously by applying decisively forward cyclic input to gain airspeed (1–2 sec). Once sufficient airspeed is achieved (20–30 kts), adjust the pitch attitude to level the helicopter and finally raise the collective back to the desired power setting.

- The Vuichard recovery technique differs in that the pilot is required to use the collective pitch, while applying lateral cyclic and maintaining heading control with the pedals. Thus, this technique is designed to escape the column of descending air by moving laterally.

Keep in mind there are still examiners who do not recognize the Vuichard recovery as legitimate for the purposes of passing a checkride.

[PH.VIII.E.K6; FAA-H-8083-21]

15. **What precautions should a pilot take during the recovery from VRS to avoid other hazardous flight conditions?**

During the recovery from VRS, a pilot should take precautions to avoid entering other hazardous flight conditions such as over-speeding the rotor system, losing altitude too rapidly, or encountering obstacles. The pilot should monitor rotor RPM and airspeed carefully while recovering, ensuring they remain within safe operational limits. Controlled and gradual adjustments to the collective and cyclic are important to prevent abrupt changes in flight dynamics. The pilot should also maintain spatial awareness and altitude awareness to avoid ground or obstacle collisions, especially if the VRS recovery is taking place at low altitudes. Maintaining a steady, controlled recovery process is crucial for ensuring overall flight safety.

[PH.VIII.E.K6; FAA-H-8083-21]

16. What are the key indicators a pilot should recognize that suggest the onset of VRS in helicopter flight?

The key indicators a pilot should recognize for the onset of VRS include a sudden and uncommanded increase in descent rate, despite applying more collective pitch. Other signs include a loss of efficiency in the rotor system as indicated by increased vibrations, a feeling of sinking or settling, and reduced response to control inputs. Pilots may also observe an abnormal increase in power requirement without the expected increase in climb performance. Recognizing these indicators promptly is crucial for effective response and recovery from VRS.

[PH.VIII.E.R1; FAA-H-8083-21]

17. What strategies can a pilot employ to mitigate the risk of entering VRS during critical phases of helicopter flight?

Pilots should employ strategies such as maintaining a forward airspeed during descents to ensure adequate airflow through the rotor disc. Avoiding high descent rates (over 300 feet per minute) is also crucial, especially when operating near or below ETL. Pilots should be vigilant about their power usage and avoid situations where high power is combined with low airspeed. Regular training and practice in recognizing and recovering from VRS scenarios, along with thorough preflight planning and situational awareness, are also key to mitigating the risk.

[PH.VIII.E.R1; FAA-H-8083-21]

18. What are the risks associated with entering a helicopter maneuver at a lower altitude than planned, particularly in relation to VRS?

Entering a helicopter maneuver at a lower altitude than planned increases the risk of encountering VRS due to reduced recovery space in case VRS symptoms are recognized. At lower altitudes, the pilot has less time and altitude to correct the flight path before ground impact or other hazards occur. This situation is especially critical when performing operations like hovering or slow flight, where VRS is more likely to develop due to low airspeed and high-power settings. The limited altitude may not provide sufficient room to execute effective recovery procedures.

[PH.VIII.E.R2; FAA-H-8083-21]

19. **How can continuous training and situational awareness help pilots avoid unintentionally entering VRS at low altitudes?**

Continuous training and heightened situational awareness are crucial in helping pilots avoid unintentionally entering VRS at low altitudes. Regular training, including simulator sessions, reinforces a pilot's ability to recognize and respond to VRS symptoms quickly. Familiarity with the specific helicopter's performance characteristics under various conditions, including low altitude operations, equips pilots with the knowledge to anticipate and avoid situations that could lead to VRS. Maintaining situational awareness during flight, such as constantly monitoring altitude, airspeed, and descent rate, allows pilots to stay ahead of the aircraft and make informed decisions to prevent entering VRS, especially when operating closer to the ground.

[PH.VIII.E.R2; FAA-H-8083-21]

20. **What are the risks associated with applying excessive power during a maneuver that could lead to VRS?**

Applying excessive power during a maneuver that could lead to VRS increases the risk of entering this hazardous flight condition. Excessive power can intensify the rotor downwash and airflow recirculation, which are key factors in the development of VRS. When a helicopter is in a high-power, low-air-speed descent, the rotor system is more likely to descend into its own downwash, reducing lift and rotor efficiency. Excessive power application can also strain the powerplant, potentially leading to over-torque or over-temperature conditions, which can further compromise flight safety.

[PH.VIII.E.R3; FAA-H-8083-21]

21. **How can continuous training and performance monitoring help pilots manage power application to prevent VRS?**

Continuous training and performance monitoring can help pilots manage power application to prevent VRS by reinforcing the understanding of the helicopter's powerplant limitations and the aerodynamic principles related to VRS. Regular training sessions, including flight simulations and practical exercises, improve pilots' skills in power management and their ability to recognize the onset of VRS. By consistently monitoring performance parameters such as torque, temperature, rotor RPM, descent rate, and airspeed, pilots can make more informed decisions about power application. Staying within operational limits and practicing proactive power management techniques in different flight scenarios are essential for reducing the risk of VRS.

[PH.VIII.E.R3; FAA-H-8083-21]

22. How does the risk of collision hazards increase when a helicopter is experiencing VRS?

The risk of collision hazards increases significantly when a helicopter is experiencing VRS due to the uncontrolled and rapid descent that occurs in this condition. The pilot may lose altitude quickly and unpredictably, increasing the likelihood of colliding with terrain, obstacles, or structures, especially in congested or confined areas. Additionally, the reduced maneuverability and control response during VRS can make it difficult for the pilot to avoid obstacles during the descent. When practicing VRS be sure to provide sufficient altitude as a safe buffer between your helicopter and the ground.

[PH.VIII.E.R4; FAA-H-8083-21]

23. How can a pilot assess and mitigate the risk of collision during operations prone to VRS?

To assess and mitigate the risk of collision during operations prone to VRS, a pilot should maintain situational awareness of the environment, including awareness of obstacles and terrain. Prior to conducting maneuvers such as hovering or steep approaches, pilots should conduct thorough reconnaissance of the area to identify potential hazards. Implementing risk mitigation strategies, such as maintaining a safe altitude above hazards, planning escape routes, and avoiding over-reliance on high power settings in low airspeed scenarios, can reduce the likelihood of encountering VRS. Regular training on VRS recognition and recovery techniques is also essential for enhancing a pilot's ability to respond effectively to avoid collision hazards.

[PH.VIII.E.R4; FAA-H-8083-21]

24. How do distractions in the cockpit increase the risk of encountering VRS, and what can a pilot do to manage them?

Distractions in the cockpit can increase the risk of encountering VRS by diverting the pilot's attention from critical flight parameters such as descent rate, airspeed, and power settings. To manage distractions, pilots should adhere to a strict cockpit resource management protocol, prioritize tasks based on their importance to flight safety, and minimize nonessential activities, especially during critical flight phases where the risk of VRS is higher. Effective communication and division of duties in multi-crew operations also help in managing distractions.

[PH.VIII.E.R5; FAA-H-8083-25]

25. What strategies can a pilot employ to maintain situational awareness and prevent disorientation, which may lead to VRS?

To maintain situational awareness and prevent disorientation, which may lead to VRS, pilots should continuously monitor their flight environment, including weather conditions, terrain, and any potential obstacles. Regular scanning of flight instruments and awareness of the helicopter's position and performance are essential. Pilots should also practice and be familiar with the procedures and flight characteristics of their helicopter to quickly recognize and respond to signs of VRS.

[PH.VIII.E.R5; FAA-H-8083-25]

26. How does the risk of loss of tail rotor effectiveness (LTE) relate to vortex ring state (VRS) in helicopter flight?

The risk of loss of tail rotor effectiveness (LTE) relates to vortex ring state (VRS) as both conditions can be exacerbated by similar flight regimes, particularly low-speed flight and high-power settings. While VRS primarily affects the main rotor system, leading to a loss of lift, LTE affects the tail rotor, resulting in a loss of yaw control. Both conditions can occur simultaneously or independently, particularly in hovering or slow flight operations. Recognizing and understanding the flight conditions that can lead to LTE and VRS are crucial for effective risk mitigation.

[PH.VIII.E.R6; FAA-H-8083-21]

27. What specific flight scenarios should a pilot be aware of that increase the risk of LTE occurring concurrently with VRS?

Pilots should be aware of specific flight scenarios that increase the risk of LTE occurring concurrently with VRS, such as hovering in windy conditions, performing downwind turns, flying at low airspeeds with high power settings, and conducting operations in confined areas. These scenarios can create situations where the tail rotor is less effective for a given wind azimuth, and the main rotor is susceptible to VRS due to the high descent rates and reduced airspeed. Pilots must be vigilant in these conditions and manage their flight path and power settings to avoid both LTE and VRS.

[PH.VIII.E.R6; FAA-H-8083-21]

Skills to be demonstrated:

- Complete the appropriate checklist(s).

- Clear the area.

- Select an altitude that allows recovery to be completed no lower than 1,000 feet AGL or as recommended by the manufacturer, whichever is higher.

- Establish conditions leading to VRS entry.

- Promptly recognize, announce, and recover at the first indication of VRS.

- Use single-pilot resource management (SRM) or crew resource management (CRM), as appropriate.

F. Low Rotor Revolutions Per Minute (RPM) Recognition and Recovery

Note: The evaluator must test the applicant orally on this Task if the helicopter used for the practical test has a governor that cannot be disabled. During the preflight briefing, evaluators must discuss avoiding any condition that may lead to rotor stall during the demonstration of this Task. If the skills are tested in flight, evaluators and applicants must ensure the helicopter's main rotor system remains in a safe operating range in accordance with the POH/RFM. Evaluators must not test this Task during critical phases of flight (e.g., takeoffs or landings).

1. How does a pilot recognize the onset of low rotor RPM, and what immediate actions should be taken for recovery?

A pilot recognizes the onset of low rotor RPM by listening to the helicopter and monitoring the rotor RPM gauge; in addition to Low RPM Horn audio warnings if equipped. Immediate actions for recovery include lowering the collective to decrease blade pitch and reduce drag on the rotor system and adjusting throttle or engine power to increase rotor RPM.

[PH.VIII.F.K1; FAA-H-8083-21]

2. What factors contribute to a low rotor RPM condition in helicopter flight, and how does this affect energy management?

Factors contributing to a low rotor RPM condition in helicopter flight include excessive collective pitch input, high altitude operations, heavy aircraft weight, and engine power limitations. This situation requires careful management of collective pitch and throttle (in piston engines) or collective and engine power (in turbine engines) to restore rotor RPM to its optimal range for flight.

[PH.VIII.F.K1; FAA-H-8083-21]

3. **How does wind direction and speed affect the risk of encountering low rotor RPM during helicopter operations?**

Tailwinds can decrease effective translational lift, increasing the power required to maintain altitude or perform maneuvers, potentially leading to low rotor RPM if the power demand exceeds the engine's capability. Strong crosswinds can also impact the aerodynamic efficiency of the rotor system, requiring careful power management to avoid rotor RPM decay. Pilots must be vigilant in windy conditions and adjust their flight techniques accordingly to maintain optimal rotor RPM.

[PH.VIII.F.K2; FAA-H-8083-25]

4. **How do weight and loading configurations influence a helicopter's susceptibility to low rotor RPM?**

Heavier aircraft weights increase the power required to achieve and maintain lift, pushing the engine and rotor system closer to their performance limits. Pilots must ensure that the helicopter is loaded within its weight and balance limits and adjust flight operations to accommodate the increased power demands of heavier weights, especially in critical flight phases where power margins are limited.

[PH.VIII.F.K2; FAA-H-8083-21]

5. **What role does temperature play in the recognition and recovery from low rotor RPM situations?**

Higher temperatures reduce air density, resulting in decreased lift generated by the rotor blades and reduced engine power output, both of which can lead to low rotor RPM. Pilots must be aware of the ambient temperature and its impact on the helicopter's performance, particularly in hot conditions or when operating at or near the aircraft's maximum performance limits. Preflight planning and in-flight power management must account for temperature effects to ensure adequate rotor RPM is maintained throughout the flight.

[PH.VIII.F.K2; FAA-H-8083-21]

6. **What is the aerodynamic principle behind the decrease in rotor RPM when excessive collective pitch is applied?**

The aerodynamic principle behind the decrease in rotor RPM when excessive collective pitch is applied is due to an increase in the angle of attack of the rotor blades, which increases the induced drag across the rotor system. As the collective pitch is increased, the rotor blades bite more aggressively into the air, requiring more engine power to maintain the same rotor RPM. If the engine cannot provide sufficient power to overcome the increased drag, rotor RPM begins to decrease. This phenomenon is a critical aspect of helicopter aerodynamics, especially in situations where engine power is limited.

[PH.VIII.F.K3; FAA-H-8083-21]

7. **How does translational lift affect rotor RPM, and what implications does this have for low RPM recovery?**

Translational lift occurs as a helicopter gains forward speed, improving the efficiency of the rotor system by moving through undisturbed air, which provides a more even airflow over the rotor disc. This increased efficiency can lead to a natural increase in rotor RPM as the helicopter transitions from hover to forward flight, assuming engine power settings remain constant. For low RPM recovery, pilots can utilize translational lift by moving the helicopter forward, if altitude and space permit, to improve rotor efficiency and help increase rotor RPM. Understanding the transition to translational lift is crucial for managing rotor RPM effectively.

[PH.VIII.F.K3; FAA-H-8083-21]

8. **What impact does engine power output have on a pilot's ability to recover from low rotor RPM?**

Engine power output directly impacts a pilot's ability to recover from low rotor RPM. Adequate engine power is essential for increasing rotor RPM by allowing the pilot to apply more collective pitch without causing the rotor to slow further. If the engine cannot produce sufficient power to overcome the aerodynamic drag on the rotor system, recovery from low rotor RPM may be difficult or impossible, particularly in high workload or critical flight phases. Pilots must be aware of their helicopter's power limitations and manage power usage carefully to maintain or recover rotor RPM within safe operating limits.

[PH.VIII.F.K4; FAA-H-8083-21]

9. In the context of powerplant performance, what considerations should a pilot keep in mind when operating near the helicopter's maximum gross weight?

When operating near the helicopter's maximum gross weight, a pilot must be particularly mindful of powerplant performance limitations, as the engine may be operating near its maximum capacity. This leaves less power available for increasing rotor RPM in response to low RPM conditions. Pilots should anticipate the need for more precise power management, be conservative with collective inputs, and be prepared to use all available power reserves judiciously to avoid overloading the rotor system. Additionally, understanding the performance charts and limitations provided in the helicopter's flight manual is essential for safe operation, especially during takeoffs, climbs, and maneuvers requiring significant power.

[PH.VIII.F.K4; FAA-H-8083-21]

10. What recovery techniques can pilots employ that specifically address powerplant performance limitations during low rotor RPM conditions?

To address powerplant performance limitations during low rotor RPM conditions, pilots can employ several recovery techniques, including gently lowering the collective to decrease the load on the rotor system and allow the engine to regain RPM. Simultaneously, pilots should adjust the throttle (in piston helicopters) or engine power (in turbine helicopters) as necessary to provide additional power without exceeding engine limitations. Forward cyclic inputs to gain airspeed can also assist in rotor RPM recovery by increasing airflow through the rotor system. Pilots must always be aware of the powerplant's operational limits to prevent engine damage during recovery attempts. Effective use of autorotation principles to manage rotor energy can also be crucial, especially if engine power is insufficient to recover rotor RPM directly.

[PH.VIII.F.K4; FAA-H-8083-21

11. What defines the operational limits of main rotor RPM (N$_r$) in a helicopter, and why are these limits critical for safe flight?

The operational limits of main rotor RPM (N$_r$) in a helicopter are defined by the manufacturer and are critical for maintaining the structural integrity of the rotor system and ensuring adequate lift and control authority. Operating below the minimum N$_r$ limit can lead to insufficient lift, loss of rotor control, and potential rotor stall. Exceeding the maximum N$_r$ limit risks structural damage to the rotor blades and hub from excessive centrifugal forces. Adhering to these limits is essential for safe flight, as they ensure the rotor system operates within its designed aerodynamic and structural capabilities.

[PH.VIII.F.K5; FAA-H-8083-21]

12. What role does the governor or the FADEC system play in managing main rotor RPM, and how does this assist pilots?

The governor or the Full Authority Digital Engine Control (FADEC) system plays a crucial role in managing main rotor RPM by automatically adjusting the engine power output to maintain rotor RPM within the desired operational range. For helicopters equipped with these systems, the governor or FADEC relieves the pilot from manually adjusting the throttle in response to changes in collective pitch or flight conditions. This assistance allows pilots to focus more on flight maneuvers and situational awareness, enhancing flight safety by ensuring that rotor RPM remains stable and within limits, especially during critical phases of flight.

[PH.VIII.F.K5; FAA-H-8083-21]

13. What distinguishes low rotor RPM from blade stall in helicopter aerodynamics?

Low rotor RPM refers to a condition where the rotational speed of the helicopter's main rotor falls below the optimal operational range, reducing the rotor's ability to generate lift. Blade stall, on the other hand, occurs when the angle of attack of the rotor blades exceeds the critical angle, leading to a significant loss of lift due to airflow separation over the blade surface. While low rotor RPM is primarily a power management issue, blade stall is an aerodynamic condition related to the blade's angle of attack and airspeed. Low rotor RPM if not corrected, could lead to main rotor blade stall.

[PH.VIII.F.K6; FAA-H-8083-21]

14. In what flight conditions are helicopters most susceptible to low rotor RPM and blade stall, and how can pilots mitigate these risks?

Helicopters are most susceptible to low rotor RPM during high-power demand situations, such as heavy lifting, high-altitude operations, or when aggressively recovering from a descent. Blade stall is more likely during aggressive maneuvers that require high angles of attack, such as abrupt climbs or turns. Pilots can mitigate these risks by carefully monitoring rotor RPM and blade angle of attack, especially during critical flight phases, and by adhering to recommended flight envelopes and operational procedures. Preflight planning to account for weight, altitude, and environmental conditions can also help avoid conditions conducive to these issues.

[PH.VIII.F.K6; FAA-H-8083-21

15. What are common powerplant limitations that can lead to low rotor RPM in helicopter operations, and how can pilots identify these limitations?

Common powerplant limitations that can lead to low rotor RPM include maximum torque or power output, temperature limits (such as turbine inlet temperature for turbine engines or manifold pressure limits for piston engines). Pilots can identify these limitations by referring to the helicopter's flight manual, which outlines the powerplant's operational parameters, and by monitoring engine instruments during flight. Awareness of these limitations is crucial, especially during high-power demand operations like takeoff, climb, or maneuvers requiring significant collective inputs.

[PH.VIII.F.R1; FAA-H-8083-21]

16. **How can a pilot effectively recover from a low rotor RPM condition while considering powerplant limitations?**

    To effectively recover from a low rotor RPM condition while considering powerplant limitations, a pilot should initially lower the collective to reduce the load on the rotor system, allowing the rotor RPM to increase. The pilot should then gently apply power, if available, to support the recovery without exceeding the powerplant's limitations. If the situation allows, transitioning to forward flight to gain translational lift can help increase rotor efficiency and assist in RPM recovery. Understanding the specific power plant's response characteristics to control inputs is crucial for managing the recovery process effectively.

    [PH.VIII.F.R1; FAA-H-8083-21]

17. **What is the role of the powerplant governor in managing rotor RPM, and how does its operation affect low rotor RPM scenarios?**

    By automatically adjusting the engine's power output to maintain the rotor RPM within a specified operational range. In low rotor RPM scenarios, a properly functioning governor will increase engine power to compensate for increased load or decreased airspeed, helping to prevent the rotor RPM from dropping further. However, if the governor is not operating correctly or is overridden by the pilot, the risk of entering a low rotor RPM condition increases. Understanding the governor's operation and limitations is essential for effectively managing rotor RPM.

    [PH.VIII.F.R2; FAA-H-8083-21]

18. **What preemptive measures can pilots take to mitigate risks associated with governor malfunction during flight?**

    Pilots should become proficient in manual throttle control to adjust engine power as needed to maintain rotor RPM. This includes practicing throttle adjustments in flight scenarios where governor assistance is simulated as inoperative. Understanding the specific indicators of governor performance issues for their helicopter type and conducting thorough preflight inspections can help in identifying potential problems before flight.

    [PH.VIII.F.R2; FAA-H-8083-21]

19. In the event of a governor failure leading to low rotor RPM, what recovery techniques should pilots employ?

Pilots should immediately manually adjust the throttle to increase engine power and recover rotor RPM. Lowering the collective to decrease the aerodynamic load on the rotor blades can also help increase RPM. Pilots must then stabilize the helicopter at a safe altitude and airspeed while managing throttle settings to maintain optimal rotor RPM. Overcompensating with throttle inputs must be avoided to prevent overspeeding the rotor system. Effective manual throttle control and collective management are key to safely recovering from low rotor RPM conditions caused by governor failure.

[PH.VIII.F.R2; FAA-H-8083-21]

20. How does low rotor RPM increase the risk of collision during helicopter operations, particularly in congested areas?

Low rotor RPM increases the risk of collision during helicopter operations by compromising the pilot's ability to maintain control and altitude, particularly in congested areas where precise maneuvering is required. Reduced rotor efficiency can lead to decreased lift and responsiveness, making it more challenging to navigate around obstacles or execute emergency maneuvers to avoid collisions. Pilots must be vigilant in monitoring rotor RPM and employ effective recovery techniques promptly to maintain safe control and avoid collision hazards.

[PH.VIII.F.R3; FAA-H-8083-21]

21. How do distractions and loss of situational awareness contribute to the occurrence of low rotor RPM scenarios, and what strategies can pilots employ to mitigate these risks?

Distractions and loss of situational awareness can lead to a failure to monitor critical flight instruments, including rotor RPM, especially during high workload phases of flight such as takeoff, maneuvering, and landing. Pilots can mitigate these risks by adhering to cockpit resource management principles, maintaining a sterile cockpit during critical flight phases, and practicing regular scans of flight instruments to ensure rotor RPM remains within safe limits.

[PH.VIII.F.R4; FAA-H-8083-25]

22. What is a low inertia rotor system, and why is it significant in helicopter operations with regard to low RPM recognition and recovery?

A low inertia rotor system is one where the rotor blades have relatively low mass and therefore less kinetic energy stored for a given RPM. This characteristic makes the rotor system more susceptible to rapid deceleration when power is reduced or when aerodynamic loading increases, posing challenges for maintaining rotor RPM within safe operational limits. Recognizing and recovering from low rotor RPM is critical to avoid entering a state where the helicopter does not have enough lift to maintain flight, which could lead to a potentially dangerous situation. Low inertia systems will lose RPM relatively quickly when compared to a higher inertia rotor system, the opposite is also true that low inertia systems will also recover their lost RPMs faster when compared to a higher inertia rotor system.

[PH.VIII.F.R5; FAA-H-8083-21]

Skills to be demonstrated:

• Complete the appropriate checklist(s).

• Clear the area.

• Detect the development of low rotor RPM and initiate prompt corrective action.

• Execute the recovery procedure to return rotor RPM to normal limits.

G. Antitorque System Failure

1. What are common indications of an antitorque system failure in helicopters?

Common indications of an antitorque system failure include uncommanded yaw movements, difficulty in maintaining directional control, an increase in main rotor torque indications beyond normal limits, unusual vibrations, and visual or auditory warnings from the helicopter's monitoring systems. Additionally, pilots may notice that pedal inputs (used to control the tail rotor) have no effect on the helicopter's yaw or that significantly more pedal input than usual is required to maintain directional control.

[PH.VIII.G.K1a; FAA-H-8083-21]

2. What are the potential consequences of an antitorque system failure during various phases of flight?

The potential consequences of an antitorque system failure vary depending on the phase of flight. During takeoff and landing, the failure can lead to a loss of directional control, making these critical phases of flight particularly dangerous. In hover or low-speed flight, the helicopter may spin uncontrollably. During forward flight, the effects might be less pronounced, giving the pilot more time to react and compensate for the loss of tail rotor effectiveness, but it still poses a significant risk to flight safety.

[PH.VIII.G.K1a; FAA-H-8083-21

3. How do mechanical flight control failures in helicopters manifest differently from antitorque system failures?

Antitorque failure usually falls into one of two categories. One is failure of the power drive portion of the tail rotor disk resulting in a complete loss of antitorque. The other category covers mechanical control failures prohibiting the pilot from changing or controlling tail rotor thrust even though the tail rotor may still be providing antitorque thrust.

[PH.VIII.G.K1b; FAA-H-8083-21]

4. What emergency procedures should pilots be familiar with in the event of an antitorque system failure?

Pilots should be familiar with specific emergency procedures outlined in the helicopter's POH or flight manual for dealing with an antitorque system failure. These procedures typically include immediately reducing power to decrease torque, establishing a controlled glide if altitude permits, and preparing for an autorotative landing if the situation cannot be rectified.

[PH.VIII.G.K1c; FAA-H-8083-21]

5. What is the procedure for a complete tail rotor failure?

If a complete tail rotor failure occurs while hovering, enter a hovering autorotation by rolling off the throttle. If the failure occurs in forward flight, enter a normal autorotation by lowering the collective and rolling off the throttle. If the helicopter has enough forward airspeed (close to cruising speed) when the failure occurs, and depending on the helicopter design, the vertical stabilizer may provide enough directional control to allow the pilot to maneuver the helicopter to a more desirable landing sight.

[PH.VIII.G.K1c; FAA-H-8083-21]

6. In the case of a stuck left pedal, what is the procedure?

A stuck left pedal (high power setting), which might be experienced during takeoff or climb conditions, results in the left yaw of the helicopter nose when power is reduced. The landing profile for a stuck left pedal is best described as a normal-to-steep approach angle to arrive approximately 2–3 feet landing gear height above the intended landing area as translational lift is lost. The steeper angle allows for a lower power setting during the approach and ensures that the nose remains to the right. Increase the collective smoothly to align the nose with the landing direction and cushion the landing. A small amount of forward cyclic is helpful to stop the nose from continuing to the right and directs the aircraft forward and down to the surface. In certain wind conditions, the nose of the helicopter may remain to the left with zero to near zero ground speed above the intended touchdown point. If the helicopter is not turning, simply lower the helicopter to the surface. If the nose of the helicopter is turning to the right and continues beyond the landing heading, roll the throttle toward flight idle, which is the amount necessary to stop the turn while landing.

[PH.VIII.G.K1c; FAA-H-8083-21]

7. In the case of a stuck neutral or right pedal, what is the procedure?

The landing profile for a stuck neutral or a stuck right pedal is a low-power approach terminating with a running or roll-on landing. The approach profile can best be described as a shallow to normal approach angle to arrive approximately 2–3 feet landing gear height above the intended landing area with a minimum airspeed for directional control. The minimum airspeed is one that keeps the nose from continuing to yaw to the right. Upon reaching the intended touchdown area and at the appropriate landing gear height, reduce the throttle as necessary to overcome the yaw effect if the nose of the helicopter remains to the right of the landing heading. The amount of throttle reduction will vary based on power applied and winds. The higher the power setting used to cushion the landing, the more the throttle reduction will be. A coordinated throttle reduction and increased collective will result in a very smooth touchdown with some forward groundspeed.

[PH.VIII.G.K1c; FAA-H-8083-21

8. What techniques can pilots employ to maximize control during a landing with an antitorque system failure?

To maximize control during a landing with an antitorque system failure, pilots can employ several techniques, including:

- Choosing an approach path that aligns with favorable wind conditions (preferably a headwind or quartering headwind).

- Maintaining a higher airspeed during the approach to enhance the effectiveness of the cyclic control for directional stability.

- Utilizing the collective pitch control judiciously to manage descent rate and airspeed, understanding that large or abrupt changes can affect the helicopter's yaw.

- Planning for a running landing or a slide-on landing if the helicopter is equipped with skids, to maintain directional control through to a complete stop.

[PH.VIII.G.K2; FAA-H-8083-21

9. **What key components of the antitorque system should be inspected during a preflight check to identify potential risks of failure?**

During a preflight inspection, key components of the antitorque system that should be thoroughly checked include the tail rotor blades for damage, cracks, or wear; the tail rotor gearbox for any signs of leaks or damage; the drive shafts for integrity and secure fittings; control linkages for proper connection and absence of excessive play; and the pitch change mechanism for correct operation and response. Inspecting these components helps identify potential risks of antitorque system failure before flight.

[PH.VIII.G.R1; FAA-H-8083-21]

10. **How can pilots mitigate the risk of antitorque system failure identified during preflight inspection?**

Pilots can mitigate the risk of antitorque system failure identified during preflight inspection by adhering to a strict inspection checklist that includes all components of the antitorque system. Any abnormalities or signs of wear and tear should be addressed before flight by consulting maintenance personnel. Implementing a conservative decision-making process that errs on the side of caution, such as choosing not to fly until all issues are resolved, is key to risk mitigation. Regular maintenance and adherence to the helicopter's service intervals for the antitorque system also play a crucial role in preventing failures.

[PH.VIII.G.R1; FAA-H-8083-21]

11. **How can a pilot identify the specific type of antitorque system installed on the helicopter provided for the practical test?**

A pilot can identify the specific type of antitorque system installed on the helicopter by reviewing the aircraft's pilot's operating handbook (POH) or flight manual, which includes detailed descriptions of the helicopter's systems and configurations. Understanding the type of antitorque system (e.g., traditional tail rotor, fenestron, or NOTAR) is crucial for recognizing the appropriate indications of system failure and implementing the correct emergency procedures specific to that system.

[PH.VIII.G.R2; FAA-H-8083-21]

12. **Describe the risk assessment process a pilot should follow when encountering indications of an antitorque system failure during flight in the aircraft supplied for the practical test.**

    The risk assessment process involves immediately recognizing the signs of an antitorque system failure, such as uncommanded yaw, loss of tail rotor effectiveness, or warning indicators. The pilot should then quickly evaluate the severity of the failure, considering factors like altitude, flight conditions, and proximity to suitable landing areas. Based on this assessment, the pilot must decide on the most appropriate emergency procedure, prioritizing the safety of flight and planning for an emergency landing if conditions deteriorate.

    [PH.VIII.G.R2; FAA-H-8083-21]

13. **What initial steps should a pilot take upon identifying an antitorque system failure during flight?**

    Upon identifying an antitorque system failure during flight, the pilot should immediately prioritize maintaining control of the helicopter by adjusting the collective to manage the torque effect and using cyclic inputs to maintain stability. The pilot should then establish a flight condition that minimizes the need for antitorque pedal inputs, such as a slight forward flight to enhance directional control with aerodynamic forces. Following immediate control measures, the pilot should plan for an emergency landing, selecting an appropriate site and preparing to execute a running landing or autorotation, depending on the type of antitorque system issue.

    [PH.VIII.G.R3; FAA-H-8083-21]

14. **What are the key elements of risk mitigation when dealing with an antitorque system failure?**

    Key elements of risk mitigation when dealing with an antitorque system failure include thorough preflight inspections focusing on the antitorque system's components, familiarity with the helicopter's specific emergency procedures for antitorque failure, continuous monitoring of system performance indicators during flight, and regular training in emergency procedures, including autorotation and running landings. Additionally, maintaining situational awareness and having a predefined plan for potential emergency landing sites can significantly reduce the risks associated with antitorque system failures. For checkrides pilots are encouraged to memorize their specific helicopters antitorque system failure procedures.

[PH.VIII.G.R3; FAA-H-8083-21]

H. Dynamic Rollover

1. What is dynamic rollover in helicopters, and what are its primary contributing factors?

Dynamic rollover is a phenomenon where a helicopter pivots around one of its skids or wheels and rolls over, potentially leading to a loss of control and crash if not corrected promptly. Dynamic rollover begins when the helicopter starts to pivot laterally around its skid or wheel.

For dynamic rollover to occur the following three factors must be present:

- A rolling moment
- A pivot point other than the helicopter's normal CG
- Thrust greater than weight

This can occur for a variety of reasons, including the failure to remove a tie down or skid-securing device, or if the skid or wheel contacts a fixed object while hovering sideward, or if the gear is stuck in ice, soft asphalt, or mud. Dynamic rollover may also occur if you use an improper landing or takeoff technique or while performing slope operations. Whatever the cause, dynamic rollover is possible if not using the proper corrective technique.

[PH.VIII.H.K1; FAA-H-8083-21]

2. How does lateral center of gravity (CG) affect a helicopter's susceptibility to dynamic rollover?

Lateral CG affects a helicopter's susceptibility to dynamic rollover by influencing the roll stability of the aircraft. An off-center lateral CG, where the weight is not evenly distributed from side to side, can cause the helicopter to tilt towards the heavier side. This imbalance increases the risk of one skid or wheel contacting the ground first during takeoff or landing, creating a pivot point that can initiate a rollover, especially if corrective action is not taken promptly.

[PH.VIII.H.K2; FAA-H-8083-21]

3. **What role does thrust play in the dynamics of rollover, and how can pilots manage it to prevent such incidents?**

   Thrust plays a critical role in the dynamics of rollover by providing the lifting force that can either contribute to or prevent a rollover. Excessive thrust, particularly in combination with an uneven ground or slope, can lead to one skid lifting off prematurely, creating a pivot point. Pilots can manage thrust to prevent rollover incidents by applying power smoothly and gradually, ensuring both skids or wheels lift off simultaneously and maintaining balanced lift throughout takeoff and landing phases.

   [PH.VIII.H.K2; FAA-H-8083-21]

4. **How do crosswinds contribute to the risk of dynamic rollover, and what strategies can pilots use to mitigate this risk?**

   Crosswinds contribute to the risk of dynamic rollover by exerting lateral forces on the helicopter, which can lead to unanticipated roll movements during critical phases of flight like takeoff and landing. Pilots can mitigate this risk by performing takeoffs and landings into the wind as much as possible to minimize crosswind components, adjusting flight controls to compensate for wind effects, and being prepared to abort the takeoff or landing if control is compromised.

   [PH.VIII.H.K2; FAA-H-8083-21]

5. **Discuss the impact of slope operations on dynamic rollover risk and best practices for operating on sloped terrain.**

   Slope operations significantly impact dynamic rollover risk by creating an uneven support surface for the helicopter during takeoff and landing. When one skid or wheel is higher than the other, the aircraft is more prone to tilt and potentially roll over. Best practices for operating on sloped terrain include performing thorough reconnaissance of the landing area, approaching and departing up the slope when possible, maintaining a steady hover before touchdown to assess ground firmness and slope steepness, and using cyclic control to keep the helicopter level.

   [PH.VIII.H.K2; FAA-H-8083-21]

6. What is a preventive flight technique that pilots can use during slope operations to minimize the risk of dynamic rollover?

A preventive flight technique for slope operations includes approaching the slope with the uphill skid or wheel making contact first, allowing the pilot to maintain control and assess the stability of the surface before fully committing to touchdown. Pilots should keep the cyclic control adjusted to ensure the helicopter remains parallel to the slope during this partial contact phase. Power application should be smooth and controlled, with continuous assessment of the helicopter's attitude and readiness to abort the landing if stability is compromised.

[PH.VIII.H.K3; FAA-H-8083-21]

7. How can pilots effectively use cyclic and collective controls during slope operations to prevent dynamic rollover?

During slope operations, effective use of cyclic control is crucial to maintain the helicopter's lateral balance and ensure the uphill skid contacts the ground first. The cyclic should be adjusted to keep the rotor disk parallel to the slope. Collective control should be used judiciously to manage lift and descent rate, increasing it slowly to prevent sudden shifts that could lead to rollover. Pilots should be prepared to reduce collective quickly if the helicopter begins to roll or if an unstable condition is detected.

[PH.VIII.H.K3; FAA-H-8083-21]

8. Describe the recommended recovery procedure if a pilot detects the onset of dynamic rollover during a slope operation.

If a pilot detects the onset of dynamic rollover during a slope operation, the recommended recovery procedure is to immediately lower the collective to reduce lift and minimize the rolling motion, while simultaneously applying cyclic control opposite to the direction of the roll to level the aircraft. There is a point at which beyond recovery is impossible.

[PH.VIII.H.K3; FAA-H-8083-21]

9. **What are the critical considerations for a pilot when choosing a slope for landing or takeoff to avoid dynamic rollover?**

Critical considerations when choosing a slope for landing or takeoff include assessing the slope's steepness, surface texture, and firmness to ensure it is within the helicopter's operational limits and capabilities. Pilots should also consider environmental factors such as wind direction and speed, which can affect control during slope operations. Visibility of the slope and surrounding area is crucial to avoid obstacles that may complicate the operation. Finally, pilots should always have an alternate plan in case the initial slope chosen proves unsuitable upon closer inspection.

[PH.VIII.H.K3; FAA-H-8083-21]

10. **What surface conditions are particularly conducive to dynamic rollover in helicopters?**

Surface conditions particularly conducive to dynamic rollover include uneven terrain, soft soil or mud that may allow one skid to sink more than the other, slippery surfaces such as ice or wet grass that reduce friction and control, and slopes where the helicopter is at an angle to the surface. Obstacles on the ground that may catch a skid or wheel, such as rocks, holes, or debris, also significantly increase the risk of dynamic rollover.

[PH.VIII.H.R1; FAA-H-8083-21]

11. **What risk mitigation strategies can pilots employ when landing on surfaces identified as high risk for dynamic rollover?**

Risk mitigation strategies for landing on high-risk surfaces include choosing an alternate landing site with more favorable conditions if possible, approaching the landing area with caution, and ensuring that the approach path and landing orientation minimize exposure to the identified risks. Pilots should use gentle control inputs to maintain stability and avoid abrupt maneuvers. Preparing for a quick takeoff in case of unstable contact with the surface and briefing passengers on emergency procedures are also prudent measures. Pilots should always be ready to abort the landing if conditions appear worse than anticipated upon closer inspection.

[PH.VIII.H.R1; FAA-H-8083-21]

12. What are the key considerations for a pilot when hovering at low altitude to avoid dynamic rollover due to landing gear proximity to ground obstructions?

Key considerations for a pilot when hovering at low altitude include vigilant monitoring of the helicopter's altitude and lateral movements to ensure sufficient clearance between the landing gear and any ground obstructions. Pilots must be aware of the helicopter's landing gear configuration and its implications for clearance, maintain a stable hover with minimal lateral or vertical movements, and conduct a thorough pre-hover reconnaissance to identify potential obstructions like rocks, uneven terrain, or debris that could interact with the landing gear. It's crucial to approach any landing or hovering operation with caution, especially in unfamiliar environments.

[PH.VIII.H.R2; FAA-H-8083-21]

13. What flight control inputs are critical to monitor during takeoff or landing to prevent dynamic rollover?

Critical flight control inputs to monitor during takeoff or landing to prevent dynamic rollover include cyclic positioning to maintain lateral balance, collective pitch adjustments to control lift and descent without causing abrupt changes in attitude, and antitorque pedal inputs to manage yaw without inducing unnecessary lateral motion. Proper coordination of these controls is essential to ensure a balanced lift-off or touchdown, minimizing the risk of tilting and creating a pivot point that could lead to rollover.

[PH.VIII.H.R3; FAA-H-8083-21]

14. How can excessive or abrupt cyclic inputs during takeoff or landing contribute to dynamic rollover risk?

Smooth, controlled cyclic movements are necessary to maintain level flight and prevent the onset of dynamic rollover. Excessive or abrupt cyclic inputs during takeoff or landing can contribute to dynamic rollover risk by causing the helicopter to tilt beyond its critical rollover angle, especially if one skid or wheel is already in contact with the ground, creating a pivot point. Such inputs may also lead to overcorrection, where the pilot's attempt to counteract an initial tilt results in a rollover on the opposite side.

[PH.VIII.H.R3; FAA-H-8083-21]

15. **What techniques can pilots employ to mitigate the risk of dynamic rollover associated with collective pitch inputs?**

    To mitigate the risk of dynamic rollover associated with collective pitch inputs, pilots can employ techniques such as gradually increasing or decreasing collective to maintain a stable, controlled rate of ascent or descent. This approach helps avoid sudden changes in lift that could destabilize the helicopter during critical phases of flight. Pilots should also be mindful of the helicopter's weight and center of gravity, adjusting collective inputs accordingly to maintain balance and control during takeoff and landing.

    [PH.VIII.H.R3; FAA-H-8083-21]

16. **What specific risks are associated with performing a sideward hover close to the ground, and how do they relate to dynamic rollover?**

    Performing a sideward hover close to the ground introduces specific risks such as the potential for one skid or wheel to catch on an obstruction, uneven terrain, or to sink into soft ground, creating a pivot point around which dynamic rollover can occur. This maneuver requires precise control inputs to maintain a stable hover without lateral drift that could lead to unintended contact with ground obstacles or induce a tilt, increasing the risk of rollover.

    [PH.VIII.H.R4; FAA-H-8083-21]

17. **How can pilots mitigate the risks of dynamic rollover during sideward hover operations?**

    Pilots can mitigate the risks of dynamic rollover during sideward hover operations by maintaining a higher hover altitude when lateral clearance allows, ensuring there is adequate space free of obstructions. Before initiating the maneuver, pilots should conduct a thorough reconnaissance of the area to identify and avoid potential hazards. Smooth and controlled cyclic inputs are crucial to manage lateral movement and maintain a level attitude. Pilots should also be prepared to abort the maneuver and transition to forward flight if control is compromised or if the risk of rollover becomes apparent.

    [PH.VIII.H.R4; FAA-H-8083-21]

18. How do aircraft slope limitations influence the risk of dynamic rollover during slope operations?

Aircraft slope limitations directly influence the risk of dynamic rollover by defining the maximum angle at which a helicopter can safely operate on a slope without the risk of tipping over. Exceeding these limitations increases the likelihood of one skid becoming a pivot point, leading to potential rollover if the helicopter tilts beyond its critical angle. Understanding and adhering to these limitations is crucial for pilots to assess the suitability of a landing area and to perform slope operations safely, minimizing the risk of dynamic rollover. Each helicopter has its own slope limitations, it's up to the pilot to operate within those limitations.

[PH.VIII.H.R5; FAA-H-8083-21]

19. What is the critical rollover angle in helicopter operations, and how does it contribute to the risk of dynamic rollover?

The critical rollover angle in helicopter operations is the maximum angle at which a helicopter can be tilted laterally before it reaches a point where recovery is no longer possible, and rollover becomes inevitable. This angle varies depending on the helicopter's design, landing gear configuration, and center of gravity. Exceeding this angle creates a rolling moment that can lead to dynamic rollover, especially if one skid or wheel is caught or if there's uneven terrain. Understanding this angle is crucial for pilots to maintain control inputs within safe limits during takeoff, landing, and low-speed maneuvers to avoid dynamic rollover.

[PH.VIII.H.R6; FAA-H-8083-21]

20. What is translating tendency in helicopter flight, and how does it relate to dynamic rollover?

During hovering flight, a single main rotor helicopter tends to move in the direction of tail rotor thrust. This lateral (or sideward) movement is called translating tendency. This phenomenon can affect dynamic rollover risk when a helicopter is taking off, landing, or hovering close to the ground by the helicopter's tendency to have one skid lower than the other. If not considered, this can lead to one skid/wheel potentially becoming a pivot point for rollover, especially during operations close to obstacles or on uneven terrain.

[PH.VIII.H.R7; FAA-H-8083-21]

I. Ground Resonance

1. What is ground resonance, and which types of helicopters are most susceptible to this phenomenon?

Ground resonance is a dangerous vibration phenomenon that occurs in helicopters with fully articulated rotor systems when one or more of the rotor blades become out of phase with the others, causing an imbalance. This imbalance can lead to increasingly violent oscillations that can damage or destroy the helicopter if not promptly corrected. Helicopters susceptible to ground resonance are those with fully articulated rotor systems because these systems allow for each blade to flap, lead, and lag independently, which can initiate the condition if the helicopter's landing gear does not absorb the oscillations effectively.

[PH.VIII.I.K1a; FAA-H-8083-21]

2. What preventive flight techniques should pilots employ during takeoffs and landings to minimize the risk of ground resonance?

To minimize the risk of ground resonance during takeoffs and landings, pilots should employ preventive flight techniques that include ensuring smooth and balanced landings to prevent shocks or imbalances on the rotor system. Pilots should aim for synchronized skid or wheel contact with the ground, avoiding uneven or hard landings that could initiate rotor system oscillations. It's crucial to maintain proper rotor RPM within the recommended limits, as deviations can contribute to conditions favorable for ground resonance.

[PH.VIII.I.K1b; FAA-H-8083-21]

3. What characteristics of a landing surface can contribute to the occurrence of ground resonance in helicopters?

Characteristics of a landing surface that can contribute to ground resonance include uneven terrain, surfaces with varying firmness, and those that are particularly soft or yielding. Uneven terrain can cause one skid or wheel to contact the ground before the other, creating an initial imbalance that might trigger ground resonance. Surfaces with varying firmness, such as patches of soft soil interspersed with harder ground, can affect the landing gear's ability to evenly distribute and absorb the forces upon touchdown. Soft or yielding surfaces may allow one part of the landing gear to sink more than the other, again potentially initiating an imbalance that could lead to ground resonance.

[PH.VIII.I.K1c; FAA-H-8083-21]

4. Describe the role of landing gear design in influencing a helicopter's susceptibility to ground resonance based on the landing surface.

The design of a helicopter's landing gear plays a significant role in influencing its susceptibility to ground resonance based on the landing surface. Helicopters equipped with shock-absorbing landing gear, such as oleo struts or other types of dampers, are better able to absorb and dissipate the energy from uneven or hard landings, reducing the risk of initiating ground resonance. The width of the landing gear stance also affects stability; a wider stance offers better lateral support and can help prevent the tilt that leads to ground resonance. The type of landing gear (skids vs. wheels) can also impact how the helicopter interacts with different surfaces, with wheels potentially offering better roll-over prevention on hard surfaces but skids providing a broader base of support on soft or uneven terrain.

[PH.VIII.I.K1c; FAA-H-8083-21]

5. **What specific items should be inspected on a helicopter to prevent ground resonance?**

   To prevent ground resonance, specific items that should be inspected on a helicopter include the rotor system components (such as blades, hub, pitch links, and dampers) for signs of wear, damage, or improper adjustment. Landing gear components, including shocks, struts, and dampers, must be checked for proper function and fluid levels to ensure they can absorb and dissipate landing forces effectively. Additionally, the inspection should cover the helicopter's structural integrity, focusing on the airframe and attachment points of the rotor and landing gear systems for any signs of stress, cracks, or other damage that could affect the aircraft's vibration characteristics and response.

   [PH.VIII.I.K2; FAA-H-8083-21]

6. **Describe the importance of landing gear system integrity in preventing ground resonance and the types of inspections required.**

   Landing gear system integrity is crucial in preventing ground resonance because the landing gear acts as the primary shock absorber during ground contact, damping the oscillations that could lead to resonance. Inspections should focus on the condition and operation of shock-absorbing components, such as oleo struts and dampers, checking for leaks, adequate pressure, and signs of wear or damage. The landing gear's structural components should also be inspected for cracks, corrosion, or any deformities that could compromise its effectiveness. Ensuring that all parts of the landing gear system are in good working order through regular, detailed inspections is vital for maintaining the system's integrity and preventing ground resonance.

   [PH.VIII.I.K2; FAA-H-8083-21]

7. What are the corrective actions during low rotor RPM speeds to try and prevent ground resonance?

If the RPM is low, the only corrective action to stop ground resonance is to close the throttle immediately and fully lower the collective to place the blades in low pitch.

[PH.VIII.I.K3; FAA-H-8083-21]

8. What are the corrective actions during normal rotor RPM speeds to try and prevent ground resonance?

If the RPM is in the normal operating range, fly the helicopter off the ground, and allow the blades to rephase themselves automatically.

[PH.VIII.I.K3; FAA-H-8083-21]

9. What factors may contribute to the onset of ground resonance in helicopters?

Factors that may contribute to the onset of ground resonance in helicopters include:

- *Rotor system imbalance*—An imbalance in the rotor system, such as uneven blade weight or improper blade tracking, can initiate oscillations that lead to ground resonance.
- *Landing gear issues*—Damaged or malfunctioning landing gear, particularly the shock-absorbing components like dampers or oleo struts, can fail to absorb the initial oscillations, exacerbating the resonance.
- *Uneven or hard landings*—Landing on uneven terrain or experiencing a hard landing can create an initial shock that starts an oscillatory motion, potentially leading to ground resonance.
- *Rotor RPM*—Operating the rotor system at RPM levels outside the recommended operational range can make the helicopter more susceptible to ground resonance.
- *Structural weaknesses*—Any structural weaknesses or damage in the helicopter's airframe can amplify the oscillations caused by ground resonance.

[PH.VIII.I.R1; FAA-H-8083-21]

10. How can pilots recognize the onset of ground resonance in helicopters?

Pilots can recognize the onset of ground resonance in helicopters through several indicators:

- *Vibrations*—An initial sign is a sudden and unusual increase in vibrations felt through the airframe, which may quickly escalate in intensity.
- *Audible cues*—Unusual noises from the rotor system or airframe that deviate from the normal operational sounds, indicating potential instability.
- *Visual observations*—The helicopter may begin to rock or sway on the ground, with the movement becoming progressively more violent if not addressed.

[PH.VIII.I.R2; FAA-H-8083-21]

11. What factors should pilots consider when selecting a recovery procedure for ground resonance?

When selecting a recovery procedure for ground resonance, pilots should consider current rotor RPM.

- If the RPM is low, the only corrective action to stop ground resonance is to close the throttle immediately and fully lower the collective to place the blades in low pitch.
- If the RPM is in the normal operating range, fly the helicopter off the ground, and allow the blades to rephase themselves automatically.

[PH.VIII.I.R3; FAA-H-8083-21]

J. Low-Gravity (G) Recognition and Recovery

1. What are low-G conditions in helicopter flight, and how do they occur?

Low-G conditions in helicopter flight refer to situations where the helicopter and rotor system experiences reduced gravitational forces, often due to turbulence like wind shear or abrupt and aggressive forward cyclic control inputs that unload the rotor disc, particularly in forward flight.

[PH.VIII.J.K1a; FAA-H-8083-21]

2. Why is low-G potentially hazardous for two bladed rotor systems?

Helicopters with two-bladed teetering rotors rely entirely on the tilt of the thrust vector for control. Therefore, low-G conditions can be catastrophic for two-bladed helicopters. During a pushover from moderate or high airspeed, as the helicopter noses over, it enters a low-G condition. Thrust is reduced, and the pilot has lost control of fuselage attitude but may not immediately realize it. Tail rotor thrust or other aerodynamic factors will often induce a roll. The pilot still has control of the rotor disk, and may instinctively try to correct the roll, but the fuselage does not respond due to the lack of thrust. If the fuselage is rolling right, and the pilot puts in left cyclic to correct, the combination of fuselage angle to the right and rotor disk angle to the left becomes quite large and may exceed the clearances built into the rotor hub. This results in the hub contacting the rotor mast, which is known as mast bumping.

[PH.VIII.J.K1a; FAA-H-8083-21]

3. What are common flight situations that can lead to low-G conditions in helicopters?

Common flight situations that can lead to low-G conditions in helicopters include:

- *Abrupt forward cyclic inputs*—Rapidly pushing the cyclic forward, especially during maneuvers like low level flight or quick level-off from a climb.
- *Turbulence*—Encountering severe or unexpected turbulence can momentarily unload the rotor system, especially if

the turbulence induces sudden upward movements of the helicopter.

- *Pilot overreaction*—Overcorrecting for a perceived threat or obstacle by aggressively pushing the cyclic forward, sometimes in panic or due to misjudgment.

[PH.VIII.J.K1b; FAA-H-8083-21]

4. How can pilots prevent the occurrence of low-G conditions during flight?

Pilots can prevent the occurrence of low-G conditions by avoiding abrupt or aggressive cyclic inputs, especially in forward flight. Maintaining smooth and coordinated control movements helps keep the rotor system loaded and prevents the unloading that leads to low-G conditions. Pilots should also be mindful of flight maneuvers and environmental factors, such as turbulence, which could inadvertently lead to reduced G forces on the rotor system.

[PH.VIII.J.K1c; FAA-H-8083-21]

5. What recovery techniques are recommended if a pilot encounters low-G conditions?

If a pilot encounters low-G conditions, the recommended recovery technique involves gently applying aft cyclic to reload the rotor disc and restore normal flight conditions. Pilots are advised to minimize any lateral cyclic inputs during recovery to prevent exacerbating the condition.

[PH.VIII.J.K1c; FAA-H-8083-21]

6. What effects do low-G conditions have on semirigid rotor systems?

Low-G conditions can have significant effects on semi-rigid rotor systems, primarily due to the inherent design characteristics that allow for teetering of the rotor hub. In low-G conditions, the reduced gravitational force can lead to excessive flapping of the rotor blades. This results in the hub contacting the rotor mast, which is known as mast bumping, and of blade strike on the tail boom or fuselage, especially if the rotor system becomes unstable.

[PH.VIII.J.K2; FAA-H-8083-21]

7. How do fully articulated rotor systems respond to low-G conditions?

Fully articulated rotor systems respond to low-G conditions with a potential for instability due to the independent movement of each rotor blade in the system. These systems are designed with multiple hinges (flapping, lead-lag, and feathering) that allow each blade to react independently to aerodynamic and inertial forces. During low-G conditions, the lack of sufficient gravitational force doesn't negatively affect the main rotor blades due to the centrifugal force acting on the blades, that force then is translated to the main rotor hub allowing the pilot's ability to maintain control of the main rotor and subsequently the helicopter during a low-G condition.

[PH.VIII.J.K2; FAA-H-8083-21]

8. What are the implications of low-G conditions on multi-bladed rotor systems?

Multi-bladed rotors may experience a phenomenon similar to mast bumping known as droop stop pounding if flapping clearances are exceeded, but because they retain some control authority at low G, occurrences are less common than for teetering rotors.

[PH.VIII.J.K2; FAA-H-8083-21]

9. What is mast bumping, and how is it related to low-G conditions in helicopters?

Mast bumping is a phenomenon specific to helicopters with semi-rigid (teetering) rotor systems, where the rotor hub or blades contact the mast, the vertical shaft that supports the rotor system. This can occur when the rotor system experiences excessive flapping due to abrupt maneuvers or turbulence. Low-G conditions, particularly in helicopters with a teetering rotor system, exacerbate rotor flapping because the reduction in gravitational force on the rotor disc decreases the stabilizing load, allowing greater freedom for the rotor blades to flap. If the flapping becomes severe enough, it can lead to the rotor hub contacting the mast, potentially causing catastrophic damage.

[PH.VIII.J.K3; FAA-H-8083-21]

10. **Why do certain pilot responses in low-G conditions increase the risk of mast bumping?**

    Certain pilot responses in low-G conditions increase the risk of mast bumping due to overcorrection or inappropriate control inputs. In a low-G situation, with the main rotor blades un-loaded the helicopter may roll due to the force of the tail rotor, a pilot's instinctive reaction might be to apply abrupt lateral cyclic to realign the helicopter with the horizon. However, in helicopters with semi-rigid rotor systems, such abrupt control inputs can cause excessive rotor blade flapping, increasing the risk of the rotor blades or hub striking the mast. Pilots are trained to reload the rotor system prior to correcting any roll of the helicopter.

    [PH.VIII.J.K3; FAA-H-8083-21]

11. **What specific pilot actions should be taken to avoid mast bumping during low-G conditions?**

    To avoid mast bumping during low-G conditions, pilots should:
    - *Gently apply aft cyclic*—Smoothly and gradually apply aft cyclic to increase the load on the rotor system and return to positive G conditions without causing excessive rotor flapping.
    - *Avoid lateral cyclic inputs*—Refrain from sudden lateral cyclic movements that could exacerbate rotor flapping and lead to mast bumping.
    - *Stay calm and controlled*—Maintain composure to execute deliberate and measured control inputs, avoiding overreaction that could worsen the situation.

    [PH.VIII.J.R1; FAA-H-8083-21]

12. **How do turbulence and gusty wind conditions contribute to low-G situations in helicopter flight?**

    Turbulence and gusty wind conditions can contribute to low-G situations in helicopter flight by inducing sudden and unpredictable changes in airspeed and altitude, which may momentarily reduce the load on the rotor system. When a helicopter encounters a strong gust or turbulent air, the upward airflow can cause an abrupt upward lift, momentarily unloading the rotor disc. This reduction in rotor load decreases the effective gravitational force on the helicopter, potentially leading to a low-G condition. The pilot's instinctive corrective actions to regain control and stability, especially if overcorrected with abrupt forward cyclic inputs, can exacerbate the situation, further unloading the rotor and increasing the risk of entering a low-G condition.

[PH.VIII.J.R2; FAA-H-8083-21]

13. How can pilots mitigate the risks associated with encountering turbulence or gusty winds to prevent low-G conditions?

Pilots can mitigate the risks associated with encountering turbulence or gusty winds to prevent low-G conditions by:

- *Preflight planning*—Analyzing weather reports and forecasts to anticipate areas of potential turbulence or gusty winds and planning the flight path accordingly.
- *Speed adjustment*—Adjusting airspeed to the recommended speed for turbulence penetration, as specified by the helicopter manufacturer, to enhance stability and control.
- *Altitude consideration*—Flying at altitudes that allow for more significant air mass stability, when possible, to reduce the effects of turbulence.
- *Smooth control inputs*—Applying cyclic, collective, and pedal inputs smoothly and gradually to avoid abrupt maneuvers that could lead to rotor unloading.

14. What are control inputs that can cause mast bumping in the context of low-G conditions in helicopters?

Control inputs that can cause mast bumping in the context of low-G conditions in helicopters, especially in those with two bladed, semi-rigid or teetering rotor systems, include abrupt and aggressive cyclic movements. Specifically, pushing the cyclic forward too rapidly can unload the rotor disc, creating a low-G condition that significantly increases the risk of mast bumping. Followed by sudden lateral cyclic inputs in an attempt to correct the helicopter's roll in a low-G condition can exacerbate rotor flapping, leading to potential mast bumping. These inappropriate control inputs disrupt the rotor's equilibrium, allowing the rotor hub to contact the mast.

[PH.VIII.J.R3; FAA-H-8083-21]

K. Emergency Equipment and Survival Gear

1. Are emergency locator transmitters (ELTs) required for helicopters?

No, according to 14 CFR §91.207, helicopters do not fall under the U.S.-registered civil airplane requirements.

[PH.VIII.K.K1; 14 CFR 91.207]

2. What is the purpose of an emergency locator transmitter (ELT) in helicopter operations?

The purpose of an emergency locator transmitter (ELT) in helicopter operations is to enhance the safety and survivability of crew and passengers in the event of an emergency or crash. The ELT is designed to automatically activate upon impact or can be manually activated by the crew, emitting a distress signal that aids search and rescue teams in quickly locating the crash site. This device significantly reduces the search area and time required to find survivors, increasing the chances of a successful rescue operation.

[PH.VIII.K.K1; FAA-H-8083-21]

3. What are the testing requirements for ELTs?

The testing requirements for emergency locator transmitters (ELTs) as outlined in the provided text include:

- *Battery replacement or recharging*—ELT batteries must be replaced or recharged when the transmitter has been in use for more than one cumulative hour. ELT batteries must also be replaced or recharged when 50 percent of their useful life (or, for rechargeable batteries, 50 percent of their useful life of charge) has expired, as established by the transmitter manufacturer under its approval. This requirement does not apply to batteries (such as water-activated batteries) that are essentially unaffected during probable storage intervals.

- *Annual inspection*—Each ELT must be inspected within 12 calendar months after the last inspection for proper installation, battery corrosion, operation of the controls and crash sensor, and the presence of a sufficient signal radiated from its antenna.

[PH.VIII.K.K1; 14 CFR 91.207]

4. What is the primary purpose of having a fire extinguisher as part of the emergency equipment in helicopters?

The primary purpose of having a fire extinguisher as part of the emergency equipment in helicopters is to provide a means for the crew and passengers to combat initial fires that may occur in the cockpit, cabin, or engine compartments. It serves as a critical tool for controlling or extinguishing small fires before they spread and become unmanageable, thereby enhancing the safety of all onboard and potentially allowing the helicopter to land safely or preventing the fire from causing further damage.

[PH.VIII.K.K2; FAA-H-8083-21]

5. What are the limitations of fire extinguishers in helicopter emergency situations?

Limitations of fire extinguishers in helicopter emergency situations include:

- *Limited capacity*—Fire extinguishers carry a finite amount of extinguishing agent, which may not be sufficient for large or well-established fires.
- *Type-specific effectiveness*—The effectiveness of a fire extinguisher depends on its type and the class of fire it's being used against. Using the wrong type of extinguisher on a fire can be ineffective or even exacerbate the fire.
- *Accessibility and reach*—In some emergency situations, the location or intensity of the fire may limit the ability to use the extinguisher safely or effectively.
- *Training and familiarity*—Effective use of a fire extinguisher requires training and familiarity with its operation. In a high-stress emergency situation, improper use can occur, reducing the extinguisher's effectiveness.

[PH.VIII.K.K2; FAA-H-8083-21]

6. What are the essential helicopter emergency equipment and survival gear for operations in extreme hot climates?

For operations in extreme hot climates, recommended helicopter emergency equipment and survival gear include hydration supplies such as water or electrolyte solutions, lightweight and reflective coverings or shelters to provide shade, sun protection such as sunscreen, UV-protective clothing, and sunglasses, cooling towels or vests to manage body temperature, a first-aid kit with items for treating heat-related illnesses, signaling devices for rescue, and navigation tools like GPS or maps for finding the nearest shelter or water source.

[PH.VIII.K.K3a; FAA-H-8083-25]

7. What additional equipment is recommended for helicopter operations in cold climate extremes?

For cold climate extremes, recommended helicopter emergency equipment and survival gear include insulated thermal clothing layers, waterproof and windproof outer layers, gloves, hats, and thermal socks to retain body heat, portable heaters or emergency blankets for warmth, high-energy food supplies that remain edible in cold temperatures, a first-aid kit equipped for cold weather injuries such as frostbite, ice axes, and snowshoes if terrain requires, signaling devices, and a reliable means of communication (satellite phone or radio). These items help ensure survival and aid in being located in snowy or icy conditions.

[PH.VIII.K.K3a; FAA-H-8083-25]

8. What is essential helicopter emergency equipment and survival gear for operations in mountainous terrain?

Recommended helicopter emergency equipment and survival gear for operations in mountainous terrain include a high-quality altimeter and compass for navigation, sturdy hiking boots and climbing gear for rugged terrain, thermal blankets and insulated clothing to cope with sudden temperature drops, a first-aid kit with items for treating injuries specific to falls or altitude sickness, emergency rations and water purification tablets, fire-starting tools, signaling devices such as mirrors, flares, and whistles, and a portable shelter or tent. The equipment should be lightweight and compact to not compromise the helicopter's weight limits and balance.

[PH.VIII.K.K3b; FAA-H-8083-25]

9. **What emergency equipment is required for flights in Alaska?**

The minimum equipment during the summer months is: food for each occupant for one week; one axe or hatchet; one first aid kit; an assortment of fishing tackle such as hooks, flies, and sinkers; one knife; fire starter; one mosquito head net for each occupant; and two signaling devices such as colored smoke bombs, pistol shells, etc. sealed in metal containers. In addition to the above, the following must be carried as minimum equipment from October 15 to April 1 of each year: one pair of snowshoes; one sleeping bag; one wool blanket for each occupant over four.

[PH.VIII.K.K3b; FAA-H-8083-25]

10. **What are you required to carry aboard aircraft operated for hire over water and beyond power-off gliding distance from shore?**

Approved flotation gear readily available to each occupant and at least one pyrotechnic signaling device.

[PH.VIII.K.K3c; FAA-H-8083-25]

11. **What are the essential helicopter emergency equipment and survival gear for overwater operations?**

For overwater operations, recommended helicopter emergency equipment and survival gear include personal flotation devices (PFDs) for all passengers and crew, a life raft equipped with a canopy for protection against the elements, water desalination devices or emergency drinking water packets, signaling devices such as waterproof flares, strobe lights, and mirrors, GPS and emergency locator transmitters (ELTs) for precise location tracking, sun protection gear including sunscreen and hats, hand and foot cranks for manual water removal from the raft, fishing kits for long-term survival scenarios, and a first-aid kit waterproofed or in a floating container. These items ensure individuals can survive until rescue if they need to ditch in water.

[PH.VIII.K.K3c; FAA-H-8083-25]

12. What survival gear is recommended to sustain life for 48 to 72 hours after a helicopter emergency in a remote area?

To sustain life for 48 to 72 hours after a helicopter emergency in a remote area, recommended survival gear includes water enough for each occupant, water purification system or tablets and durable water containers to ensure access to clean drinking water. High-energy, non-perishable food items such as energy bars, nuts, and dried fruits provide essential nutrition. Clothing should be layered and adaptable to changing conditions, including moisture-wicking base layers, insulation layers, and a waterproof and windproof outer layer. A compact, lightweight shelter, such as a survival tent or bivy sack, offers protection from the elements. Additionally, a sleeping bag or thermal blankets suitable for the environment help maintain body temperature.

[PH.VIII.K.R1; FAA-H-8083-25]

Skills to be demonstrated:

- Identify appropriate equipment and personal gear.

- Brief passengers on proper use of onboard emergency equipment and survival gear.

Night
Operations

9

A. Night Operations

1. How does the eye adapt to darkness, and what is the significance of this adaptation for night flying?

The eye adapts to darkness through a process called dark adaptation, where the sensitivity of the retina to low light levels increases over time, allowing for better vision in the dark. This process involves the regeneration of rhodopsin, a photopigment in the rods of the retina, which are responsible for vision at low light levels. Dark adaptation can take up to 30 minutes to complete, reaching optimal sensitivity. For night flying, understanding and allowing for dark adaptation is crucial, as it enhances a pilot's ability to see and interpret navigation lights, unlit obstacles, and terrain. Pilots are advised to avoid bright lights before and during night flights to maintain night vision.

[PH.IX.A.K1; FAA-H-8083-25]

2. What is the role of rod and cone cells in night vision, and how does this affect pilots?

Rod and cone cells play distinct roles in vision. Rod cells are more numerous, located in the peripheral retina, and are highly sensitive to light, making them essential for night vision and detecting movement. However, rod cells do not discern color, which is the primary function of the cone cells located in the central retina. Cone cells work best in bright light and are responsible for high-resolution color vision. At night, pilots rely more on rod cells, resulting in reduced color vision and resolution. This reliance on peripheral vision at night, known as off-center viewing, helps pilots detect faint light sources or obstacles in low-light conditions.

[PH.IX.A.K1; FAA-H-8083-25]

3. What is spatial disorientation, and how can pilots prevent it during night flights?

Spatial disorientation is a condition where a pilot's perception of direction, altitude, or aircraft attitude does not match reality. This condition is more common during night flights due to the lack of visible horizons and visual references, leading to reliance on vestibular and somatosensory systems that can be easily misled. To prevent spatial disorientation, pilots are trained to trust their flight instruments rather than sensory perceptions. Regular instrument training, thorough preflight planning, maintaining situational awareness, and using the horizon or artificial horizon as references can help prevent disorientation. Pilots are also advised to avoid sudden head movements and to be particularly cautious in conditions where visual cues are limited, such as over water or in featureless terrain at night.

[PH.IX.A.K1; FAA-H-8083-25]

4. How is night scanning different from day scanning?

Night scanning, like day scanning, uses a series of short, regularly spaced eye movements in 10° sectors. Unlike day scanning, however, off-center viewing is used to focus objects on the rods rather than the fovea blind spot. When looking at an object, avoid staring at it too long. If staring at an object without moving the eyes, the retina becomes accustomed to the light intensity and the image begins to fade. To keep it clearly visible, new areas in the retina must be exposed to the image. Small, circular eye movements help eliminate fading. Also, move the eyes more slowly from sector to sector than during the day to prevent blurring.

[PH.IX.A.K1; FAA-H-8083-25]

5. What personal equipment is considered essential for pilots during night flights in helicopters?

Essential personal equipment for pilots during night flights in helicopters includes a flashlight with a red or white light option to preserve night vision while allowing for map reading and cockpit instrument checks. Spare batteries for all electronic devices are crucial to ensure functionality throughout the flight. Additionally, wearing a watch with a backlight can help pilots keep track of time without impairing their night vision.

[PH.IX.A.K2; FAA-H-8083-25]

6. What considerations should be made for using flashlights and cockpit lighting during night flights?

When using flashlights and cockpit lighting during night flights, pilots should consider the impact on their night vision. Red or dim white light is preferred for preserving night vision while providing adequate illumination for reading maps, checklists, and instrument panels. Adjustable intensity settings can help balance between preserving night vision and ensuring readability. Flashlights should be secured to prevent them from rolling away or causing distractions. Cockpit lighting should be adjusted to the lowest practical level that still allows for safe operation of the aircraft, reducing glare and reflection.

[PH.IX.A.K2; FAA-H-8083-25]

7. What are the basic helicopter equipment and lighting requirements for night operations according to aviation regulations?

14 CFR §91.205(c) specifies that helicopters operating at night must be equipped with:

F – Fuses (spare set or three of each type, if fuses are used)

L – Landing light (if for hire)

A – Anti Collision lights

P – Position lights (AKA navigation lights)

S – Source of electrical power

[PH.IX.A.K3; 14 CFR 91.205]

8. What additional equipment might be required for helicopters to conduct night operations in certain airspace or under specific regulations?

For night operations in certain airspace or under specific regulations, helicopters might be required to have additional equipment beyond basic lighting. This can include radio navigation and communication equipment compatible with the airspace requirements, a functioning transponder with altitude reporting for controlled airspace, and, where applicable, ADS-B (Automatic Dependent Surveillance-Broadcast) equipment for real-time precision tracking. For operations over water or remote areas, emergency flotation devices or rafts.

[PH.IX.A.K3; 14 CFR 91.205]

9. **What types of lighting systems are used to identify airports, heliports, helipads, landing areas, runways, and taxiways for helicopter pilots?**

Lighting systems used to identify airports, heliports, helipads, landing areas, runways, and taxiways for helicopter pilots include runway edge lights, which outline the edges of runways at night with white or amber lights; taxiway lights, typically blue, guiding pilots along taxi paths; approach lighting systems (ALS), aiding in the transition from instrument to visual flight for landing; heliport/helipad lighting, including perimeter lights for outlining the landing area, often green, yellow, or white; and obstruction lights, which mark obstacles such as buildings, towers, and cranes, usually with red or white flashing lights to warn pilots of potential hazards. These systems are crucial for navigation and safe operation during night flights and low visibility conditions.

[PH.IX.A.K4; FAA-H-8083-25]

10. **How do obstruction lights enhance safety for helicopter operations?**

Obstruction lights enhance safety for helicopter operations by clearly marking tall structures, such as buildings, towers, antennas, and construction cranes, which could pose a collision hazard during flight. These lights are typically red or white and can be steady or flashing, making them visible against a variety of backgrounds at night or during adverse weather conditions. By alerting pilots to the presence of obstructions, these lights allow for timely avoidance maneuvers, especially during low-altitude operations common to helicopters, thereby significantly reducing the risk of collision and enhancing overall flight safety.

[PH.IX.A.K4; FAA-H-8083-25]

11. **What is pilot-controlled lighting (PCL), and how does it work for helicopter pilots?**

Pilot-controlled lighting (PCL) is a system that allows pilots to activate or control the intensity of airport or heliport lights from the cockpit, typically through a series of radio transmissions on a designated frequency. This system is especially useful at smaller airports or heliports without 24-hour tower services. By keying the aircraft's microphone, pilots can turn on runway, taxiway, and approach lights, often with the ability to adjust the brightness to suit current visibility needs. PCL enables pilots to ensure adequate lighting for takeoffs, landings, and taxiing during night operations or in low visibility conditions, enhancing safety and operational flexibility.

[PH.IX.A.K4; FAA-H-8083-25]

12. What techniques can helicopter pilots use for night orientation and navigation?

Helicopter pilots can use several techniques for night orientation and navigation, including reliance on illuminated landmarks, such as roads, cities, and towns, to guide their path. GPS and other navigational aids like VORs (VHF Omnidirectional Range) are essential for precise navigation when visual references are limited. Pilots should frequently cross-reference their position using these aids to ensure accuracy. Preflight planning with detailed route maps and understanding the terrain and obstacles along the flight path are crucial. Additionally, if available, pilots can use night vision goggles (NVGs) to enhance their ability to see terrain and obstacles in low-light conditions.

[PH.IX.A.K5; FAA-H-8083-25]

13. What are effective chart reading techniques for night flights?

Effective chart reading techniques for night flights include using a dimmable, red cockpit light to illuminate charts without impairing night vision. Pilots should familiarize themselves with the chart details during preflight planning to minimize the need for extensive chart reading in flight. Organizing charts and flight documents for easy access during the flight can reduce cockpit workload. Electronic flight bags (EFBs) with adjustable screen brightness settings can also be useful for accessing charts digitally while preserving night vision. Briefing on key waypoints, frequencies, and procedures before reaching critical phases of flight can reduce the reliance on real-time chart reading under low-light conditions.

[PH.IX.A.K5; FAA-H-8083-25]

14. How can pilots maintain night vision effectiveness during flights?

To maintain night vision effectiveness, pilots should allow their eyes to adapt to darkness before flying, which can take up to 30 minutes. They should avoid looking directly at bright lights and use red cockpit lighting to preserve night vision. If exposure to bright light is unavoidable, pilots should close one eye to help maintain some degree of dark adaptation in the other. Wearing sunglasses during the late afternoon can help prepare the eyes for night flying by reducing exposure to bright sunlight.

[PH.IX.A.K5; FAA-H-8083-25]

15. What are the key considerations for helicopter pilots during night taxi operations?

During night taxi operations, helicopter pilots should prioritize visibility and situational awareness. This includes using appropriate lighting, such as landing lights for illuminating the taxi path and position lights to indicate the aircraft's presence to others. Pilots must be vigilant for obstacles not easily visible at night, including parked aircraft, ground equipment, and personnel. Slow and deliberate movements are recommended to allow time to detect and react to hazards. Pilots should also be familiar with the airport or heliport layout and any specific night operation procedures it may have. Effective communication with ground control is crucial for receiving taxi instructions and updates on ground traffic.

[PH.IX.A.K6; FAA-H-8083-25]

16. What lighting equipment is essential for helicopters to conduct safe taxi operations at night?

For safe taxi operations at night, helicopters must be equipped with functioning position lights (red for left, green for right, and white for the tail) to indicate their orientation and movement direction to other pilots and ground personnel. Anti-collision lights (red or white flashing lights) are essential to enhance the aircraft's visibility. Landing lights should be used to illuminate the taxi path, although pilots should be mindful of directing these lights away from other aircraft or personnel to prevent dazzling. Pilots should also have a flashlight handy for cockpit management and in case of a need to inspect the aircraft or navigate on foot in poorly lit areas.

[PH.IX.A.K6; FAA-H-8083-25]

17. How can helicopter pilots interpret the position and direction of other aircraft at night based solely on position lights?

Aircraft are equipped with a red light on the left (port) wingtip, a green light on the right (starboard) wingtip, and a white light on the tail. By observing these lights, pilots can determine the orientation and relative movement direction of other aircraft:

- *Red and green visible*—If both the red and green lights are visible, the aircraft is facing towards or flying perpendicular to the observer. If the red light is on the right and the green on the left, the aircraft is moving towards the observer. If the green is on the right and the red on the left, the aircraft is moving away or across the observer's path.

- *Only red visible*—If only the red light is visible, the aircraft is moving left to right from the observer's perspective, showing its left side.

- *Only green visible*—If only the green light is visible, the aircraft is moving right to left from the observer's perspective, showing its right side.

- *Only white visible*—If only the white taillight is visible, the aircraft is moving away from the observer.

[PH.IX.A.K7; FAA-H-8083-25]

18. What are common visual illusions that helicopter pilots might experience during night flying, and how can they affect flight operations?

Common visual illusions experienced by helicopter pilots during night flying include:

- *Autokinesis*—Stationary lights can appear to move when stared at in darkness for several seconds. This can lead to disorientation and incorrect judgments about the movement of other aircraft or obstacles.

- *False horizon*—Stars, city lights, or cloud formations can be misinterpreted as the true horizon, leading to improper aircraft attitude adjustments.
- *Black hole illusion*—Occurs during a night approach over unlit terrain or water, creating the illusion of being at a higher altitude than actual, potentially leading to a dangerously low approach.
- *Size-distance illusion*—At night, a lack of visual references can make it difficult to accurately judge the size and distance of objects or lights, leading to misinterpretations of an aircraft's altitude and speed.
- *Runway width illusion*—A narrower-than-usual runway can create the illusion of being higher than actual during an approach, while a wider runway can create the opposite effect.
- *Runway and approach lighting illusions*—Bright runway lights or approaches over lit areas can give the impression of being closer than actual, while dim lights or approaches over dark areas may appear farther away.

[PH.IX.A.K8; FAA-H-8083-25]

19. What are the benefits of using autopilot or automation systems during night operations in helicopters?

The benefits of using autopilot or automation systems during night operations in helicopters include enhanced situational awareness, reduced pilot workload, and increased flight safety. Automation can maintain stable flight by controlling altitude, airspeed, and heading more precisely than manual flying, especially in the dark when visual references are limited. It allows pilots to focus more on navigation, monitoring aircraft systems, and looking out for traffic or obstacles. Autopilot systems can also execute complex flight paths and approaches with high accuracy, contributing to safer operations in challenging conditions. Additionally, the use of automation can help mitigate pilot fatigue by reducing the physical and cognitive demands of flying at night.

[PH.IX.A.K9; FAA-H-8083-25]

20. How can pilots identify and assess collision hazards specific to night operations?

Identifying and assessing collision hazards specific to night operations involves several strategies:

- *Preflight planning*—Carefully plan the flight path by studying maps and NOTAMs (Notices to Air Missions) for information on potential hazards like construction cranes, tall buildings, or temporary obstacles that may not be well-lit or visible at night.

- *Situational awareness*—Maintain high situational awareness by continuously monitoring air traffic control communications, radar services, and TCAS (traffic collision avoidance system), if available, to be aware of other aircraft in proximity.

- *Use of lighting*—Proper use of aircraft lighting, including navigation, anti-collision, and landing lights, can significantly enhance the visibility of your helicopter to other pilots. Understanding how to interpret the position and navigation lights of other aircraft helps in assessing their direction and altitude.

- *Visual scanning techniques*—Employ effective visual scanning techniques to overcome the limitations of night vision, such as using peripheral vision, which is more sensitive to light and movement in low-light conditions, to detect other aircraft.

- *Night vision equipment*—If certified and available, use night vision goggles (NVGs) to enhance visual capability during night operations, improving the ability to identify other aircraft and obstacles.

[PH.IX.A.R1; FAA-H-8083-25]

21. How can pilots identify and assess the risk of runway incursion during night operations?

Identifying and assessing the risk of runway incursion during night operations involves several key practices:

- *Preflight planning*—Review the airport or heliport layout thoroughly before the flight, paying special attention to runway and taxiway configurations, noting any areas that are complex or have a history of incursions.

- *Briefing*—Conduct a comprehensive briefing that includes a review of the airport's lighting systems, such as runway and taxiway lights, and any specific procedures for night operations at the airport.
- *Enhanced situational awareness*—Maintain high situational awareness during taxi, takeoff, and landing phases. Recognize that visibility is reduced at night, making it harder to see signage, taxiway markings, and other aircraft.
- *Communication with ATC*—Keep clear and constant communication with air traffic control (ATC), confirming clearances and readbacks, especially for runway crossings or instructions to enter or vacate runways.
- *Use of airport diagrams*—Have an airport diagram readily accessible and use it to visually track your position on the airfield during taxi operations, especially at unfamiliar airports.
- *Lighting systems knowledge*—Understand the airport's lighting systems, including the color coding of lights used on taxiways, runways, and their thresholds, to help in navigating and avoiding unauthorized runway entry.

[PH.IX.A.R2; FAA-H-8083-25]

22. What strategies can pilots employ to mitigate risks related to distractions, task prioritization, loss of situational awareness, or disorientation in night operations?

To mitigate risks related to distractions, task prioritization, loss of situational awareness, or disorientation during night operations, pilots can use several strategies:

- *Preflight planning*—Comprehensive preflight planning ensures familiarity with the flight route, airspace restrictions, weather conditions, and airport layouts, reducing the likelihood of surprises that can lead to distractions or disorientation.
- *Prioritizing tasks*—Adopting a methodical approach to task management, prioritizing tasks based on their criticality to flight safety (e.g., aviate, navigate, communicate), helps maintain focus on essential operations.

(continued)

- *Maintaining situational awareness*—Continuously monitoring flight instruments, navigational aids, and ATC communications enhances situational awareness. Regularly updating mental models of the aircraft's location and flight status is crucial.

- *Limiting cockpit distractions*—Minimize nonessential activities and conversations in the cockpit, especially during critical phases of flight like takeoff, approach, and landing.

- *Use of automation wisely*—Appropriately using automation to reduce workload while remaining vigilant and ready to take manual control if the situation demands.

- *Training and proficiency*—Regular training and practice, including simulator sessions that focus on night operations, instrument flying, and emergency procedures, improve a pilot's ability to manage disorientation and maintain situational awareness.

- *Visual scanning techniques*—Practicing effective visual scanning techniques that minimize the reliance on a single visual cue and prevent fixation on specific instruments or outside lights can help avoid visual illusions and disorientation.

- *Health and wellness*—Ensuring adequate rest before night flights and managing fatigue can significantly reduce the risk of losing situational awareness or becoming disoriented.

[PH.IX.A.R3) FAA-H-8083-25]

23. How can pilots identify risks associated with visual illusions and night adaptation during all phases of night flying?

Pilots can identify risks associated with visual illusions and night adaptation during night flying by being aware of conditions that commonly lead to these phenomena:

- *Autokinesis*—Occurs when a stationary light appears to move if stared at for several seconds, leading to potential misjudgment of flight path or altitude adjustments.

- *False horizon*—Pilots may misinterpret sloping cloud formations, city lights, or star patterns as the true horizon, leading to improper aircraft orientation.

- *Black hole approach*—Flying into a poorly lit area with no surrounding lights can create an illusion of being at a higher altitude than actual, potentially resulting in an undershoot.
- *Size-distance illusion*—Lights or objects may appear farther away and larger or closer and smaller than they are, affecting altitude and speed perception.
- *Runway width illusion*—A narrower or wider runway than usual can falsely indicate a higher or lower altitude during approach, respectively.
- *Night adaptation*—The eyes' adaptation to darkness can be compromised by sudden exposure to bright lights, reducing the ability to see in low-light conditions.

[PH.IX.A.R4; FAA-H-8083-25]

24. How can pilots identify the difference between night currency and proficiency in the context of night operations?

Identifying the difference between night currency and proficiency involves understanding the definitions and implications of each:

- *Night currency*—refers to meeting the regulatory requirements for flying at night, which typically involve completing a specific number of takeoffs and landings at night within a certain period. Currency ensures that a pilot has recently experienced night flying but does not necessarily reflect the pilot's comfort level, skill range, or ability to handle complex situations that might arise during night operations.
- *Night proficiency*—goes beyond currency, encompassing a pilot's comprehensive skill set, confidence, and ability to safely conduct a variety of night flying operations under different conditions. Proficiency includes adeptly managing navigation, communication, aircraft control, emergency procedures, and understanding and dealing with night-specific challenges such as visual illusions and reduced visibility.

[PH.IX.A.R5; FAA-H-8083-25]

25. What weather phenomena can significantly reduce visibility during night operations, and what is the recommended mitigation strategy to maintain safety?

Fog, low clouds, and precipitation can significantly reduce visibility during night operations. The recommended mitigation strategy includes thorough preflight weather assessment, en route weather updates, and readiness to divert to an alternate destination if weather conditions deteriorate below safe minimums. Pilots should also ensure they are proficient in instrument flying skills to manage unexpected instrument meteorological conditions (IMC).

[PH.IX.A.R6; FAA-H-8083-25]

26. How can a pilot mitigate the risk associated with reduced celestial and terrestrial navigation cues during night operations in adverse weather conditions?

To mitigate the risk associated with reduced navigation cues during night operations in adverse weather conditions, a pilot should rely on flight instruments and navigation aids to maintain situational awareness. Using GPS, VOR, and other navigational systems can help compensate for the lack of visual references. Additionally, maintaining proficiency in instrument flying and having a well-thought-out flight plan with clear waypoints and alternates are crucial for safe navigation.

[PH.IX.A.R6; FAA-H-8083-25]

27. How should a pilot assess the impact of inoperative navigation lights on night operations, and what are the appropriate mitigation actions?

The impact of inoperative navigation lights on night operations can significantly affect the visibility of the helicopter to other aircraft, increasing the risk of mid-air collisions. The appropriate mitigation actions include checking all navigation and anti-collision lights during preflight checks, repairing any inoperative lights before night operations.

[PH.IX.A.R7; FAA-H-8083-25]

28. **What are the considerations and mitigations for operating with an inoperative landing light during night landings?**

    Operating with an inoperative landing light during night landings increases the difficulty of visualizing the landing area and recognizing obstacles. Pilots should consider the following mitigations: conduct a thorough preflight to ensure all other lights and equipment are operational, plan landings at well-lit heliports or airports to compensate for the lack of a landing light, increase approach and hover checks to ensure obstacle clearance, and if possible, delay the operation until the equipment can be repaired or use an alternative helicopter.

    [PH.IX.A.R7; FAA-H-8083-25]

29. **How can a pilot prepare for the possibility of inoperative cockpit instrumentation lighting during night operations?**

    To prepare for inoperative cockpit instrumentation lighting, pilots should ensure that portable, battery-operated lights are available and functioning as a backup. Pilots should be familiar with the location and operation of these lights and practice using them during night flight training. Additionally, ensuring that all necessary charts and materials are accessible and can be illuminated without impairing night vision is essential.

    [PH.IX.A.R7; FAA-H-8083-25]

Postflight
Procedures
10

A. After Landing, Parking, and Securing

1. Describe the standard procedure for safely shutting down a helicopter's engine after a flight.

The standard procedure for safely shutting down a helicopter's engine after a flight includes allowing the engine to cool down at idle to prevent thermal shock, following the manufacturer's recommended shutdown sequence to avoid damage to the engine and components, engaging the rotor brake if applicable once the rotor RPM is within the specified range, turning off avionics and electrical systems, and finally, turning the ignition switch to the OFF position and recording flight and engine times as required.

[PH.X.A.K1; FAA-H-8083-21]

2. What are the critical steps involved in securing a helicopter after the last flight of the day?

Securing a helicopter after the last flight of the day involves conducting a thorough postflight inspection to check for any damage or leaks, ensuring that all switches are in the OFF position, applying rotor and control locks as necessary to protect against wind damage, securing doors and windows to prevent unauthorized access and weather damage, attaching tie-downs or moving the helicopter into a hangar to protect against strong winds or inclement weather, and finally, covering sensitive components such as the pitot tube and exhaust outlets to prevent debris and insect obstruction.

[PH.X.A.K1; FAA-H-8083-21]

3. How should a pilot perform a postflight inspection, and what key areas should be emphasized during this inspection?

A postflight inspection should be performed methodically, starting from one point of the helicopter and moving around in a consistent direction to ensure no areas are overlooked. Key areas to emphasize include checking the main rotor and tail rotor blades for nicks, cracks, or other damage, inspecting the landing gear for integrity and tire condition, examining the fuselage for structural damage or fluid leaks, ensuring all fasteners and cowling are secure, checking the engine and transmission areas for signs of leaks or overheating, and verifying that all antennas and external equipment are securely attached. Any anomalies should be documented and addressed before the next flight.

[PH.X.A.K1; FAA-H-8083-21]

4. What information should a pilot include when documenting an in-flight discrepancy found during or after a flight operation?

When documenting an in-flight discrepancy, a pilot should include a clear and concise description of the issue, the flight conditions or phases during which the discrepancy was noted (e.g., altitude, airspeed, weather conditions), any actions taken by the crew to address or mitigate the issue during flight, the status of the discrepancy at the end of the flight (resolved, unresolved, or worsened), and the date and time of the occurrence. It's also helpful to note any relevant cockpit indications, warning lights, or system malfunctions observed.

[PH.X.A.K2; FAA-H-8083-21]

5. Describe the process for reporting a postflight discrepancy to maintenance personnel and ensuring it is addressed before the next flight.

The process for reporting a postflight discrepancy involves completing the appropriate section of the aircraft's maintenance log or discrepancy report with detailed information about the issue observed. The pilot should communicate directly with maintenance personnel to ensure they understand the nature and severity of the discrepancy. The maintenance team should then assess the reported issue, perform the necessary repairs or adjustments, and officially document the resolution in the aircraft's maintenance records. The pilot should verify that the discrepancy has been resolved by reviewing the maintenance log and, if necessary, conducting a preflight check or consultation with maintenance staff before the next flight.

[PH.X.A.K2; FAA-H-8083-21]

6. What are common postflight activities that could distract a pilot from properly securing the helicopter, and how can these distractions be mitigated?

Common postflight activities that could distract a pilot include debriefing with passengers, immediate planning for the next flight, handling paperwork, and personal phone calls or messages. To mitigate these distractions, pilots should follow a strict shutdown and securing checklist before attending to any non-operational tasks. Establishing a routine that prioritizes aircraft securing tasks can help ensure that all necessary steps are completed without omission. Additionally, setting clear boundaries with passengers and crew about postflight procedures can minimize interruptions until the helicopter is properly secured.

[PH.X.A.R1; FAA-H-8083-2]

7. Explain how establishing a standardized postflight procedure can help mitigate risks associated with activities and distractions during this phase.

Establishing a standardized postflight procedure helps mitigate risks by creating a consistent sequence of actions that pilots follow after every flight, reducing the likelihood of omission due to distractions. A standardized checklist ensures that all critical tasks, such as securing the aircraft, performing postflight inspections, and documenting discrepancies, are completed in an orderly and methodical manner. This routine becomes habitual, increasing efficiency and safety, and allowing pilots to systematically complete tasks even in a distracting environment. Regular training and practice of these procedures reinforce their importance and help pilots maintain focus on postflight duties, regardless of external distractions.

[PH.X.A.R1; FAA-H-8083-2]

8. What are the primary risks associated with parking a helicopter in a congested area, and how can a pilot assess these risks before landing?

Primary risks associated with parking a helicopter in a congested area include the potential for colliding with ground obstacles, vehicles, or other aircraft; causing injury to persons in the vicinity due to rotor wash; and damaging property or the helicopter itself with rotor blades. A pilot can assess these risks before landing by conducting a thorough pre-landing reconnaissance of the intended parking area, looking for safe ingress and egress routes, identifying clear areas free of obstacles, and considering the effects of rotor wash on nearby objects and people.

[PH.X.A.R2; FAA-H-8083-21]

9. **Describe the steps a pilot should take to ensure compliance with airport-specific security procedures during postflight operations.**

A pilot should first familiarize themselves with the specific security procedures of the airport by reviewing published materials or consulting with airport operations. Steps include securing the aircraft according to the airport's guidelines, which may involve specific locking mechanisms for the aircraft and hangar, ensuring that all identification and access badges are displayed correctly, and reporting any security concerns or breaches immediately to airport security or management. Pilots should also participate in any required security briefings or training sessions offered by the airport to stay updated on current procedures and threats.

[PH.X.A.R3; FAA-H-8083-2]

10. **What are the key safety considerations a pilot must assess before allowing passengers to disembark the helicopter on the ramp?**

Ensuring the rotor blades have completely stopped to avoid the risk of injury from rotor wash or contact, checking the surrounding area for other aircraft operations or ground vehicles to prevent accidents on the ramp, and assessing environmental conditions such as slippery surfaces or adverse weather that could affect passenger safety. Additionally, the pilot should ensure that passengers are briefed on the safest path to exit the helicopter and move clear of the area always avoiding walking back towards the tail rotor.

[PH.X.A.R4; FAA-H-8083-21]

Skills to be demonstrated:

- Minimize the hazardous effects of rotor downwash during hovering.

- Park in an appropriate area, considering the safety of nearby people and property.

- Complete the appropriate checklist(s).

- Conduct a postflight inspection and document discrepancies and servicing requirements, if any.

- Secure the helicopter.

Glossary

Pro Tip: To help you study, create flashcards from the following terms and definitions.

Advancing blade—The blade moving in the same direction as the helicopter or gyroplane. In rotorcraft that have counterclockwise main rotor blade rotation as viewed from above, the advancing blade is in the right half of the rotor disc area during forward movement.

Airfoil—Any surface designed to obtain a useful reaction of lift, or negative lift, as it moves through the air.

Aircraft pitch—When in reference to an aircraft, the movement about its lateral, or pitch, axis. Movement of the cyclic forward or aft causes the nose of the helicopter or gyroplane to pitch up or down.

Aircraft roll—The movement of the aircraft about its longitudinal axis. Movement of the cyclic right or left causes the helicopter or gyroplane to tilt in that direction.

Angle of attack—The angle between the airfoil's chord line and the relative wind.

Autorotation—The condition of flight during which the main rotor is driven only by aerodynamic forces with no power from the engine.

Axis of rotation—The imaginary line about which the rotor rotates. It is represented by a line drawn through the center of, and perpendicular to, the tip-path plane.

Blade coning—An upward sweep of rotor blades because of restraining the fore and aft movement of the rotor blade.

Blade feathering—The rotation of the blade around the span-wise (pitch change) axis.

Blade flap—The ability of the rotor blade to move in a vertical direction. Blades may flap independently or in unison.

Blade lead and lag—The fore and aft movement of the blade in the plane of rotation. It is sometimes called hunting or dragging.

Blade loading—The load imposed on rotor blades, determined by dividing the total weight of the helicopter by the combined area of all the rotor blades.

Blade root—The part of the blade that attaches to the blade grip.

Blade span—The length of a blade from its tip to its root.

Blade stall—The condition of the rotor blade when it is operating at an angle of attack greater than the maximum angle of lift.

Blade tip—The part of the blade furthest from the hub of the rotor.

Blade track—The relationship of the blade tips in the plane of rotation. Blades that are in track will move through the same plane of rotation.

Blade twist—The variation in the angle of incidence of a blade between the root and the tip.

Blowback—The tendency of the rotor disc to tilt aft in forward flight as a result of flapping.

Center of pressure—The point where the resultant force of all the aerodynamic forces acting on an airfoil intersects the chord line.

Centrifugal force—The apparent force that an object moving along a circular path exerts on the body constraining the object and that acts outwardly away from the center of rotation.

Centripetal force—The force that attracts a body toward its axis of rotation. It is the opposite of centrifugal force.

Chord line—An imaginary straight line between the leading and trailing edges of an airfoil section.

Chord-wise axis—A term used in reference to semirigid rotors describing the flapping or teetering axis of the rotor.

Cyclic feathering—The mechanical change of the angle of incidence, or pitch, of individual rotor blades independently of other blades in the system.

Delta hinge—A flapping hinge with a skewed axis so that the flapping motion introduces a component of feathering that would result in a restoring force in the flap-wise direction.

Disc area—The area swept by the blades of the rotor. It is a circle with its center at the hub and has a radius of one blade length.

Disc loading—The total helicopter weight divided by the rotor disc area.

Dissymmetry of lift—The unequal lift across the rotor disc resulting from the difference in the velocity of air over the advancing blade half and retreating blade half of the rotor disc area.

Flapping hinge—The hinge that permits the rotor blade to flap and thus balance the lift generated by the advancing and retreating blades.

Ground effect—A usually beneficial influence on rotorcraft performance that occurs while flying close to the ground. It results from a reduction in upwash, downwash, and blade tip vortices, which provide a corresponding decrease in induced drag.

Hunting—Movement of a blade with respect to the other blades in the plane of rotation, sometimes called leading or lagging.

Inertia—The property of matter by which it will remain at rest or in a state of uniform motion in the same direction unless acted upon by some external force.

Induced drag—That part of the total drag that is created by the production of lift.

Induced flow—The component of air flowing vertically through the rotor system resulting from the production of lift.

L/D_{MAX}—The maximum ratio between total lift (L) and total drag (D). This point provides the best glide speed. Any deviation from the best glide speed increases drag and reduces the distance you can glide.

Load factor—The ratio of a specified load to the total weight of the aircraft.

Parasite drag—The part of total drag created by the form or shape of helicopter parts.

Pendular action—The lateral or longitudinal oscillation of the fuselage due to it being suspended from the rotor system.

Pitch angle—The angle between the chord line of the rotor blade and the reference plane of the main rotor hub or the rotor plane of rotation.

Profile drag—Drag incurred from frictional or parasitic resistance of the blades passing through the air. It does not change significantly with the angle of attack of the airfoil section, but it increases moderately as airspeed increases.

Resultant relative wind—Airflow from rotation that is modified by induced flow.

Retreating blade—Any blade, located in a semicircular part of the rotor disc, where the blade direction is opposite to the direction of flight.

Retreating made stall—A stall that begins at or near the tip of a blade in a helicopter because of the high angles of attack required to compensate for dissymmetry of lift.

Solidity ratio—The ratio of the total rotor blade area to total rotor disc area.

Span—The dimension of a rotor blade or airfoil from root to tip.

Symmetrical rotor—An airfoil having the same shape on the top and bottom.

Teetering hinge—A hinge that permits the rotor blades of a semi-rigid rotor system to flap as a unit.

Tip-path plane—The imaginary circular plane outlined by the rotor blade tips as they make a cycle of rotation.

Translating tendency—The tendency of the single-rotor helicopter to move laterally during hovering flight. Also called tail rotor drift.

Translational lift—The additional lift obtained when entering forward flight, due to the increased efficiency of the rotor system.

Transverse-flow effect—A condition of increased drag and decreased lift in the aft portion of the rotor disc caused by the air having a greater induced velocity and angle in the aft portion of the disc.

Under-slung—A rotor hub that rotates below the top of the mast, as on semi-rigid rotor systems.

Unloaded rotor—The state of a rotor when rotor force has been removed, or when the rotor is operating under a low-G or negative-G condition.

Vortex ring state—A transient condition of downward flight (descending through air after just previously being accelerated downward by the rotor) during which an appreciable portion of the main rotor system is being forced to operate at angles of attack above maximum. Blade stall starts near the hub and progresses outward as the rate of descent increases.